Papers in Mediaeval Studies 15

Frontispiece. Mural painting (Town Hall, Wismar, Germany) from ca. 1400, showing a small boat transporting stockfish and beer in the harbour. Photo: Jan Bill.

Cogs, Cargoes, and Commerce: Maritime Bulk Trade in Northern Europe, 1150-1400

edited by

Lars Berggren, Nils Hybel and Annette Landen

PONTIFICAL INSTITUTE OF MEDIAEVAL STUDIES
TORONTO

NATIONAL LIBRARY OF CANADA CATALOGUING IN PUBLICATION DATA

Main entry under title:
Cogs, cargoes, and commerce : maritime bulk trade in northern Europe, 1150-1400.

(Papers in mediaeval studies, ISSN 0228-8605 ; 15)
Papers presented at a conference entitled: New markets for new goods: the emergence of large scale trade in northern Europe, 1150-1400, held in Malmö, Sweden, 19-21 February 1997.
Includes bibliographic references and index.
ISBN -0-88844-815-5

1. Shipping – Europe, Northern – History – To 1500 – Congresses. 2. Bulk carrier cargo ships – Europe, Northern – History – To 1500 – Congresses. 3. Europe, Northern – Commerce – History – To 1500 – Congresses. I. Berggren, Lars, 1951– II. Hybel, Nils, 1948– III. Landen, Annette, 1956– IV. Pontifical Institute of Mediaeval Studies. V. Title: New market for new goods: the emergence of large scale trade in northern Europe, 1150-1400 VI. Series.

HF395.C64 2002 387.5′44′09480902 C2002-901013-6

Pontifical Institute of Mediaeval Studies
59 Queen's Park Crescent East
Toronto, Ontario, Canada M5S 2C4

Printed in Canada

Contents

Illustrations and Tables

Plates

FIGURES

Chart

Tables

Preface

Beer is one of the essential ingredients in this book, indeed it can be said to have provided the initial source of inspiration for it. In fact, the whole thing began in a pub when a number of participants from various sections of the International Medieval Congress in Leeds 1995 met over a pint of beer and started to chat about trade and transport of heavy goods–such as beer–in Northern Europe during the Middle Ages. Herring, grain, pottery, timber, stone, salt, iron and other items of inglorious but voluminous everyday consumption soon entered into the discussion in which everybody present seemed to be in possession of important pieces of a whole that, alas, could only be vaguely discerned. Before long, we had reached the conclusion that scandalously little had so far been done to bring together the results of research carried out in this field within a wide range of disciplines, and that the least we could do to improve the situation was to arrange a seminar on the subject.

That the enthusiasm for the project had less to do with the temporary effects of beer than with genuine scholarly interest was soon made manifest by the determination with which the participants in the discussion set to work to bring about the seminar. Within a year an organising committee had managed to secure both the necessary funding and the participation of some twenty eminent scholars representing a wide range of different disciplines and countries. The event itself took place in Malmö, 19-21 February 1997, more precisely at *Fridhemsborg,* the "Swe-Dane" publisher Einar Hansen's magnificent villa overlooking the straits of Öresund and with the skyline of Copenhagen on the horizon. In this most appropriate place general historians, economic historians, art historians, medieval and maritime archaeologists from Denmark, Sweden, Germany, Great Britain and Canada gathered to discuss questions of cogs, cargoes and commerce in the light of their recent research.

The title chosen for the seminar was "New Markets for New Goods. The Emergence of Large Scale Trade in Northern Europe 1150-1400." The overall picture that emerged during the three days was not one of dramatic change and commercial revolution but rather one of comparatively peaceful and steady growth. For while it is probably correct that North European trade in bulk commodities entered a phase of expansion around the middle of the twelfth century, it is also true that this development to a very large extent built on pre-existing structures. The trade in basic commodities, such as timber, grain, salt and pottery, that had been going on since time immemorial now expanded both in terms of volumes and of geography, while important new items–for instance beer, stone and various stone products–were gradually introduced into the system. Ships, trade routes and commercial networks changed, old centres declined and new ones emerged–but by and large nothing of all this came about in a "revolutionary" fashion, although the long-term effects were profound. Focusing attention firmly on the basic commodities of everyday life rather than on the objects of more or less conspicuous consumption thus produced a new and in a sense truer picture of the forces, mechanisms and pace of change.

The insights gained in and through the seminar were clearly of great importance for the history of Medieval Europe, and it was decided that at least a substantial selection of the contributions had to be made available to a larger public. Such decisions are easily taken but harder to realise. Some of the studies presented at the seminar were nearly finished at the time and could rapidly be revised and completed in the light of the discussions, while others needed more thorough rethinking and recasting. Another task of translating, correcting, and harmonising the terminology of scholars representing so many different countries and disciplines was to require efforts of a magnitude that had not been foreseen. Nevertheless it is the contention of the editors that their efforts were well spent–the result is a highly useful and thought-provoking volume on an important subject of current and growing interest.

The Malmö seminar was organised by a committee consisting of Lars Berggren, Nils Hybel, Annette Landen and Bjørn Poulsen, and was made financially possible through the generous sponsorship of Einar Hansen's research fund (Einar Hansens Forskningsfond). Apart from the authors of the articles in this volume, a number of other scholars also made valuable contributions to the seminar: Detlef Kattinger (Greifswald University, Germany) presented his research on the trade in wax and furs between England and the Baltic; Ebbe Nyborg (The National Museum, Copenhagen) discussed the importation of stone, lead and bronze for ecclesiastical buildings in Denmark; Per Kristian Madsen (The Antiquarian Collection in Ribe, Denmark) examined the importance and activities of Ribe within the Hanseatic League; Anders Ödman (The Historical Museum, Lund, Sweden) introduced current research on iron production and trade in medieval Denmark. All the authors of the present volume have greatly benefitted from the knowledge conveyed in these expositions, and from the insightful remarks of other participants in the discussions.

The task of editing the volume has been carried out by Lars Berggren, Nils Hybel and Annette Landen (of whom the latter is also responsible for the bibliography, and for the harmonisation of footnotes and references). The contributions of non-English authors have been translated and/or corrected by Alan Crozier (L. Berggren), Stacey M. Cozart (B. Poulsen), Gillian Fellows-Jensen (J. Bill), and Jennifer Paris (N. Hybel and R. Hammel-Kiesow). This part of the work and the final publication have been made possible by financial aid from Einar Hansens Forskningsfond, Ebbe Kocks Stiftelse, Hielmstierne-Rosencroneske Stiftelse, Nordenstedtska Stiftelsen, the Danish Research Council for the Humanities (Statens Humanistiske Forskningsråd), the Faculty of Humanities of the University of Copenhagen, and the Danish National Research Board ("Netværket Danmark og Europa i Senmiddelalderen"). Finally, we thank the Pontifical Institute of Medieval Studies for publishing the volume in their series, and especially its director of publications, Dr Ron B. Thomson, not only for converting a package of data files into a handsome book, but also for improving its content.

Lars Berggren and Annette Landen

Introduction

Nils Hybel

Commercialisation is a key topic in social and economic history as old as this historical discipline itself. The early socio-economic historians of the nineteenth century considered the history of the second millennium AD to be an evolutionary or a revolutionary process of commercialisation. Medieval society was assumed to be basically founded on a subsistence economy and enforced and customary social and economic relations. It was maintained that medieval markets were undeveloped and that money only penetrated the agrarian sector during the high Middle Ages and consequently the majority of the medieval population was subject to serfdom. Some historians even found a mover of this state of things in commercialisation, on equal terms with the social antagonisms of the Marxists, the demographic repercussions of the Black Death (F. Seebohm, R. Ernle) or the lord's and peasants' joint interest in creating liberal social and economic conditions for the increasing of agricultural productivity (Thorold Rogers). For late nineteenth-century historians like Erwin Nasse, W. von Ochenkowski and W.J. Ashey, commercialisation was not merely the destination of history, it was also considered a historical mover towards commercialisation. Economic history was considered the story of a continuous ascent of unilinear progress from barbaric primitiveness to the developed societies of modern times. The core of progress was commercialisation and this materialised as a rise in the market economy and the transformation of the personal ties of serfdom into the legally reciprocal, clearly-defined, impersonal free relations of copy-hold and wage labour.

Around the time of the First World War the idea of fluctuating levels of economic activities and commercialisation emerged in medieval research. Henri Pirenne depicted the commercial history of the Middle Ages in terms of a blocking of the Mediterranean trade in the early Middle Ages, the flourishing commercial development of the high Middle Ages and the setbacks of the late Middle Ages. During the depression in the 1930s this idea was refined in respect to the latter period. The works of Wilhelm Abel, Marc Bloch, C.A. Christensen and Michael M. Postan revealed, more or less simultaneously, the concept of a late medieval crisis involving the entire socio-economy of society. The view that the medieval economy had its declines, its setbacks, as well as its advances, extended the scope of research on the whole medieval period. The idea of fluctuating levels of medieval socio-economy was pushed back into the twelfth and thirteenth centuries, for example in Postan's studies from the 1930s and 1940s of the chronology of labour services and the rise of a money economy. Most of the studies still focused on commercialisation but commerce was no longer considered an important agent of historical change, even though a few attempts to bring back variants of this doctrine were made in the post-war period. In his critique of Maurices Dobb's book *Studies in the Development of Capitalism,* from 1946, Paul M. Sweezy defended a classical commercial standpoint and in the 1950s W.C. Robinson and Johan Schreiner launched a monetary alternative to Postan's mariginal land theory.

From the 1940s the dominating trend in economic history was to ascribe the fluctuations of economic activities and commercialisation primarily to structural changes—especially demographic. With Dobb's book a "neo-Marxist" theory appeared, and in the 1950's a "neo-Malthusian" theory was formulated by Michael Postan and Wilhelm Abel. At that time these theories appeared as strongly marked, mutually incompatible bodies of thought, but from the 1960s on there was a tendency for the "neo-Malthusian" and "neo-Marxist" positions to merge, and lead away from mono-causal explanatory models. They agreed that the population growth of the high Middle Ages turned into a demographic decline before the Black Death some time in the first half of the fourteenth century, and that this demographic swing grew from a complex pattern of causes arising in the thirteenth century. Thus, it was agreed that the exploitation of the peasants increased, that the volume of the landlords' investments was inadequate, that pressure on the available land increased, that agricultural productivity tended to drop, and that climate and epidemics had an important demographic effect on an already vulnerable socio-economic situation. Yet there were still clear dividing lines between the two bodies of theory in their different emphases on which of these factors should be seen as determinants of demographic decline. The "neo-Malthusians" continued to seek the ultimate reason for the demographic downturn in an insoluble conflict between nature and society—the exhaustion of the soil caused by the increasing population pressure of the high Middle Ages—whereas the "neo-Marxist" investigation of the causes of the declining population was rooted in a social conflict between lord and peasant—the increasing exploitation of the peasants likewise caused by increasing population pressure.

Already in 1962 Anthony Bridbury turned some of this learning on its head. He claimed that agricultural productivity increased after the great loss of population in the plague epidemics in the second half of the fourteenth century and based this statement on indications of manufacturing, commercial and urban developments. Bridbury demonstrated that there is no simple and unequivocal relationship between population development and economic and commercial change. Later it has been proved by others (among them the writer of this introduction) that the empirical preconditions for the structuralist theories are dubious. There is no documentation for the existence of a general "Malthusian" situation in Northern Europe in the first half of the fourteenth century. The documentation for the "neo-Marxist" claims of overexploitation and a consequent deterioration in the reproductive conditions of the peasants towards 1300 is equally doubtful. And there is just as little proof of a general population decline before 1348.

A new approach to the study of medieval social and economic history has been derived from these successive and successful attacks on the structuralist paradigms in the years witnessing the break-down of the Iron Curtain and what seems to be the global victory of a market economy. See for example R.H. Britnell, *The Commercialisation of English Society 1000-1500* (Cambridge 1993) and Edward Miller and John Hatcher, *Medieval England, Towns, Commerce and Crafts 1086-1348* (London 1995). Firstly, the dichotomies subsistence/market economy and personal/impersonal relations are not viewed so stringently; and, secondly, as a simplification, commercialisation is increasingly considered a mere process of growth and dispersal. Commercial activities have existed in Northern Europe in various forms since prehistoric times, with varying importance for the development of the societies in the region. Subsistence and exchange economies have always been linked, just as the alternative of looting or trading. Personal "feudal" relations are by no means more original or archaic than impersonal commercial ones—they have probably coexisted for as long as we can trace the history of human societies in this part of the world, just as well as agriculture, crafts and trade. The Middle Ages did not experience a transition from a natural economy to a market economy. Trade was an integral part of the medieval economy on a local and regional scale in Northern Europe, as it was between this part of Europe and other parts of the world—Southern Europe and the Orient. All economic sectors were closely related and mutually dependent upon one another. Medieval farmers and rural and urban craftsmen were linked to merchants and consumers at home and overseas.

The present volume is a contribution to this modern trend in economic history offering a new perspective on the history of trade from the high to the late Middle Ages. It is the first collection of essays concentrating on the interregional bulk trade in Northern Europe, providing a picture of the volumes and the chronology of the most important bulk commodities from the middle of the twelfth to the end of the fourteenth century.

In spite of the lack of systematic and comparative studies of the medieval bulk trade in Northern Europe before 1400, historians have generally agreed that the history of trade in medieval Northern Europe can be divided into a phase dominated by an exchange of luxuries and a phase of increasing importance of bulk trade, but the chronology of this process has been a matter of dispute. Some have argued that bulk commodities were "pushed" into the markets of Western Europe as a consequence of colonisation and the foundation of new towns in the east from the middle of the twelfth century, and that long-distance bulk trade became an important economic factor around the middle of the thirteenth century. According to others, bulk commodities were rather "pulled" by late medieval urbanisation into the West. Whereas some of the landed aristocracy grew poorer from the end of the fourteenth century, urban capital and spending power increased due to proto-industrialisation and the development of crafts and commercial activities. Urban prosperity attracted eastern bulk commodities to the markets of Western Europe where they put a strain on, for instance, the grain markets by connecting them with price zones where grain was considerably cheaper because of lower production costs.

Both readings are more likely to be reflections of changes in the supply of historical source material rather than of the actual development of medieval trade in Northern Europe. In the high Middle Ages trade in the Baltic and the North Sea changed hands. In the first half of the twelfth century German merchants still had only a fairly modest share of the commerce. Trade in the Baltic was principally in the hands of the Gotlanders, and Scandinavians were the leading traders also in the North Sea. The Norwegians were the most important traders in the North Sea, but Danish and Swedish, Flemish, Saxon and Frisian merchants were found here too. During the next hundred years commerce in the North Sea and the Baltic was to fall under the domination of German merchants who had an unusual organisational talent. They created one of the most unique, flexible and powerful institutions of the Middle Ages, the Hansa, and town organisations from which abundant written sources have been handed down to us. The impression that bulk trade in Northern Europe was a novelty in the middle of the twelfth century to a great extent depends on this change of leadership, and the subsequent change in the supply of literary evidence for the study of trade in the North Sea and the Baltic.

In principle the same methodological objection can be raised against the idea that large-scale trade had its roots some two hundred years later, at the end of the fourteenth century. Ignoring adequate pre-Black-Death sources, in particular the earliest English poundage rolls examined by contributors to this anthology, the scholars arguing for this chronology have been misled by Hanseatic sources, because these do not allow quantitative calculations of the ratio between high-value goods and bulk commodities before the Lübeck and Hamburg poundage rolls of 1368/69. By ignoring the fact that the modest bulk trade in the decades of pandemics in the second half of the fourteenth century was, compared with trade in the fifteenth century, a reflection of the drastic demographic regression, and by overlooking the abundant evidence of bulk commodities in North European trade in the pre-plague period presented in this volume, the decline in bulk goods in the decades after the Black Death has been interpreted as a beginning rather than as a downswing in a trade that had been in operation for centuries.

The present volume provides ample evidence that the history of medieval trade cannot be divided into a phase dominated by an exchange of luxuries followed by a phase of increasing bulk trade. The contributors convincingly demonstrate how long-distance trade with bulk commodities affected consumption patterns, technology and agricultural specialisation centuries before the Black Death ravaged the demographic development of Europe. Bulk trade was certainly not exclusively a late medieval phenomenon—the question is rather if its beginnings in Northern Europe can be delimited back in time to the twelfth century. The international bulk trade seems to be older: several of the present articles indicate that it has a much longer history. In fact beer seems to have been the only product becoming a trade commodity after 1150. The beginning of the long distance trade in stone, pottery, timber and grain fades into the distance, even though the specific export of stone products from Gotland can also be dated within the period concentrated on here. Thus, strictly speaking, international bulk trade was not an innovation of the mid-twelfth century. This book sheds light on important aspects of its expansion, and shows how it developed from an incidental activity to a regular trade during the two and a half centuries from 1150 to 1400.

In the opening article Bruce Campbell accentuates the expanding trade at all levels during the thirteenth century by pointing out that the total volume of English exports at the beginning of the fourteenth century, as compared with the Gross Domestic Product, reached a level which it did not notably exceed for centuries. At this time demand and production and transportation costs were clearly more essential for the development of trading patterns than national borders. The proto-industrialised towns in the Netherlands and non-agricultural Western Norway bought English raw materials, fuel and victuals on equal terms with domestic producers and consumers; all depended on the market in which the commodities could be sold with profit. Grain and firewood from Kent, cloth, grain, dairy produce and herrings from East Anglia, wool from central and southern England, hides and coal from the north-east, and hides and tin from south-west England were exported to markets abroad.

The Danish realm was also being integrated in a North European interregional market during the thirteenth century. Björn Poulsen describes how, in the thirteenth and fourteenth centuries, cloth, beer, iron and salt were imported while agricultural products and herring became increasingly important exports. From the early twelfth century Danish horses were known, and appreciated, in Europe, and in the next century there is evidence of horses exported to Germany, England and Flanders. Together with hides, fat, tallow, herrings and bacon, horses were the chief Danish export to the urbanised parts of north-western Europe, whereas extensive cattle exports did not begin before the end of the fourteenth century. During the twelfth century, as Denmark became a supplier of herring and agricultural products to markets in Northern Germany and the Netherlands, the country was gradually integrated in the trade structure centred on the German towns.

The important role in the bulk trade played by Lübeck—the leading German town on the south coast of the Baltic Sea—is demonstrated in Rolf Hammel-Kiesow's article. The golden age of the town lasted nearly two hundred years, from the early thirteenth to the late fourteenth century, and coincides with the emergence of bulk commodities in the commercial activities of the town. Basing himself not only on written sources but also on important architectural features, Kiesow argues that before 1200 Lübeck was primarily a port of transshipment of high-value goods, and that from the beginning of the thirteenth century the town became an exchange centre for Lüneburg salt, grain, flour, beer, herring and stockfish. Transshipment via the Lübeck-Hamburg axis was particularly important for the transport of high-value goods, such as wax, furs and cloth, between east and west, whereas for good reasons it was probably more convenient to ship bulky products *ummeland*, i.e., from the Baltic and the Scanian markets via the Skagerak round the Skaw into the North Sea and vice versa. Kiesow traces this traffic back into the twelfth century and describes the part Lübeck merchants may have played in the *ummelandsfart* from the thirteenth century.

A presentation of crucial technological preconditions for the development of long-distance bulk trade in Northern Europe is given in Jan Bill's account of the significant changes in the construction and size of the cargo ships. Major technical changes around 1200 made it possible to build larger and cheaper ships that contributed to reducing freight rates and stimulating bulk trade. Archaeological and written evidence shows how cargo capacities were steadily increasing in the period dealt with in the various articles of this book. The commercial ships do not, however, seem to have come close to the technical limits of contemporary shipbuilding, because no known cargo ship reached the size of the largest contemporary warships. An increased demand for commercial tonnage was apparently not the sole stimulus for the development of medieval shipbuilding technology.

Judging from the development of the interregional trade in victuals, building material, pottery and stone products, the demand for, and presumably also the actual tonnage of the North European mercantile fleet, increased from the middle of the twelfth to the start of the fifteenth century. Even though trade with some of these heavy and/or bulky low-value commodities may already have had a long history by the beginning of our period, the five articles dealing with the history of the trade in special bulk commodities give an overall impression of how the bulk trade developed from an incidental activity to a regular trade.

This was indeed the case with the trade in beer. Richard Unger's contribution shows that even though beer-making has a history going back to the early Middle Ages, beer did not become a trade commodity until about 1200. During the thirteenth and fourteenth centuries the trade in beer changed radically, partly because of technological improvements in beer production. In the thirteenth century German brewers discovered how to maximise the ability of hops to give durability to beer without raising the alcohol level by increasing the amount of grain used, and industrial brewing of beer for export was established first in Hamburg and Bremen, later in the Baltic towns of Rostock and Wismar. The German North Sea towns then supplied the Netherlands while the Baltic towns exported beer to Scandinavia until, in the fifteenth century, the brewing technique in Holland had reached the stage where local brewers were able to oust the

Germans from both the Dutch and the Flemish markets; and at about the same time the domestic Scandinavian brewers could successfully compete with the Germans. In the late Middle Ages the German export of beer changed direction geographically but also in respect to the types of beer traded. Since hopped beer of good quality could now be produced in many different places, exporters turned to more expensive high-quality sorts of beer. To some extent, then, the beer export industry shifted from a relatively low-value bulk commodity to a more high-value item that could better absorb the transportation costs.

Unlike the trade in beer, the one in pottery already had a long history in Northern Europe. Studies of medieval pottery have revealed that pottery was probably never made by every household or even in every village. In the twelfth century pottery seems to have been produced in a few locations, either rural, combined with agriculture or forestry, or in towns, but such goods were rarely transported over very long distances. Before 1150 there is only faint archaeological evidence of trade in pottery between the countries around the North Sea and between this region and the Baltic region. Alan Vince's contribution shows how this pattern changed quite rapidly by the middle of the twelfth century. There is abundant evidence of the importation of pottery from the Netherlands, the Rhineland, Eastern England and Northern France to Scandinavia and the Baltic in the following period.

Stone products had also been traded since time immemorial but a regular long- and medium-distance trade in sizeable stone goods seems to have started only towards the end of the twelfth century. At that time the island of Gotland, one of the strongholds of the east-west trade in Northern Europe, started to develop an industry that soon supplied the Baltic and the North Sea regions with various stone products. Using geological methods Lars Berggren and Annette Landen have identified thousands of stone objects—among them some eight hundred baptismal fonts—exported from Gotland between roughly 1150 and 1400. Lars Berggren shows that this industry probably reached its maximum output during the period ca. 1250-1350, when fonts, grave-stones, and a variety of architectural products were exported to destinations as widely apart as Bergen, Tartu, Umeå, Wilamów and Bruges. At least during this period Gotlandic stone exports constituted a true bulk trade that can be calculated in several thousands of tons annually. The profitability of the trade probably depended on the possibilities of transporting extremely heavy items along with large quantities of lighter goods, and when the opportunities for such multi-commodity freights sank drastically after the middle of the fourteenth century the whole stone industry declined rapidly.

The conversion to Christianity of Scandinavia and the Baltic provided a major stimulus to the spread of Gotland's stone products. The progress of the Church and colonisation were indeed also important preconditions for the expansion of long-distance trade in timber and grain. Wendy Childs' examination of the import of timber to England shows how Baltic timber became increasingly important on the English market in the fourteenth century. England was not particularly short of timber in the Middle Ages and imports were never really large scale. Nevertheless some types of timber may have been essential for special industrial, military and naval purposes and the trade could have had an important impact on the economy in the immediate hinterlands of the principal timber-importing ports, Hull and Lynn. The import of timber to England can be traced back to the thirteenth century. In the first decade of the fourteenth century Norway seems to have been the chief exporter of timber to England, but some time after 1310 the balance of the import turned in favour of Baltic timber. Despite the drastic demographic downturn there was an increase in the import of both timber and its by-products—such as tar, pitch and ashes—in the fourteenth century. This development was possibly connected with the rise of the English cloth industry. During this century England began to produce cloth on a scale allowing exports to the Baltic in exchange for timber and other merchandise. But probably the comparative cost structures in England and the Baltic also helped to make the trade profitable.

Earlier research has demonstrated how different price and cost zones prevailed in Eastern and Western Europe in the fifteenth century, but if this was also the case in the previous centuries has not yet been established. Nils Hybel's contribution shows that it is perhaps not too rash to assert that different price and cost structures came into existence simultaneously with the colonisation of the hinterland of the south-eastern coasts of the Baltic Sea. It is undoubtedly in this context that the grain imported from the Baltic to grain-growing England, documented in the closing article in this anthology, must be understood. The grain route from the Baltic to the North Sea is proved to have been in full operation by the start of the fourteenth century at the latest. The overseas grain trade from the English North Sea ports was dominated from the second half of the thirteenth century by the export of wheat to Norway, but in the first decade of the following century it declined. At the same time imports of oats and primarily rye from Germany and the Baltic region became increasingly important, supplemented by wheat imported from France, Spain, Portugal and probably Italy to the Channel ports. The import of rye seems to have reached a maximum in the 1320s but, like the import of timber, the quantities imported were very modest; nevertheless it is possible to argue that the grain imports affected local prices and perhaps also the development of prices on a more general scale.

There is hardly any doubt that by the middle of the twelfth century, trade in bulk commodities in the North had entered a phase of increasing importance for the future of all Europe. Between 1150 and 1400, then, it developed from an incidental activity to a regular part of an increasingly internationalized North European economy. The volume and the geography of the trade expanded, but compared with the total of goods produced in Northern Europe it was modest. Nonetheless, the overseas bulk trade became an important factor of the medieval economy with strong influence on every day life.

From the end of the thirteenth century urbanization together with agricultural specialization in Western Europe created a rapidly expanding market for foodstuffs and timber—mainly for specific industrial and building purposes. Grain from the distant fields of Eastern Europe became the daily bread of West European town dwellers—sometimes even of those living close to or in the middle of arable districts—and timber and animal foodstuffs came from Scandinavia and the Baltic region to the growing towns of North-western Germany, the Netherlands and Eastern England. This trade not only stimulated urbanization and the early growth of industrial production but also affected the development of prices and influenced the formation of agricultural production and forestry in the West. The spread of Gotlandic stone products, the production of pottery centralized in a few locations and the commercialization of the German beer production from about 1200 did not only influence consumption and patterns of production, it also affected fashion, religious practice, common habits and traditions. The exchange of goods brought the populations of Northern Europe in closer contact, changing lifestyles and making them more uniform, thus providing a precondition for the pre-industrialization in the West and the spread of European civilization in the North.

The Sources of Tradable Surpluses: English Agricultural Exports 1250-1350[1]

Bruce M. S. Campbell

During the long thirteenth century expanding trade at all levels—local, regional, national and international—transformed the relationship between population and the land.[2] Trade liberated individual cities, regions, and states from a narrow and exclusive dependence upon their own agricultural sectors for foodstuffs, fuel, draught power and a wide range of organic raw materials. Rates of demographic and economic growth thereby became attainable which exceeded the biologically determined reproduction rates of plants and animals. As rural population densities and urban concentrations built up in core areas of economic activity so a widening orbit of trade enabled these areas of mounting land scarcity to circumvent Ricardian constraints and meet a growing proportion of their needs by drawing upon regions of relative land abundance. Imports of such land-extensive products as timber, pitch, wax, furs, wool, hides, live animals on the hoof, and low-yielding grain served, in effect, as land substitutes. In return, regions economically reliant upon the production of a narrow range of basic primary products gained access to the bullion, quality manufactures and specialized produce of more developed regions, typically cloth, craft wares of many sorts, and wine. This Smithian process of reciprocal exchange, once initiated, proved self-perpetuating for much of the thirteenth century.[3] Its dynamism derived from a combination of market growth and falling transaction costs, the former underpinned by population growth, the latter by advances in the technology and organization of trade and commerce. Such developments proved propitious for farmers whose involvement in the expanding

[1] My thanks to the participants in the 1997 Malmö conference, "New Markets for New Goods: the Emergence of Large-Scale Trade in Northern Europe 1150-1400," for their comments upon an earlier version of this paper and to Ken Bartley for producing Figures 2 and 4.

[2] Lopez 1971; Persson 1988; Grantham 1999.

[3] Grantham 1995.

commercial nexus increased almost everywhere. Greater access to expanding markets promoted specialization. Farmers began to capitalize upon their comparative advantage, thereby raising the mean productivity of agriculture as a whole and counteracting the opposing tendency towards diminishing returns.[4] The expanding volumes of agricultural produce (processed and unprocessed) entering trade and the growing distances over which they were traded provide evidence of these developments.

Commercial growth in this period was a pan-European and inter-continental phenomenon. Within northern Europe the epicentre of that growth was Flanders. It was the southern focus of the North Sea trading region and was strategically located at the intersection between the north-south and east-west trans-European trade routes. Here developed "the most populous cluster of large cities in western Europe—probably in all Europe".[5] Collectively, Bruges, Ghent, and Ypres had a population of at least 150,000 on the eve of the Black Death; adding the many lesser towns would raise this figure to at least 250,000.[6] Commerce and manufacturing—mass-produced textiles in particular—together provided the lifeblood of this remarkable urban conglomeration, which represented the single greatest north-European concentration of demand for food, industrial raw materials (principally high-quality wool), and fuel (both wood and coal). Flanders became the one trading partner common to all countries bordering the North Sea and Baltic. England may have exchanged produce and merchandise with Ireland, Scotland, Scandinavia, north Germany, Holland, Brabant, Normandy, France, Spain and Italy, but it was to Flanders that the bulk of all English exports were sent.[7] This was to the obvious benefit of those parts of England most convenient to those east- and south-coast ports which serviced that trade: Newcastle, Hull, Boston, Lynn, Yarmouth, Ipswich, London, Sandwich, and, to a lesser extent, Southampton. Indeed, the very fact that Newcastle, Hull, Boston and Lynn were new urban creations of the eleventh and twelfth centuries bears witness to the vigour with which England's North Sea trade had expanded during the twelfth and thirteenth centuries.[8] By the close of the latter century Boston and Hull were respectively the second and third most important ports in the land, both profiting from

[4] Persson 1988: 63-103; Overton & Campbell 1991: 9-22.
[5] Russell 1972: 112.
[6] Information supplied by Professor Erik Thoen, University of Ghent, Belgium.
[7] Lloyd 1982: 108-109.
[8] Beresford 1988: 463-465, 467f, 473f, 515f; Miller & Hatcher 1995: 196f.

their close trading links with Flanders.

E. Miller and J. Hatcher have recently estimated English exports to be worth approximately £302,000 at the opening of the fourteenth century.[9] Apart from significant quantities of lead, tin and coal, over 90 percent of these exports were of direct or indirect agricultural provenance. Wool and cloth were the most prominent of these items, followed by hides, some grain, and small amounts of firewood. For this point in time G. D. Snooks and N. Mayhew have recently offered alternative Gross Domestic Product (GDP) estimates of £4.1 million and £4.7 million respectively.[10] The basis on which Snooks' estimate has been made is unclear and the high base population of 6.0 million upon which it depends inflates Mayhew's estimate. In fact, a significantly smaller population of 4.25 million is more plausible, given known patterns of land-use and levels of crop yield. Recalculating GDP by Mayhew's method using this lower population estimate yields a national income of £3.7 million.[11] This is a far from robust figure. If not seriously wide of the mark, it suggests that English exports may already have been worth at least 6.5 percent and perhaps as much as 8 percent of GDP. Agricultural exports constituted an even greater proportion —probably in excess of 10 percent—of the nation's gross agricultural production. Four centuries later, at the end of the seventeenth century, exports were still worth only 5-6 percent of an admittedly larger GDP and during most of the first half of the nineteenth century they accounted for 9-11 percent of national income.[12] Moreover, even with the aid of corn bounties payable under the Corn Laws, direct exports accounted for only 8 percent of gross agricultural output by the middle of the eighteenth century.[13] Crude as these comparisons may be, they highlight both the scale and the economic significance of the agricultural export trade which had developed by ca. 1300, which is all the more remarkable given the pressure of domestic demands upon the agricultural sector as the national population attained its medieval peak. Indeed, it was upon the wealth created by trade that the population was increasingly reliant for at least part of its support.

Throughout the thirteenth century exports almost certainly exceeded

[9] Miller & Hatcher 1995: 213.

[10] Snooks 1995: 50, and Mayhew 1995: 57-59.

[11] Campbell 2000b.

[12] Deane & Cole 1969: 28f.

[13] Overton 1996: 89, 146.

imports and thus yielded a healthy positive trade balance and a steady inflow of bullion, ensuring a stable currency for the greater part of that century. Growing bullion stocks, sound money and an increasing money supply together lubricated the wheels of commerce while the lure of commercial profits encouraged fuller participation in the market.[14] Trade grew at all levels: Miller and Hatcher estimate that exports trebled in real value over the course of the century and internal trade must have grown at least commensurately.[15] Exports thus grew faster than the concurrent increase in population and constituted one of the more dynamic components of the economy, generating both income and employment. The lure of profitable export markets encouraged greater investment and specialization on the part of English agricultural producers than could otherwise have occurred. The export trade also underpinned much domestic urban growth, which in turn provided farmers with further incentives to invest, specialize and innovate. No English port gained more from its involvement in international trade than London. It was already the leading English port at the beginning of the thirteenth century and during the course of that century it doubled its share of the expanding volume of trade so that by that century's close it was handling over a third of all English exports.[16] A growing proportion of that trade was in the hands of denizen merchants. London was the only English port to maintain connections with all parts of the continent and the only port concerned with every branch of trade. Much of the city's physical growth derived from this expanding commercial role. By ca. 1300 it had grown to become the second largest city north of the Alps (after Paris) with a population of 70-75,000 inhabitants.[17] It was thus a major centre of demand in its own right. Agricultural specialization, of which there is clear evidence, in London's immediate hinterland was therefore an indirect result of that city's heightened involvement in international trade.[18]

The patterns of agricultural specialization which evolved within London's provisioning hinterland were a microcosm of the wider patterns of commercial specialization emerging within the nascent North Sea trading region. Trade, whatever its scale and the distance over which it is conducted, is selective. Whether commodities were worth trading depended upon

14 Mayhew 1995: 71-74.

15 Miller & Hatcher 1995: 214.

16 Miller & Hatcher 1995: 196, 214; Keene 1989b: 99-111.

17 Campbell et al. 1993: 9-11; Nightingale 1996: 95-98.

18 Campbell et al. 1993: 111-144.

Figure 1. England's principal North Sea and Channel ports and associated navigable rivers, ca. 1300. Map: Alf Dahlberg, Lund. Source: Langdon 1993: 4f.

their costs of production, ability to withstand costs of carriage and still be sold at an advantage, perishability, and the availability of suitable means of transport. Other things being equal, the cheapest, bulkiest, and most perishable commodities and those produced by the most intensive and expensive methods in areas of high land rents were those traded over the shortest distance, using, wherever possible, water rather than land transport. Firewood, hay, fodder crops, fresh milk, vegetables and brewing grains are good examples. Over greater distances traded commodities had to be cheaply and, therefore, extensively produced, non-perishable, and either possess a high value relative to their bulk or be exceptionally cheap to transport. Such commodities included furs, wax, wool, wheat, wine and live animals on the hoof.[19]

The Ports and Their Hinterlands

Proximity placed the extreme south-east of England at the lowest cost-distance from Flanders and neighbouring regions of the continent. No major English port was closer to the continent than Sandwich on the east Kent coast (Figure 1). In fact, it and its subsidiary ports from Faversham on the north Kent coast to Winchelsea on the south coast were closer in cost-distance to the entire continental coast between the Schelde and the Somme than they were to London.[20] Circa 1300 they handled approximately 3 to 5 percent of the nation's overseas trade, the bulk of it in the control of foreign merchants.[21] The high unit value commanded by arable land within the immediate hinterland of these ports identifies eastern Kent as an area of exceptionally high economic rent and consequently of intensive, high-cost methods of production (Figure 2).[22] The region's physical advantages for arable production were one component of these high rent levels. Above average population densities and the absence of rigid manorial structures and communal agrarian institutions were others. But superimposed upon these were the overlapping influences of two major urban centres of demand: London to the west and the great Flemish cities across the Channel to the east, both accessible by sea. This convergence of

19 *Von Thünen's Isolated State:* xxiii-xxxviii, 149-157.

20 Campbell et al. 1993: 182.

21 Miller & Hatcher 1995: 214.

22 Campbell et al. 1993: 128-144.

demand ensured that grain sold at a premium. Faversham was the grain market downstream of London most frequented by that city's corn-mongers. Sandwich, at a greater cost-distance from London, was a less important source of metropolitan supply. Instead, merchants from Picardy and Flanders, including men from the great city of Ghent, were as likely to be encountered in its grain market.[23] By 1300 east Kent appears to have been a significant exporter of grain.[24] This trade was only profitable because east Kent specialized in producing wheat and barley, respectively the winter and spring grains most capable of bearing the costs of carriage, while the short sea crossing kept freight costs low.

Low transport costs were even more critical to the small but locally significant export trade in oats—the lowest valued and bulkiest of the grains—from the south coast ports of Sandwich, Romney, and Rye, all of which were considerably closer in cost-distance to Picardy and Flanders than London.[25] The reclaimed and highly fertile soils of the Stour, Romney and Walland Marshes were especially suited to the production of high-yielding oats, which could be delivered direct from the farm to the coastal ports. The potentially punitive cost of overland transport was thereby kept to a minimum. Canterbury Cathedral Priory's Romney Marsh demesnes of Appledore and Fairfield and its demesne of Ebony on the adjacent Isle of Oxney were all major producers and sellers of oats.[26] Their distinctive commercial profiles reflect the unique combination of environmental and economic opportunities presented by these strategically located coastal marshlands.[27]

The commercial proximity of these small ports on the south-east coast of England to urban markets across the Channel is also apparent in the trade that grew up in firewood. Medieval cities required fuel—typically wood, but also charcoal, coal and peat—in quantity yet it was one of the bulkiest of all commodities to transport.[28] Consequently, commercial production of firewood, as J. H. von Thünen's land-use model demonstrates,

[23] Campbell et al. 1993: 180.

[24] Gras 1926: 293; Lloyd 1982: 56. Cf. Nils Hybel's article below, pp. 225f.

[25] Miller & Hatcher 1995: 185.

[26] Campbell & Power 1989: 33; Campbell et al. 1993: 116-118, 160; Campbell 1995b: 144, 151.

[27] Cheese produced from the flocks and herds stocked in the rich marshland grazings was a small but regular export of the port of Winchelsea in the early fourteenth century: Pelham 1929: 107-111.

[28] Galloway et al. 1996: 447-451.

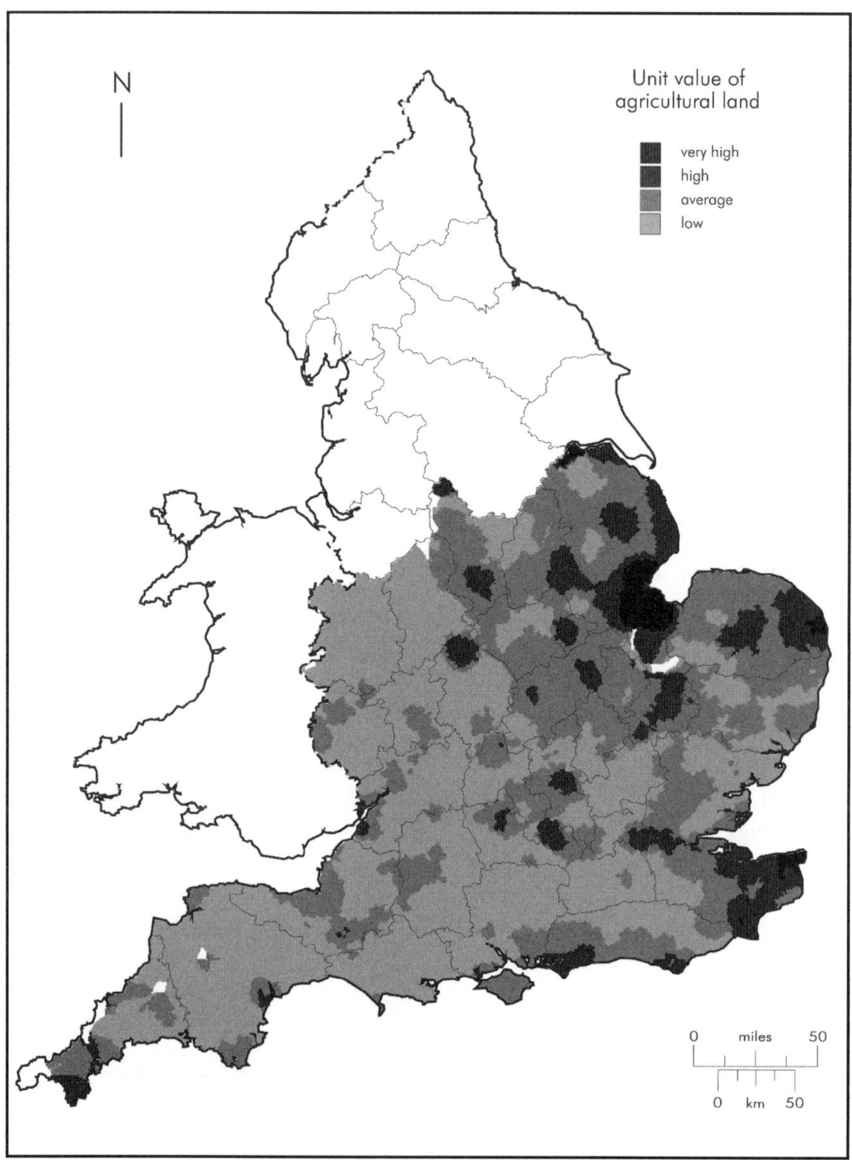

Figure 2. The unit value of agricultural land in England, 1300-1349, according to the *Inquisitiones Post Mortem*. Source: all extant and legible *IPM* extents dated 1300-49 in the PRO, London.

Figure 2:

Method:

K. Bartley and B.M.S. Campbell, "*Inquisitions Post Mortem*, G.I.S., and the Creation of a Land-use Map of Pre Black Death England," *Transactions in G.I.S.* 2 (1997).

Variables:

(unit value grassland : unit value arable) x 2.0
(unit value meadow : unit value arable) x 1.5
(unit value meadow : unit value pasture) x 1.5
(unit value arable) x 1.2

Definition:

Land Category	Mean unit value of arable (pence)	Mean ratio (unit value : unit value) of:		
		grassland to arable	meadow to arable	meadow to pasture
very high	16.2	1.1	1.3	2.9
high	7.0	2.2	2.8	3.3
average	4.3	3.6	4.3	3.9
low	2.6	5.7	6.5	5.3
all	3.9	4.5	5.3	4.3

was only viable at a close cost-distance to the market.[29] The intensively managed woodlands of southeast Kent and the southern Weald enjoyed just such a location. Coppicing ensured that these commercially lucrative woodlands were managed on a sustainable basis. In the late thirteenth century, as wood prices soared, they became major appreciating assets, returning an income per acre as great and sometimes even greater than the intensively cropped arable in the same vicinity. The 150-acre Reinden woods above Folkestone yielded an annual income of 9½ pence an acre in the 1270s.[30]

Since transport costs rose rapidly with distance, proximity of the woodlands to the coastal ports and such navigable rivers as served them was vitally important. Charcoal and timber remained commercially viable at a slightly greater range than faggots since they both commanded a higher value relative to their bulk. Winchelsea, serviced by the navigable lower reaches of the rivers Brede and Rother, was the natural outlet for this trade and thereby ranked as "the greatest exporter of timber and fuel in England

[29] *Von Thünen's Isolated State:* 106-123.

[30] Witney 1990: 34.

throughout the Middle Ages".[31] Wealden faggots, charcoal, timber and oak bark for tanning were regularly purchased in quantity by merchants from Normandy, Picardy, Flanders, Zealand and Eastland.[32] Small quantities were also exported from the northern Weald via the Medway. Sustaining this trade and the intensive management methods upon which it depended was the expanding demand of the great manufacturing centres of the Low Countries. So insatiable was their need of fuel that the trade in faggots and charcoal from Kent and Sussex was complemented by a similarly sea-borne (if, albeit, long distance) trade in coal from Newcastle.[33]

The high economic rent and correspondingly intensive methods of agricultural production which prevailed in much of Kent left only limited potential for commercial wool production. Although sheep were kept in many parts of the county they often took second place to cattle and swine (Figure 3). Often they were kept more for their manure than their wool. At this date Kentish sheep were very much an adjunct of the county's intensive arable husbandry and the coarse fleeces which they produced sold at prices well below the national average (Figure 4). Some of this wool was sold overseas. At the opening of the fourteenth century Sandwich handled 1.7 percent of all wool exports by bulk, less by value (Figure 3).[34] For foreign merchants seeking wool, larger supplies of higher quality were to be found elsewhere.

By the opening of the fourteenth century London had established itself as England's single greatest mart for wool. 35 percent of all unprocessed wool by bulk—the product of over 3.5 million sheep—passed through the port and its subsidiaries plus substantial additional quantities worked up as broadcloth and worsted (Figure 3).[35] Many foreign merchants came specifically seeking these commodities, especially the wool so necessary to the urban textile industry on the continent. For others, whose primary purpose was to bring wine, general merchandise and a range of high-quality raw materials, wool and cloth constituted the most profitable available return cargoes. Increasing numbers of English merchants were also engaged in the trade.[36] Given the vast quantities of wool being sent abroad via London it

[31] Pelham 1928; Pelham 1929: 106-12; Pelham 1936a: 322; Gardiner 1996: 133f.

[32] Pelham 1936a: 322; Witney 1990: 34.

[33] Pelham 1936a: 321f; Hatcher 1993: 26, 473f.

[34] Carus-Wilson & Coleman 1963: 41; Lloyd 1982: 220.

[35] Childs 1996: 130f.

[36] Carus-Wilson & Coleman 1963: 41-46; Pelham 1936a: 306-308.

is something of a surprise to discover that agricultural producers in the city's extensive hinterland tended to be more concerned with meeting the capital's own formidable and expanding demands for food, fuel and raw materials than with producing wool for export. Certainly, wool was produced within the London region but usually more as a secondary than a primary activity (Figure 3).

Whereas over 90 percent of demesnes within a ten-county area around London sold grain and live animals, only 70 percent sold wool. Of the gross income generated by the sale of agricultural produce, 9 percent was contributed by wool.[37] Sales of grain and live animals loomed far larger and would have been more prominent still had less of both been transferred for consumption elsewhere on the estate. As in Kent, sheep were more likely to have been kept as a useful component of mixed-farming systems geared towards grain production, than as an end in themselves. This is hardly surprising. Like all large cities, London required grain in quantity. The high prices, which Londoners were prepared to pay for their grain drew in supplies from a hinterland, in normal years, of 4,000 square miles. These same high prices effectively precluded London from becoming a regular exporter of grain.[38] The same applied to firewood, the supply of which was becoming increasingly inadequate to the capital's needs. London's zone of regular firewood supply extended to 12 miles by land and 50 miles by water and for industrial purposes was increasingly augmented by coal shipped down the coast from Newcastle.[39] Nor, more surprisingly, was London a significant exporter of hides, even though cattle husbandry was strongly developed in the metropolitan hinterland and meat animals were regularly driven to the city for slaughter.[40] Most hides were presumably absorbed by the capital's own substantial leather-working industry which catered to the single greatest market for leather goods in the kingdom. The residuum of hides left over for export was only a fraction of the original supply.

Wool alone, in processed and unprocessed forms, was therefore London's sole agricultural export of consequence. The volume of this trade bears tribute to the city's role as a major *entrepot* and collecting centre. Some of this wool was produced within the London region itself (Figures

[37] Campbell 1995: 147-150.

[38] Campbell et al. 1993: 27.

[39] Galloway et al. 1996: 455-467.

[40] Pelham 1936a: 315f; Lloyd 1982: 219; Power & Campbell 1992: 236f; Shaw 1956: 357.

3 and 4). For instance, within the Thames basin the presence of strong market opportunities for meat, milk, hides and wool encouraged all but the heaviest soiled demesnes and those within the immediate environs of the capital to stock both sheep and cattle.[41] The bulk of London's wool exports came, however, from further afield. Wool as a product was more profitably produced in regions of low economic rent than those of high and within farming systems characterized by semi-extensive and extensive methods of production. As the returns to the 1341 wool tax indicate, wool was a significant product of England's commonfield heartland, especially wherever limestone wolds and chalk downs created pasture in abundance (Figure 4). In the 1270s merchants licensed to export wool were active in many of the towns of central and southern England (Figure 3).[42] Much of the wool that they traded probably came from peasant producers. In the 1290s Pegolotti lists many monastic houses in the same area from which wool could also be obtained (Figure 3).[43] To all classes of producer in England's land-locked interior the international wool trade represented a commercial lifeline since, once shorn, graded and packed, wool was often the sole agricultural product capable of withstanding the costs of transport to distant markets. "There can be no doubt that London was the main outlet for the wool of central England, the Cotswolds, and the Welsh March."[44] The finest and highest valued wools, produced in the Welsh borderland (Figure 4), were brought the longest distance. The sheep that produced these finer wools were less productive and required more nourishing feed and greater care than coarser-wooled breeds. They were therefore at their greatest comparative advantage in the land-locked western interior of England, where there was an abundance of suitable pasturage, population densities were below average, and levels of economic rent were generally low. In such regions only a high-valued, low bulk, non-perishable product was capable of being sold with profit at a distance. The returns to the 1341 wool tax nevertheless demonstrate that the quantities of wool produced in these western districts were relatively small (Figure 4).

London's success in capturing the wool supply of a wide area of southern, south-eastern, eastern, central and west-central England left only residual amounts for export via the lesser ports of the south and east coasts

41 Campbell & Power 1989: 31-36.

42 Donkin 1973: 120-123.

43 Pelham 1936b: 242f; Donkin 1973: 122.

44 Lloyd 1977: 132.

(Figure 3). Ipswich, for instance, although a busy port with old established trading connections across the North Sea handled less than 3 percent of all wool sent overseas in the opening decade of the fourteenth century.[45] Yarmouth in the same decade exported only fractionally more.[46] This is all the more paradoxical given the apparent prominence of sheep farming within Norfolk and Suffolk. On the evidence of the lay subsidy returns of 1327 and 1332 and the wool tax returns of 1341 no English county was more densely populated with people and sheep than Norfolk (Figure 4).[47] This combination implies that East Anglian sheep were more intensively managed than those elsewhere, the low prices commanded by their coarse fleeces testifying to the essentially subordinate role of sheep within the mixed-farming systems of which they formed a vital element.[48] Nor was this specialization in the production of coarse wool economically irrational: such wools had the merit that per unit area they returned a higher yield at less cost than their finer and higher-priced alternatives. Moreover, the manure produced by these foldcourse sheep was integral to the maintenance of arable production. Instead of exporting wool, Yarmouth sent abroad significant quantities of cheap, light worsted cloth, often woven with a linen warp spun from the flax and hemp produced in quantity within the region by the many small producers.[49] Using the region's cheap and abundant labour force to add value to these relatively low-grade raw materials by processing them into a higher-grade product created a commodity better able to enter overseas trade. The high rural population densities associated with the development of domestic industry and presence within the region of a major provincial city—Norwich—nevertheless ensured that the bulk of all food produced was retained for consumption within the region. Although some grain was exported—principally high-yielding wheat and high-grade malted barley—it was only a tiny fraction of total production.[50]

[45] Butter—a land-extensive product—and bacon also featured among Ipswich's exports, which included modest quantities of grain: Postan 1987: 171; Lloyd 1982: 52, 218.

[46] Carus-Wilson & Coleman 1963: 41; Lloyd 1977: 69, 134f.

[47] Campbell 2000a:13. Based upon a national analysis of the number of recorded taxpayers per vill in the 1327 and 1332 lay subsidies using data supplied by R. E. Glasscock of St John's College, Cambridge.

[48] Bailey 1990.

[49] Sutton 1989; Lloyd 1982: 51; Childs 1996: 129f.

[50] Saul 1975: 226, 368-371.

Yarmouth, in 1334 the highest taxed port after London and York with the kingdom's second largest mercantile marine after London, lay on the outermost periphery of that city's grain provisioning zone.[51] In terms of cost-distance, however, Flanders was closer (Figure 1).[52] The influence of overseas demand is perhaps to be seen in the exceptionally high unit value of arable land within Yarmouth's immediate hinterland (Figure 2) and associated intensity and innovativeness of husbandry methods (which closely resembled those practised within the hinterland of Sandwich).[53] It is nevertheless significant that throughout the first half of the fourteenth century the prior of Norwich preferred to send the surplus grain from his top-yielding demesnes of Hemsby and Martham the 30 miles by boat to the priory in Norwich rather than deliver it by cart to the quayside in Yarmouth a mere 7 miles away.[54] Perhaps Yarmouth's grain trade had once been much larger; certainly, it grew in volume following the Black Death when Norfolk became a county of excess grain production.[55] But in the first half of the fourteenth century the needs of Norfolk's own expanding population were paramount and participation in the international grain trade was decidedly limited and quite possibly declining. It was therefore the harvest of the sea rather than the harvest of the land for which Yarmouth was internationally most renowned. The port was England's single greatest herring fishery. By 1340 its autumn herring fair was attracting about 500 ships and as many as 700 individuals, including merchants and dealers from some 50 continental settlements. At the trade's peak in the 1330s over 5,000 metric tons of herrings were being exported, with Gascony the single greatest customer.[56]

As a town and port Yarmouth was very much a creation of this commercializing age, built on a sand spit and with the sea to the east and the navigable rivers Bure, Yare, and Waveney to the west. Kings Lynn, at the opposite end of the county and at the mouth of the navigable River Ouse, was an even more remarkable growth and, with its subsidiary ports of Burnham, Holkham, Wells and Blakeney on the north Norfolk coast, served

[51] The port's merchant fleet probably included 100 vessels of 100 tons or more: Saul 1982: 76-80.

[52] Campbell et al. 1993: 61, 70.

[53] Campbell 1983; Power & Campbell 1992: 233-236.

[54] Norfolk Record Office DCN 60/15 and 60/23.

[55] Saul 1975: 226, 368-371.

[56] Saul 1982: 77f; Saul 1983: 33-42; Lloyd 1982: 51.

a far more extensive and diverse agricultural hinterland (Figure 1).[57] It sent modest quantities of wool and hides plus some cloth overseas but was chiefly noted as the east-coast port most actively engaged in the grain export trade.[58] Between 1304 and 1307 alien merchants alone sent 3,500-5,500 quarters a year overseas.[59] In cost terms Lynn, like Yarmouth, was closer to Flanders than London and the former, of course, exercised the stronger demand. Lynn had also long traded grain northwards, up the coast to Scotland and across the North Sea to Norway, both of which were deficient in home-produced bread grain.[60]

As a grain *entrepot* Lynn enjoyed conspicuous advantages. An extensive network of navigable rivers—the Great Ouse, Nene, Cam, Little Ouse and Wissey—provided cheap access to a wide and varied hinterland (Figure 1).[61] Investment in boats, warehouses and granaries—all available for hire and well-documented in the royal purveyance accounts—provided the commercial infrastructure necessary to service this waterway system.[62] Nor was there any major city to compete for surplus produce and drive up prices and land values, with the result that (except on the exceptionally fertile reclaimed silt soils close to Lynn) production methods remained relatively extensive and unit costs comparatively low. There are signs that producers within Lynn's hinterland were responding to commercial opportunities and adopting more intensive and innovative methods but progress lagged some way behind the leads set by eastern Norfolk and eastern Kent.[63] Sale prices of grain were well below the national average, ensuring that grain produced in the east midlands of England could be sold with profit in overseas markets.[64] The activities of grain merchants trading through Lynn have been documented by N. S. B. Gras.[65] Because the hinterland of Lynn was a recognized source of surplus grain it attracted the repeated attention of the royal purveyors from the 1290s in their quest for grain to provision the royal armies in Scotland and France. It is no coincidence that

57 Parker 1971: 1-18; Langdon 1993: 3-7.

58 Carus-Wilson 1962-63: 182-201; Lloyd 1982: 49, 109.

59 Gras 1926: 289. Cf. Nils Hybel's article below, pp. 223.

60 Gras 1926: 114f, 172f; Carus-Wilson 1962-63: 185; Lloyd 1982: 151-153.

61 Gras 1926: 62f.

62 Campbell 1995b: 81.

63 Power & Campbell 1992: 233-236; Hogan 1988; Ravensdale 1974: 114-120.

64 Farmer 1988: 743f.

65 Gras 1926: 170-176.

Lincolnshire, Cambridgeshire, and Huntingdonshire were the most frequently purveyed counties in England.[66] Strong commercial demand found expression in an unusually great differentiation of farming types within this region, which echoed that prevailing within the more highly commercialized hinterland of London. Agriculturally this diversity was the region's most distinguishing feature.[67]

Across the Wash another new town, Boston, plied an even more active trade with the continent. Unlike Lynn, Boston exported only small amounts of grain and dealt primarily in wool and cloth: its wide hinterland, increasingly encroached upon by London, embraced much of eastern and north central England.[68] In the 1270s it had handled more wool than any other port, but by the opening decade of the fourteenth century it had been eclipsed by London (Figure 3). Nevertheless, a quarter of all English wool exports was still passing through Boston plus significant quantities of cloth.[69] A majority of that trade was in the hands of foreign merchants, prominent among them dealers from Italy, Brabant, Flanders, north Germany, northern France and Cahors.[70] The bulk of the wool traded through Boston was produced within the Fenland, Lincolnshire and the north-east midlands, some of it being brought considerable distances overland. The port developed as the natural outlet for the quality wools produced in the oolitic limestone country which stretched diagonally across England from Lincolnshire in the north-east. The wools produced in the Kesteven and Lindsey divisions of Lincolnshire were second only in quality to those of Monmouthshire, Herefordshire, and Shropshire (Figure 4). They came from areas of extensive mixed farming where the arable was generally subject to biennial or triennial fallowing and there was an abundance of permanent pasture to support the flocks.

Within the reasonably well documented seigniorial sector, specialized sheep-corn demesnes were a characteristic feature of the oolitic zone, as well as the chalk downs of southern England focusing upon Salisbury Plain (Figure 3). It is on the Wessex downlands that the largest flocks and highest stocking densities are recorded and this may be one of the few

66 Maddicott 1975 and 1987: 301; Campbell 1995b: 95f.

67 Power & Campbell 1992: 240, 242.

68 Gras 1926: 282; Lloyd 1982: 215.

69 Carus-Wilson & Coleman 1963: 41; Childs 1996: 128f; Lloyd 1977: 64.

70 Carus-Wilson & Coleman 1963: 41; Carus-Wilson 1962-63: 186; Lloyd 1977: 66f, 85f.

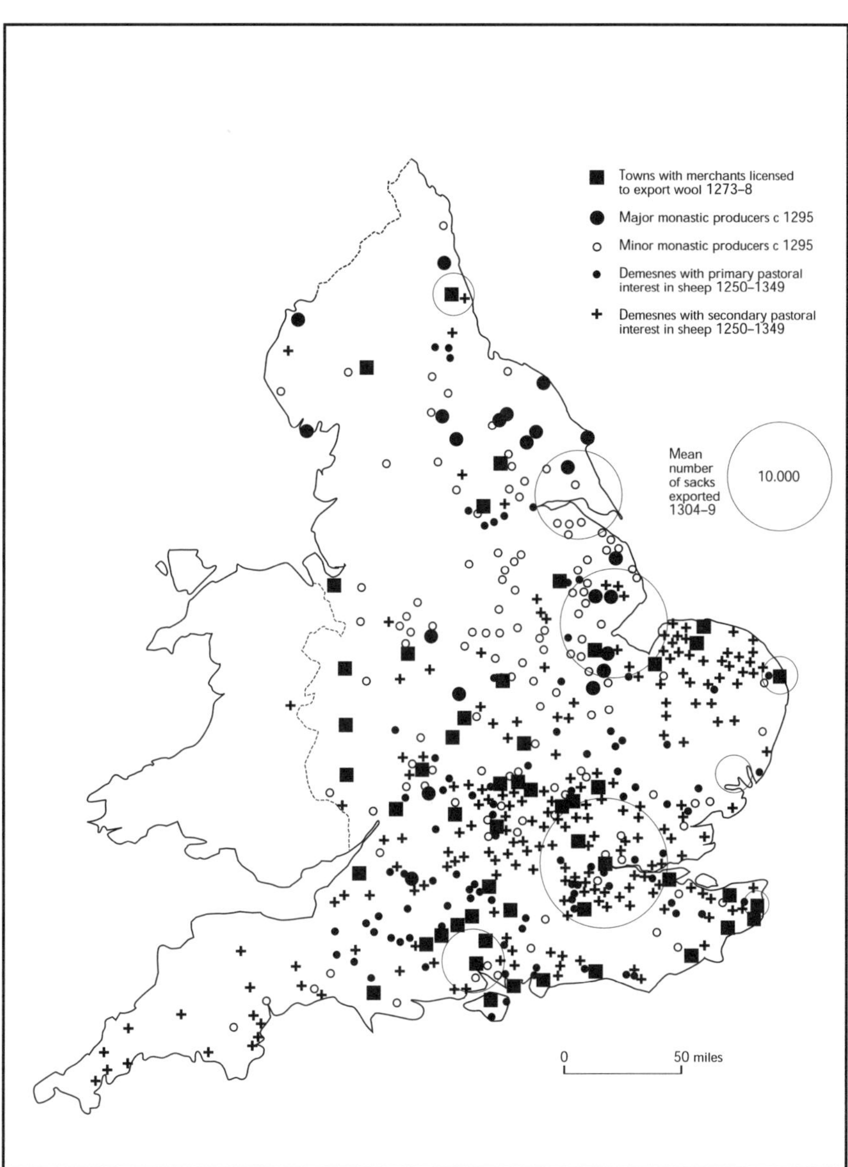

Figure 3. England: evidence of the production and export of wool, ca. 1300. Map: Alf Dahlberg, Lund. Source: Donkin 1973: 122; Carus-Wilson and Coleman 1963: 41; Campbell 2000: 109, 112, 114.

areas where at this date seigniorial flocks eclipsed peasant flocks.[71] Here some version of sheep-corn husbandry was the dominant farming system.[72] Many of these demesnes pursued a dual policy of producing grain by relatively extensive methods for estate consumption and sale in local markets and wool for bulk sale in distant markets. Evidence of specialization in commercial wool production is apparent in the separation of sheep into specialized breeding and wool-producing flocks, respectively of ewes and wethers. On the greatest estates flock management was sometimes organized at an estate rather than manorial level, often with separate sheep accounting and the transfer of wool to centralized warehouses where it could be graded and packed and sold in bulk to foreign buyers. The bishops of Winchester, for instance, sent all their wool to Wolvesey Palace in Winchester and sold it from there.[73] Foreign buyers, many from southern Europe, shipped it out through Southampton, the principal wool-exporting port on the south coast.[74] Southampton also shipped out substantial numbers of hides, more in fact than any other port bar Newcastle. Many were re-exports.[75] That the supply of hides was well in excess of the needs of local leather production is perhaps indicative that Southampton traded rather than processed primary products.

The south coast trade could not, however, match the east coast trade. Southampton handled only 8 percent of wool exports in the opening decade of the fourteenth century compared with the 35 percent handled by London, 25 percent by Boston, and 17 percent by Hull (Figure 3).[76] The last was the most northerly port involved in sending significant quantities of wool overseas. Another new town, it stood at the mouth of the most extensive system of navigable rivers in the country (Figure 1).[77] In accordance with this location it plied an active trade up and down the British coast and across the North Sea and dealt in a wide range of commodities.[78] Grain was both exported and imported, together with a range of other agricultural

[71] Postan 1962.

[72] Power & Campbell 1992: 237.

[73] Farmer 1991: 399f; *The Pipe Roll of the Bishopric of Winchester 1301-2*, 1996: xx; Campbell 1995b: 141.

[74] Platt 1973: 69-77; Lloyd 1977: 69f, 126.

[75] Pelham 1936a: 315f; Platt 1973: 78-84; Lloyd 1982: 224.

[76] Carus-Wilson & Coleman 1963: 41.

[77] Beresford 1988: 511f; Langdon 1993: 3-7.

[78] Lloyd 1982: 151f.

products and small quantities of cloth, but at the opening of the fourteenth century the mainstays of its export trade were hides and wool.[79] Hull's immediate hinterland, like those of most other east-coast ports, was distinguished by above average unit land values and innovative methods of husbandry.[80] Such attributes are indicative of relatively high levels of economic rent arising from the convergence within the same narrow area of strong domestic and overseas demand. Nevertheless, the wider hinterland served by Hull was characterized by below average population densities and extensive rather than intensive methods of production.

Notwithstanding the prominence of several of the northern Cistercian monasteries as major suppliers of wool to Italian merchants, the returns to the 1341 wool tax indicate that the north-east of England outside the East Riding of Yorkshire was not an especially important wool-producing region (Figure 4).[81] Adverse environmental conditions were a major reason for the coarseness of much northern wool and hence its low price. Moreover, many northern flocks suffered high mortality levels and the various forests and chases still harboured several natural predators. These natural disadvantages for wool production could be overcome, but it required capital and entrepreneurship in order so to do. The better-organized northern abbeys—Fountains and Kirkstall in Yorkshire and Newminster in Northumberland—were consequently among the few significant northern producers of high-quality wools.[82] Nor were sheep integral to the mixed-husbandry of the region in the way that they were on the downs and wolds of southern England where peasant-owned flocks were far more fully developed. Hence the importance attached to cattle rearing as witnessed by the lively trade in hides.

Further north again low wool prices further discouraged large-scale commercial wool production (Figure 4) and cattle consequently eclipsed sheep altogether. In contrast to many of their pampered southern counterparts, these northern cattle were reared extensively, usually in upland vaccaries.[83] Surplus stock were driven south for sale to lowland arable farmers requiring replacement animals and urban butchers who would fatten them

[79] Gras 1926: 287; Lloyd 1977: 65f, 127-130; Lloyd 1982: 150, 214; Childs 1996: 127f; cf. Nils Hybel's article below, pp. 220-222.

[80] Mate 1980.

[81] Donkin 1978: 82-102.

[82] Farmer 1991: 395-397.

[83] Donkin 1978: 69-79; Miller 1975.

up and slaughter them for meat.[84] Because cattle rearing was the economic mainstay of much of the northern rural economy Newcastle-upon-Tyne was the leading English port for the export of hides, handling a third of the total trade.[85] In contrast, it was responsible for only 4 percent of wool exports by bulk (less by value) (Figure 3). The port's other great export, of course, was coal, the demand for which was growing among industrial users in the coastal towns that fringed the North Sea. Several thousand tons a year were sent to a wide area stretching from Normandy to the Baltic.[86]

TABLE 1. STRUCTURE OF THE ENGLISH EXPORTS IN AGRICULTURAL PRODUCE, CA. 1300

Proximity to Flanders	Principal Ports	Main agricultural commodities traded	Methods of production
Zone 1	Sandwich	Grain, coarse wool	Intensive
	Winchelsea	Oats, firewood	Intensive
Zone 2	London	Wool, cloth	Intensive and semi-Intensive
Zone 3	Ipswich	Cloth, dairy produce	Semi-intensive
	Yarmouth	Some grain, cloth, herring	Intensive – extensive
Zone 4	Kings Lynn	Grain, some coarse wool	Semi-intensive and semi-extensive
	Boston	Wool (including fine wool)	Semi-intensive and extensive
	Southampton	Wool, hides	Semi-extensive
Zone 5	Hull	Wool, hides, some grain	Mostly extensive
Zone 6	Newcastle	Hides (and coal)	Extensive (and Intensive)

84 Atkin 1994: 14f; Farmer 1991: 377-392.
85 Pelham 1936a: 315f; Lloyd 1982: 211.
86 Pelham 1936a: 321f; Blake 1967: 12-16, 21.

It was the Flemish market which exercised the single greatest gravitational pull upon the export trade of these ports on the east and south-east coasts of England. The powerful "von Thünen field of force" exercised by that market is apparent in the choice of agricultural commodities traded and methods of their production, both of which varied with cost-distance from Flanders (Table 1). Commodities such as oats and firewood, with a low value relative to their bulk, were traded over the shortest distances (Zone 1). Their production was closely tied to coastal locations and immediate access to water transportation. In contrast, long-distance trade involving long-overland hauls to coastal ports was restricted to non-perishable agricultural commodities with a high unit value, most notably fine wool (Zone 4). The products traded over the greatest distances also tended to be produced by the most land-extensive methods, since low production costs were necessary to offset high transportation costs. Closer to overseas markets the costs of transportation were lower with the result that more intensive methods of production became viable. Indeed, exposure to strong overseas demand could drive up economic rent to levels which justified adoption of the most land-intensive methods of all: close management of sustained-yield, coppiced woodland is one example, continuous cropping of high-yielding grain is another. It is no coincidence that progressive and productive methods of grain production were common to the immediate hinterlands of Sandwich, Yarmouth, Lynn and Hull. The one notable exception to all this is London, whose own demand for agricultural products drove up prices and rent levels and thereby precluded the London region from becoming a significant supplier of grain, fuel or hides to the export market. Wool, processed and unprocessed, was therefore the principal mainstay of its export trade.

The Commodities Traded

Lucrative as exports of firewood were to owners of woodland in privileged parts of Kent and Sussex, they were of trifling significance at a national scale. The volumes involved were far too small; nor, given available resources, levels of domestic demand, and prevailing transport costs was there much prospect of them ever become much larger. Similar factors restricted the scale and relative significance of the grain export trade. Gras reckoned that at least 13,000 quarters a year were being exported by alien merchants at the beginning of the fourteenth century.[87] If so, the trade would have been worth at most £4,000. Gras's estimate should be compared with the 3,800 quarters of wheat, 20,400 quarters of oats, 5,800 quarters of barley, and 3,200 quarters of beans and peas requested in 1296 by Edward I for the provisioning of his army in Gascony.[88] Such a substantial shipment for military purposes reveals a clear expectation that tradable surpluses of at least comparable magnitude were normally available. Miller and Hatcher's recent estimate of the value and composition of English exports includes grain with general merchandise, whose collective annual value they estimate at £26,000.[89] If grain and grain products contributed a third of that value they would have been worth £8,500-£9,000, a sum equivalent to about 30,000 quarters of wheat.

30,000 quarters was sufficient grain to feed a city the size of Norwich for a year at a *per capita* consumption of 1.65 quarters. In normal years, London (a city of 70-75,000 inhabitants ca. 1300) consumed approximately 100-130,000 quarters of grain which it drew from a provisioning hinterland of some 4,000 square miles.[90] At corresponding levels of yield and rates of disposal an area of 1,000 square miles would have been sufficient to supply the export trade. This is equivalent to a fifteenth of all the arable land in the country; less if the grain trade was smaller. It is an intriguing coincidence that roughly the same proportion of the national agricultural area commanded unit valuations of land that were well above the national average and therefore indicative of high economic rent. The bulk of this high-valued land was concentrated within the immediate hinterlands of those east-coast ports known to have been most actively involved in the overseas grain trade: Rye, Sandwich and Faversham in Kent, Yarmouth and Kings Lynn in Norfolk, and Boston, Grimsby and Barton-upon-Humber in Lincolnshire (Figure 2).[91] As such it reflects the selective and highly circumscribed penetration of overseas demand reinforced by the concentrated demand for grain of the port towns themselves. Nevertheless, the vast majority of all arable land in England was as yet little touched by either of these demands. Away from the ports and the metropolis most arable pro-

87 Gras 1926: 111. Cf. Nils Hybel's article below, pp. 220-227.

88 Prestwich 1972: 120f.

89 Miller & Hatcher 1995: 213.

90 Campbell et al. 1993: 31-36, 72-77.

91 Campbell 1998.

ducers had to be content with the small-scale demand of local markets.[92]

The high unit transport costs which precluded arable producers from participating in overseas trade unless they were on, or had riverine access to, the coast did not apply to pastoral producers, or at least not to the same extent.[93] Hides were one of the most commercialized of all agricultural products and it was a rare port which did not export at least some.[94] In the 1280s Newcastle, Southampton, Hull and Exeter shipped the largest quantities (there are no statistics for Bristol), which identifies the north-east and south-west of England as the areas of greatest surplus hide production.[95] Both are regions of below average population density at some remove from the more developed parts of central and south eastern England where domestic leather production is likely to have been most fully developed. About 45,000 hides were annually being exported by the end of the thirteenth century, worth at least £2,340 and perhaps as much as £5,600 (assuming a mean price per hide of 2s. 6d.).[96] On a rough estimate, this is equivalent to perhaps a seventh of the annual national output of cattle hides and probably no more than an eighth of the combined national output of cattle and horse hides.[97]

The limited aggregate value and small output proportions of the firewood, grain and hides sent overseas at the beginning of the fourteenth century renders the scale and value of the combined wool and cloth trades all the more remarkable and exceptional. On Miller and Hatcher's estimation wool (85.5 percent) and cloth (5.5 percent) together worth an impressive £274,000 accounted for 91 percent by value of all English exports.[98] According to the customs accounts 41,310 sacks of wool were annually exported during the years 1304-09. Since each sack contained the fleeces of at least 240 sheep it required at least 10 million sheep to supply the export trade alone. Yet more sheep were involved in producing the

92 Farmer 1991: 329; Campbell 1997.

93 Overton & Campbell 1992: 393f.

94 Campbell 1995b: 172.

95 Pelham 1936a: 315f.

96 Miller & Hatcher 1995: 213; Campbell 1995b: 172.

97 Demesne stocking densities imply a national seigniorial herd of approximately 750,000 animals. The national herd is likely to have been at least three times as great. If all cattle died or were slaughtered after 7 years 320,000 cattle hides would have been produced per year.

98 Miller & Hatcher 1995: 213.

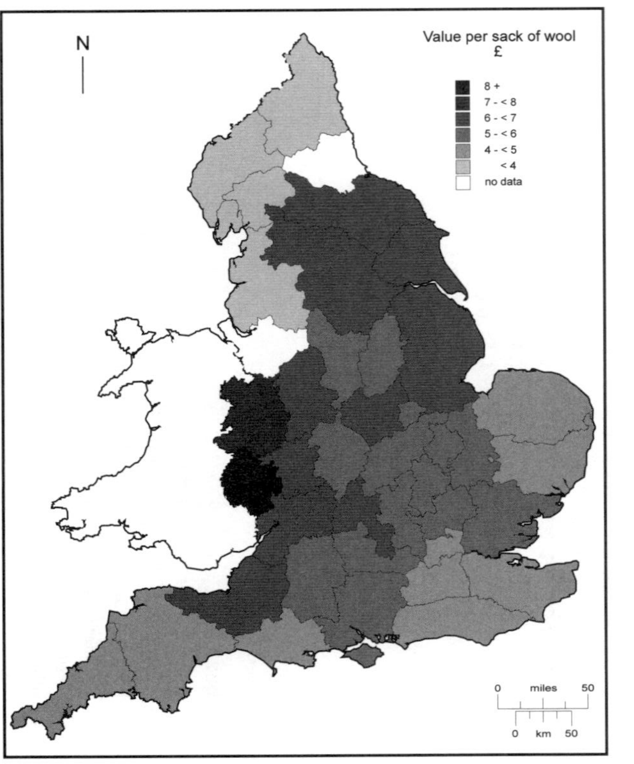

Figure 4A. Regional wool prices according to the 1337 Nottingham schedule. Source: Ormrod 1991: 178f.

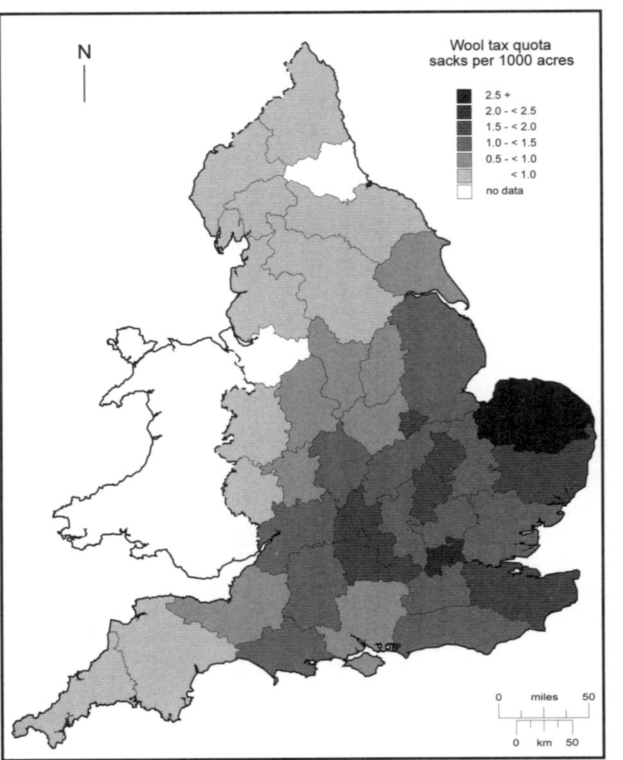

Figure 4B. Wool tax quota in 1341. Source: Ormrod 1991: 178f.

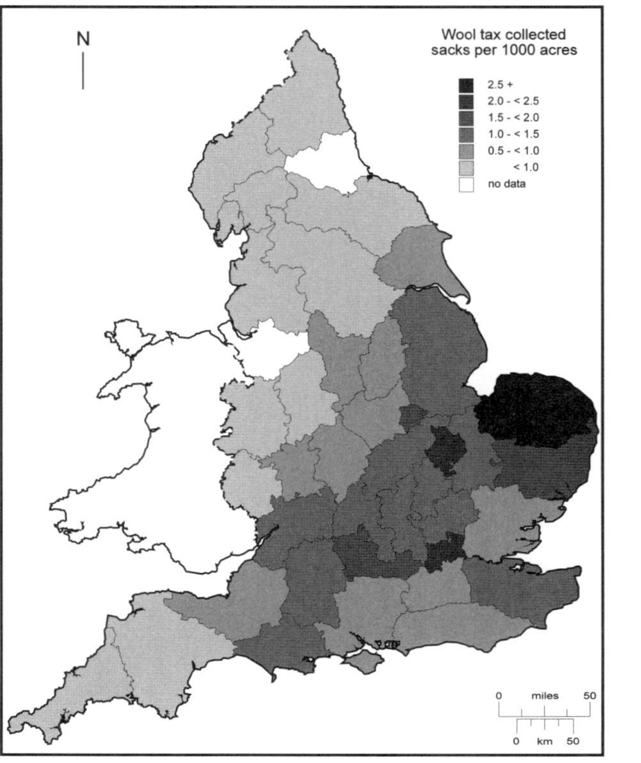

Figure 4C. Wool tax collected in 1341. Source: Ormrod 1991: 178f.

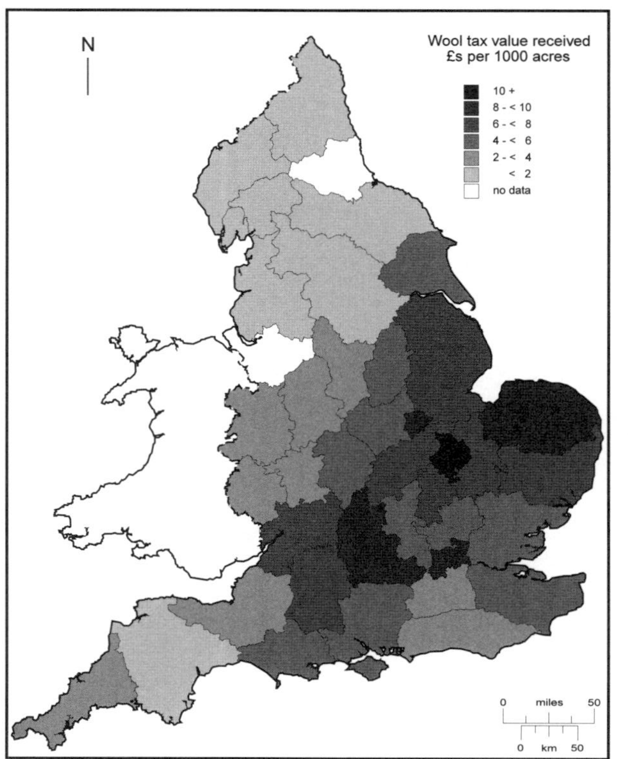

Figure 4D. Wool tax value received in 1341. Source: Ormrod 1991: 178f.

wool exported as cloth. In 1341 when the crown was granted a tax of one fifteenth of all the wool produced in the kingdom over 25,000 sacks were collected, which was equivalent to the product of over 6 million sheep.[99] The scale of this tax levy, when taken in conjunction with the 22,844 sacks exported that same year (the product of 5.5 million sheep), implies a vast national flock, so vast in fact that domestic consumption of wool must have far exceeded that sent abroad.[100] Moreover, as the returns to the 1341 wool tax make plain, that flock—like the population which it outnumbered several times over—was concentrated disproportionately within the lowland arable counties of central, eastern and southern England (Figure 4), thereby confirming R. Trow-Smith's observation that "hurdled arable flocks" were "the true basis of medieval sheep husbandry".[101]

Although the largest flocks were maintained by lords, on the evidence of recorded stocking densities the national demesne flock cannot have numbered more than about 2.5 million animals.[102] It follows that the vast majority of sheep were in non-seigniorial ownership. Consequently, it was the enterprise of rectors with their own glebe lands, freeholders, substantial customary tenants, and many others that underwrote production of England's premier export commodity. Presumably, sheep were better suited to the limited capital resources of peasants than the cattle, which were more heavily invested in by most lords. Nowhere was the dichotomy between predominantly cattle-owning lords and sheep-owning peasants more pronounced than in Norfolk, the county which made the single heaviest contribution to the 1341 wool tax (Figure 4) even though the stocking density of sheep on demesnes within the county was well below the national average.[103] Possibly here, as in Suffolk, Cambridgeshire, Huntingdonshire, Bedfordshire, Northamptonshire, and Rutland, the limited interest of lords in sheep farming left greater opportunities for others to exploit.[104]

The evidence of the wool tax leaves little doubt that most English wool was produced by small producers operating in lowland, mixed-farming

[99] In 1338-39 a similar tax had raised 14,000 sacks: Ormrod 1991: 176-181.

[100] Carus-Wilson & Coleman 1963: 46. Of course, much of the wool received as tax would subsequently have been exported.

[101] Trow-Smith 1957: 142.

[102] Campbell 2000b.

[103] Overton & Campbell 1992: 385f.

[104] Trow-Smith 1957: 141.

contexts (Figures 3 and 4).[105] Nevertheless, for large-scale sheep farming to be feasible at all required substantial amounts of permanent pasture, for, apart from some milk fed to young lambs and grain and legumes consumed as winter-feed, it was upon grass that medieval sheep were mostly fed. True, many a lowland flock was folded on the arable, but this was more for the dung that the sheep contributed to the soil than for the grazing which the fallow afforded to the sheep. Consequently, for sheep to be so numerous there must still have been a sufficiency of pasture. In 1800 there were on average 1.5 acres of pasture for every 1.0 acre of arable and there is no reason to suppose that in 1300 the ratio was any less.[106] Sheep-pasture was often managed in common and could be of many types, typically, downland sheep-walks, sandy heathlands, fresh- and salt-water marshes, moorland and rough pasture. Within the seigniorial sector sheep were kept on upland and lowland, on light-land and heavy-land, on wolds and downs and in fens and marshes. The breed of sheep, type of grazing, and method of management all affected the weight and quality of the fleece.[107] The prices commanded by English wools generally increased from south-east to north-west, the finest wools produced in Shropshire and Herefordshire generally selling for twice the price of the coarse wools produced in far greater quantity in Norfolk, Suffolk and Kent (Figure 4).[108] The coarsest wools of all, however, were produced in the south-western counties of Devon and Cornwall and, above all, the north-western counties of Cumberland, Westmorland and Lancashire. The latter was the English region with least comparative advantage in wool production.

It was English wools of medium and fine quality, produced by semi-extensive and extensive methods in areas of below-average economic rent, that were most sought after by foreign buyers and most capable of withstanding the costs of long-distance transportation, rather than the coarse wools produced by more intensive methods, even though the latter were produced in greater quantity. These coarse wools stood a greater prospect of being traded internationally if they were processed into cloth. The regions of most active medium- and fine-wool production were mostly endowed with an abundance of woldland and downland pastures, were

[105] Power, E. 1941: 29-31; Ormrod 1991: 177; Waugh 1991: 60f; Bridbury 1992: 185f.

[106] Overton & Campbell 1996: 290.

[107] Ryder 1984.

[108] Munro 1978.

remote from major urban markets, and in every case lay well outside the regular grain-provisioning hinterland of London (Figures 3 and 4). Their predominantly land-locked character made wool the best prospect for long-distance trade: only furs and live animals were capable of withstanding costs of overland carriage over greater distances. The profits which these sheep-farming counties derived from the wool trade is apparent in the fact that most supported above average levels of per capita taxable wealth in 1327 and 1332.[109]

It follows that England's greatest international comparative advantage ca. 1300 lay in the semi-extensive and extensive production of wool and hides, both high-value, grass-based pastoral products exported mostly raw for processing elsewhere. Its comparative advantage for cloth was much weaker, although manufacture of cheap worsteds appears to have held up somewhat better against foreign competition than high-quality broadcloths. Continental manufacturers could produce quality cloths at a more competitive price provided that they could obtain adequate supplies of fine wool, hence the buoyancy of Flemish and Italian demand for English wools. That demand penetrated deep into the English countryside and ensured that even in the remote Welsh borderland agricultural producers contributed to international commodity flows.

Economic Rent, Cost-Distance, and the Export Trade in English Agricultural Produce

England ca. 1300 was an active supplier of agricultural products to the international market. The commodities that it exported were those capable of being sold with profit in foreign markets: grain and firewood from Kent, worsted cloth, grain, dairy produce, and herrings from East Anglia, medium and fine wools in great quantity from central and southern England, hides and coal from the north-east, and hides and tin from the south-west. Transport costs played a large part in determining which of these were worth sending overseas. So, too, did the relative strength of domestic demand, which competed with international demand for many of these products, driving up prices and production costs to levels which at times stifled the prospect of any export trade developing. London, for instance, sent little agricultural produce abroad (its own needs were too great), apart from

[109] See above, n. 47.

wool, which it mostly obtained from some distance.

Handling trade could, however, be more profitable than producing the commodities being traded. London was not alone in owing much of its twelfth- and thirteenth-century growth to the expanding volume of commerce handled by its port. Newcastle, Hull, Boston, Kings Lynn, Yarmouth, Ipswich, and Sandwich all grew vigorously during the same period. It was through these North Sea ports that overseas demand penetrated England, driving up levels of economic rent (Figure 2) and promoting greater differentiation of land-use and methods of agricultural production. Its impact was greatest wherever navigable rivers enabled individual ports to tap a wide hinterland (Figure 1). Intensive coppicing to produce firewood spread inland from Winchelsea via the rivers Rother and Brede; rivers rather than roads linked Yarmouth—fronted by the sea and backed by extensive marshes—to its populous and richly productive hinterland; and it was the navigable rivers Ouse, Nene and Welland which served as the umbilical cord linking the otherwise land-locked east midlands to the ports of the Wash. It is in these eastern parts of England, even more than the wool-producing country further inland, that the benefits of fuller participation in international trade are most clearly to be seen. Here, steepening contours of economic rent generated widening differentials in land values and product prices. Land-use and farm enterprise both became more specialized and further market growth was thereby facilitated.[110]

This was a commercial system capable of fuller development and elaboration. Yet in 1300 it was nearing its climax. Over the next half century a succession of physical and biological shocks would reduce the output of agriculture and decimate populations.[111] Heightened warfare on many fronts would increase the risks and costs of trade.[112] To finance war English kings would impose duties on trade and tax their subjects heavily and repeatedly, introducing novel direct taxes upon wool and grain.[113] The wool trade became a pawn in a political game. The outbreak of the Hundred Years War between England and France gave licence to increased piracy on the North Sea and in the English Channel, and exposed the south-coast

[110] Britnell 1995: 14-19; Campbell 1997.

[111] Campbell 1991.

[112] Munro 1991: 120-130. On the impact of the Anglo-Scottish war upon the trade and commerce of Newcastle and north-eastern England see McNamee 1997: 225-27.

[113] Maddicott 1987: 329-351.

ports to French attacks. Italian banks collapsed as monarchs and others defaulted on their loans, sending shock waves through the European monetary system.[114] Commercial recession replaced commercial expansion and as trade, at least internationally, contracted, agricultural producers almost everywhere began the often-difficult process of readjusting to an altered economic world.

[114] Fischer 1996: 30-45.

The Widening of Import Trade and Consumption around 1200 A.D.: a Danish Perspective

Bjørn Poulsen

THE NEW GOODS

A number of new goods seem to have reached Denmark in the period 1150-1350. The Danish chronicler Saxo, writing about 1200, recounts the story of Duke Knud Lavard, who in the 1120s appeared at a royal wedding provocatively dressed "in the Saxon manner". He was dressed in purple robes, not in the sheepskin coats worn by the others present.[1] If we are to believe Saxo, it was still considered provocative to wear foreign cloth thirty years later. Around 1150 the Danish king Svend Grathe started to dress in the German fashion and even to request his men of the *hird* to do the same.[2] The result was, Saxo disapprovingly remarks, that the King's court became occupied by "dressed-up noblemen instead of the usual persons dressed in peasants' clothes". In respect to meals, too, Svend Grathe allegedly abandoned the good old ways for "foreign delicacies and fine table manners." We should regard the stories of Saxo more as a reflection of his own time around 1200 than of the situation of some years previously, but there is no doubt that the writer felt that he was describing something new and dangerous to the traditional order.

Another example of a commodity with such characteristics is found in the biography of the Viborg bishop, Gunner, written some time after his death in 1250. It includes a description of the bishop's attitude to drinking. Bishop Gunner was a sober man who drank out of silver cups that he always brought with him on journeys—according to the biography, this was the habit of the nobles and leaders of the time. His favourite drinks were Danish beer and mead. Furthermore, it is stated: "at that time Saxon beer and the new cups had not as yet reached our country as commodities and very few liked this drink". This inspires the biographer to tell a terrible

[1] Saxo Grammaticus 1913: 56.

[2] Saxo Grammaticus 1913: 97.

story of what happened later, when this sort of beer had arrived at the residence town of the bishop, Viborg.[3]

Saxo and Bishop Gunner's biographer were not alone in reacting against the import of foreign cloth and beer. In a decree issued in Helsingborg in 1283, King Erik Glipping, apparently trying to restrict the use of imported cloth, ordained that nobody should wear clothes that had been made of small pieces of fabric (*uestes in minutas partes incisas*).[4] In the same spirit it is also stated: "if anybody wishes to wear his clothes for a year or more, it should not be reckoned as a shame." A subsequent section maintained the following: "no-one, after Whitsun, should import, sell, or drink German beer". The punishment fixed for breaking this law was a heavy fine of forty *marks* per barrel. However, the import and use of the new goods could not be stopped. Foreign cloth and beer continued to gain ground in Denmark during the thirteenth century and these goods were not the only imported goods that changed Danish patterns of consumption and social norms.

According to the customs tariff in the oldest Danish town law from Schleswig, customs duties in the twelfth century were levied on each person crossing the town border.[5] This early law is therefore not particularly well suited for giving an impression of the goods in trade. The spectrum of imported goods only becomes evident in the Danish town laws from the second half of the thirteenth century. Of course, this can be seen as a consequence of the fact that customs duties had become customs on commodities, but it probably also reflects a change in the commodities traded. As an example of this, we can take a look at the law of Haderslev of 1292 which included a tariff.

Haderslev is situated on the east coast of Jutland, where several roads crossed. The customs tariff is divided into three parts that, to some degree, show us the passage of goods on these different roads. Smaller vessels could sail into the town, and in the town law it is explicitly mentioned that lime, wood and millstones arrived on ships. We find this information in the first section of the tariff, which mainly refers to goods considered to constitute the cargo of the ships, such as manufactured animal products, grain, beer, herring, salt, copper, tar and millstones. Apparently, this is a list of

[3] *Scriptores Minores*, vol. 2, 1922: 272f; *Viborgbispen Gunners Levned* 1892:23; Søgaard 1953:261-284.

[4] Similar edicts were issued by the Norwegian king in 1314 and 1315. Cf. Nielsen 1981: 2-5.

[5] *Danmarks Gamle Købstadslovgivning*, v. 1, 1951: 1-17. See also Jessen 1996: 7-22.

goods traded by ships in the Baltic. The next section has the headline "On wine customs", and may be interpreted as a list of goods en route to or from Ribe via the road connecting Haderslev and Ribe. This at least applies to cloth and wine. It is mentioned that the wine is transported in normal casks (Danish: *fade*), and in casks called *askøefatt*.[6] The so-called *drifftrug*—cleaned rye, maybe from southern Denmark or the southern shores of the Baltic—was probably on its way overland from Haderslev to Ribe.[7] Finally, the tariff included a third article that concentrated on the ferry service from Årøsund to Assens.[8] In this is mentioned the transport of horses, cattle, sheep, pigs and salt, and it would seem to reveal an early phase of the transfers that took place from the early fifteenth century as part of the growing international cattle trade.[9]

Against this background it is possible to divide the goods mentioned in the law into domestic products and foreign products imported to Denmark (see Table 2 below). In 1292 quite a large number of goods were imported to Haderslev: beer, wine, cloth and the metals iron, steel, copper, led, and presumably also tar. Tar, *"lest pick i trafen tunne, lesttiœre"*, most probably came from the east Baltic areas, presumably by way of Lübeck, since it was stored in barrels of *trafe*, that is, from the river Trave. There is also reason to believe that most of the millstones were foreign imports.[10]

Other town laws with tariffs confirm that the goods stocked in Haderslev were rather typical for Denmark around 1300. A customs tariff from Flensburg, dated to ca. 1300, contains the same goods as the Haderslev tariff as well as a few more. The additional agricultural items are hops, beans and nuts. The group of luxury goods is augmented by small articles (German: *Kramgut*), wax and furs.[11] The supply of fish was apparently also larger in Flensburg, but otherwise the tariff of this town only differs by giving more detailed information on some wares, such as salt, that could be bought from their Frisian places of production.

The presence of a broad spectrum of commodities in Danish towns in the thirteenth and fourteenth centuries is supported by many other sources.

6 As has been noticed, *"askøefatt"* was derived from *Auxois* in Burgundy.

7 Cf. Kalkar, vol. 1, 1881: 381.

8 Cf. *Atlas over Fyns kyst i jernalder, vikingetid og middelalder* 1996:112f.

9 Cf. Blanchard 1986: 427-460.

10 On the import of millstones from Mayen, see Madsen 1967: 9-11; Carelli & Kresten 1997.

11 On the trade in small wares, see Enemark 1981b.

TABLE 2. COMMODITIES MENTIONED IN THE CUSTOMS TARIFF OF HADERSLEV, 1292

Article	Origin: Denmark	Origin: Foreign
I. Agricultural and forest products	wheat, rye, barley, oats	rye (*driftrug*)
	malt, flax, sweet gale	
	cattle, sheep, pigs, horses	
	butter, meat, tallow, fat, hides, honey	
	wood, spear-shafts	
		tar
II. Fish products	herring, whale oil	
III. Raw materials	salt	salt
	iron	iron, steel
		copper, lead
		lime
IV. Manufactured goods	beer	beer
		wine
		spears
	homespun, linen	cloth
		line
		millstones

Source: *Danmarks Gamle Købstadslovgivning*, vol. 1, 1951: 267-276

Danish agricultural products and herring seem to dominate the trade, as was the case in the late Middle Ages and later. Characteristically, in the year 1316, a customs tariff for the whole realm mentions trade in grain, oxen, cows, sheep, butter, fat, tallow, meat, hides, horses, haddock, herring from Scania (Skåne), and nuts as well as cloth.[12] A levy on the sale of beer is included in a separate section. Apart from the cloth, and maybe the beer, these are Danish agricultural bulk goods.

The customs tariffs give us an indication of what was transported in and out of town and country. An account from the year 1319 proves that one was able to buy basic goods in Danish towns. The account deals with the expenses of 15 vassals from Rügen in the service of the Danish king and

[12] *Diplomatarium Danicum*, 2nd ser., vol. 7, no. 407.

travelling through his realm (Table 3, p. 38). The account is not particularly impressive, but it shows that German beer, meat, bread and salt were on sale daily in the towns.[13] Anyone with enough money could buy their basic food in the market place.

To sum up, Danish written sources give us the impression that the supply of goods in the period 1200-1350 became quite differentiated. As pointed out by Helen Clarke some years ago, archaeology does not say much about the bulk trade with agricultural and forest products.[14] But, certainly, archaeology supplies us with much useful evidence when discussing the goods traded on the Danish market. For instance, written sources contain little on the trade in building material and stones. We are told that in 1254 the people of Copenhagen were using "timber, stone, iron and lime" to build houses, and in 1289 the town lord of Copenhagen gave them a permission to quarry limestone on the island of Saltholm.[15] In 1290 lime is mentioned in the tariff of Haderslev, and lime and limestone (*brœnd liim, eldœr liimstien*) appear in Flensburg ca. 1300. But on the basis of the few known written sources that exist, we remain ignorant of details concerning the import of building stones, baptismal fonts,[16] stone coffins, lead for roofing or cast copper products like pots or bells. Only the study of the material artefacts can tell us, for example, about the widespread import, mainly from Lübeck, of bronze or copper pots for Danish households from the thirteenth to the fifteenth century. [17] On the basis of north German material, Max Hasse has suggested that until the late twelfth century, a town household contained only about 1-2 kilograms of metal tools, while around 1350 it normally had 20-100 kilograms of these;[18] most likely this also applied to households in Danish towns. Surveys of the Danish use of limestone from Gotland and tufa from the Andernach region on the Rhine south of Cologne have recently demonstrated that large quantities of stone were imported. The Rhinish stone was used to build churches in southwest Jut-

13 Likewise it has been noted that in fourteenth-century Swedish provincial towns it was normally possible to buy German goods like wine and beer; see *Raven van Barnekows räkenskaper för Nyköpings fögderi 1365-1367,1994: 55.*

14 Clarke 1985: 113-120.

15 *Diplomatarium Danicum*, 2nd ser., vol. 1, no. 138; *Diplomatarium Danicum*, 2nd ser., vol. 2, no. 396 (*Lapides ad calcem*).

16 See Lars Berggren's article, below, pp. 170, 175ff.

17 Cf. Drescher 1976: 307-320; Liebgott 1989: 253-257; Bitsch 1997.

18 Hasse 1979: 7-83.

TABLE 3. EXPENSES OF 15 VASSALS FROM RÜGEN IN THE SERVICE OF THE DANISH KING, TRAVELLING THROUGH DENMARK, 1319 (AFTER 30TH SEPTEMBER)

Time	Town/Goods bought	Price
Tuesday evening	Ringsted	
	4 barrels of beer	8 *mark*
	bread	4 *mark*
	1 cow	4 *mark* and 4 *ørtug*
	4 sides of bacon	4 *mark* and 6 *ørtug*
	2 sheep	1 *mark*
	8 chickens	12 *ørtug*
	firewood and salt	1 *mark*
	2 *dromt* oats for fodder	4 *mark*
Wednesday morning	Ringsted	
	2 sheep	1 *mark* and 4 *ørtug*
	butter	18 *ørtug*
	eggs	6 *ørtug*
		Total: 29 Scanian *mark*
Wednesday evening	Nœstved	
	1 cow	4 *mark* and 2 *ørtug*
	2 sheep	28 *ørtug*
	2 sides of bacon	2 *mark* and 4 *ørtug*
	12 chickens	8 *ørtug*
	bread	2 *mark* and 4 *ørtug*
	2 barrels of German beer	4 *mark* and 2 *ørtug*
	1 barrel of Danish beer	1 *mark*
	oats	2 *mark* and 2 *ørtug*
Tuesday morning	Nœstved	
	2 barrels of beer	4 *mark* and 4 *ørtug*
	bread	2 *mark*
	2 sheep	1 *mark* and 2 *ørtug*
	2 sides of bacon	1½ *mark*
	honey	16 *ørtug*
	firewood and salt	1 *mark*
	fodder	4 *mark* and 4 *ørtug*
		Total: 35 *mark in copper money*

Tuesday evening	Vordingborg	
	2 barrels of beer	4 *mark*
	for the carriers	2 *ørtug*
	beef and mutton	3 *mark* and 2 *ørtug*
	bread	1 *mark* and 2 *ørtug*
	firewood and salt	20 *ørtug*
	fodder, 1 bundle	1 *mark*
		Total: 10 *mark* and 2 *ørtug sjællandsk*

Source: *Diplomatarium Danicum*, 2d ser., vol. 8, no. 147

land during the period ca. 1175 to 1250, while stone from Gotland was used all over the country for a number of different purposes—mainly architectural and sculptural—from ca. 1200 onward.[19] Also local and daily trade can be traced through finds of bones and plants in the Danish towns.[20]

In the following, I shall principally limit my comments to written sources, concentrating on the changes in three main groups of imported goods: firstly, I shall discuss cloth and beer in greater detail; secondly, I shall make some observations on iron and salt, and, finally, I shall make some general comments on the commercialisation of the Danish economy from the twelfth to the fourteenth century.

Cloth and Beer

Foreign cloth had been imported to Denmark since prehistoric times.[21] The descriptions of Saxo from around 1200, however, should be regarded as indications of the increased use of foreign cloth. Admittedly, the material is scant, but if one can trust the written sources, the Danish market opened up for foreign cloth during the thirteenth century.

About 1200, Arnold of Lübeck noticed that the Danes were wearing linen as well as scarlet and purple cloth, a novelty at the time. A number of

19 See Lars Berggren's article below, pp. 144-146. Cf. also Jacobsen 1937: 14.

20 See for instance Greigh 1983 and Hatting 1987.

21 Jørgensen 1992.

TABLE 4. PRICES FIXED FOR CLOTH IN DENMARK BY KING ERIK MENVED, 13 MARCH 1304

Type	Origin	Price, in Danish *Mark*
Pannus Gandauus	Ghent	40
Pannus Ypœrsk	Ypern	36
Pannus Orthinburg	Aardenburg	24
Pannus Brygist	Bruges	24
Pannus Popœrst	Poperinghen	18
Pannus Nyuœlst	Nivelles	18
Pannus Thornist	Tournai	18
Pannus thyuk sayn ("saie grasse")	Flanders	13
Pannus Auœrst	Antwerp	9
Panni alii (Other sorts of cloth, not to be sold without special permission):		
Branband	Brabant	
Ængilsk	England	
Langlaken		

Source: *Diplomatarium Danicum* 2nd ser., vol. 5, no. 310.

testaments from the late thirteenth century contain some evidence of the different types of cloth. In 1261 a wealthy nobleman from Zealand, Peder Olufsen of Karise, possessed one piece of blue cloth. In 1293 the widow of a nobleman bequeathed a number of foreign pieces of cloth to her family, among them cloaks of blue, yellow and brown (Danish: *brunert*) cloth as well scarlet red ones.[22] She donated these valuable clothes to her daughters and other persons of rank, whereas her donation to the lepers of Nœstved consisted only of common homespun and linen.

The cloth was sealed at its place of production, at least from the thirteenth century onward, but most datable finds of seals from Denmark are from the fifteenth century or later. However, a lead seal from Douai from about 1350 (1342-60) was found at the marketplace in Dragør. Another seal, found in the town of Svendborg, dates back to ca. 1270–1300; regrettably, we do not know the place of production.[23] The types of cloth traded are better indicated in a royal decree from the year 1304.[24] That year the

22 *Diplomatarium Danicum,* 2nd ser., vol. 4, no. 67.

23 Orduna 1995.

24 *Diplomatarium Danicum,* 2nd ser., vol. 5, no. 310.

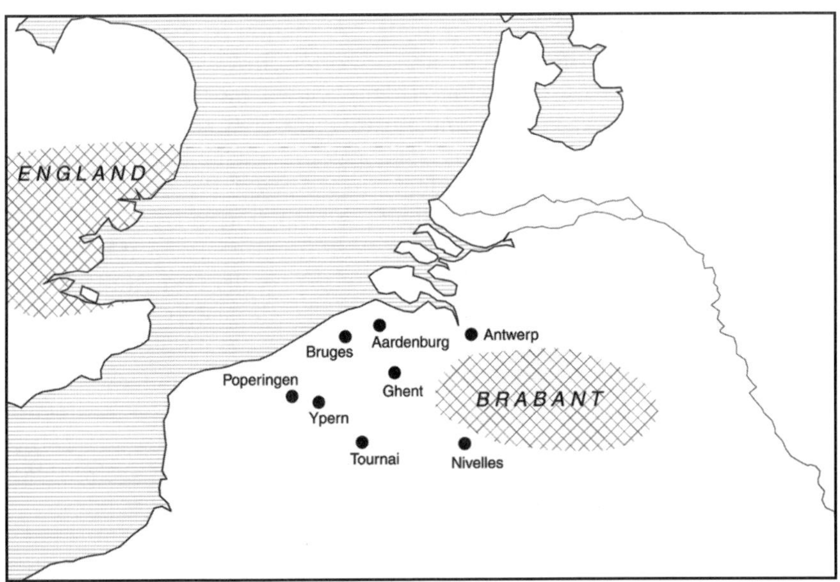

Figure 5. Centres of production of cloth imported into Denmark. Map: Jens Kirkeby, University of Aarhus.

Danish king Erik Menved fixed maximum prices for a number of foreign cloth types that must have been commonly sold (Table 4). Here there is cloth from the important Flemish centres of production—Ghent, Ypres, Bruges and Tournai—along with smaller ones like Poperinge and Aardenburg, as well as Nivelles and Antwerp in Brabant. If we map the centres of production we get the distribution shown in Figure 5. It is evident that cloth on the market mainly stemmed from the cloth-producing regions of Northern France and the Netherlands.

As a rule, foreign merchants imported cloth, even if customs rolls from King's Lynn, Yarmouth and Boston from about the year 1300 testify to some export of English cloth to Denmark on both English and Danish ships.[25] From charters given to the towns of Deventer and Harderwijk it is evident that towns in the northern Netherlands also exported cloth directly to the Danish market from about 1300.[26] The importance of import via Ribe, and

25 Information kindly provided by Wendy R. Childs, University of Leeds.

26 *Diplomatarium Danicum,* 2nd ser., vol. 7, no. 410 (1316); *Diplomatarium Danicum,* 2nd ser., vol. 9, no. 311(1326); *Diplomatarium Danicum,* 2nd ser., vol. 12, no.

of the direct relation to centres of cloth production in the Netherlands, should not be underestimated. The main exporters, however, were undoubtedly German towns on the Baltic. This is shown by charters given to, among others, Lübeck, Wismar and Rostock, as well as by documented sales.[27] Before 1330, the aristocrat Duke Knud of Halland and Samsø, for instance, bought scarlet and silk cloaks in Lübeck.[28] From the mid-thirteenth century, it became a major issue for the citizens of Danish towns to prevent foreign merchants from selling cloth retail. Only on the Scanian market were exemptions made to the otherwise prevalent rule that foreigners were allowed to bring the cloth only to Danish dealers.[29] From 1254 and onward, most Danish town laws include sections maintaining that foreigners are not allowed to cut cloth or linen at the marketplaces.[30]

A couple of account books from Hanseatic merchants of the fourteenth century reveal more details about the sale of cloth to Danish traders. One of these merchants was Hermann Wittenborg of Lübeck who in the 1330s sold cloth from Flanders to the town of Ribe.[31] Among his sales to the citizens of Ribe were eight pieces of cloth from Diksmuide for a price of 9 *mark* per piece, and seven pieces from Aardenburg for 8 1/2 *mark* per piece. In the 1350s Johannes Wittenborg, the son-in-law of Hermann Wittenborg, sent his servant to the Scanian market each year to sell cloth (from Bruges and other places), beer, and spices such as pepper, ginger and nutmeg.[32] A merchant from Hamburg, Vicko von Geldersen, also sold cloth to Denmark, more precisely to Flensburg, Schleswig and the Scanian market in the years 1367-79. In Flensburg he sold almonds, figs, caraway

---

89 (Ribe 1338).

27 Charters for trade with cloth: *Diplomatarium Danicum,* 2nd ser., vol. 9, no. 5 (1323); *Diplomatarium Danicum,* 2nd ser., vol. 9, no. 294 (1326); *Diplomatarium Danicum*, 2nd ser., vol. 10, no. 39 (1328).

28 *Diplomatarium Danicum,* 2nd ser., vol. 10, no. 204.

29 *Diplomatarium Danicum*, 2nd ser, vol. 9, no. 294.

30 *Diplomatarium Danicum,* 2nd Ser., vol. 1, no. 50 (Copenhagen 1254); *Diplomatarium Danicum,* 2nd ser., vol. 4, no. 121 (Copenhagen 1294); *Danmarks Gamle Købstadslovgivning,* vol.1, 1951: 273 (29; Haderslev 1292); *Danmarks Gamle Købstadslovgivning,* vol. 1, 1951: 119 (36; Flensburg ca. 1300); *Diplomatarium Danicum,* 3rd ser., vol. 1, no. 215 (Aabenraa 1335).

31 *Das Handlungsbuch von Hermann und Johann Wittenborg* 1901: 4f (nos. 24 and 32).

32 *Das Handlungsbuch von Hermann und Johann Wittenborg* 1901: 19 (no. 75), 42 (no. 278).

(*amigdalis et de ficubus, de git*), and cloth from Bruges, Ghent and Bergen op Zoom along with cloth termed grey and red. To a merchant from Schleswig he sold white cloth from Bruges for a price of 43 *mark*.[33] Since von Geldersen did not allow credit in the Scanian market, his dealings there are not revealed by his account book. However, it mentions several agents who were sent to the market to buy barrels of herring. In 1379 von Geldersen, together with two other merchants, built a ship (*Kogge*); its maiden voyage went to Scania, and there is no reason to doubt that its cargo, at least in part, consisted of cloth from Flanders.

As the prices reveal, the richly coloured foreign cloth was generally an expensive article, and there are almost no indications that it was sold to people outside the ranks of nobility, clergy and wealthy burghers.[34] That it could nevertheless be found in the possession of peasants seems to be indicated by a passage in the law (*birkeret*) of Lund from ca. 1326 exemplifying things that could be stolen in a peasant home.[35] But in all probability common people had to be content with homespun and linen, and leave foreign cloth to the wealthy.[36]

Foreign beer was much more democratically distributed. In twelfth-century Denmark, beer was made both in towns and the countryside.[37] The peasants brewed their own and manors, monasteries and towns produced steady quantities. A brewery (*braxatorium*) is mentioned in a will from 1257, and in the following years much information on brewers and brewing appears in the towns.[38] The technique used in making hop beer was adop-

[33] *Das Handlungsbuch Vickos von Geldersen* 1895: (nos. 70, 106, 125, 126, 240, 277, 382)

[34] P. Chorley posed the question of whether cloth remained a luxury article in Chorley 1987: 349-379.

[35] *Danmarks Gamle Købstadslovgivning*, vol. 4, 1961: 12 (49: "Tagher bonde af andrum bonde klede œller swerdh œller anner thing hwat som thet œr, bøde thre, marc for raan œller wœri ich meth tylter eth").

[36] In the Borough custom of Aabenraa from 1335, a coat made of grey homespun is mentioned as suitable clothing for seamen: *Diplomatarium Danicum*, 3rd ser., vol. 1, no. 215. Cf. also Richard Unger's article in this volume.

[37] On the history of beer in medieval Denmark, see Kjersgaard 1978:84-99.

[38] Erslev 1901: 7, line 7 ("... et *braxatorium*"); *Danmarks gamle Købstadslovgivning*; vol. 3, 1955:165ff (Roskilde 1268; 25 "*Item braxatores similiter puniantur*"); Erslev 1901: 50(1302, "*Item Ascerobraxatori*").

ted in the towns around this time.[39] Hops and malt from barley made a good spicy beer that was economical to transport. In the town law of Copenhagen from 1254, the manufacturing of malt is not mentioned, but the technique appears in the revised version from 1294 as well as in the law of Flensburg from around 1300. An inventory from 1328, from the castle of Copenhagen, mentions eight barrels of bog myrtle and four barrels of beer marked as hop beer.[40]

The first written evidence of the import of hops for domestic beer production dates to the year 1300, when hop is mentioned in the customs tariff of Flensburg.[41] In 1338 foreigners sold hops in Aabenraa in measures of *dromt* (German: *Drömt*, ca. 300 litre) and *pund*.[42] But there are indications that hop beer was already being imported to Denmark in the first part of the thirteenth century, i.e., some years before it is mentioned in the biography of Bishop Gunner of Viborg. A customs duty on beer, levied in 1231 at the ferry passage between Zealand and Falster, seems to indicate an ongoing import of beer from the new German towns in the south.[43] Almost at the same time, a law applicable to the Scanian market explicitly mentions that German merchants brought their *trave-beer*.[44] In 1269 the town law of Ribe refers to the import of mead and beer; the beer presumably being imported by foreigners, even if this is not stated.[45] In 1281 the town lord of Copenhagen issued a decree fixing the measures of *trave-beer*, *mensuram trafnisiœ*.[46] The following reason is given for this: "up to now the beer (...) has been sold without a fixed measure and with a small reduction, to the loss of the buyers and to the detriment of the souls of the sellers". This may be taken to mean that German beer was a new product for which the rules of trade had not yet been fixed.

For a long period of time beer was apparently imported only from Lübeck—presuming that *trave-beer* did not also mean beer from Wismar imported by way of Lübeck. In the account book of the Lübeck merchant

[39] For the spreading of the technique, see Unger 1992: 281-313. Cf. Irsigler 1996:377-397.

[40] *Diplomatarium Danicum,* 2nd ser., vol. 4, no. 121; *Diplomatarium Danicum,* 2nd ser., vol. 10, no. 53.

[41] *Danmarks Gamle Købstadslovgivning,* vol. 1, 1951: 119 (38), 129 (96).

[42] *Diplomatarium Danicum,* 3rd ser., vol. 1, no. 215.

[43] *Kong Valdemars Jordebog,* vol. 1, 1926: 20. Cf. Venge 1987: 16.

[44] Enemark 1982b: 703.

[45] *Diplomatarium Danicum,* 2nd ser., vol. 2, no. 145.

[46] *Diplomatarium Danicum,* 2nd ser., vol. 3, no. 5.

Johan Wittenborg we find a clear case of beer export from Lübeck. In 1358, Wittenborg sold 14 *last* 2 *dromt* malt to a brewer named Claus von Vemeren, and there is no doubt that the brew made from this malt was sold at the Scanian market.[47] We do not know if von Vemeren actually undertook brewing directly at the Scanian market, but this possibility cannot be excluded. *Trave-beer* is mentioned in Danish documents, wills and borough customs between 1299 and 1338 as well as later on.[48] This kind of beer was served at memorial meals in the monasteries and was commonly sold at the town fairs. When the small Schleswig castle of Brink (on the west coast of Jutland) bought two barrels of beer for 14 *skilling grot* in 1388, the beer was still of the *trafnisie* type.[49] However, at that time the Lübeck export was declining, and from the mid-fourteenth century the charters show that the importers of beer to the Scanian markets included merchants of Stralsund and Rostock, besides people from Lübeck.[50] In 1342, for instance, a letter mentions beer from Rostock, Stralsund and Wismar on the Danish market.[51] From the second half of the fourteenth century, in fact, the beer of Wismar dominated the Danish market. Wismar beer was consumed in the Trinity Guild of Flensburg in 1362, and in 1388 the only foreign beer known to the Flensburg town council was Wismar beer.[52] From around 1400, large quantities of beer were imported from the thriving brewing town of Hamburg, which prior to this date had been supplying primarily the Netherlands.

[47] *Das Handlungsbuch von Hermann und Johann Wittenborg* 1901: LXXII, 42,45.

[48] *Diplomatarium Danicum*, 2nd ser., vol. 5, no. 27 (Monastery of Esrom 1299); *Diplomatarium Danicum*, 2nd ser., vol. 5, no. 328 (monasteries in Lund 1304); *Diplomatarium Danicum*, 3rd ser., vol. 1, no. 215 (Aabenraa1335); *Diplomatarium Danicum*, 2nd ser., vol. 12, no. 89 (Ribe 1338). In the years 1365-67 the only foreign beer found in Sweden seems to have been trave-beer; see *Raven van Barnekows räkenskaper för Nyköpings fogderi 1365-1367*, 1994: 54, 152, 154, 156, 158,160, 162, 168, 174, 226.

[49] "Regnskabet for Ribebispens gård Brink 1388-89", 1993:316-336. A late example of "*trafnisie*" being served in Denmark was recorded in 1408; see Erslev 1901: 181.

[50] *Diplomatarium Danicum*, 2nd ser., vol. 9, no. 294. Cf. Stefke 1989: 468-72.

[51] *Diplomatarium Danicum*, 3rd ser., vol. 1, no. 272, 275, 279.

[52] In 1362 members of Flensburg guilds drank Wismar beer, see *Danmarks Gilde-og Lavsskråer fra Middelalderen* 1899-1900: 265 (5). In 1388 beersellers in Flensburg were authorised to sell Wismar beer; see *Danmarks Gamle Købstadslovgivning*, vol. 5, 1961: 121 (16).

At the Scanian markets, German beer was sold by the Hanseatic merchants from their booths.[53] However, apart from this one case, only Danes reserved the right to sell beer retail. The sale of both German and Danish beer in barrels, jugs, mugs and pots was now quite common in towns. As mentioned above, a party of noblemen from Rügen bought 2 barrels of German beer and 1 barrel of Danish beer in the town of Nœstved one night in 1319.[54] Likewise, a section of the Aabenraa town law of 1335 mentions the serving of Danish beer as well as *trave-beer* imported from Lübeck.[55] Normally, the price of German beer was twice that of Danish beer. The sales outlets were (market) booths mentioned already in the Schleswig borough custom of ca. 1200 as well as in the Copenhagen borough custom of 1254.[56] From 1284 onward it is frequently mentioned that the sellers were usually women—or *ølkunœ* ("brewing woman"), in the expression of the time.[57]

Specialised taverns became increasingly common. Around 1260 a "brewing woman" ran a tavern in the countryside near the main road of Schleswig, the so-called *hœrvej* (German: *Heerweg*), and it seems as if the peasant population was involved in the beer industry both as producers and consumers.[58] The Roskilde borough custom of 1268 mentions beer brewed in the countryside and taken into town to be sold for cash, *per denarios*.[59] That peasants also sold beer in the countryside is revealed by a royal decree of 1316 stating "every peasant who sells beer should pay the Bailiff 6 shilling sterling a barrel".[60] We must conclude that beer was widely consumed in all layers of society, some of it locally produced, some of it imported. A combination of small and large-scale transportation of beer was surely a precondition for this consumption.

[53] *Diplomatarium Danicum*, 2nd ser., vol. 9, no. 294; *Diplomatarium Danicum*, 2nd ser., vol. 10, no. 39.

[54] *Diplomatarium Danicum*, 2nd ser., vol. 8, no. 147.

[55] *Diplomatarium Danicum*, 3rd ser., vol. 1, no. 215.

[56] *Diplomatarium Danicum*, 3rd ser., vol. 1, no. 138 (Copenhagen1254). Cf. *Diplomatarium Danicum*, 2nd ser., vol. 4, no. 121 (Copenhagen 1294).

[57] *Danmarks Gamle Købstadslovgivning*, vol. 1, 1951: 122 (57).

[58] *Danske Helgeners Levned* 1893-94: 393.

[59] *Danmarks Gamle Købstadslovgivning*, vol. 3, 1955: 165ff(20: "..*quod autem de piscibus est predictum, de potu (a rure ferendo) et per denarios uendendo uolumus observari*").

[60] *Diplomatarium Danicum*, 2nd ser., vol. 7, no. 407.

IRON AND SALT

Furnaces for smelting iron dating back to about 1100-1300 have been found in northern Germany and Denmark, and in Schleswig-Holstein a growth of 15% in the number of furnaces can be documented in relation to the preceding Viking Age sites.[61] To a certain degree, the western Danish demand could be covered by domestic production and there was even room for limited export to other parts of Denmark. Until the late sixteenth century, a limited production went on in Jutland. More importantly, however, eastern Denmark experienced a significant growth in iron production from about 1100 to 1300. It has been possible to document the rapid expansion of iron production in northern Scania during this period and up to the fourteenth century; investigations have likewise shown a new production of iron in the province of Halland from at least the twelfth century.[62]

Analyses of iron finds made by Vagn F. Buchwald show us the places from which iron could be imported.[63] Slags and nails from the medieval smiths of northern Zealand, for instance, are interpreted as being made of iron from Halland. A whole "toolchest" from the twelfth century was found near the village of Veksø on Zealand; four pieces of iron tools from the chest can be attributed to Zealand or Jutland, five to South Norway and six to South Halland.[64]

A few written sources support the claim that eastern Denmark supplied the rest of Denmark with iron in the twelfth and thirteenth centuries. As early as 1197, the Zealand monastery of Sorø was given the locality of Tvååker in Halland, "where one can obtain iron from the soil", and five years later an "ironmill" is mentioned at the same place.[65] When another Zealand monastery, Esrom, purchased a farm in Halland in the 1170s, it was presumably motivated by the wish to obtain iron. For the same reason, in 1301 Esrom monastery obtained the right to freely buy timber, wood and iron pieces, *clauos ferreos*, in the town of Helsingborg.[66]

The investigations carried out by Anders Ödman indicate that around

[61] Steensberg 1952; Jöns 1992/1993: 41-55.

[62] Personal communication from Anders Ödman, The Historical Museum, University of Lund; Olsson 1995.

[63] Buchwald 1992: 265-286; Buchwald 1995: 108-126.

[64] Engberg & Buchwald 1995: 70.

[65] *Diplomatarium Danicum,* 1st ser., vol. 3, no. 223; *Diplomatarium Danicum,* 1st ser., vol. 4, no. 67.

[66] *Diplomatarium Danicum,* 2nd ser., vol. 5, no. 148.

1200 the archbishop of Lund received his share of the Scanian iron production. A written source throws some light on the bishop's income in iron. In a complaint from 1257—which lists a number of payments that the official of the Danish king, the *gældker,* had appropriated from the bishop's court in Lund—besides meat, vegetables, salt, and wine, iron is mentioned: *trecenta frustra ferri,* 300 pieces of iron.[67] This iron was probably rent or duty paid by the archbishop's tenants.

From the twelfth century onward a considerable amount of iron was produced in the most eastern part of the Danish realm, northern Blekinge, and in the Swedish province of Småland.[68] The Swedish town of Kalmar gained importance as an export harbour for iron. In the customs tariff of Flensburg from ca. 1300 we find "*Kalmars iœrn*" and "*Blekungs iœrn*"—i.e., iron from Kalmar and Blekinge—in addition to *climpiern* (sold in hundreds), which must have been local or Swedish iron.[69] Iron from central Sweden was also imported to Denmark quite early. About 1200, Saxo mentions a part of Sweden called *Järnbäraland*: literally, the area from which one carries out iron. Iron mining had become common in central Sweden at this time, and advanced technology with hearths was used.[70]

Little is known about the distribution of iron, but as the practice of the monastery of Esrom shows, large-scale consumers could go directly to the places of production to purchase the iron. The Danish borough customs show that in the thirteenth century iron was commonly sold at the market places, as is made clear, for instance, by the law of Flensburg. In the customs tariff of Haderslev of 1292, besides the measure of iron in hundreds, *hundert klimpiern,* a smaller measure is also mentioned, *iernmees*.[71] Although there are not many written sources, archaeological evidence shows that the iron trade expanded during the period 1100 to 1300.

The production and trade of salt also experienced growth.[72] From the twelfth or the thirteenth century production was developed in several

[67] *Acta Processus Litiuminter Regem Danorum et Archiepiscopum Lundensem,* 1922: 28. Cf. Skyum-Nielsen 1994: 75.

[68] Nihlén 1932.

[69] *Danmarks gamle Købstadslovgivning,* vol. 1, 1951: 113 ff (98: "*... for hundrith climpiern. eldœr blekungs iœrn. eldœr kalmœrs iœrn, sœx penning*"). Cf. Stenholm 1986: 92-94.

[70] Cf. Kumlien 1956: 482-490.

[71] *Danmarks gamle Købstadslovgivning,* vol. 1, 1951: 267 ff.

[72] Madsen 1977: 269-294.

places in Denmark. Investigations done by Jens Vellev have recently given solid evidence of salt production on Lœsø, an island where it is quite easy to dig wells with a high concentration of saltwater.[73] Large-scale salt production went on here in the early fourteenth century, with the Chapter of Viborg as the driving force. The chapter owned the whole island and was paid a levy on the salt kettles, and the levy was sent by ship to Viborg's harbour town, Hjarbœk, every year; in the fifteenth century this constituted at least 648 barrels of salt. Local peasants carried out the production on the island, but the ownership of the salt kettles could be split up in shares owned by citizens and clergy on the mainland. Peasants also produced salt in other parts of Denmark.

In Frisia salt was produced in a very special way: by burning turf and turning it into salt. The production of turf salt was presumably very large about 1100-1350.[74] The borough customs of Schleswig and Flensburg mention only this type of salt, which was transported by wagon from the west coast to the east coast. The west coast town of Ribe remained the most important place for the sale of North Friesian salt during the Middle Ages, and Ribe's large customs income from the salt trade in 1231—40 *mark*—presumably derived for the most part from Frisian salt. The twelfth-century borough customs of the east Swedish town of Söderköping reveal that Ribe's re-export of Friesian salt was larger than could be expected: it mentions salt from Ribe (*ripärä salt*), Lüneburg (*travesalt*), and also French and Norwegian salt.[75]

Lüneburg salt was imported to Denmark from German towns, especially from Lübeck, from around 1200, and from the mid-thirteenth century we may assume that the so called "*ummelandfahrer*"[76] coming from the Netherlands to the Scanian markets brought French salt with them. The Scanian markets, of course, were the largest consumers of salt. The customs books of Lübeck, the *Pfundzollbücher* of 1368-69, show us that in this year salt to a value of 60,000 *mark* was exported from Lübeck, corresponding to one third of the town's total export. One third of this salt, about 20-24,000 barrels, went to the Scanian markets each year.[77]

[73] Vellev 1993.

[74] Poulsen 1991: 279-292.

[75] Yrwing 1968: 219-242.

[76] See p. 55.

[77] Enemark 1982a: 705.

INTERDEPENDENCIES IN PRODUCTION, TRADE AND CONSUMPTION

About 1200, Arnold of Lubeck noted that the Danes who formerly dressed in seamen's clothes "are now wearing scarlet and fur as well as purple and linen because they are now making large profits from the fish markets taking place in Scania each year, and to which merchants from the neighbouring areas are coming, taking with them gold, silver and other goods to buy their herring (...) Their country is likewise rich in good horses because of the rich pastures".

We can take Arnold's comments as an indication that something new was happening in Danish trade about 1200, even if we tend to place the breakthrough some decades before. This should be seen as a consequence of the market created by the newly founded German towns of the Baltic from the middle of the twelfth century. Broadly speaking, the demand for horses and herring was a product of new patterns of consumption in Europe: a new feudal class demanded stallions for their warfare, and the spread of Christianity created an expanding market for fish.[78] The increased salt production and the import of salt to Denmark constituted a necessary precondition for the emergence of the international herring fisheries. In the same way, increases in the export of meat were dependent on salt supplies. Even if the salting of herring had gone on for a number of centuries before 1200, the emergence of the international Scanian markets must have caused a sharp rise in the demand for salt. German beer seems to have reached the Danish market some time shortly after 1200, and the import of foreign cloth rose simultaneously.

In early medieval Denmark, as in the rest of Europe, the agrarian sector experienced growth and change.[79] The introduction of new tools caused a rise in grain production: the balanced sickle, for example, became common, the plough with mouldboard and heavy coulter was used (archaeological finds date to ca. 1000-1100), and horses were now employed as draught animals thanks to new harness forms. The processing of the increased grain production was facilitated by the construction of mills. A decisive factor in this agricultural revolution lies in the increased supply of iron, as it was the

[78] On the use and consumption of war horses, see Davis 1989; cf. Hyland 1997. The important topic of horse breeding is dealt with by Gladitz 1997. The increased use of horses, also in agriculture, has been demonstrated by Langdon 1986.
[79] Poulsen 1997.

prerequisite for the making of most of the new tools.[80]

This new agricultural complex seems to have been introduced in Denmark in the period 1000 to 1100. The chronology of the iron supply, however, is very important, and the evidence of an explosion in the Danish iron production in the twelfth and thirteenth centuries suggests that we should move our dating of the agricultural revolution up in time and pay less tribute to the eleventh century than is normally done. Agricultural innovation seems nevertheless to have taken place somewhat before the introduction of the rest of the goods discussed in this paper. For these products, which form part of a restructured urban culture, the period 1200-1300 must be termed revolutionary.

NEW PLACES OF EXCHANGE AND NEW CONSUMERS

From the Viking Age onward we are able to follow the urbanisation of Denmark. In his survey of Danish urban economy, Anders Andrén maintains that until about 1200 the towns mainly served as *points d'appui* for royalty and the Church, and that it was not until the thirteenth century that they assumed the role of distributors of commodities to any great degree.[81] Between the mid-1100s and 1270 many Danish towns were founded, and the urban network was filled out in the period up to 1350. Thus, by the thirteenth century a nation-wide system of market towns existed. In this century, most of the population was involved in the commodity economy. The weekly markets connected town and country, but agrarian and urban producers also met outside the towns. One example is the fair held each year outside the gates of the monastery of Æbelholt between June 15th and 29th from at least the 1260s, where, among other things, horses were traded.[82] From around 1300, if not before, it was also possible to find countryside taverns that sold beer to members of the local rural society in exchange for payment in money.[83]

There is no doubt that the amount of money in Denmark increased considerably between the year 1100 and 1330. Particularly in the last part

[80] For a list of tools possessed by a Danish peasant ca. 1200, see Engberg & Buchwald 1995: 70.

[81] Andrén 1985; cf. Andrén 1994.

[82] *Diplomatarium Danicum,* 2nd ser., vol. 1, no. 461.

[83] *Diplomatarium Danicum,* 2nd ser., vol. 7, no. 407.

of the period, 1300-1330, it seems that a huge number of coins were minted.[84] From an account of 1282, listing the amounts that the Papal Chamber had received in tithes, we get an idea of how much money was in circulation. The tithe from nine Danish towns and dioceses is calculated as 55,203 1/2 *mark* (or 13,248,840 Danish *penninge*) in Danish money alone.[85]

From about 1200, at the large markets in Scania all groups of society were in possession of cash. The archbishop of Lund could arrive at the market, as he did in the 1250s, with 1,000 *mark* "to make his most necessary purchases".[86] Most landowners headed for the market, as documented by a law from around 1200 demanding that peasants (Danish: *landbo*) should pay their annual rents before the 15th of August so that their lords could buy the things needed at the Scanian market. Peasants were certainly also present in large numbers. A source from around 1200, for instance, tells us of the presence of a peasant from Halland with 17 *penninge* in his pocket.[87] Foreign capital was brought in by Hanseatic merchants; in 1358, for instance, the servant of a Lübeck merchant brought 160 *mark* in silver money to the Scanian markets, besides the articles of salt and ginger.[88]

Written sources as well as finds of coins indicate that in the thirteenth century money was more widespread in society than ever before. A study of stray finds of Danish coins seems to show that coin circulation was common in towns from about 1150-1200, while the countryside did not become monetized until the middle of the thirteenth century.[89] There is probably good reason to analyse this problem again, both in light of the fact that money rents seem to be paid commonly by peasants in Scania as early as the twelfth century, and that according to numismatic studies, the use of money was spreading in the eleventh century.[90] A growing number of archaeological finds of local marketplaces, often dating back to the eighth and ninth centuries and situated near water as well as inland, perhaps ought to make us place less emphasis on the commercial break-

84 Jensen 1992.
85 *Diplomatarium Danicum*, 2nd ser., vol. 3, no. 33.
86 *Diplomatarium Danicum*, 2nd ser., vol. 5, no. 105.
87 *Danske Helgeners Levned* 1893-94: 361f.
88 *Das Handlungsbuch von Hermann und Johann Wittenborg*, 1901: 42 (no 278).
89 Poulsen 1979.
90 Cf. Hårdh 1976.

through around 1100-1300 than is normally done.[91] One can also observe the widespread use of foreign goods in Danish villages as early as the eighth and ninth century. For example, quernstones of basalt lava from the Rhine area seem to have reached every farm and village of Western Jutland. Presumably, Ribe distributed this kind of goods to agrarian producers, who in turn supplied the town with their products.[92]

It is nevertheless indisputable that new commercial channels came into existence in the period 1100 to 1300. This was not only the case in urban areas, but also in a broader commercial context. About 1200, in the Baltic, the old sea routes of the Viking Age were used. About 1080, Schleswig succeeded Hedeby as the commercial centre of the Schlei and became one of the main points of the old route heading from Eastern Europe and Novgorod. In Schleswig (as in Hedeby), people from Frisia, the Rhine area, Niedersachsen and Westphalia met others from Gotland, Sweden, Norway, Wenden and Russia. A Danish town with connections westward was still central to Baltic trade around the year 1200.

However, Danish dominion ended with the defeat of King Valdemar II at Bornhöved in 1227, and the Danish and Nordic lead in the sea trade disappeared. Even if the connections between Ribe and Flanders/England during the thirteenth century are not to be underestimated, the future lay with the German towns. While Schleswig was reduced to regional importance, and in the 1230s abandoned its harbour constructions, the German towns flowered: Wismar, Rostock, Stralsund, Greifswald, Stettin, Danzig, Elbing—and first and foremost Lübeck.[93] Denmark now became part of a trade structure centred on the German towns of the Baltic. The German towns, although they were not large in an international context, were both consuming Danish agricultural products and producing manufactured products for the Danish market. The new commercial structure of the Baltic therefore had decisive effects on Danish import and export. At the same time, the herring markets in Scania came into existence from the middle of the twelfth century, taking the form of international fairs for Baltic and West European commodities from about 1200 onward. In Danish historiography these markets are regarded as the prime gate of import from abroad to Danish towns; it is documented that the value of the import to Scania from

[91] Ulriksen 1990; Christensen & Johansen 1991; Nilsson 1990; *Atlas over Fyns kyst i jernalder, vikingetid og middelalder* 1996: 194-200.

[92] Jensen 1990.

[93] Vogel 1977; Vogel 1989.

Lübeck was five and four times as high for the years 1399 and 1400 as the import to the rest of Denmark.[94]

By around 1200 an international fair (i.e., the one in Scania) and a dense network of market towns in close contact with the German market and other parts of northern Europe existed in Denmark. It was mainly ships that maintained the connections. I shall not discuss the development of shipping, but it should be emphasised that this form of transportation, so easily accessible in Denmark, decisively furthered the ongoing market integration. Transport by ship was much less expensive than land transport: a chronicler writing in about 1200 noted that the town of Roskilde was located on the sea and not inland because this spared the merchants the expense of renting carts.[95] A more precise indication of an awareness of the benefits of sea transport is to be found in a law from the second half of the thirteenth century, the so-called *Thords artikler*, in which it is stated that a barrel of beer should cost one half more in inland towns, the *akselstœder,* than in the sea towns.[96]

In conclusion, from the thirteenth century and onward Denmark became a still more integrated part of the North European market. The country had trade connections with England and Flanders, but Denmark in particular became part of the Hanseatic trade system centred in the German towns of the Baltic. Cloth, beer, iron, salt and many other products were supplied from abroad, and a broad commercial network of towns, merchants and consumers was able to circulate all the goods imported.

[94] Arup 1925; Christensen 1957: 76; Enemark 1988.

[95] *Krøniker fra Valdemarstiden*, 1900-01:13.

[96] *Danmarks Gamle Landskabslove,* supplementary volume to vol. 4, 1951-61: 89.

Lübeck and the Baltic Trade in Bulk Goods for the North Sea Region 1150-1400

Rolf Hammel-Kiesow

The German town of Lübeck, founded in 1143, was at the height of its importance for the east-west trade from the early thirteenth to the second half of the fourteenth century. It played a key role in the trade between Western Europe and the Holy Roman Empire on the one hand, and the Scandinavian countries and the Baltic region on the other. In the traditional view of the trade between the Baltic region and the North Sea region, nearly all western goods *en route* to the east and eastern goods travelling west had to be unloaded and reloaded in Lübeck from sea-going ship to barge and cart or vice versa. During the second half of the fourteenth century direct shipment of bulk goods, such as grain, timber or salt, between the North Sea and the Baltic Sea increased, and Lübeck's importance in bulk-goods trade consequently decreased—at least in comparison with its trade in high-quality products. This applied, however, only to the direct east-west trade; the town's importance for the transport of goods from the Baltic Sea region to central and southern Germany remained constant.

This traditional picture is founded on precious little information. There are only a few written sources dealing with Lübeck's bulk-goods trade in the thirteenth century; they are somewhat more abundant in the fourteenth century but then mostly relate to the trade in luxury goods such as furs, wax and cloths. In the following it will be questioned whether it is correct to maintain that the two sea regions, from early Hanseatic time up to the fourteenth century, were connected virtually only by the land link Lübeck-Hamburg.[1]

Concerning the commodities traded, the traditional view portrays Lübeck in the second half of the twelfth century as a trading-place and port of transshipment mainly for high-value goods such as cloth, furs and wax.

[1] Daenell 1902: 9 f.; Rörig 1928: 158; Dollinger 1989: 301, 512. A fairly recent archaeological study even discusses totally separate trading areas during late medieval and early modern trade; van Haster 1991: 211.

But by the end of this century at the latest, bulk goods such as herring and salt supplemented these high-value goods.[2] The increasing demand for foodstuffs caused by the growth of the European population in the thirteenth century meant that herring and salt became the fundamental commodities traded in Lübeck for at least 400 years. So fundamental were they that it was said that Lübeck was built upon herring-barrels.[3]

By far the most important fishing grounds in Europe in the thirteenth and fourteenth centuries were those of Scania, which was also the busiest centre for curing and trade with herring. Scania's importance for Lübeck already in 1201 was so great that the town surrendered to King Knut VI of Denmark, when he arrested the merchants of Lübeck and seized their vessels at the markets of Skanör and Falsterbo. Important fishing grounds were also found along the coasts of the Isle of Rügen, near Stralsund; here Lübeck obtained privileges concerning herring exports in 1224.

The strong position achieved by Lübeck in the herring trade was a result of its trade with salt from Lüneburg. Even if this salt trade was far from monopolised by Lübeck merchants, by the end of the fourteenth century they were purchasing roughly 50% of the annual production of the Lüneburg salt-works (there is evidence of this from 1368/69). Lüneburg salt was not only used for curing fish but also exported on a large scale to the Baltic area.[4]

At the turn of the thirteenth century, Lübeck traded in bulk goods from the western Baltic (herring, salt, grain and presumably beer) and from Norway (stockfish). Salt was only sent into the Baltic region via Lübeck, and to certain extent this was also the case with herring. Grain and beer, presumably from Holstein and Mecklenburg, were shipped to Norway. All other bulk goods were brought from the east to Western and Central Europe via Lübeck. The traditional view holds that the connection between the Baltic and the North Sea was made using the land link via Lübeck-Hamburg but not directly by sea.

[2] There is now evidence—mainly archaeological—that the herring trade already had great importance for the coastal region of the south-western and southern Baltic before the twelfth century; Benecke 1982; Leciejewicz 1985; Leciejewicz 1991; Jahnke 2000, chapter 1, "Einleitung".

[3] Dollinger 1989: 289.

[4] Hammel-Kiesow 1998a. The production of Lüneburg salt itself increased from 5200 tons in 1205 to approximately 16000 tons at the end of the thirteenth century.

The role of Lübeck as a link between east and west was shared in late summer every year by the herring markets of Skanör and Falsterbo, which are recorded since the twelfth century and were established as international fairs towards the middle of the thirteenth century. Merchants from the Netherlands, England and other parts of Western Europe came to the Scanian fairs by ship, sold their goods, and bought herring and Baltic commodities taken to the fairs by Scandinavian merchants and by merchants from the newly-settled towns on the southern and eastern coasts of the Baltic. The *ummelandfart* (the sea route round the Skaw, northern Jutland) is first recorded in a charter given to Kampen merchants by the Danish king in 1251.[5]

This document, however, does not necessarily indicate the start of the direct route from Western Europe to the Scanian markets, and the Baltic Sea. Indeed, it seems more likely that the direct route was used even before 1251. But with what frequency? And did the ships sail on from Scania to the Baltic ports? The answer to these questions would indicate the importance of trade with bulk commodities via Lübeck before the second half of the fourteenth century.

In my opinion it is not too far-fetched to imagine considerable *ummelandfart* before the 1250s. Ever since the end of the twelfth century the sea route from the island of Gotland in the Baltic Sea to Norway and further on to the English east coast is well recorded. German merchants of the Baltic cities, primarily Lübeck merchants we presume, joined the Gotlandic merchants in the so-called *Gilda communis* and sailed together with them to Norway and England.[6] German merchants, especially from the Wendish towns Lübeck, Wismar, Rostock and Stralsund, visited Norway on their own from the beginning of the thirteenth century at the latest. On getting closer trade connections with England and Flanders, it was only a small step to sail from the top of the Skaw in the direction of Boston or Bruges. This was of course far more dangerous since gales were frequent and the west coast of the Jutland peninsula lacked natural harbours. For this reason the direct route between the Baltic and the North Sea region was used only by ships carrying bulk goods; for very valuable goods Lübeck remained the most important port of transshipment.

[5] *Diplomatarium Danicum*, 2d ser. vol.1, no. 50; *Hansisches Urkundenbuch* 1, 1876, no. 411.

[6] Kattinger 1999: 184 f.

Studies in Hanseatic history in the decades after World War II do not (at least not directly) deal with the topic of Baltic bulk goods—the first monograph on Baltic herring fishery and trade was published in 2000.[7] And hardly any attention has been paid to the other bulk goods from the region, such as grain, tar, pitch, potash, etc., even though the overall picture of trade between Western and Eastern Europe emphasises the essential importance of Baltic bulk goods. In the main these were raw materials and foodstuffs necessary for the economic growth and prosperity of Flanders and England and, later on, of the northern Netherlands.[8] Nevertheless, more recent studies do deal with the *ummelandfart* in both directions, which is said to have taken place in a small number of cases with bulk commodities already in the second half of the thirteenth century,[9] but no study presents the few pieces of evidence we actually have. In what follows, I will therefore give a description of the part Lübeck merchants may have played in the *ummelandfart* with respect to their trade in bulk goods.

Written Evidence

The written sources for Lübeck trade fall in three periods.[10] In the first, which began in the middle of the twelfth and came to a close in the middle of the thirteenth century, no figures at all are recorded for bulk commodities. Chronicles, privileges and even the famous toll rolls from Damme and Thourout[11] on the route to Bruges (1252) give hardly any information.

The second period—from the third quarter of the thirteenth to the middle of the fourteenth century—gives better information through the account books (*Handelsbücher*) of some Lübeck merchants, some customs accounts recorded in England, and also the so-called *Niederstadtbuch*, a ledger maintained by the city authorities for private debts. But, like the lists of commodities carried by wrecked or captured ships, these sources only give information concerning individual cases. However, they do allow us in some cases to reconstruct the ratio between high-value goods and bulk goods.

7 Jahnke 2000 (see note 2 above).
8 See, e.g., Postan 1973.
9 Weczerka 1973: 46, 51; Fritze et al. 1974: 72; Stoob 1995: 137.
10 According to Dollinger 1989: 275-78.
11 *Hansisches Urkundenbuch* 1, 1876, no. 432, 435.

The third period that began in the second half of the fourteenth century, is characterised by a far greater wealth of sources, most of them of the same type as in the second period. However, the most important ones are new: the so-called *Pfundzollbücher*. The *Pfundzoll* were customs imposed on ships and commodities in towns of the Hanseatic League during times of war. The great importance of this source is that for specific harbours and specific years it lists nearly all the ships, the weight and the value of almost all commodities which arrived in and sailed from a harbour.[12] Of course there are gaps, but in spite of them these sources allow us for the first time to reconstruct nearly all the seaborne trade for a specific town. In this way we are able to get a rough picture of the relationship between high-value goods and bulk goods.

This short overview shows that the Lübeck evidence gives no figures allowing us to determine the proportions of high-value and of bulk goods, not even in individual cases, before the third decade of the fourteenth century. No rough overall relationship can be established for the time before 1368/69, i.e., when a large and ever-increasing share of the bulk goods passed Lübeck by on its way through the Sound. For the period in which it must have been important, both in value and in volume (1150/1200-1350/1400), there are only few sources with qualified evidence and even a total lack of "hard figures."

Growth and Decline of Population and the Development of the Economy

Population growth, mainly in Western Europe, in the twelfth and thirteenth centuries led to an increasing demand for foodstuffs and raw materials. In the course of the thirteenth century the newly settled coastal regions of the southern and eastern Baltic, and their hinterlands, increasingly provided these commodities.

There must have been a serious recession in the bulk-goods trade after the Black Death in the second half of the fourteenth century. This is important from a methodological viewpoint because the above-mentioned *Pfundzollbücher*, which give a rough ratio between high-value goods and bulk commodities, do not exist before 1368/69 when heavy population losses had already taken place. In contrast to historians believing in an

12 The records for the Baltic region are given in Jahnke 1998 (see list 163-170).

increasing trade (with high-value goods only?) after the first epidemics, I presume that the heavy losses of one-third, or even half of the population in many parts of Europe must consequently have led to a downswing in trade with bulk commodities. There is evidence throughout Europe of a severe economic downswing after the late 1370s when the de-population effects of the third wave of the Black Death had culminated and led to consequences for the level of rents, prices and the demand for certain commodities. In Lübeck and Genoa the value of the seaborne trade shows a considerable decrease, as in England too.[13] The output of silver coins also shrank dramatically, in Lübeck in the second half of the fourteenth century, in other European countries and towns mainly between 1395 and 1415.[14] The only exception—as far as we know—was the Netherlands where only few died during the Black Death epidemics. The figures Arne Nedkvitne gives for the trade with stockfish between Norway and England also show an extreme downswing. At the beginning of the fourteenth century approximately 2000 tons (1 ton = 1000 kg) of stockfish per year were brought to the eastern harbours of England (1200 tons by German merchants, especially from Lübeck, 500 tons by English and 300 tons by Norwegian merchants). From 1365 to 1400 stockfish exports to England had sunk to roughly 470 tons, about a quarter of the amount traded at the beginning of the century. Even if this shrinkage does not apply to the entire stockfish trade, it seems clear that this development was due to population decreases and smaller production in Norway as well as in England[15] (and in other countries to which stockfish was exported, even if there are no figures like those found for England). The figures given in the *Pfundzollbücher* for 1368/69 must therefore be smaller than those (unknown ones) for Lübeck's seaborne trade half a century earlier.

This assumption may be substantiated by evidence of trade with bulk goods in the twelfth and thirteenth centuries to which less importance has hitherto been attached.

[13] For Lübeck see Hammel-Kiesow 1993a. For Genoa and England see Peter Spufford, "The Scale of Commercial Activity," a paper delivered at a conference in Lübeck in 1993; also Spufford 2000: 201-205f.

[14] North 1994.

[15] Nedkvitne 1976a. See also Nedkvitne 1983b: 33-61. For an overview see Helle 1980: 32f. For the former period see Helle 1967. Stockfish constituted about 83% of the whole Norwegian export to England which seems to have been more important than the export from Bergen/Norway to Lübeck.

THE TOPOGRAPHICAL INFRASTRUCTURE OF THE LÜBECK HARBOUR[16]

To some degree the topographical infrastructure of the Lübeck harbour reflects the history and development of the town's trade (Figure 6). In the oldest part of the port, which we think goes back to the twelfth century, were the landing-places for vessels from Rostock, Stockholm, Wismar, Novgorod and Riga, all places which Lübeck merchants visited already in the twelfth and at the beginning of the thirteenth century. Vessels from Bergen in Norway, from the markets of Skanör and Falsterbo, from Prussia and Courland had landing-places in areas of the port which were extended in the early thirteenth century, the time when Lübeck merchants started to visit the markets of these regions.

According to this pattern of development the port of Lübeck was divided into two specific areas according to the nature of the goods that were loaded and unloaded there: in the oldest area high-value goods such as furs, wax and cloth were unloaded, whereas the extended area constituted the port for bulk goods such as herring, grain and beer.[17]

Grain must have been an item of much importance in Lübeck trade.[18] It came to Lübeck from Mecklenburg, Holstein and the county of Ratzeburg, and Prussia too from 1280, mainly for transport to the west. The status of the southern Baltic coast as a region of surplus grain production is well documented from the second half of the thirteenth century. Moreover, at the end of the thirteenth century, the Wakenitz River was dammed for a third time to obtain enough waterpower to be able to construct larger grain mills. However, the capacity of these mills is unknown, and neither do we know if they were fully occupied in supplying the town's population with flour. Certainly flour is well documented as one of Lübeck's exports, chiefly being supplied to Bergen.

There were many granaries in both harbour areas. At the turn of the thirteenth/fourteenth century, twenty-two granaries were located on the sea harbour (Figure 6) and a further seventeen on the domestic port (Figure 7). This leads to the conclusion that large amounts of grain were brought in by sea. But much must also have come from the county of Holstein to Lübeck via the Trave River, or been sent from Lübeck to Hamburg

16 See Hammel-Kiesow 1999.

17 See Hammel-Kiesow 1996.

18 For the Lübeck grain trade see Rörig 1958a: 190 f.; Rörig 1958b: 555-559, 564 f.; Rörig 1958c: 221 note 7, 238.

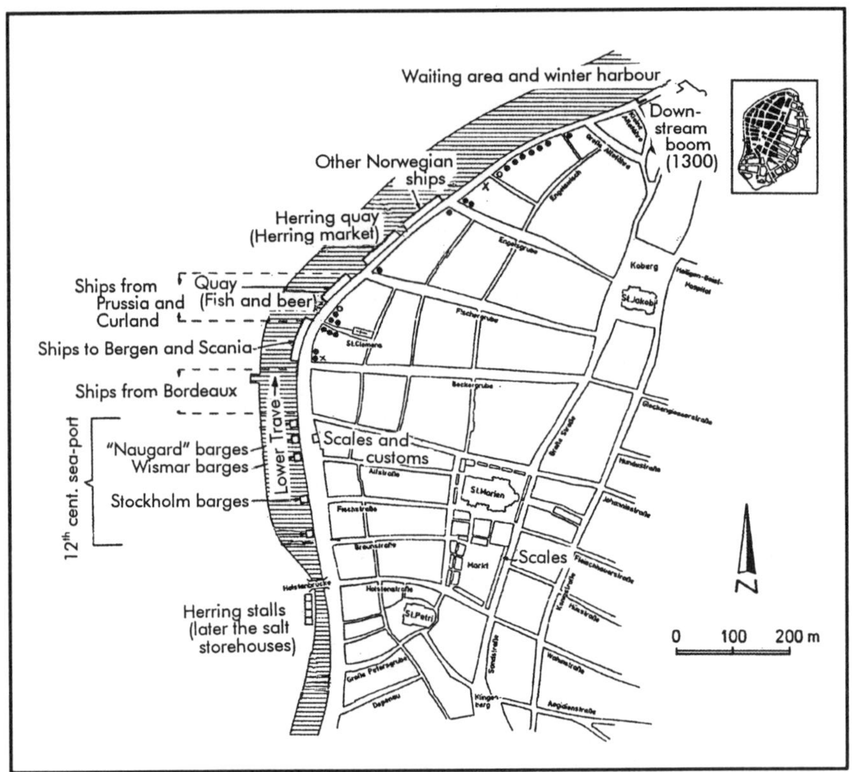

Figure 6. Lübeck Sea Harbour showing the location of the granaries
- ● Granary recorded 1284-1315
- o Granary recorded after 1315
- x Granary–exact position not known

Map: Rolf Hammel-Kiesow, Lübeck.

on the same river; grain would have travelled from the county of Ratzeburg on the river Stecknitz. Unfortunately, the buildings whose function can be clearly identified by their descriptions in the *Oberstadtbücher* do not exist any more, and only a few traces of them have been found. Therefore we know nothing of their storage capacity.

There is, however, an eighteenth-century drawing of the later, so-called Arsenal in the north of the town, which in those days was called the *domus civitatis*, and was used as a granary. It was the same type of building as one

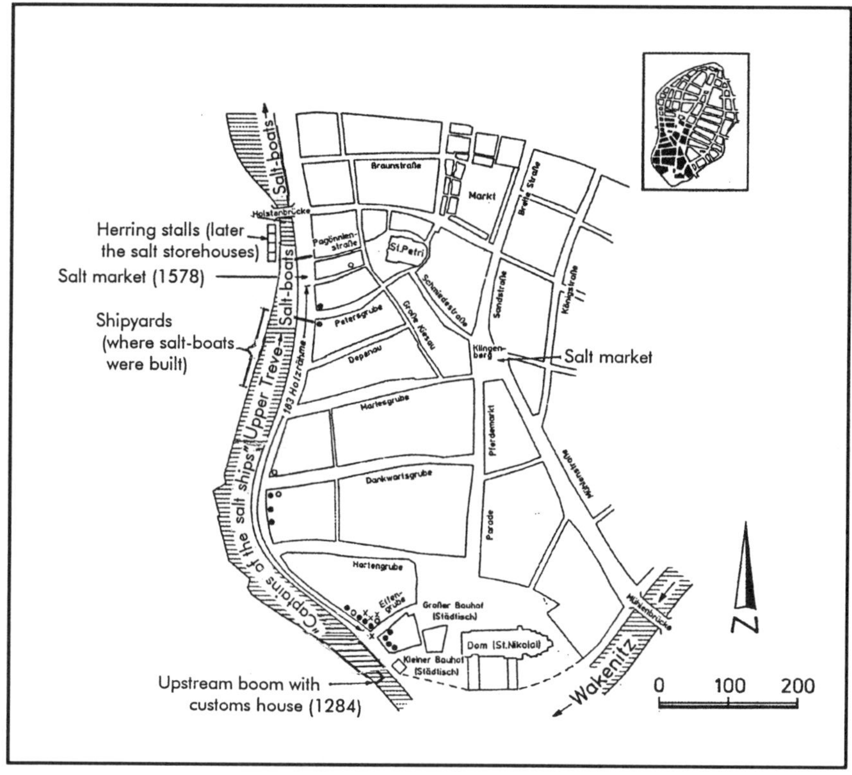

Figure 7. Lübeck Domestic Harbour showing the location of the granaries
- ● Granary recorded 1284-1315
- o Granary recorded after 1315
- x Granary–exact position not known

Map: Rolf Hammel-Kiesow, Lübeck.

which was, or rather still is situated in the domestic port. During the sixteenth century this was converted into a salt store, as was the Arsenal, and in the late seventeenth century it was rebuilt and became one of the most valuable buildings of the early modern town according to seventeenth- and eighteenth-century tax documents. Here we can at least find the remains of the grain store in its fireproof walls, and note that the facade remained unchanged although the function of the building underwent total alteration.

Plate 1. *Salzspeicher* (storage houses for salt) near the Holstentor at the end of the nineteenth century; up until the sixteenth century they were used as storehouses for herring. Photo: Museum für Kunst und Kulturgeschichte der Hansestadt Lübeck.

Judging by the entries in the *Oberstadtbücher*, a large number of grain stores in the town's harbour areas were converted into salt stores in the sixteenth century. The records of grain stores of around 1300, in comparison to the salt lofts and salt stores of the sixteenth century,[19] clearly reflect the decline of the grain trade through Lübeck and the flourishing of the trade with Lüneburg salt which, however, culminated between 1525/6 and 1571/2.[20] The herring houses—the famous Lübeck *Salzspeicher*—near the Holstentor were converted into salt stores at the same time (Plate 1).

[19] The storage building An der Obertrave 43/44, for example, was recorded in 1301 as *domus frumenti*, in 1539 as *solthus*. I am grateful to Margrit Christensen who allowed me to use the results of her research; see her *Kleinbürgerlicher Wohnungsbau in Lübeck. Grundstücksentwicklung, Baustruktur und Sozialtopographie im 16. und 17. Jahrhundert* (forthcoming).

[20] Hammel-Kiesow 1998a: 64 ff.

ARCHITECTURAL EVIDENCE—THE *DIELENHAUS*

In the last quarter of the thirteenth century, with the great increase in stone structures, house types became standardised in Lübeck. There is documentation for a wide range of building types in the second and third quarters of this century, but after ca. 1500 virtually only the so-called *Dielenhäuser* were built.[21]

Typically the *Dielenhaus* consisted of a large, high, single room on the ground floor (possibly already with a *Dornse*, a small, separated room beside the entrance, used as an office, *scrivekamere*), sometimes a very low first storey and three to four lofts under the roof. Where the ground allowed it, a cellar construction was built, usually in merchants' houses of vaulted construction (Plate 2).

The storage lofts appear to have been primarily constructed for bulk goods because their loading capacity was insufficient for barrel-packed commodities. The storage capacity of a *Dielenhaus* far exceeded the provisions necessary for a normal household. One *Last* of grain, about two tons, needs ten square metres of floor space.[22] On the lower floor of a *Dielenhaus*, where the storage space is unrestricted by the slope of the roof, an average of 160 square metres could have stored 16 *Last* or 32 tons of grain. In the fourteenth century there were about 500 merchants in Lübeck, some owning more than one property,[23] giving a lower storage-room capacity for the whole town of 8,000 *Last* or 16,000 tons of grain. In other words, there would have been sufficient storage space for the provisions of around 46,000 people for one year (350 kg per head/year). But this does not take into account the storage capacity of the lofts, nor the capacity of the *Dielenhäuser* that were not owned by merchants, nor, most importantly, the capacity of the storage houses mentioned above. The latter ones would have had room for another 16,000 tons of grain.[24] It should be noted that

[21] Scheftel 1997; Hammel-Kiesow 1998b: 103-105.

[22] Hennings 1956.

[23] Hammel-Kiesow 1988: 56 f.

[24] A highly hypothetical calculation can be made for the storage house in the area of the domestic port (see Figure 6). It has a surface of ca. 670 square metres, which would be sufficient to store 67 *Last* or 134 tons (see note 22). If we calculate for three floors only, the storage capacity would have been 134 *Last* or about 400 tons. If we now assume a similar capacity for the 39 storage houses existing at the beginning of the fourteenth century, we get a storage room capacity of another 16,000

Plate 2. Lübeck, vaulted cellar, Schüsselbuden 2, used as a store room for goods that could be kept in a slightly damp atmosphere. Photo: Jens Holst, Hoisdorf/ Stralsund.

Lübeck had around 20,000 inhabitants at this time. If we compare this with the annual grain consumption in London (at the end of the thirteenth century approximately 27,900 tons for both food and drink) we see that Lübeck's storage capacity (over 32,000 tons) would have been more than sufficient for the estimated grain requirement of London's 100,000 inhabitants.[25] To put these figures into perspective, they should be compared to the "rather substantial amount of grain" exported from England between 1377 and 1461—which averaged no more than 3,861 quarters (= 653 tons) *per annum*.[26]

We do not know when the east-west grain trade through Lübeck came to an end. It must have declined simultaneously with the increasing trade via the direct route from Prussian and Livonian harbours to Western Europe. This began in the second half of the fourteenth century but would only have threatened Lübeck's trade from the last quarter of the fifteenth century. Grain was an important commodity for western destinations—at first to Bruges and later direct to other ports and to the bays of Bourgneuf, to Portugal and Spain, where it was exchanged for salt.

It is interesting to note that, as far as we now know, trusses (*Unterzüge*) and *Hausbäume*, which increased the loading capacity of the lofts, came into being in the fifteenth-century *Dielenhäuser*. This could indicate that the bulk goods storage spaces, after the decline in the grain trade, were now rebuilt to accommodate other, heavier items.[27] The number known of such cases is, however, too small to offer a solid basis for this hypothesis.

The *Dielenhaus* had further storage spaces: the first storey, which was possibly also used as living quarters, but above all the cellar.[28] This served as store for goods that ought to be kept in a somewhat damper atmosphere,

---

tons of grain, which would have been sufficient for another 46,000 people a year—indeed a very hypothetical calculation.

25 For London see Campbell *et al.* 1993: 35, who give 165,000 quarters (1 quarter = 281.904 litres). To convert this volumetric measurement into kilograms, we have to reduce it by 0.6 (see Rahlf 1996: 44, a study which I recommend highly to all who deal with grain history because of its methodological precision concerning the use of historical grain prices and quantities of grain); the resulting sum is 27,908,500 kg.

26 Jenks 1985: 503; Jenks gives 841 tons because he uses another factor to convert litres of grain into kilograms.

27 I am grateful to Jens-Christian Holst for this hypothesis.

28 Holst 1986.

Figure 8. Lübeck–map of cellars. Black: vaulted cellars; grey: cellars with trabeated ceilings. Map: Jens Holst, Hoisdorf/Stralsund.

such as cloth and furs, while the upper storey was kept for goods needing dry storage.

The storage capacity of the cellars was enormous. For the exhibition "Pfeffer & Tuch für Mark & Dukaten" (The Lübeck Treasure Trove), the present writer made a reconstruction of the cellar of a Lübeck merchant house from around 1530. The goods are shown in barrels, bales and sacks, which correspond in size, contents and price to our present knowledge of trade in Lübeck in the first half of the sixteenth century. Only half of the cellar is filled with goods, which have a value of 1.3 million DM in today's currency, or roughly 580,000 US dollars or 665,000 Euro (2001 rates).

A glance at the cellar plan of the town (Figure 8) shows how many vaulted cellars (the black ones), were constructed in Lübeck as a rule in the thirteenth and at the latest in the early fourteenth century.[29] This information gives an idea of the quantity and value of the goods stored in the houses of the Lübeck merchants in the Middle Ages and in Early Modern times.

The development of the infrastructure of the Lübeck sea harbour, as well as the evidence of storage-houses mentioned in the entries of the *Oberstadtbücher,* and architectural history revealing the storage capacity of the *Dielenhaus*, prove the existence of the bulk goods trade (which was never in doubt anyway). The question now is the nature of these bulk goods and whether some travelled to England and Flanders by ship—through the Belt or Sound and round the Skaw.

Bulk Goods in the Trade with England

At the beginning of the thirteenth century it seems that German merchants from the Baltic region travelled to England, at first together with Scandinavian merchants from Gotland.[30] The question of whether the Gotland mer-

[29] Holst 1986: 117.

[30] The first evidence of a merchant from the Baltic region in London is a safe-conduct given in July 1223 to Gilbert of Schleswig, a subject of the Duke of Lüneburg; see Lloyd 1991: 17 and note 5.

The presence of Lübeck merchants in London before 1226 is proved indirectly by an imperial charter (*Reichsfreiheitsprivileg*) from 1226, which ruled that the merchants from Cologne and Tiel had to stop exacting illegal tolls from Lübeck merchants in London; Lloyd 1991: 18.

In the same year the merchants of Gotland successfully claimed in the *curia regis*

chants (mentioned in contemporary English sources) were actually Scandinavians or Germans is, I think, solved by the study of Detlef Kattinger which proves that indigenous Gotlandic merchants and Germans collaborated in the so-called *gilda communis*, first in the Baltic region and subsequently in trade with England too.[31] They shipped furs and wax to England where the goods were sold especially to the court and to noblemen.[32] We do not know whether these merchants travelled from the Baltic Sea through the Sound to Norway and then onwards to England, or whether they chose the Lübeck-Hamburg route. There is evidence of both: at the turn of the thirteenth century for the route via Norway, and somewhat later, in 1237, for the Lübeck-Hamburg route.[33] Here again is the

---

that they should be exempt from lastage and other customs throughout England, and that they had never paid any before the last war, presumably the disturbance of 1223-24; Lloyd 1991: 17.

In Boston and Lynn the earliest evidence dates back to the twelfth century and consists of non-specific references to "Easterlings" (*Estrenses*); Lloyd 1991: 39. *Estrenses* meant people coming from E(a)stland, i. e., the Baltic region or even "the parts beyond the North Sea" including Denmark; see Nils Hybel's article below, p. 221; Behrmann 1997.

[31] Kattinger 1999: 233-264. Lloyd 1991: 17, emphasises that "it is quite clear that merchants of Lübeck and other towns of the north-German mainland did not automatically share in Gotland privileges in England," which may be true concerning the meaning of "automatically" but not concerning the close connection between Lübeck and other north-German and Gotlandic merchants proved by Kattinger.

[32] E.g., *Hansisches Urkundenbuch* 1, 1876, no. 475 a.a. 1255.

[33] Norway route: Kattinger 1999: 233 f. This route was to become one of the most important for the trade of the Wendish towns from Lübeck to Stralsund up until the sixteenth century; see below.

Lübeck-Hamburg axis: *Hansisches Urkundenbuch* 1, 1876, no. 281; Kattinger 1999: 251-254. A charter granted in this year (1237) by King Henry III of England to *omnibus mercatoribus de Guthland[ia]* was kept in the Lübeck archives. In the archives of the town of Wesel, situated on the lower Rhine, and of the Westphalian town of Soest, are copies of this charter, which show that merchants of these towns traded in England together with Gotlandic merchants.

For the land route see, too, the charters granted by the counts of Holstein for the burghers and merchants from Riga in 1251 (*Hamburgisches Urkundenbuch* 1, 1907, no. 562), for *universis mercatoribus Romani imperii* in 1253 (*Hansisches Urkundenbuch* 1, 1876, no. 454), for all merchants coming from Gotland in 1255 (*Hansisches Urkundenbuch* 1, 1876, no. 483); Kattinger 1999: 308-314, who interprets these charters as a reaction to the charter which King Abel granted to the *um-*

question of what the first written evidence really proves. Perhaps the merchants of the *gilda communis* chose the direct way round the Skaw because the first written evidence of this is dated only fourteen years later, 1251.

Ever since the last third of the thirteenth century there is evidence of the import to England of bulk goods from the Baltic region by early Hanseatic and this means by Lübeck merchants too. Bulk goods were shipped to ports on the east coast, e.g., Boston and (King's) Lynn,[34] and comprised many kinds of timber, woodland products like potash,[35] pitch and tar, as well as copper (from Sweden), herring[36] and stockfish. Norwegian stockfish, timber and herring were the only bulk merchandise originating east of England but not from the Baltic. Nevertheless, timber and herring were Baltic products too. The Baltic merchants also imported sturgeons, butter, grease, litmus, anise, wool, iron and silver; and they sold goods produced in the Hanseatic towns themselves, such as linen, hardware, products made of wood, as well as beer. The chief imports seem to have been raw materials, which may have superseded high-value items, though we have no firm statistical background for the assumptions.[37]

---

melandfarer, p. 312 (see below). The Lübeck-Hamburg axis and then the transport from Hamburg to England is mentioned for the commodities of Lübeck merchants and other merchants from the *regnum theutonicum* in a letter from King Rudolf I to King Edward I in 1282; *Urkundenbuch der Stadt Lübeck* 2:1, 1858, no. 54 (= *Hansisches Urkundenbuch* 1, 1876, no. 892).

34 It is surprising that in London there are almost no records of fish and timber products, which made up the bulk of German imports on the English east coast. This was despite the fact that Lübeck merchants were among the permanent residents of London. And those northern products which do appear in the London customs accounts, viz. wax, furs and copper, were not imported directly but had been stapled in Flanders; Lloyd 1991: 38.

35 In 1295 a vessel belonging to Heinrich Rekelinchusen from Riga, loaded with ashes, was seized in England; *Hansisches Urkundenbuch* 1, 1876, no. 1179.

36 Jahnke 2000: chapter III.10.7 "Der Heringshandel nach England"; his results for the beginning of the fourteenth century are based on Hybel 1996. In 1291 merchants from Staveren, Friesland, Stralsund, Greifswald, Harderwijk and Lübeck seem to have imported herring to Lynn; Jahnke 2000, who cites Kunze 1891, no. 14, pp. 13 f. In 1296 German merchants named Wolf and Tidemann from Stralsund and Albert from Holland had sent three vessels loaded with herring and other commodities from Germany and from the Netherlands to Ravensworth in the county of York; *Hansisches Urkundenbuch* 1, 1876, no. 1207.

37 Kunze 1891: XLV, the list of imported commodities given above.

Until recently it was not known whether grain from the Baltic was exported to England in the thirteenth century,[38] but now Nils Hybel has proved that grain, especially rye, was shipped to England some time in the thirteenth century, and that by the turn of the century this was a regular traffic.[39] The chronicler Matthew Paris was the first to mention German grain in England; in 1258 the people of London were saved from famine by overseas grain. Probably the 50 or more ships which carried the grain to England were from the *regnum theutonicum*.[40] Even if there is no proof that ships from the Baltic were among them, it seems highly likely because only a few years later, in 1262, there is evidence of English merchants purchasing grain in Rostock.[41] A list of duties from 1275 shows that rye, wheat and barley were exported from Greifswald, mainly by Hanseatic merchants,[42] and one can suggest that some of the Pomeranian grain travelled to England. A quarter of a century later it seems as if the closest connections between England and a Baltic port were those with the Pomeranian town of Stralsund.[43] In 1278 Wislaw II of Rügen decreed that freight and

[38] Lloyd 1991: 42, says that it is a moot point whether any grain came to England from the Baltic before the 1320s. Schulz 1911 (1978): 14, thought that a grain trade existed but only to a slight degree. Neither of these authors had the following evidence which, of course, makes a Baltic grain route to England not absolutely clear: in 1257 a merchant named Johann from Lübeck brought oats valued at 4 pounds, 10 s, 10 d to the king's court, *Hansisches Urkundenbuch* 1, 1876, no. 502; in 1260 there is mention of grain and other commodities destined for London travelling in a ship belonging to Salomon from Hamburg, *Hansisches Urkundenbuch* 1, 1876, no. 554; see below the evidence of grain exported from Livonia by Lübeck merchants (note 85).

[39] See Nils Hybel's article below, pp. 233-240. I therefore only give evidence concerning the grain trade of Lübeck and the Wendish towns.

[40] Carus-Wilson 1973: 96.

[41] *Mecklenburgisches Urkundenbuch* 2, 1864, no. 953.

[42] *Hansisches Urkundenbuch* 1, 1876, no. 746.

[43] See Lloyd 1991, table 1, Hanse ships in Yorkshire ports, 1304-9; from Stralsund 32 vessels (from Lübeck 14, from Rostock 5); from Hamburg, the only port on the North Sea, 25 vessels of the total of 84 coming from eight ports.

Ships from Stralsund sailed to the harbours of Boston, Lynn, Kingston upon Hull and Ravensworth; Fritze 1984: 59. Stralsund seems to have been the Baltic port most favoured by English merchants in the fourteenth century; in the first half of this century grain, timber and herring were the most important export commodities; Fritze 1961: 137 ff.; 156 ff.

handling charges on typical Baltic goods including rye were payable half before departure from the port of Stralsund and half on arrival in Flanders or England.[44] Without any doubt this evidence indicates direct overseas shipping from Stralsund to England and Flanders.

The same conclusion can be drawn from a treaty made between Edward I and Richard de Alemannia in 1283-84. Richard was a citizen of Lynn and a merchant of the King. He expected to travel to Estland and Norway to buy grain and other merchandise for sale in England.[45] Grain which has to be (loaded in Lübeck? and) unloaded in Bruges is mentioned among other Baltic bulk goods in the Lübeck ship and sea laws (mainly concerning the route to Flanders) of 1299.[46] There is therefore no doubt that it was also shipped to England when there was need of it—and a possibility to profit from the trade. It seems that the grain of unknown origin that was exported to England by German merchants not only came from the hinterland of the river Elbe, especially from the Altmark, but from the Baltic region too. An agreement between the city of London and German merchants made in 1282 allowed that grain "brought into the city by Hanseatic merchants might be sold from their hospices and granaries within forty days, unless the king or the city authorities needed to order otherwise because of dearth."[47] Furthermore at the beginning of the fourteenth century German merchants co-operated closely with the grain traders of London to supply the people of this city in times of shortage as, e.g., in 1302 when Parliament was supplied.[48]

From the beginning of the fourteenth century England imported grain annually from the Baltic—supplies coming from Lübeck in the west to Thorn in Prussia in the east—even if the quantities imported were very modest. Overseas trade was not restricted to years of poor harvests, years of warfare, or times when grain prices were high. Such factors only affected the grain trade.[49] This result allows us to obtain a picture of the trade with England involving other Baltic products such as timber,[50] pitch, tar, potash

[44] *Hansisches Urkundenbuch* 1, 1876, no. 868; *Pommersches Urkundenbuch* 2, 1881, no. 1091, pp. 367-68; cf. Nils Hybel's article below, p. 219, note 13.

[45] Public Record Office, C. 66, 103; see Nils Hybel's article below, p. 216.

[46] *Urkundenbuch der Stadt Lübeck* 2:1, 1858, no. 105, 20.

[47] Lloyd 1991: 21; *Hansisches Urkundenbuch* 1, 1876, no. 902.

[48] Carus-Wilson 1973: 96.

[49] See Nils Hybel's article below, p. 233.

[50] See Wendy R. Childs' article in this volume, passim.

and so on, for which there are no figures from the English poundage.

We do not know the volume of trade in other bulk commodities from the Baltic,[51] though a few sources give a glimpse of it. It is worth noticing that the first ship from Lübeck recorded in an east-coast harbour occurs in connection with the export of wool in 1275[52] and therefore refers to the well known route Lübeck-Bergen-Eastern England-Flanders (in other cases Flanders-Eastern England)-Lübeck. In 1291 Johannes Hamer from Lübeck, as well as two other German merchants, were accused by the royal falconer of failing to hand over duties payable to him in the port of Lynn. Commodities belonging to these three merchants, it is said, were loaded on to 140 ships; e.g., herring, copper, butter, a variety of timber, ham, cheese, fells, ash and *harpoys*, a mixture of pitch, tar and resin for caulking vessels.[53] Three years later in the port of Newcastle the mayor and bailiffs arrested eleven cogs belonging to the merchant Johann from Lübeck (was he identical with Johann Hamer?); during this action five barrels of herring, four barrels of beer, 20 shillings sterling and other commodities were stolen from a burgess of the town of Newcastle.[54] In 1294/5 fifty merchants who had come *ummeland* on their way to Flanders were arrested in Ravenser; twenty-three came from towns in Friesland or Ijssel towns, sixteen from Stralsund, three from Lübeck, two from Greifswald, one from Rostock and one from Riga. Herring was the most important commodity for thirty-five

[51] For the volume of Norwegian stockfish imported to England, see note 15 above.

[52] An account of the dues collected on wool, woolfells, and hides exported from Hull, 27 June 1275-27 April 1276: "La neef Jon Hegman de Lubike"; five of twelve merchants who had commodities carried by this ship came from Lübeck too; Gras 1918: 23, 229 f. Another six merchants "de Lubike" are mentioned in this account (237, 240-242) but no other ship coming from the same town. Detailed research in the account on merchant's names that do not reveal a region or town might show that other merchants came from the Baltic.

[53] Kunze 1891: no. 14, 13-15. See note 36 above.

[54] *Urkundenbuch der Stadt Lübeck* 2:1, 1858, nos 131, 132 (= *Hansisches Urkundenbuch* 1, 1876, nos 1165, 1166); see also *Urkundenbuch der Stadt Lübeck* 1, 1843, no. 633 a.a. 1293 (=*Hansisches Urkundenbuch* 1, 1876, no. 1184); *Urkundenbuch der Stadt Lübeck* 2:1, 1858, no. 133 a.a. 1296.—In 1295 the city of Lübeck complained about the seizure of seven of its ships at Newcastle, Ravenser and Yarmouth; Lloyd 1991: 37 (Public Record Office E159/68, m. 61).

Some time before 1307 Norwegian pirates stole 7910 pounds of copper and other commodities destined for England from two German merchants; *Hansisches Urkundenbuch* 2, 1879, no. 110.

of the merchants.[55]

In 1303 beans and "pro brasio" (?) were exported from Boston on a "navis Hermanni de Lubik" as well as salt, cloth, honey and bed-clothes on a further three Lübeck ships and by other Lübeck merchants (in one case on a ship of "Gerardi de Rostok").[56] In the same year stockfish, fish, oil and goatskins were imported to Boston on at least six Lübeck ships, which again refers to the route via Norway, England and Flanders mentioned above.[57] Two cogs from Stralsund, *una bussa* from Wismar, two cogs from Lübeck, as well as a vessel of unknown type from Stralsund, ran the blockade against the port of Lynn in the first half of 1303;[58] we can therefore guess that the number of vessels from the Baltic visiting this port in normal years was somewhat greater.[59] The amount of herring brought to the ports of Scarborough, Whitby and Ravenser between 1304/05 and 1308/09 by English fishermen and Hanseatic merchants ranged from 397 *Last* (4,764 barrels; 1308/09) to 806 *Last* (9,672 barrels; 1304/05). At the same time Hanseatic merchants also visited the ports of Lynn and Yarmouth and traded herring.[60] Only in a few cases is it possible to decide whether the imported herring came from Scania or Norway, i.e., caught near Bohuslen and Marstrand. Apart from the English and Norwegian merchants, merchants from towns ranging from Zeeland (the Netherlands) to Lübeck were

[55] Nedkvitne 1983b: 52 (*Diplomatarium Norvegicum* 19, 1910, no. 395, note 1).

[56] Gras 1918: 32, 275, 277, 279 (navis Arnaldi Crouse de Lubik), 282 f. (navis Johannis Wale de Lubik), 286 (navis Antonii de Lubik).

[57] Gras 1918: 33, 289 (navis Henrici de la Porte de Lubik), 290 (navis Hermanni de Lubik), 291 (navis Frederici de Lubik), 292 (presumably a ship of Edbright de Lubik), 294 (navis Johannis Wale de Lubik; see note 56), 299 (navis Hermanni de Lubik), 300 (navis Antonii de Lubik; see note 56).

[58] *Hansisches Urkundenbuch* 2, 1879, no. 40; see Sartorius Freiherr von Waltershausen 1830: 306-311.

[59] Further evidence of direct shipping from Lübeck and from the Baltic to England: A ship belonging to a London merchant loaded in Lübeck for England with wax and other commodities valued at 600 mark sterling was captured at the mouth of the river Elbe by people from Hamburg; *Hansisches Urkundenbuch* 2, 1879, no. 166 a.a. 1310; see also no. 168. At the same time a vessel belonging to the merchant Heinrich Daniel from Kingston upon Hull loaded with ashes, timber, flax, *pice* (pitch; *picula?*), bitumen and other commodities for England, was attacked and robbed on its way from the Baltic (*de partibus Estlandie*) near the isle of Heligoland by people from Kampen; *Hansisches Urkundenbuch* 2, 1879, no. 167.

[60] See Jahnke 2000 and Hybel 1996.

later engaged in this trade.[61] On February 26th, 1323 129 *Last* (1,548 barrels) of Norwegian herring were imported to England by merchants from Lübeck and Harderwijk.[62] Finally 1200 tons of stockfish sent to England annually by German merchants, especially Lübeck merchants in the first decade of the fourteenth century, would have been carried in at least 20 ships, a figure which is, of course, based on estimation.[63] This figure fits the 22 German cogs that carried fish to the harbour of Lynn in 1302.[64]

In summary, two factors were responsible for the increasing bulk-goods trade between the Baltic region/Norway and England in the second half of the thirteenth century. Firstly, the early Hanseatic merchants gained control of an ever-increasing part of the Norwegian export trade because of their grain imports to Norway, and, secondly, skippers and merchants became accustomed to the direct route from the Baltic to the North Sea region through the Sound and round the Skaw. With regard to the Norwegian-English connection, in the course of time the German merchants took over a well-established trading route but did not open up new markets. They were not the only merchants engaged in this trade. Up until the second decade of the fourteenth century there is evidence of English, Norwegian and Gotlandic merchants on this route[65] and on the route from Norway to Flanders.[66] The increasing amounts of grain available in the newly-colonised regions of the southern Baltic coast, gave the German merchants, from Lübeck to the Prussian towns,[67] much economic influence on Nor-

[61] Jahnke 2000: chapter IV.2.3. "Der Handel mit Bohuslenhering am Ende des 13. Jahrhunderts."

[62] Jahnke 2000: chapter IV.2.2. "Die Heringsperiode [der Bohuslen-Fischerei] am Ende des 13. Jahrhunderts."

[63] The ships carried about 40 *Last* (1 *Last* = ca. 2 tons); Nedkvidne 1983: 579; one has to make allowance for the fact that ships carried mixed freight not just stockfish.

[64] *Hansisches Urkundenbuch* 2, 1879, no. 40, p. 21.

[65] See, e.g., Kattinger 1997: 163-172; Susse, who owned some ships, was engaged in trade between Gotland and Norway, England and Flanders with traditional commodities such as furs and wax as well as herring and timber for shipbuilding. His activities are recorded from ca. 1300 until ca. 1325. He became a burgess of Lynn where Hanseatic merchants accused him of having seized copper on the open sea.

[66] See below notes 89-92.

[67] Prussian merchants actively traded with Pomeranian towns, especially Stralsund and Greifswald, but also with Norway. It seems obvious that they sailed from Norway to England too. In the late thirteenth century it seems as if there was rivalry

wegian fish exports. Merchants from the Wendish towns in particular but also from Bremen appropriated much of the Norwegian exports of stockfish and winter herring. That Lübeck merchants tried to monopolise this trade can be seen from a complaint filed by the *Englandfahrer* from Stralsund who were hampered by Lübeck merchants in their trading.[68] At all events, in the early fourteenth century the stockfish trade with England was dominated by Lübeck merchants, but merchants from Stralsund, Rostock, Hamburg as well as Norway were still engaged in it too.[69] Stockfish was imported mainly at the ports of Boston and Ravenser (but only until the 1320s), herring at Hull and Lynn.[70]

We assume that it was mainly the merchants of the Wendish towns situated in the Baltic region (Lübeck, Wismar, Rostock, Stralsund and Greifswald) that began to use the direct route from the Baltic to Western Europe from the middle of the thirteenth century at the latest. We do have evidence of this dating from 1275. Vessels which departed from ports east of the river Oder are only recorded by English sources in a few cases until the fourteenth century.[71] Unfortunately we do not know whether timber from the Baltic, which was imported into England from the end of the thirteenth century, was shipped directly or whether it was unloaded and reloaded in Lübeck for transport on the Lübeck-Hamburg axis. As a return freight the Baltic vessels generally carried salt, which was exported from Hull, Boston and Lynn, and could be sold at the herring markets in Scania.[72] Otherwise cloth was the only export to the east.

---

between Prussian and Lübeck merchants in Norway; Czaja 1995: 21-38, 43-55.

68 *Hanserecesse* 1:1, 1870, no. 28.

69 Lloyd 1991: 40 f.

70 Lloyd 1991: 40 f.

71 Lloyd 1991: 41. Gras 1918: 3, 159, 165, refers to "A list of local customs due in the port of Ipswich (?), 1303 (?)", in which commodities from Danzig (Denske) were free whether by count or by weight; in this case the trade from Danzig to England would have constituted a remarkable amount and it is a question whether the Danzig merchants would have achieved the privilege by travelling in Lübeck or Hamburg ships.

In 1291 a ship of Johan de Dantzige loaded with gold, silver and sturgeon valued at £120 was wrecked near Green in the county of Kent; probably it was on its way to Danzig with bullion for the Crusaders (CP 40/89/113). I am grateful to Stuart Jenks, Erlangen, for this hint.

72 Lloyd 1991: 42 f., is of the opinion that the export of salt "explains the prevalence of Stralsund ships, with the salt customed in the name of the masters"; but

Flanders

The first evidence of the trading of Lübeck and Hamburg merchants with Flanders dates to the middle of the thirteenth century, therefore somewhat later than such trade with England. Probably the strong position of Flemish merchants trading with the east up until the middle of the thirteenth century, especially with Hamburg and the Altmark with its large amount of grain, was the reason for this. Their influence waned already in the second half of the century because the Flemish merchants were unable to recover their outstanding money.[73] Their balance of trade was positive because there was not sufficient return commodities from Hamburg and the hinterland of the Elbe to Flanders. Merchants from Lübeck and Hamburg on their way to Flanders, paid duty in Utrecht in 1244 on grain, flax, hemp, tallow, tar, pitch, timber, potash, herring, stockfish and salt—bulk goods from the Baltic region except for the last two or three commodities.[74] We have

---

there is no evidence that Stralsund merchants or Stralsund ships traded in the name of the master of the Teutonic Order.

[73] Reincke 1942/1943: 51-164; van Werveke 1963: 67; based on Rörig 1940: 20 f. It seems that Flemish merchants had sent grain from the Altmark on the route through Hamburg to Flanders already at the end of the twelfth century; there is no definite evidence before 1238 when the Altmark grain trade is mentioned in a charter for the town of Aardenburg; Rörig 1940: 54 f. A customs account from the Utrecht fairs dated about 1178—forged but probably trustworthy with regard to its contents—gives evidence of merchants from the Rhineland, from Friesland, Saxony and Scandinavia as visitors, selling grain, wine, herring, salt from Zeeland, and ore; Henn 1989: 42.

For the activities of Friesian merchants in the Baltic during the thirteenth century see below notes 93-95.

[74] *Hansisches Urkundenbuch* 1, 1876, no. 334. See further the list of commodities imported from and exported to the sea in the customs roll of the town of Dordrecht (1287); *Hansisches Urkundenbuch* 1, 1876, no. 1033.—The customs order issued for Hamburg by the counts of Holstein (1262/63) mentions primarily grain, moreover ashes, copper and other commodities. In connection with merchants of the margrave of Brandenburg, Flanders is given as destination for these commodities.; *Hansisches Urkundenbuch* 1, 1876, no 573. The commodities came from the hinterland of the river Elbe because merchants from Lübeck, Gotland and Riga paid no duty in Hamburg and further because only merchants from the Elbe regions are mentioned in the order. This example shows how difficult it is to decide where certain bulk goods came from if their origin is not mentioned. Grain and ashes were products of the Altmark and Brandenburg, as well as the Baltic, while copper was

already heard of the freight and handling charges for Baltic bulk commodities laid down in 1278 by Wislaw II of Rügen; half had to be paid before departure in the port of Stralsund and half on arrival in Flanders or England,[75] which is evidence of the direct route round the Skaw in the last quarter of the thirteenth century. In 1294 Philip IV, the French king, in the course of his war against England, requisitioned in French ports numerous ships belonging to merchants from Lübeck, Gotland, Riga, Wismar, Rostock, Stralsund and Elbing, as too ships from Kampen and Hamburg.[76] The Count of Flanders granted liberties to the burghers of Lübeck in 1298 concerning their trade and the same rights as had had the Hamburg merchants for some time on the Zwin and in the other regions of Flanders, namely "...*ubicunque navigio eosdem contigerit applicari.*"[77]

At the end of the thirteenth century the direct route round the Skaw became integrated into the legal security network built up by the towns since the third decade of the century.[78] In 1298 the bishop of Ribe granted the burghers of Lübeck the right to possession of all their goods if shipwrecked within the borders of his bishopric, to which the dangerous northwestern coast of Jutland belonged. A year later the archbishop of Lund granted them the same rights.[79] In the same year, 1299, the first fleet (of warships) from the so-called *Seestädte*, i.e., towns situated on the coast of the Baltic Sea and of the North Sea (*exercitus Ciuitatum maritimarum*), is mentioned in the waters off Harderwyk. This fleet consisted of ships from Lübeck, Prussian towns and other *civitatibus maritimarum.*[80] In the same year there is evidence in the Lübeck shipping and sea laws mainly concerning the route to Flanders, of the *ummelandfart* as well as of handling charges for the loading/unloading of commodities from the Baltic region:

---

mined in the Harz region as well as in Sweden.

75 See note 44. *Hansisches Urkundenbuch* 1, 1876, no. 868.

76 *Urkundenbuch der Stadt Lübeck* 1, 1843, nos 517, 519 (=*Hansisches Urkundenbuch* 1, 1876, nos 1173, 1175).

77 *Hansisches Urkundenbuch 1, 1876,* no. 1279 (=Urkundenbuch der Stadt Lübeck 1, 1843, no. 677).

78 See Jenks 1995: 514 ff.; Hammel-Kiesow 1998b (see especially pp. 80-84).

79 *Urkundenbuch der Stadt Lübeck* 1, 1843, nos 687, 691 (=*Hansisches Urkundenbuch* 1, 1876, nos 1295, 1303).

80 *Urkundenbuch der Stadt Lübeck* 1, 1843, no 728 (=*Hansisches Urkundenbuch* 1, 1876, no 1331). In 1309 cogs of the "Easterlings" did great damage to English and Scottish vessels; *Hansisches Urkundenbuch* 2, 1879, no. 143.

grain, wax, copper, *tenes* (bars), *blies* (?), beer, pitch, tar, ashes, timber (*wagenschot, lit holt*), lard and *wede* (wood?).[81]

Concerning grain, there are the same problems for Flanders as for England. In the traditional view, exports of grain from the regions in the "far" east of the Baltic to Flanders, even up to the middle of the fifteenth century, were restricted to years of poor harvests and famine because of the high cost of transport.[82] Comparable to the results achieved by Nils Hybel for English grain imports,[83] a similar grain import to Flanders can be imagined when the demand for it was great even though there is only little evidence. The customs roll of the town of Dordrecht (1287) mentioned above, contains the first evidence of grain *van Oestland* as well as *een Tra-[v]eton[ne] vlas*, meaning a ton of flax from Lübeck.[84] Moreover it is possible that Livonian grain was sold by Lübeck merchants to the regions of western Europe at the end of the thirteenth century; in 1299 they received a charter issued by the *Landmeister* of the Teutonic Order in Livonia, which permitted them to buy, sell and export grain and other commodities without any restriction.[85] Two years earlier, in 1297, the Danish King Erik VI Menved had ordained "that restrictions on the grain export from Reval could only be imposed in exceptional cases."[86]

Herring was another bulk commodity imported to the northern Netherlands already before the middle of the thirteenth century as shown by the charter granted in 1251 by the Danish King Abel to the *ummelandfarer*.[87]

81 *Urkundenbuch der Stadt Lübeck* 2:1, 1858, no. 105, 10, 20, 21. The Hamburg sea law from 1292 provides evidence of the *ummelandfart* from Scania to Flanders; Kiesselbach 1900: 87 f.

82 Lesnikov 1957/58: 613 f.

83 See Nils Hybel's article below, pp. 227-241.

84 *Hansisches Urkundenbuch* 1, 1876, no. 1033.

85 *Urkundenbuch der Stadt Lübeck* 1, 1843, no. 701 (=*Hansisches Urkundenbuch* 1, 1876, no. 1309); grain *(annona)* is the only commodity mentioned explicitly in the charter. Moreover, as a result of new negotiations grain and the other commodities had been inserted as an addition in a charter granted a year earlier (*Urkundenbuch der Stadt Lübeck* 1, 1843, no. 688 = *Hansisches Urkundenbuch* 1, 1876, no. 1301, 06. 01. 1299). We can therefore assume that the Lübeck merchants were interested in the Livonian grain trade.

86 See Nils Hybel's article below, p. 233; *Diplomatrium Danicum* 2d ser., vol. 4, no. 260.

87 *Hansisches Urkundenbuch* 1, 1876, nos. 411, 423.

At the end of the thirteenth century much of the imported herring must have come from the Norwegian Sea where, near Bohuslen, there is evidence of burghers from Bremen and of the towns on the river Ijssel fishing for herring from 1288. But fishing must have taken place there far earlier (since *progenitorum temporibus*). Ships from the Wendish towns were also fishing for herring there.[88]

The herring must have been an important foodstuff for the—in medieval terms—densely populated towns and countryside of Flanders.[89] In Damme in 1323 a special staple for herring was even established.[90] We do not know to what extent Hanseatic merchants exported herring from Scania to Flanders. There is no statistical data before the second half of the fourteenth century, when between 1374/75 and 1379 the imports of all merchants to Sluys, where a second staple had been established, ranged between 1,060 and 2,482 *Last* a year (12,720 and 29,784 barrels). The Sluys staple was less important than that at Damme. At the latter, between December 1382 and May 1383, Hanseatic merchants alone had to pay taxes for 612 *Last* (7,344 barrels) herring, whereas at Sluys their share was 279 *Last* (3,356 barrels). [91] Unfortunately we do not know anything about the competition between the remarkable fisheries of the southern North Sea and English Channel, on the one hand, and herring imported by German merchants on the other, before the end of the thirteenth century. Norwegian stockfish, already mentioned in the oldest tax documents from Damme (1252), was also brought to Flanders by Norwegian merchants up until the 1320s. However, they were ousted by merchants from northern Germany in the following years.[92]

Friesian merchants are first mentioned as "Friesians coming from

[88] *Hansisches Urkundenbuch* 1, 1876, nos. 1040, 1045, 1095 (a.a. 1292), 1153 (a.a. 1294), 1299 (a.a. 1298 = the Wendish towns planned to make a complaint in the name of all towns assembled in Lübeck in this year to the king of Norway against a herring tax which they thought was unfairly high), 1316 (a.a. 1299).

[89] Jahnke 2000 (see note 2 above), chapter III.10.8 "Der Handel über Schelde, Maas und Rhein", has no evidence before the fourteenth century. Nedkvitne 1983b: 51-54; in 1294/5 35 merchants who had come *ummeland* on their way to Flanders had been arrested in Ravenser with herring as most important commodity; see above, note 55.

[90] van Werveke 1963: 71.

[91] Jahnke 2000: chapter III. 10.8 "Der Handel über Schelde, Maas und Rhein."

[92] Bugge 1906: 96 f.

Eastland" in a customs roll from Utrecht, dated 1122.[93] These merchants had probably chosen the route via the port of Schleswig on the North Sea axis up the rivers Eider and Treene to Hollingstedt and from there the short land route to Schleswig. The chronicler Heinrich of Livonia reported that around 1200 Friesian ships sailed in Gotlandic and Livonian waters, and in 1198 the *Alberti Chronica Slavorum* mentions that Friesians and people from other regions equipped themselves for their journey to Livonia with vessels, weapons and foodstuffs in Lübeck.[94] For this reason one cannot be sure whether some of the Friesians had not already chosen the direct route round the Skaw. By the second half of the thirteenth century at the latest they sailed directly through the Sound to acquire foodstuffs, especially grain, from the southern Baltic coast. There is evidence of grain from Denmark and from *Slavia*, i.e., the coast of Mecklenburg and Pomerania, being exported to Friesland during the great famine of 1272; in 1273 the town of Greifswald is mentioned in this connection and in 1284 merchants of Rostock sold a large amount of rye to the town of Dordrecht.[95]

Moreover the northern Netherlands, especially the counties of Holland and Zeeland but also the bishopric of Utrecht, were important for the Hanse merchants because the trading routes to Flanders passed through these territories, both by land and by sea.[96] The towns of these regions played an important role in the trade with Scania from the first half of the fourteenth century,[97] and with the towns on the southern shore of the Baltic[98] as well as Norway[99] and Sweden[100] (from 1332 to 1360 Scania be

93 *Hansisches Urkundenbuch* 1, 1876, no. 8; Häpke 1913: 172. For the former period see Ellmers 1986.

94 Häpke 1913: 174.

95 Häpke 1913: 181-183.

96 See, e.g., the customs-privilege granted by Willem, count of Hennegau, Holland, etc., to all merchants "van Oestlande" (this included the regions south of the North Sea, too), who came over sea with "fully loaded" ships to the town of Dordrecht; *Bronnen tot de Geschiedenis van den Oostzeehandel* 1:1, 1917, no. 71 (= *Hansisches Urkundenbuch* 2, 1879, no. 232).

97 Seifert 1997: 38-40. Jahnke 2000: chapter II.10. 8., III.10.9.

98 Before 1300 commodities belonging to merchants from Harderwijk were stolen and some burnt "super terram Gellandie", i.e., on the way between Pomerania and the isle of Rügen (it is unclear whether this concerns only the goods transported by other people or by the merchants themselves too?); *Bronnen tot de Geschiedenis van den Oostzeehandel* 1:1, 1917, no. 55 (= *Urkundenbuch der Stadt Lübeck* 1, 1843, no. 728; *Hansisches Urkundenbuch* 1, 1876, no. 1331).

longed to the king of Sweden and Norway). As for bulk goods, notwithstanding the early customs rolls there is only little evidence: herring was brought back by Dutch merchants from Norway and Sweden, wood (*lignum*), grain, pitch, tar, ashes from Prussia[101] and train-oil from Estonia.[102] Therefore there were close connections between Lübeck and the Wendish towns,[103] on the one hand, and towns on the Ijssel and the Zuidersee, on the other, from the second half of the thirteenth century.[104] In

---

No example of the direct route from Danzig to Harderwijk with furs is mentioned before 1370; *Bronnen tot de Geschiedenis van den Oostzeehandel* 1:1, 1917, no. 366 (= *Urkundenbuch der Stadt Lübeck* 3, 1871, no. 713); this shows, again, how difficult it is to interpret the evidence we have. One has to compare this late evidence with the fact that merchants from Danzig had paid no customs in Ipswich (?) at the beginning of the fourteenth century (see note 71).

99 *Bronnen tot de Geschiedenis van den Oostzeehandel* 1:1, 1917, no. 37-39 (= *Hansisches Urkundenbuch* 1, 1876, nos. 993, 996, 997) a.a. 1285 when "Lewart, Groninge, Stoveren, Campe, Swolle, Deventer, Sutphan, Herderwic et Mudhen" were involved in a conflict with the king of Norway on the side of (later) Hanseatic towns.

100 Eric, duke of Sweden, granted his protection to the Kampen burghers and their trade (1313) and granted them a charter concerning the tax on herring, the felling of trees and the "Rechtssprache" (1314); *Bronnen tot de Geschiedenis van den Oostzeehandel* 1:1, 1917, nos. 72 (=*Hansisches Urkundenbuch* 2, 1879, no. 234), 74 (*Hansisches Urkundenbuch* 2, 1879, no. 248).

101 Merchants from Harderwijk lost their timber (valued at 200 gulden) to soldiers of the "exercitus civitatum maritimarum ... super terram Gellandie" (see note 98) [about 1368]; *Bronnen tot de Geschiedenis van den Oostzeehandel* 1:1, 1917, no. 363 (*Hanserecesse* 1:1, 1870, no. 509); see also no. 504 (*Hanserecesse* 1:3, 1870, no. 486).

102 From Reval to Doesborg; *Hansisches Urkundenbuch* 4, 1896, no 815 a.a. 1385.

103 In 1313 two burghers from Zutphen sold some real property in Rostock; they had acquired it by law (in the court of the town) because of the debts of the former owner ("hereditatem unam cum iusticia prosecutam"); it seems obvious, that these were trade debts; *Bronnen tot de Geschiedenis van den Oostzeehandel* 1:1, 1917, no. 73 (*Mecklenburgisches Urkundenbuch* 6, 1870, no. 3647).

In 1346 and 1347 cogs from Kampen and Harderwijk, which brought cloth to Rostock, are mentioned in the account book of Johann Tölner, mayor of the town; *Mecklenburgisches Urkundenbuch* 6, 1870, no. 175, 183.

104 Later, in 1340, the towns of Lübeck, Stralsund, Rostock, Wismar, Kampen, Staveren, Harderwijk and the other towns of the Zuideree and all merchants were granted a privilege by Count Johan [III] of Holstein concerning conduct and pro-

this connection mention should be made of letters written by Zwolle and Kampen in 1294,[105] well known to all students of Hanseatic history. Both towns thanked the council of Lübeck for trying to keep the Friesians and the Flemish out of the Baltic. According to a decision about wages for "schipmen", it seems to have been common for ships from Kampen to sail to Riga, Reval, Pernau and Stockholm (12 *olde groten*) as well as to Gotland and Prussia (9 *olde groten*) and to Kolberg, to the Wendish towns and to Lübeck (6 *olde groten*) in the middle of the fourteenth century.[106] The same can be deduced from a *Willkür* of the town of Amsterdam concerning misdemeanours (torts) of its burghers in the Nordic kingdoms, in Prussia, in the Wendish towns, in the *Oestersschen* towns and in the whole of *Oestlande*.[107] Around 1378 the Prussian towns made an agreement with the skippers from Kampen and from the towns of the Zuiderzee that shows that Prussian merchants commonly sent their goods on Dutch ships.[108] A further sign of close connections is that a councillor from Danzig owned a sixth part of a ship from Zutphen.[109]

Regarding the second half of the fourteenth century, there is good reason to agree with the traditional view of the history of trade between the Baltic and the North Sea region. From this time there is a large amount of

---

tection for their goods and themselves on the route between Lübeck and Hamburg; *Urkundenbuch der Stadt Lübeck* 2, 1858, no. 712. The evidence shows clearly that both the direct route round the Skaw and that on the isthmus of the Jutland peninsula were used by merchants. It is still a question to what degree bulk goods were carried on the route between Lübeck and Hamburg, after the *ummelandfart* had become more common.

[105] *Hansisches Urkundenbuch* 1, 1876, nos. 1154, 1155.

[106] *Hansisches Urkundenbuch* 3, 1882-86, no. 230, a.a. 1352; see also *Bronnen tot de Geschiedenis van den Oostzeehandel* 1:1, 1917, no. 521 (*Hansisches Urkundenbuch* 4, 1896, no. 999; *Hanserecesse* 1:3, 1870, no. 489) a.a. [1390]; *Bronnen tot de Geschiedenis van den Oostzeehandel* 1:1, 1917, no. 528 (*Hanserecesse* 1:3, 1870, no. 492) a.a. [1390].

[107] *Hansisches Urkundenbuch* 3, 1882-86, no. 553 about 1360.

[108] See also *Bronnen tot de Geschiedenis van den Oostzeehandel* 1:1, 1917, nos. 441, 495 (*Hansisches Urkundenbuch* 4, 1896, no. 599, 882 = *Hanserecesse* 1:2, 1870, no. 348b, p. 474).

[109] See also *Bronnen tot de Geschiedenis van den Oostzeehandel* 1:1, 1917, no. 455 (*Hansisches Urkundenbuch* 4, 1896, no. 691); see also also *Bronnen tot de Geschiedenis van den Oostzeehandel* 1:1, 1917, no. 458 (*Hansisches Urkundenbuch* 4, 1896 no. 705).

evidence showing that the direct route through the Sound and round the Skaw was used increasingly. Nevertheless, the evidence referred to above for England, as well as for Flanders and the Ijssel towns, proves that this direct route had by then already been in use, and probably in good use, for more than 100 years.

TRADE WITH BULK COMMODITIES AFTER THE SECOND HALF OF THE FOURTEENTH CENTURY

What evidence do the figures for bulk trade in the late fourteenth and late fifteenth century reveal? Can they help to interpret the evidence from the thirteenth and early fourteenth centuries?

The first surviving Lübeck poundage list is from the year 1368. Unfortunately the trade with bulk commodities is poorly recorded, because the list only shows goods for which the tax was paid in the port of Lübeck. The poundage on timber, ashes, flax and other bulk commodities had to be paid in the ports in the east from where these goods were exported and where the skippers were given a receipt for this. These receipts, which in Lübeck had to be handed over to the poundage clerk, have been lost (except roughly 3.5% of the Danzig receipts). Based on this imperfect evidence, ashes seem to have been imported to Lübeck in 1368 for not more than 303.5 *Mark lübisch*, timber for 189 *Mark lübisch*. For this reason it is useless to give further figures for eastern bulk commodities because they are far too unreliable for use in statistical interpretation.[110] There are insufficient records for grain quantities too as grain was not liable to poundage. Here we can only rely on hypothetical prognoses, such as those already shown above,[111] for any idea of the amounts in question.

The only reliable evidence of bulk goods is for salt and herring because these commodities originated in the town of Lüneburg and in Scania. In the Lübeck exports for the year 1368, Lüneburg salt took third place with 61,600 *Mark lübisch* after cloth (160,500 *Mark lübisch*) and fish (70,800 *Mark lübisch*). This is the equivalent of 7,600 tons, or about 56,000 barrels, and made up about 50% of Lüneburg's production capacity, measured by production for the year 1388. As the salt needed for the processing of her-

[110] For the poundage list see *Die hansischen Pfundzollisten des Jahres 1368,* 1935. For the interpretation of the figures Weibull 1967 is very important.

[111] See note 24.

ring on the Scanian markets amounted to 1,150 tons in 1368, and can be calculated to 2,040 tons by the end of the century, the majority of the salt exported via Lübeck must have been sent to the countries around the Baltic Sea.

Later the total export of Lüneburg salt via Lübeck fell from the 56,000 barrels to about 31,000 barrels on average annually from 1492 to 1496. At that time, however, Lübeck's trade was in deep crisis. In the first half of the sixteenth century the turnover rose enormously. An average of about 80,000 barrels was exported annually via Lübeck; the highest figure, 95,676 barrels, is for the year 1521. As shown above, this was the time that many granaries were converted into salt stores. In the last quarter of the century the number of barrels of salt exported annually fell to around 47,000, and in 1680/81 the level was roughly 30,000. This short survey reveals that the import of cheaper sea-salt (*Baiensalz*) from north-west France, and later also from Portugal and Spain, which had begun in the fourteenth century, did not threaten the trade with Lüneburg salt until the seventeenth century, and the greatest turnover was achieved in the sixteenth century.[112]

Trade in Scanian herring fell from 76,000 barrels in 1368 to 15,000 barrels annually between 1492 and 1496, but unlike the salt trade it made no subsequent recovery. Dutch herring took over the market in both Central Europe and the Baltic Sea region. By the end of the seventeenth century only 3,000 barrels of herring were traded annually via Lübeck harbour, and to a large extent the provenance of the contents was Dutch rather than Scanian.[113]

By the end of the fifteenth century, the population of Europe had largely recovered from the heavy losses caused by the Black Death. Figures were not as high as before, but the demand for foodstuffs and raw materials may have been nearly as high as in the early fourteenth century. However, changing patterns in production, technology and the way of life caused alterations in supply and demand. The carrying capacity of ships, for instance, had increased and it was now possible to send greater quantities of goods per shipment than one or two centuries earlier—a fact that may have influenced the volume of bulk goods sent from the Baltic to Western Europe.

[112] Hammel-Kiesow 1998a.

[113] Hammel-Kiesow 1993b.

There is no doubt that direct shipping between the Baltic and the North Sea region increased enormously in the course of the fifteenth century. The question, however, is to what degree this development impaired the trading activities of Lübeck merchants and the trade via Lübeck. It seems as if during the first half of the fifteenth century the Lübeck merchants managed to maintain their strong position in trade connections between east and west. When, for instance, an English fleet captured the Hanseatic Bayen fleet in 1449, sixteen ships belonged to Lübeck merchants and fourteen to Danzig. I think that the number of Lübeck ships on the direct route round the Skaw decreased because of the withdrawal of Lübeck merchants from trade with England after 1468 in the course of the Anglo-Hanseatic disturbances, on the one hand, and the serious competition from ships and merchants (in that sequence) from Holland and Zeeland since the 1470s when these areas were forced to obtain all their grain from the Baltic, on the other. The paucity of sources means that we have no knowledge of the amount of commodities belonging to Lübeck merchants transported on, e.g., Dutch ships. Nevertheless it appears impossible for them to have kept their former position in the east-west trade during the second half of the fifteenth century, when the economy of Lübeck suffered a general decline.[114]

This decline cannot, however, be viewed merely as a consequence of the direct route by which eastern commodities now bypassed Lübeck. As we have seen, the direct route had been in use since the middle of the thirteenth century, later on though by an increasing number of ships. Therefore I think that in the thirteenth and early fourteenth centuries trade was organised less regionally and shipping more regionally. This means that much of the merchandise from the eastern Baltic, Livonia and Prussia was taken to the ports of the Wendish towns. There it was unloaded and reloaded on to ships belonging to these towns (as shown by the Stralsund freight and handling charges of 1278) and carried to its destination in north-western Europe. It seems as if only a small portion of the eastern Baltic goods was shipped directly from, e.g., Reval, Riga or Elbing to England and Flanders. The reason for this seems to have been the special organisation of the international seaborne trade (see Figure 9). At the same time we have evidence of a similar regionally based sea-traffic between the Bay of Bourgneuf and Bruges. There a similar development took place. In the course of the second half of the thirteenth century ships from Hamburg, for example, sailed to La Rochelle, but the bulk of Bayen salt was carried

114 Hammel-Kiesow 1988: 63-66, 83, 99-101.

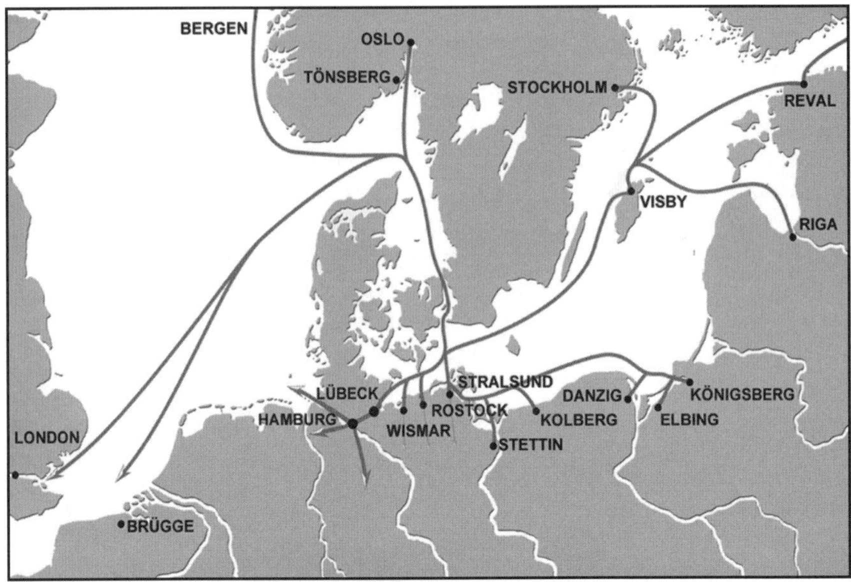

Figure 9. The regionally organised shipping in the thirteenth and early fourteenth centuries. Note the central position of the Wendish towns in the seaborne trade between the Baltic and north-western Europe. Map: Jens Holst/Lars Berggren.

by Flemish and French ships to Bruges where it was sold by, among others, merchants from northern Germany. It was not earlier than the last quarter of the fourteenth century that greater numbers of Hanseatic ships from the Baltic sailed directly to the salt harbours on the western coast of France and took over a great part of this trade.[115]

In addition, even Lübeck's wholesale trade was organised regionally at that time. The entries in the register of merchants' associations in the Lübeck *Niederstadtbuch*, which recorded private debts, as well as the account book of Hermann and Johann Wittenborg (the latter mayor of the town, decapitated in 1363) show that trade in the Baltic and trade with north-western Europe was organised independently.[116] Johann Wittenborg, for instance, sold his Baltic goods in Lübeck although he was very active in

115 Agats 1904: 48-52; Jenks 1996: 259 f.

116 Cordes 1998: 214-25; Hammel-Kiesow 1982.

trade with Flanders too—and vice versa. There is no proof of any direct sales by Lübeck merchants of Baltic goods to England or Flanders, as was common fifty years later—as shown by the example of Hildebrand Veckinchusen[117]—but this may partly be due to the lack of sources. The evidence we do have allows us to draw the conclusion that the merchandise exported to these countries—except, of course, in cases where direct shipping has been proved—had been purchased in Lübeck or other Wendish towns. I presume that it was knowledge of this pattern of trade that led to the traditional view of a lack of direct shipping between the Baltic and northwestern Europe.

When the mainly regionally organised shipping of bulk goods from East to West ended in the course of the fourteenth century (but continued for the transport of high-value goods), the Lübeck sailors and merchants lost the intermediary position they had held in this trade in the thirteenth and at the start of the fourteenth century. Merchants and sailors from the eastern Baltic now brought an ever increasing share of the bulk goods produced in their region to the countries in western Europe without Lübeck merchants being involved.

We have now seen that Lübeck merchants traded bulk commodities from the Baltic to Western Europe; what is still lacking is firm evidence that the bulk goods passed through Lübeck, i.e., were unloaded and loaded on to Lübeck ships. The idea that this was the case is based on the traditional view that, until the middle of the fourteenth century, nearly all merchandise on its way from the Baltic was given this treatment. Concerning grain there is, I think, no doubt about this, though we do not know whether the grain stored in the lofts of the Lübeck *Dielenhäuser* as well as in the granaries was imported only short distances, e.g., from Holstein, Stormarn, Lauenburg and Mecklenburg, or that the Livonian grain, mentioned above,[118] was shipped using the direct route to Flanders. Salt and herring, which are recorded quite well, were not products of the eastern Baltic. And, as we have seen, the poundage list for 1368 shows fewer entries for Baltic bulk commodities, for known reasons.

Then the question is what the fifteenth-century evidence reveals concerning the situation at an earlier time. The sea traffic between Lübeck and Danzig, which had become the most important Prussian port from the end of the fourteenth century, was still very heavy up to the second half of the

[117] Cordes 1998: 235-60; Hammel-Kiesow 1991.

[118] See note 85.

century. Not before 1475 did the number of Lübeck ships sailing to Danzig decline, though then rapidly.[119] This means that there was plenty of cargo for the vessels on the Lübeck-Danzig route before 1475. Because of the structure of east-west Baltic trade, they must also have had sufficient cargo on their way from Danzig to Lübeck. This structure implies that, apart from Lüneburg salt and Scanian herring, only high-value goods of small volume were shipped from Lübeck to the eastern Baltic. In return, Lübeck imported foodstuffs and raw materials of large volume from the Baltic.

The change around the year 1475 was probably caused by the Dutch, who began at that time to import nearly all the grain they needed from the Baltic, because their grain import regions in France had been closed to them by the French King.[120] They probably began also to carry other bulk goods besides grain on the direct route, as proved for the Wendish towns from the end of the thirteenth century. This could only have enhanced the overall development that intensified from the middle of the fourteenth century. Loss lists of captured or wrecked ships dating from 1438 to 1458 indicate that Danzig and Livonian ships of the Bayen fleet sailed west carrying the well known Baltic commodities as bulk goods.[121]

On the other hand, the transport of bulk commodities such as timber, hemp, flax, pitch, tar and tallow is proved for the Lübeck-Hamburg axis for export by sea by the *Zertifikate* from the end of the fifteenth and the beginning of the sixteenth centuries.[122] Around 1500 the trade with bulk goods via Lübeck-Hamburg-Western Europe must therefore have been profitable in spite of competition from the direct route with its—as we seem to think—cheaper freight rates. So, until the beginning of the sixteenth century at least two trade routes from the Baltic to Western Europe still existed, also for bulk commodities. There are no statistics allowing us to compare the value and volume of the bulk goods on the different routes. There is none the less reason to believe that the direct route was much more important for bulk goods. With respect to high-value goods, Lübeck was able to keep its position as a port of transshipment until the nineteenth century, though with a slight decrease in volume of traffic.

119 Schildhauer 1968.

120 van Uytven 1975: 1109-1120.

121 *Bronnen tot de Geschiedenis van den Oostzeehandel* 1:2, 1917, no. 2205, pp. 796-834 (damage lists; cargoes of Prussian and Livonian ships 1438-1458).

122 Vogtherr 1993, see especially 53 ff., edition of the *Zertifikate*; Jahnke 1996.

Final Remarks

It is difficult to trace the development of the direct shipping route from the Baltic Sea to the North Sea. It seems as if the first step was the route through the Sound to Bergen in Norway. We do not know for certain whether indigenous Gotlandic merchants, accompanied somewhat later by their German companions in the *Gilda communis*, were the first to use this route, or whether they were German merchants on their way from Gotland. Neither do we know which commodities they carried to Norway. It can only be assumed that they were the typical goods such as furs and wax, which were exported from Russia or from the hinterland of the river Daugava. The Gotlandic-German skippers and merchants did not sell their commodities in Norway (a demand for wax there is, I think, out of the question, and did the Norwegians really need furs?) but shipped them to Eastern England, at first presumably on Norwegian ships sailing the well-established route from Norway to Eastern England. Here there is sufficient evidence of merchants of the *Gilda communis* importing large quantities of furs and wax. Furthermore there is a lack of evidence that would prove that they all—as traditionally supposed—should have taken the southern route using the Lübeck-Hamburg axis. Of course, we do not know to what extent the Gotland-Norway-Eastern England route was used, nor when the merchants from Gotland began to cross the North Sea on the Bergen-Eastern England route with their own ships. The traffic through the Sound to Norway must have become heavier by the 1240s and 1250s at the latest. At roughly this time, merchants of the Wendish towns formed closer trade connections with Norway because of the grain exported from their hinterland stretching from Holstein to Pomerania, the Scanian fairs reached a climax, and merchants of the Wendish towns may have begun to visit the Bohuslen fisheries. The Scanian fairs had become attractive for merchants from the North Sea ports, mainly the Netherlands, but also from Friesland.

In this situation it is my opinion that increasing numbers of skippers did not take the relatively secure, but longer, route via Norway to and from Western Europe but chose to use the shorter though far more dangerous route round the Skaw. The first mention of the direct route—in the well-known and often-cited charter granted by King Abel of Denmark to the *ummelandfarer* in 1251—is therefore purely incidental. Indeed it refers to a well-established route. The direct overseas route from Lübeck and the Wendish towns to England and Flanders, then seems to have been common already in the second half of the thirteenth century. There is some evidence, though slight, of ships from ports in the eastern Baltic too. Of course, there are no statistics for this early time. But the quality of the evidence given above shows very clearly, in my opinion, that there was a regular traffic through the Danish Sounds and *ummeland,* the Skaw—as well as on the traditional route via Lübeck—Hamburg. From the beginning of the fourteenth century the evidence from England shows a fluctuating, but continuous, annual import of grain and timber from the Baltic.[123] Large quantities of herring from Scania and Bohuslen were taken to England too. Merchants from the Wendish towns, including Lübeck, were those primarily engaged in this trade. The traditional view, which holds that the direct route was not regularly taken before the second half of the fourteenth century, must therefore give way to the new interpretation of the evidence.

The strong position achieved by the Wendish towns through their role as transshipment ports for the sea traffic from the Baltic to the North Sea region, and vice versa, fits the leading part they played in the organisation of the Hanse. A recent study points out that the constitutional organisation of the Hanse was comparable to that of an assembly at a royal court. The town of Lübeck played—*cum grano salis*—the part of the king, the Wendish towns that of the crown council, and all other members that of the *Stände* (assembly).[124] Such political importance must have been rooted in economic strength. However, the basis of this economic strength is not clearly elucidated, nor is the reason why four rather large and densely populated cities (Lübeck, Wismar, Rostock, Stralsund) could develop in a relatively small region on the south-western coast of the Baltic in the thirteenth century and achieve such political importance. Herring and salt, which were, of course, very important for the origin of the first German settlements, followed by grain and beer after the rural areas had been colonised, as well as trade connections with central and upper Germany[125] are not, in my opinion, a sufficient basis. Neither can these factors explain why the economic strength of the Wendish towns decreased after the fourteenth century and never recovered afterwards. But if these towns had the function, in a regionally organised trade system, of transshipment ports for goods travelling from the Baltic to north-western Europe, and only lost this function because of the increasing use of the direct route through the Sound and round the Skaw, they would originally have had the economic strength which led to political influence. The towns would have been the informa-

[123] See Nils Hybel's and Wendy S. Childs' articles below, passim.

[124] Pitz 1994: passim; Hammel-Kiesow 2000: 68 ff., 83.

[125] Schich 1997: 73 f.

tion centres for all trade matters for merchants from north-western Europe and from the eastern Baltic, and this too would have given them political power. But this economic strength would have been lost after the middle of the fourteenth century.

As mentioned above, I presume that the heavy population losses were the reason why the volume of Lübeck trade recorded in 1368 was only a fraction of that reached in the years before the Black Death. There is little statistical evidence but if one thinks of the fall in stockfish imports to England from 1300/10 to 1365/1400, one can get an idea of what may have happened, even if the reduction in such imports might indicate a change in the structure of North-European trade that could have occurred without the Black Death. Elsewhere I have shown that the economic strength, and hence the volume of Lübeck seaborne trade, fell drastically from 1368 up to the 1520s.[126] It was not before the early 1530s that it recovered although without reaching the (recorded) peak of 1368 which, as we have seen, was probably only a fraction of the volume attained before this time.

[126] Hammel-Kiesow 1993a. For the economic decline see Hammel-Kiesow 1988.

The Cargo Vessels

Jan Bill

Introduction

Between 1150 and 1400 the cargo ships of northern Europe changed significantly in terms of construction as well as of size. Partly we can ascribe these changes to the growing demand for cargo space caused by the emerging bulk trade. Still, the changes may have come about against a more complex background than this; the social and political changes in society that went hand in hand with the growing specialisation of the North European economy also influenced the preconditions for shipbuilding and seagoing trade. Thus they are also reflected in the documentary and physical remains of this seafaring that survive for us to study today. In the present article, I will briefly examine some of the changes that can be observed in the course of a longer period of time, between AD 1000 and AD 1600.[1] In this wider time perspective, changes taking place around the mid-twelfth or in the late fourteenth century may be more easily detected and interpreted. I will first focus on the changes in size and cargo capacity, as these are undoubtedly the parameters that attract the most attention when considering how maritime history and archaeology can contribute to economic history in general. Next, some observations concerning changes in construction and finish will be reported and discussed, and in the final part, some brief conclusions will be drawn concerning the representativity of the size parameter as a reflection of the need for cargo capacity.

Changes in Cargo Capacity 1000-1600

The changes in cargo capacity are one of the fundamental issues investigated by maritime historians, and several studies have been published that are more thorough than anything that can possibly be achieved in the pre-

[1] For the earlier and later part of this period, reference can also be made to two new articles on the topic by Crumlin-Pedersen 1999 and Hocker 1999.

sent article. The reason why it is still relevant to deal with the problem here is primarily that a growing amount of high quality archaeological data on the development of shipbuilding technology and cargo capacity is becoming available—data that were not available for the major works that have been written on the topic, for example the books by Heinsius, Ellmers and Unger, published between 1956 and 1980.[2] These new data are based on detailed analyses of actual hull remains of medieval vessels, excavated, recorded and reconstructed according to high ship-archaeological standards.[3] The reconstructed hull shapes can be considered very accurate in the case of well-preserved vessels and provide a firm basis for cargo capacity calculations.[4] Such reconstructions, which have been carried out for both of the two large, medieval shipbuilding traditions in northern Europe, the clinker-built vessels and the cogs, also give us the opportunity to make coarser but still reasonably accurate estimates for ships that have not been or cannot be reconstructed to the same standards, but which can nevertheless be said to be similar in shape and construction to fully-analysed finds.

More uncertainty is associated with determining the load waterline of ancient vessels; for Scandinavian ships, a draft of 60 per cent of the height amidships is usually chosen, with reference to the thirteenth-century Grágás law text from Iceland, while for the calculation of the Bremen cog, a more modest value of only 53 per cent was used.[5] It is unlikely that any general rule concerning load waterlines ever existed in the Middle Ages that covered more than a limited number of ship- and voyage-types. Even small changes in draft may have significant influence on the calculated cargo capacity of a reconstructed vessel. As we shall see, however, the changes in cargo capacity over time are fortunately sufficiently marked to make such uncertainties negligible in the overall picture.

The value of the new, archaeological data is chiefly that they can be used to validate and supplement the relatively scarce information concerning the eleventh to fourteenth centuries that can be found in written sources. Before doing so, however, it is important to consider the representativity of the archaeological finds. A recent study, including in total 64 finds of wrecks or ship remains from medieval Denmark dated to the period 1000-1600 demonstrates that local crafts and vessels, used in the coastal

[2] Heinsius 1956; Ellmers 1972; Unger 1980.

[3] Crumlin-Pedersen 1977.

[4] Bill 1991b.

[5] Crumlin-Pedersen 1985: 86; Lahn 1992: 250.

zone, appear to be over-represented in the material.[6] This implies that statistical analyses cannot be applied in order to determine average cargo capacities and total shipping capacity on the basis of the archaeological material. It also implies that the largest ships of various periods may be gravely underrepresented or entirely missing in the material. Still, the largest of the ships actually found do provide minimum figures for the maximum ship sizes of their time. In the following, ship finds of northern Europe whose cargo capacity can reasonably be reconstructed either independently or by analogy will be presented as the basis for an evaluation of the development of ship sizes in northern Europe during the period AD 1000-1600. Explicit warships, for example oared long ships or late medieval and early modern naval vessels, have been omitted, and so have also the smaller cargo ships. "A small cargo ship" has been defined arbitrarily as one having a cargo capacity of less than 20 tons in the eleventh and twelfth centuries, less than 50 tons in the thirteenth and fifteenth centuries and less than 100 tons in the sixteenth century.

Clinker-Built Vessels

Clinkerbuilt vessels are defined by being built of overlapping planks, fastened together by iron or wooden nails. Such vessels were being built over extensive parts of northern Europe, and the clinker tradition was dominating in medieval Scandinavia, England, Scotland and Ireland. Load waterlines are calculated according to the Grágás load line, unless stated otherwise.

Hedeby 3 was found in the harbour of Hedeby in 1981.[7] Only a few essential timbers have been raised, including the keelson and some framing timbers from various stations in the hull. A dating to ca. 1025 has been established on the basis of dendrochronology, which also points to a local origin for the vessel. In spite of the limited number of salvaged parts, the reconstruction, based on Skuldelev 1 (see below), can be considered to be fairly accurate. The calculated cargo capacity is 60 tons.

Skuldelev 1 was excavated in 1962 as a part of a sea-route blockage north of Roskilde.[8] About sixty per cent of the hull is preserved, and recent-

[6] Bill 1997b: 109-125.

[7] Crumlin-Pedersen 1997.

[8] Olsen & Crumlin-Pedersen 1968: 96-110.

ly a dating to ca. 1050 has been provided by dendrochronology, against master curves from western Norway.[9] The reconstruction is very accurate and the cargo capacity has been calculated to 24 tons.[10]

Roskilde 4 was excavated in 1997 in the harbour area of the medieval town.[11] The lower part of the hull is preserved almost in the entire length of the vessel, along with parts of the starboard side. The first dendrochronological dating of the find points to a construction in ca. 1108.[12] The calculated cargo capacity of ca. 55 tons is preliminary, as the ship has not yet been reconstructed, but because of the vessel's close similarity to the Lynæs find (see below), the estimate is probably fairly accurate.

Lynæs 1 was excavated in 1975 off a Viking-Age and medieval fishing site near the entrance of Roskilde Fjord.[13] Only about twenty per cent of the hull is preserved, mainly consisting of the starboard bow. Dendrochronological examination shows that the vessel was built ca. 1140 in western Sweden and that repairs were carried out after 1167.[14] The calculated cargo capacity is 60 tons, based on a model and a reconstruction of the vessel.

The Bergen ship is the name given to a collection of re-used ship timbers found in constructions made immediately after one of several devastating fires in the Norwegian town of Bergen. Some of the timbers were charred, and it is believed that they originate from a large vessel, damaged by fire and scrapped and re-used afterwards. Dendrochronological analyses have recently demonstrated that the ship timbers, previously believed to represent two ships, all belong to one vessel, constructed around 1187-88.[15] The dimensions of the timbers are huge, and although only a very tentative reconstruction can be made, the find has been included here because it is without doubt proof of the existence of very large clinker-built ships in the twelfth century. The calculated cargo capacity of 120 tons apparently represents a conservative estimate but should nevertheless be used with care.[16]

Ringaren is the remains of a large clinker-built ship, investigated by divers in a number of years from 1974. The building of the ship has been

9 Bartholin 1998.
10 Crumlin-Pedersen 1985: 87.
11 Bill et al. 1998.
12 Bonde 1997.
13 Crumlin-Pedersen 1979b.
14 Daly 1998; Daly 1999.
15 Bartholin 1999.
16 Christensen 1985; Christensen 1989; Crumlin-Pedersen 1985.

dated by dendrochronology to ca. 1542. The investigations have been published, although poorly, by Svenwall in 1994. Later investigation by Simon Adey-Davies has demonstrated that the published reconstruction is too large by a factor of approximately 1.4. If the reconstruction is otherwise correct, the cargo capacity can be calculated to around 110 tons, with a suggested draft of only 51 per cent of the height amidships.[17]

Cogs

Cogs are defined by being built with a bottom with edge-to-edge planking that transform into clinker planking towards the stem and stern. The ship-sides are entirely clinker-built. The cog is probably Frisian in origin, but found widespread use in the areas influenced by the Hansa during the High Middle Ages. Load waterlines are calculated according to the load line published for the Bremen cog, unless stated otherwise.[18]

The Kollerup cog was excavated in north-west Jutland, where it had been shipwrecked on a sandy beach and quickly covered with sand. It was thus quite well preserved, to about 50 percent. With a dendrochronological dating to ca. 1150 it is probably the oldest cog known so far.[19] It is lower and more slender than later cogs and its cargo capacity of 35 tons has therefore been calculated on the basis of the Grágás load waterline.

The Rutten cog, also known as A57, is one of the Ijsselmeer finds. Only the bottom part survives and it has been dated to around 1250 on the basis of dendrochronology and ceramics found inside the vessel.[20] Its cargo capacity so far can only be roughly estimated on the basis of the size of the flat bottom, which is slightly longer and considerably wider, but also a little more rounded than that of the Bremen cog. The hull shape deviates clearly from that of the Kollerup cog. If it was indeed comparable in shape to the Bremen cog, the vessel may have been able to carry up to 160 tons.

The Bremen cog was raised in 1962 and was found to have an extremely well preserved hull (Figure 10). Dendrochronological analyses have de-

[17] Adey-Davies 1997; Rönnby & Adams 1994; Bill 1997b: 187f.

[18] Lahn 1992.

[19] Crumlin-Pedersen 1979a; Crumlin-Pedersen 1989; Andersen 1983; Daly 2000; file no. MAJ 98 at the Institute for Maritime Archaeology, National Museum of Denmark.

[20] Oosting 1987; Reinders & Oosting 1989: 111; Vlierman 1996: 56, 74.

monstrated that its timbers were felled 1379-80. It has been subject to intensive research and the cargo capacity has been calculated to 84 tons, with, as stated above, a draft of 53 per cent of the total height amidships.[21]

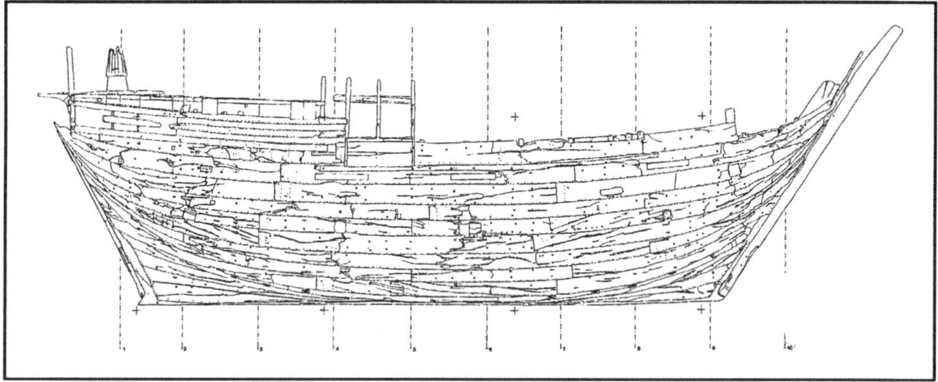

Figure 10. The Bremen Cog, 1380: Photogrammetrical recording. The ship was lost after launching, but before it had been completed. Some uncertainty therefore remains about minor details in the construction, but hull shape and cargo capacity could be established with great accuracy. Overall length: 23.27 m. Drawing: Deutsches Schiffahrtsmuseum, Bremerhaven.

WRITTEN SOURCES

In common with the archaeological finds, the written sources illustrating ship sizes in the period have limitations in terms of representativity and reliability. Sources from the thirteenth century or earlier that directly reveal the cargo capacities of large ships are rare, and sources from all periods have been prone to deliberate exaggeration or understatement in the past. For example, there may be reason to doubt the claim of the Danish king in 1423 that many Hanseatic cogs passing through the Sound had sizes of 200 *Last* or more, as this was used as an argument to increase customs.[22] On the other hand, we must admit that the argument would have had little effect, were it not at least possible to construct ships of this size. In general, cus-

[21] Ellmers 1979; Hoheisel & Baykowski 1994; Lahn 1992.
[22] Bill et al. 1997: 196.

toms accounts may be regarded as the most reliable sources for cargo sizes, as these represent cargoes actually transported rather than estimates. Furthermore, exaggerations must in general have been limited, in order not to obstruct trade; the opposite problem, that the cargoes did not fully occupy the capacity of the vessels, may moderate the picture of the development of ship sizes somewhat but can hardly be of great importance: if most large vessels sailed half-empty, there would have been little reason to construct them to this size.

In spite of the shortcomings of the written sources, I will not attempt a calculation of cargo capacities based on, for example, the sizes of crews and passenger numbers (as done by Heinsius).[23] The value of such calculations is very limited, as they inevitably have to be based on unverifiable assumptions concerning the relationship between such numbers and cargo capacity. In contrast to the archaeological record, however, we may assume that large ships were more likely than smaller ones to find their way into the written records because of their economic importance and also because they were impressive by their size alone. Both motives, however, may easily have led to exaggeration of their size. This is why information from narrative sources, as well as from sources in which exaggeration may have improved the effect of the document, calls for extra cautious treatment. In the following overview, the written sources will therefore be divided into two classes according to their assumed credibility. Evidence from customs accounts and the like will be categorised as superior to narrative or polemic sources. With respect to the minimum size of vessels included in the examination, the same criteria will be applied as used when evaluating the archaeological material.

Another problem, specifically related to the historical character of these sources, is the use of different units of weight and volume. Here, use is primarily made of sources giving the cargo capacity in *Last* or *tun*. As is commonplace in ship-historical literature, one *Last* is set to the equivalent of two metric tonnes, and one *tun* to one metric ton, unless stated otherwise.[24] These equations are of course imprecise, since definitions varied with time and place, but a common North European weight and measure system was indeed in place during most of the period dealt with here.[25] It is therefore unlikely that the fluctuations in the definitions of the *Last* and

[23] Heinsius 1956: 90-102.

[24] See, e.g., Vogel 1915a: 553-560; Heinsius 1956: 82-87; Ellmers 1972: 46.

[25] Witthöft 1989.

tun were so large that they prohibit a tentative use of historical data to illustrate the trends in development of ship sizes.

The historical evidence considered here is presented in chronological order. The overview is very cursory and includes only a part of the historical evidence available. Most of the information is found in the publications of Heinsius (1956), Friel (1995), Barfod (1990) and Mortensøn (1995).

1212: Two ships with cargoes from Ghent and Ypres are arrested in Sandwich and Winchelsea with cargoes of 100 and 120 tuns of wine, representing cargo capacities of ca. 50 and 60 *Last* respectively.[26]

1214: Ships of 40 *Last* mentioned as being present in Bristol.[27]

1289: A source from 1419 mentions that Edward I (1272-1307) had the right of first choice of wine from ships arriving in the port of London with cargoes of ten tuns, nineteen tuns, twenty tuns, one hundred tuns and two hundred tuns.[28]

1304: Royal decree from the Danish king that the traditional leidang ships on Zealand should be replaced by a smaller number of large cogs, each of 50 *Last*.[29]

1318: A ship, Nicholas, belonging to a London merchant, was robbed of 178 tuns and 9 pipes of wine plus miscellaneous other goods when anchored near Sandwich.[30]

1327: A mention of the ship of Herbert Hamer from Bremen, 40 *Last*.[31]

1327: Documentary evidence for English ships paying customs on more than 200 tons of cargo.[32]

1341: A mention of a ship of 100 *Last* in Livonia.[33]

(1390): Late fourteenth century: A mention of evers from Kampen and Harderwijk, 70 *Last* each.[34]

1411: A mention of Danzig's krejer, 90 *Last*.[35]

1412: The Hanseatic Diet stipulates that ships are not to be built larger than

[26] *Hansisches Urkundenbuch* 1876: 93. Heinsius 1956: 87.

[27] Heinsius 1956: 99.

[28] *Liber Albus* 1861: 217. Here after Marsden 1996: 31.

[29] *Diplomatarium Danicum*, 2d ser., vol. 5, no. 310.

[30] *Calendar of Close Rolls*, 1313-1318, 1893: 594; Hutchinson 1994: 96f.

[31] *Diplomatarium Danicum*, 2d ser., vol. 9, no. 447.

[32] *Calendar of Memoranda Rolls* 1326-1327, 1968: 128-133. Friel 1995: 33f., note 19, 202.

[33] *Liv-, Est- und Curländische Urkunden-Regesten* 1881.

[34] Heinsius 1956: 210.

[35] Vogel 1915a: 501f.

100 herring *Last*.[36]

1414: The cog John of King Henry V, reported to have a size of 220 tons, is lost off the Breton coast.[37]

1422: A krejer of 70 *Last* is reported to be in Kiel.[38]

1423: Erik of Pomerania claims that many Hanseatic cogs passing through the Sound now have cargo capacities of 200 *Last* and that the toll must therefore be increased.[39]

1438: Hollanders capture Prussian salt ships of up to 225 *Last*.[40]

1444-45: Bordeaux customs accounts demonstrate that English ships were being loaded with cargoes exceeding 300 tons.[41]

1450-51: One English ship on an expedition to Normandy and five on an expedition to Gascony exceed 300 tons in size.[42]

1509: The Danish king has arrested a Lübeck holk of ca. 80 *Last*.[43]

1518: From toll accounts from Aalborg, Denmark, a minimum size of 106 *Last* has been calculated for Hans Lange's ship.[44]

1553: The Danish king ships 32 *Last* of rye and 122 *Last* of malt to Amsterdam with a hulk, 'Øholken'.[45]

1555: The town of Ribe is ordered by the king to equip a ship of 100 *Last* for a military expedition; if such a large ship cannot be harboured at the town, they may choose a smaller one.[46]

1556: The Danish king sends a "fyrblase" (presumed to be a ship made of pine, probably built in the Baltic) to Halland (in today's Sweden) to load 100 *Last* coal.[47] As this was probably charcoal, the measure probably represents volume rather than weight; if the vessel was undecked, the 100 *Last* may not quite represent 200 tons.

1560-62: A list of the ships built in Lübeck is a very rich source for illustrating the ship sizes of the time. It reveals ship sizes from 60-200 *Last*, the four

[36] *Hanserecesse* 1:6, 1870, no. 69, 41.

[37] Friel 1995: 26.

[38] Barfod 1990: 23.

[39] See footnote 22.

[40] *Bronnen tot de Geschiedenis van den Oostzeehandel 1122-1499,* 1917: no. 2205.

[41] British Library Add. MS. 15524. Friel 1995: 33f., note 19, 202.

[42] Public Record Office E364/92 A, M and N; Friel 1995: 33f., note 19, 202.

[43] Barfod 1990: 105.

[44] Rigsarkivet, Copenhagen. Reg. 108 A. Nr. 25. 1518-22. Toldregnskaber fra Aalborg og Rødby. Here from Poulsen 1996a: 47.

[45] Mortensøn 1995: 44f.

[46] *Kancelliets brevbøger 1551-55*: 371.

[47] Mortensøn 1995: 127.

largest measuring 150, 150, 150 and 200 *Last*. In 1560, the largest vessel measures 200 *Last*; in 1561, 130 *Last*; and in 1562, 150 *Last*.[48]

1561: A Dane, Steffen Løitzer, sends two ships of 100 *Last* to Iceland to collect sulphur.[49]

1562: The Danish king orders two ships of at least 100 *Last* to be sent to Iceland to collect train oil and sulphur.[50]

1568: The Copenhagen merchant Marcus Hess is allowed to send a vessel of 100 *Last* to Narva with salt.[51]

1583: A list of shipped cargoes from the Aalborg company in Lübeck shows that the largest ship going to Aalborg this year took a cargo of 130 *Last*.[52]

1597: A report on ships arriving at San Lucar, Spain, between 7 October and 19 November, shows the Danish ships in the salt trade to be of sizes ranging between 100 and 160 tons.[53]

1599: Court documents reveal that Herman von Dellden, Copenhagen, owned 3/16 of a ship of 250 *Last*; his adversaries in the case also had shares in the vessel.[54]

Ship Sizes in the Middle Ages

In Figure 11, the data from the archaeological and historical sources have been presented together. As can be seen, the two data types supplement each other well chronologically. It can also be seen, however, that the large ships documented in the written sources from the fourteenth century onwards are absent from the archaeological record. But as written records from before 1300 are very few, it is still relevant to question whether we see the largest ships of the early part of the period in this material at all. An answer cannot be given on the basis of the figure but, as we shall see later, constructional changes documented in the course of the twelfth and thirteenth centuries may imply that an increase in size actually did take place at this time.

48 Archiv der Hansestadt Lübeck. Altes Senatsarchiv. Lastadie 4/1.

49 Mortensøn 1995: 195.

50 Mortensøn 1995: 152.

51 *Kancelliets brevbøger 1566-70*: 327.

52 Archiv der Hansestadt Lübeck. Hansestadt Lübeck, Schonenfahrer. Befrachtungsbuch der Aalborgfahrer 1576-1604. Here from Poulsen 1996a: 57.

53 Mortensøn 1995: 157f.

54 Mortensøn 1995: 225.

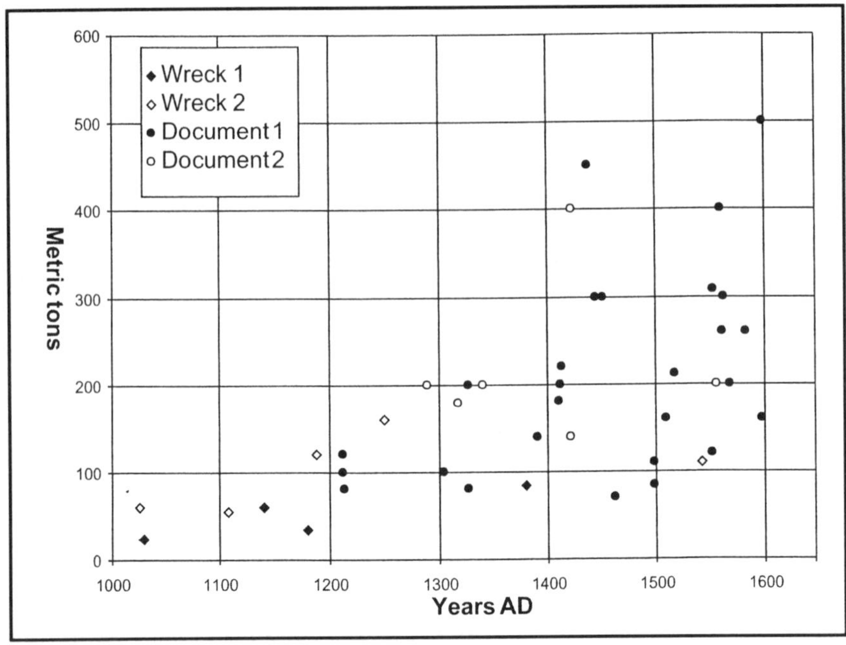

Figure 11. Archaeologically and historically documented cargo capacities, AD 1000-1600, in northern Europe. The graph shows an overall trend of exponential growth, but also tendencies towards a step-like development. It appears that the growth suddenly gained speed in the late twelfth century, that it was quite stagnant in the fourteenth century and that it again accelerated around 1400. However, the amount of data is small, and new archaeological finds may change the picture. "Wreck 1" and "Document 1" refer to the more reliable figures for cargo capacities; "Wreck 2" and "Document 2" refer to less reliable ones. Graphics: Claus Pedersen.

The figure gives the overall impression that cargo capacities were steadily on the rise from around 1150 and onwards, while the situation during the preceding 150 years was more or less stagnant. This is, however, a picture that may need some adjustments. On the basis of archaeological evidence, the tenth to twelfth centuries have elsewhere been pointed out as a very important period for the development of specialised cargo ships in northern Europe, and it has been suggested that in some areas this kind of ship was not even being used before the tenth century.[55] These studies, however, deal almost exclusively with Scandinavian vessels and thus tell us little about, for example, the cross-Channel trade. It is interesting to note that one of the few comprehensive North European collections of ship finds from the eleventh to the thirteenth centuries outside Scandinavia, the material excavated in Dublin, also seems to indicate a sudden growth in vessel size in the last part of the twelfth century. Whether this is the result, as suggested by McGrail, of the change from Hiberno-Norse to Norman rule in 1169, or whether it reflects a more general growth in shipping, is of course impossible to say on the basis of the Dublin material alone.[56] The complete answer to the question about the growth in cargo capacity in early medieval northern Europe cannot be given until relevant ship archaeological material from the southern shore of the Channel turns up in quantity—few of the finds from this period made so far have survived and been recorded in a way that makes them suitable for analysis. The Utrecht boat, which has recently been dendrochronologically dated to 997 by Ellen Jansma, is the outstanding exception. It is not known, though, how the size of this vessel, with its modest cargo capacity of 13 tons for its 17.35 m length, relates to the general pattern of ship sizes of its time, just as the original purpose of the boat is disputed.[57]

The geographical aspect of these data also encompasses the question of regional variation in seafaring. Although the main bulk of sources relates to the Baltic and North Sea area, many of the largest ships belong to the context of Atlantic trade, especially the wine trade between England and Bordeaux. It is not surprising that some of the largest ships of northern Europe were to be found here, especially from the thirteenth up to the fifteenth century. This indicates that for seafaring in the North Sea and Baltic regions, shipbuilding technology was always sufficiently ahead of the actual needs to be able to provide ships of the desired capacity. Limits for growth in ship size in these regions may have been economic in nature or they may have been set by the restrictions created by the riverine location of most larger towns. Indeed, the decision taken by the members of the Hanseatic League at their meeting in 1412 not to build ships larger than 100 herring

[55] Bill 1997a: 188-190; Crumlin-Pedersen 1999.

[56] McGrail 1993b: 98.

[57] Cargo capacity according to van der Wijk 1933, length as displayed today. Ellmers has advocated for an even smaller cargo capacity of only 8-10 tons: Ellmers 1972: 257. See Vlek 1987, for research history.

Last must have been caused by the problems involved in maintaining sufficient water depth; apart from the maximum capacity, the only other specification concerning size that is given is that the draught when loaded shall not exceed six Lübeck *Ellen*, an *Elle* being a length measure equivalent to two feet or about 58 cm.[58] Only the largest North European ships of the fourteenth century could carry as much as 100 *Last* of herring but in the early fifteenth century the figure was perhaps not any longer as impressive —and the decision made at the 1412 meeting could not have been enforced very strictly—since the Danish king only eleven years later was able to postulate that Hanseatic ships of double that size were passing through the Sound.

In the late part of the period reviewed here, commercial seafaring in northern Europe probably never came close to the technical limits of contemporary shipbuilding. This is clearly illustrated by the size of the purpose-built, military vessels of the late fifteenth century and, above all, the sixteenth century. The two Danish royal flagships, *Engelen* from 1509 and *Maria* from 1517, probably measured above 800 tons.[59] These figures seem to represent ships considerably larger than the largest contemporary merchant vessels, taking up to 450 tons cargo. Even more staggering are the sizes of the great English ships, *Jesus*, built in 1416 and measuring 1,000 tons, and *Grace Dieu*, built in 1418 and measuring 1,400 tons.[60] These ships were all purpose-built warships, even though they were not yet specifically constructed for the use of cannons. Instead, they were fighting platforms, as naval tactics still aimed at boarding and man-to-man combat as the final, decisive part of a naval battle. Every stimulus was thus in place for constructing these ships as large as possible, and indeed the triple clinker planking of the *Grace Dieu* may be taken as a sign of a shipbuilding technology being pressed to its limits in order to match increasing demands for size. The last, large, clinker-built English warship, the *Great Galley*, was launched in 1515, and measured 800 tons; but at that time carvel-built ships, similar to *Engelen* and *Maria*, were also being constructed in England, e.g., the now famous *Mary Rose* from 1514, which measured "only" 600 tons.[61]

[58] Witthöft 1989: 535; my gratitude to Christina Deggim for information on this topic.

[59] Probst 1990; Probst 1994.

[60] Friel 1995: 52; McGrail 1993a: 46.

[61] Friel 1995: 35.

The presence of very large, clinker-built vessels prior to the introduction of carvel construction is important, as it shows that these giants, which —as far as we know—had no predecessors in terms of size, were not made possible because of new technology. They were being built in a shipbuilding tradition that, by the end of the fifteenth century, had been dominant in northern Europe for a millennium. Consequently, the change from clinker to carvel did not mean that new possibilities in terms of larger carrying capacity became available for North European seafaring; the advantages of carvel technique are rather to be found in other areas, probably in savings in construction and maintenance costs. This further supports the viewpoint that size was not a problem for North European builders of merchant vessels, neither in the final phase of the clinker-built large ships, nor in the early phase of the carvels. Thus the maximum vessel sizes that we know of from written and archaeological sources, at least from around 1300 and onwards, are likely to reflect fairly well the actual maximum needs at the time and place from where we have evidence of them.

Constructional Changes ca. 1000-1300

During the early phase of the period in consideration, constructional changes that lend some credit to the suggestion of a sudden growth in ship sizes shortly before or around 1200 can certainly be observed. Again we must remember that the archaeological sources are skewed towards Scandinavia, but since we are now dealing with technical issues which can be studied without requiring the same degree of preservation of source material, the tendency is less marked than when investigating cargo capacities. The first issue to be discussed here is the introduction of through-beams, which, in the opinion of the present author, represents a major change in the structural layout of the shell-built vessels that was necessary in order to be able to increase the height, and thus the cargo capacity, of the hull.

Through-beams are horizontal beams, inserted across the hull and protruding through the planking of the ship's sides. They form an integrated structure together with the ship's sides, as their ends are locked in slots between two successive strakes (Figure 12). As such, they form very rigid connections between the two sides of the ship, a quality which is further enhanced by the very massive, vertical knees connecting the beams with the strakes above them. The Bremen cog, built in 1380, is the classical example of this construction but the same elements can be found in many other ship finds, for example in a small, clinker-built cargo carrier and ferry

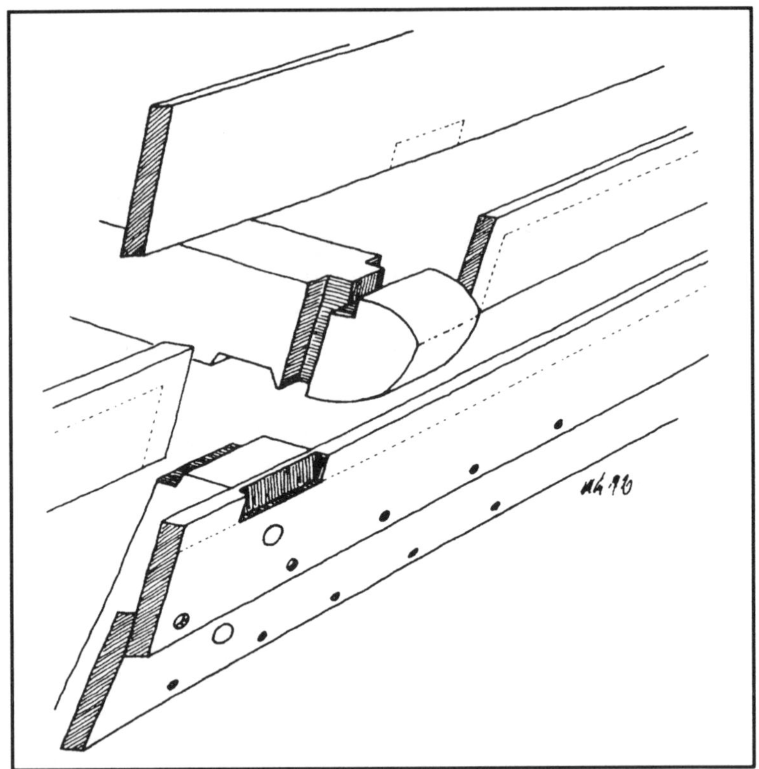

Figure 12. Exploded view of the anchoring of a through-beam into a clinker-built ship's side. This example is reconstructed on the basis of the Lille Kregme cog, built ca. 1358, probably in Pomerania. Drawing: Morten Gøthche.

vessel from around or shortly before 1300, the Gedesby ship (Figure 13).[62]

The difference between the through-beam system and the exclusively internal beam system, which is found in all early medieval North European vessels, may be the more restricted flexibility of the former system. The internal beam system, as illustrated by numerous Scandinavian finds from the eleventh up to the thirteenth century, relies entirely on tree-nailed con-

[62] Bill 1991a; Bill 1997b.

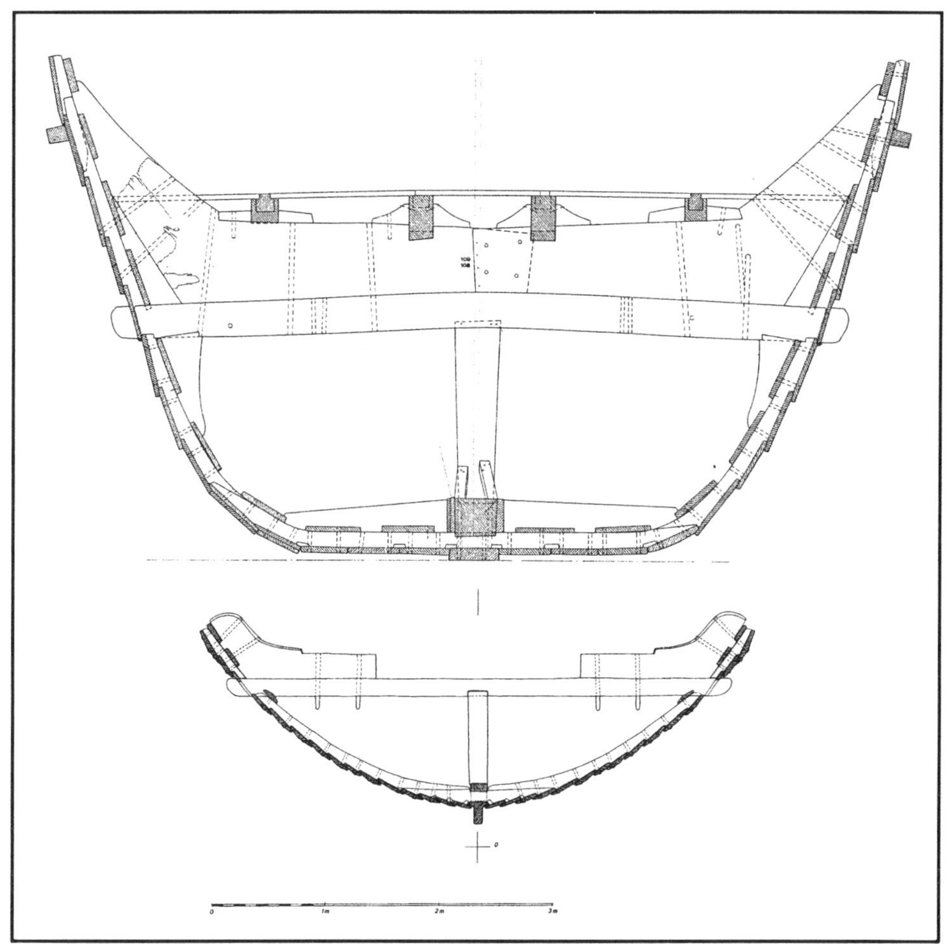

Figure 13. Reconstructed section at the mast frames of (top) the Bremen cog, 1380, and (bottom) the Gedesby ship, ca. 1300. Drawings: (top) Deutsches Schiffahrtsmuseum, Bremerhaven; (bottom) Christian Lemée.

nections between the beam system and the shipsides. It is therefore vulnerable to hull deformations that increase the beam of the ship. While twisting and hogging—the latter being the phenomenon in which the central section of the hull gets pushed upwards relative to the ends owing to surplus buoyancy in this area—cause the beam of the hull to decrease, sagging causes it to increase. Sagging occurs when the buoyancy in the central part of the hull is insufficient to carry the combined weight of this portion of the hull and the cargo stored there. The central part of the ship will thus "hang" between the fore and aft, carried by surplus buoyancy there. Owing to flexibility, the central part of the vessel will sink relative to the ends of the ship and cause the upper parts of the sides to open. Through-beams, with their firm grip on the planking, appear to be the shipbuilders' adequate response to avoid this, and thus a response to the need for ships that could carry increasingly larger and heavier cargoes in the growing bulk trade.

It is a question, however, whether this is the only reason for inserting the through-beams. The theoretical concepts of hogging and sagging are based on the idea of the ship as a skeleton-built structure, where the framing system provides the main part of the structural strength of the ship, and where decks form a very important strength component. The ships that saw the introduction of through-beams were very different from this. They were shell-built structures, where the individual planks were fastened together and formed a flexible unit responsible for a major part of the structural strength. The flexibility of this shell was controlled by the insertion of frames but these were neither as closely spaced, nor—owing to the lack of deck beams in every frame—as rigid as in later, skeleton-built vessels. It may well be that these differences, compared with skeleton-built vessels, set narrower limits for the size of ships without through-beams than did the problem of hogging and sagging. This question, however, can only be illuminated by future analyses of the structural strength of well-preserved and accurately reconstructed ship finds.

The oldest archaeological examples in northern Europe of the through-beam in its medieval function as a reinforcement of the hull—it has been suggested that in northern waters it was developed from the Roman threnus, a through-beam designed to take the quarter rudders of Roman ships —can only be dated back as far as the late twelfth century. The Bergen ship, dendrochronologically dated to around 1187, appears to be the earliest example (Figure 14). The character of the find—a collection of ship timbers, re-used in house foundations made during the reconstruction of the Bergen harbour area after a major fire—unfortunately makes a size estimate of the vessel difficult.[63]

[63] Bartholin 1999; Christensen 1985: 178-192; see Englert (forthcoming) for a discussion of the new datings.

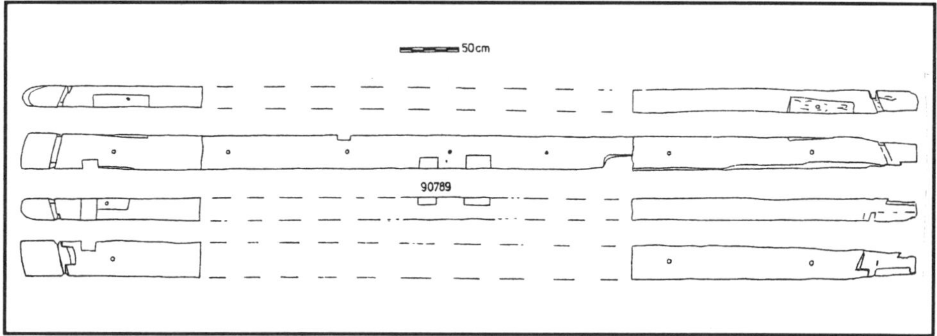

Figure 14. Through-beams from the Bryggen excavations, demonstrated by dendrochronology to belong to the "Big Ship" built in 1187-88. Drawing: Christensen 1985.

The first iconographic evidence appears to be the town seal from Dunwich (1199) and other early examples are those from Winchelsea (1274), Harderwijk (1280), and Damme (1309). The dates represent the earliest known use—the seal stamps themselves may be older. We also find through-beams represented in thirteenth-century book illustrations, for example in an English manuscript known as the Bodleian Apocalypse.[64] It may be significant that the first archaeological example found so far also represents a big ship of its time, as there are plenty of finds of contemporary, smaller finds without through-beams. However, the example of the Gedesby ship shows that at least by the end of the thirteenth century, small vessels had adopted the same framing system. It is noticeable that the Kollerup cog from ca. 1150 did not have through-beams, as this is a very consistent feature in later cog finds.[65]

Parallel to the introduction of through-beams, a series of other changes took place in North European shipbuilding, the general character of which was that they made the production of ships less laborious and thus contributed towards a lower tonnage/cost ratio. These changes have been examined most thoroughly for the Scandinavian and Baltic area, where they are perhaps also most marked. In 1992 the Swedish archaeologist Björn Varenius published his doctoral thesis, *Det nordiska skeppet* (The Nordic Ship),

[64] Bodleian Library, Oxford. MS Bodley 401, f. 55v.

[65] Andersen 1983: 23-27.

in which he argued very convincingly for the hypothesis that prior to the introduction of Christianity, the ship played an important symbolic role in Scandinavian society, and that this was the raison d'être for the very refined shipbuilding tradition that existed in the North during the Viking Age. A gradual erosion of this tradition from the twelfth up to the sixteenth century was seen as being the result of a loss of this symbolic importance, making the economic aspects of shipbuilding and seafaring the dominant design factor.[66]

More recent studies, concentrating on the Danish material, have demonstrated the change to be less gradual than indicated by Varenius, and with a marked focal point in the thirteenth century. In the course of the thirteenth century, decorative features such as mouldings disappeared, scarves and other joinery were made in cruder, cheaper ways (Figure 15) the quality of the planking material decreased markedly and the complex, internal framing system was replaced by a much simpler one, involving protruding beams.[67] Comparisons with ship finds from other parts of northern Europe show many of the same changes taking place here, although frequently somewhat earlier. As the change towards a markedly less elaborate shipbuilding practice took place quite suddenly two and a half centuries after Christianity became the official religion of the North, it is difficult to maintain Varenius' hypothesis without modification. The ship was not gradually loosing its symbolic importance and therefore falling prey to the mechanisms of the market economy. As shipbuilding is a handicraft, the skills of which were handed down from one generation to the next, such a relatively sudden change is probably to be seen as reflecting a marked reshaping of the organisation of shipbuilding. It may be that what is reflected is the change from a seafaring dominated by magnates in the countryside, maintaining the values and aesthetics of the past, to one thoroughly moulded by the tougher economic climate in the urban environment that developed so rapidly at exactly the same period as that in which bulk-commodity trade started to flourish.

The examples of changes in construction and finish, which also take place in the smaller vessels, show that although an increase in the size of the largest ships certainly coincided with the emergence of bulk trade, the changes that took place are too complicated to be explained by this parameter alone. Depending on the character of the trade, as well as on the

[66] Varenius 1992.

[67] Bill 1995; Bill 1997b.

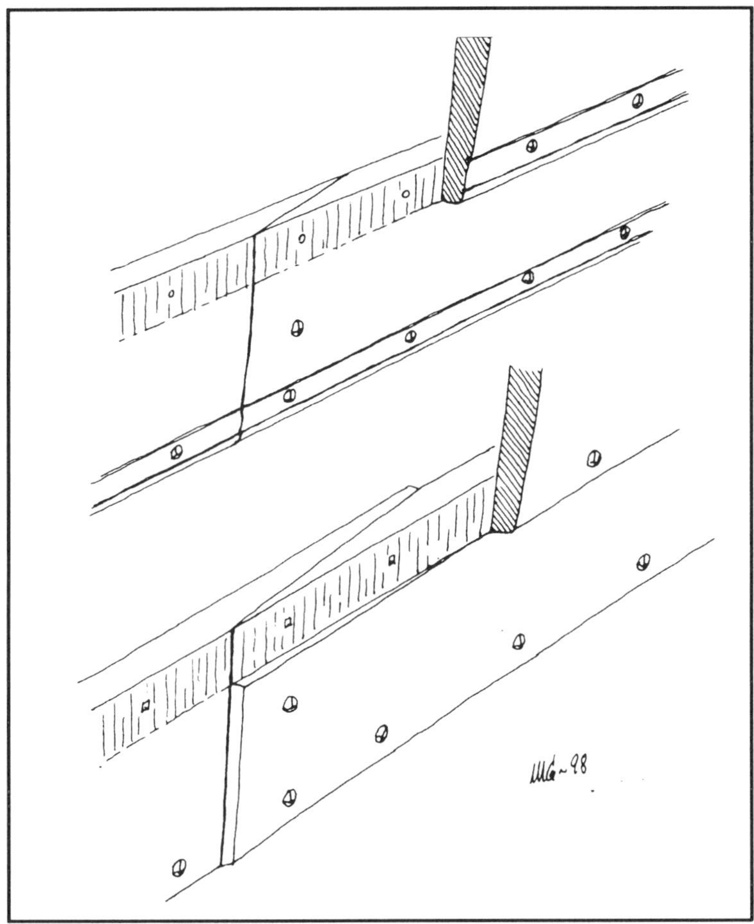

Figure 15. Examples of changes in shipbuilding techniques in high medieval Denmark. Decorative mouldings disappeared gradually, and the plank scarfs became longer and more hastily made. Drawing: Morten Gøthche.

distances and waters to be covered, the best answer to a rising demand for cargo capacity may not always be to increase the size of the individual vessels. Sometimes an increase in the number of vessels may be a better response to such a need, as may very well have been the case in southern

Scandinavia in the Middle Ages. The archipelagic character of the landscape meant that there was a great need for relatively short sea-borne transports of agricultural produce. This was the case both internally inside the country and for export to nearby urban centres in northern Germany and the Netherlands. Studies of the development of shipping as a reflection of changes in the economy and societal organisation therefore have to focus on constructional and decorative features, as well as on size and efficiency, if more detailed conclusions are to be drawn.

Conclusion

The combination of written and archaeological sources documents for northern Europe a very marked growth in ship sizes during the Middle Ages. Starting somewhat earlier, the growth gains momentum during the second half of the twelfth century and continues at least into the fifteenth. The introduction of through-beams at the latest in the 1180s seems to be of essential importance to the process, and goes hand in hand with other changes, resulting in a cheaper, more economical mode of construction. This indicates that the invention of the through-beam was the result of a pressure on shipbuilders to provide larger ships for trade purposes.

During the high and early late Middle Ages, the maximum size of ships continued to rise steeply. However, with the construction of very large purpose-built warships in the early fifteenth century, it becomes apparent that at this time trade needs are not to the same extent driving the shipbuilding industry to its technological limit. The construction of large warships on the basis of a modified version of the traditional clinker technique indicates that existing techniques around 1400 had a not yet exploited potential, which could be activated when the need, the money and the infrastructure was present.

On the basis of this short examination, it appears that ship building technology in northern Europe at least to some extent may have restricted the growth in bulk cargo trade in the twelfth century. For the remaining part of the Middle Ages no such signs can be seen, and we must assume that during this period shipbuilding technology was not a limiting factor in the development of trade.

Beer: A New Bulk Good of International Trade

Richard W. Unger

Beer making already had a long history by the early Middle Ages. In one form or another it probably dated from the early centuries of settled agriculture. The skill had spread widely so that among farmers brewing was common in medieval Europe. Brewers worked in the countryside, in monasteries and in castles to produce drinks for local consumption. The quality of the drink was low in terms of taste if not of strength. The product also had to be drunk young, that is before it turned too sour. Beer was not a commodity of trade, that is not until about 1200.

Brewing appeared in the growing towns of the eleventh and twelfth centuries. It was just like rural brewing in every way. As a place emerged for specialist brewers in towns those producers invested more in equipment, especially in kettles, which made it possible for them to increase output and efficiency.[1] The products of the urban industry began to turn up as items of incidental trade in the thirteenth century. The volume was never large but the exchange went on for centuries. With England and the Low Countries English ale surfaced in Dutch ports just as the similar Dutch product appeared in customs records of English ports. At the port of Great Yarmouth, for example, in the twelve months from 1 May 1398 on average 8,000 litres per month entered from the Low Countries. At little more than 25 litres per day the volume did not make an impression on English consumption.[2] The trade around 1400 was, like the trade two centuries before, dependent on ships making occasional and even regular trips, tramping along the coast or across the North Sea. Once the trip was undertaken and a principal good or goods taken on to cover the cost of the trip then any other commodities could be carried at low prices. The ships carried beer for the crew anyway so if the captain could sell a few of the barrels in the next port then it could yield an unanticipated but welcome profit.

1 Unger 1992: 281f, and Van Vilsteren 1994: 14-19.

2 Kerling 1954: 110f, 114, 216-220.

The trade in beer changed dramatically in the thirteenth and fourteenth centuries from being an incidental one to being a principal trade for many ships and shippers. The change was made possible by improvements in the technology of beer production. Hops had long been known in Europe. In the twelfth century hops were just one of a number of different additives brewers used to lend taste and appearance to their products as well as give some durability.[3] It may well have been brewers in Bremen in the late twelfth century who discovered how to draw the maximum gain from using the plant. Hops have certain oils which, extracted and in solution in beer, destroy or inhibit certain bacteria,[4] which meant the beer could last much longer than any of its predecessors, up to six months and more without going so sour as to be undrinkable.[5] Before the technical change of around 1200 the way to keep beer from deteriorating was to produce a drink with a high alcohol content, the alcohol acting as a preservative. Raising the alcohol level meant increasing the quantity of grain used since the alcohol was produced from fermentable matter. Beer with hops could be made with a lower alcohol content and still survive so brewers needed to use less grain in making it. Hops were not cheap and the new beers were heavily hopped but even so it seems likely that they were probably less expensive to produce than beers without hops. Of higher quality, greater durability and with no increase in price the new kind of hopped beer quickly became a commodity of long distance trade.

The sources of beer exports, beginning some time in the course of the thirteenth century, were the German port towns on the North Sea. Towns on the Baltic later joined them.[6] Bremen appears to have been the first to become involved in the trade. She continued to export beer throughout the Middle Ages but found herself superseded by the greatest centre of beer production in northern Europe, Hamburg. One chronicler called the town the "*Brauhaus der Hansa*".[7] Hamburg, compared to Bremen, had better access to raw materials and enjoyed equal or better access to transportation links with the markets for hopped beer. Hamburg was almost completely laid waste in a devastating fire in 1284. The rebuilding which followed established the basis for the subsequent industrial growth. The trade in

[3] Moulin 1981: 120f, 124-127.

[4] Ashurst 1971: 31f; De Clerck 1957: 54f, 69, 307, 322, and Hough 1985: 73-85.

[5] Doorman 1955: 17, and Pasteur 1879: 16f, 21.

[6] Huntemann 1971: 9, and Smit 1914: 31.

[7] Bing 1909: 212.

beer from Hamburg started in the thirteenth century but it was in the fourteenth that the industry in the town grew rapidly.[8]

Among Baltic ports that followed the pattern in Hamburg, Rostock developed a brewing industry for export in the fourteenth century but Wismar proved to be a more important a source for beer in the region.[9] Oddly Lübeck, the largest port and town along the coast and political leader of the Hanseatic League, does not seem to have developed an export industry. Lübeck, like virtually every town of any size in northern Germany, the Low Countries, Britain or Scandinavia, in the thirteenth and fourteenth centuries did produce beer but it produced principally for the domestic market. The competition of other nearby towns and the many alternative economic activities open for investment and effort in Lübeck may explain the small export sector. Even later than urban centres of the Wendish coast, towns further east in the Baltic, developed brewing. Gdansk had a sizeable industry by the fifteenth century. Low quality grain which came to the port, not of a quality for shipment to distant markets, could be converted to beer. Gdansk exported beer to the West as the market for beer changed, but that was at the end of the Middle Ages.

Not just beer but hops themselves became a commodity of trade. Wismar had hop gardens as early as the 1250s. In the fourteenth century, Lübeck looked outside the gardens within her walls, importing hops from as far away as Thuringia. By then Wismar imported hops from villages in Poland. Fairs were even devoted to the sale of hops and town governments on the north German coast laid down regulations for the hops trade.[10] Hops became an export good for Sweden in the fifteenth and sixteenth century, forming for example 14% of total exports by value in 1491.[11]

The markets for the new higher quality hopped beer were, in the first instance, the towns in north Germany, that is the member towns of the Hanseatic League. Those regional markets were of little interest compared to markets further afield where potential for profit from shipping hopped beer was much greater. The north German port towns tended to specialise,

[8] Bing 1909: 210, 217f, 237, 242f, and Bracker 1994: 28.

[9] Techen 1915: 264-266, 299. See Bjørn Poulsen's article (above, pp. 34f, 42-44) on the importing of beer into Denmark from Rostock, Wismar and Stralsund in the fourteenth century.

[10] Techen 1915: 318-322. Presumably the hops imported into Denmark from 1300 came from north Germany. See Bjørn Poulsen's article above, pp. 33, 42.

[11] Thunæus 1968: 71f.

the division of export markets going back to the late fourteenth century if not earlier. The Wendish towns were producers for Scandinavia with Rostock, Stralsund and especially Wismar as the centres for shipment overseas. Rostock was already known for exports to the North in the fourteenth century. Beer from Lübeck and also from Lüneberg on occasion even got shipped through Hamburg to the North. Gdansk supplied the eastern Baltic, especially Estonia, Latvia and Lithuania. Hamburg, the biggest exporter, sent its beer principally to potentially the most lucrative markets, the Low Countries, England and the towns of the lower Rhine.[12] The towns of Holland, Brabant but especially Flanders offered large population concentrations and high income levels, all not far from the sites of production. Beer from Bremen appeared on the Netherlands market in 1274. Hamburg beer is mentioned in Gouda in 1357 though it certainly was being sold in Holland well before that date.[13] Bremen beer was reported in Groningen in 1272 and by 1318 Hamburg beer was drunk there too. A trade along the North Sea coast had existed through Frisia since before the time of Charlemagne. Throughout the fourteenth century, Frisian traders carried Hamburg beer. Only grain was a more frequently exported good.[14] Wismar beer turns up in import records at Enkhuizen in 1448 but rarely after that,[15] perhaps because it got the generic name of Hamburg beer.

Beer from Bremen and Hamburg was heavy, strong and expensive. It was not a product for the poor.[16] The obstacle to success for German beer exporters in the Low Countries was competition from other drinks. At the lower end of the market, there was locally produced beer, inexpensive but of inferior quality. At the upper end hopped beer faced the favoured drink of the wealthy in Flanders, wine. The price of Hamburg beer in Flanders was apparently about the same as that for good wine. Of course there were fluctuations over time. However, in general the hopped beer from the north German coast was of such high quality that it still sold, replacing wine to some degree at the tables of the better off in Bruges, Ghent and other Flemish towns.[17]

12 Abel 1981: 22; Bing 1909: 224f, 235f, 245-247, 284; Dollinger 1964: 141, 275, and Schlosser 1981: xvi, 83-89.

13 Doorman 1955: 18, and Gemeente Archief Gouda, 37.

14 Berkenvelder 1963: 138-140, 143-145, 153, 156.

15 Gemeente Archief Hoorn, 481[287-9]. Techen 1916: 201f.

16 Pinkse 1972: 113f.

17 Abel 1981: 20-23, and Huntemann 1971: 16, 22-25, 55f.

England or rather Britain was also a logical market given its location and the other trades which connected the Hanse ports to England and Scotland. Merchants, however, found a resistance to hopped beer in England. There is ample evidence dating from the fifteenth century that consumers but even more producers of traditional ale tried to stop the import and production of hopped beer. There is among English historians an incorrect insistence that hopped beer did not arrive in the country until it appeared at Winchelsea in 1400.[18] The presumption, long made, is that no hopped beer was imported into England in the thirteenth and fourteenth centuries even though German brewers were making it, shipping it and selling it elsewhere along the North Sea littoral. The presumption seems almost certainly wrong. The existence of German merchant factories with resident populations in London and King's Lynn meant that there must have been at least a few drinkers of hopped beer in the country. English records do not indicate the import of hopped beer but a search of German documents might indicate the scale and scope of beer imports to England. Even if there were imports, though, the volume was small.

Scandinavia, on the other hand, proved to be fertile ground for German beer exporters. Geography again dictated the potential. By the mid twelfth century ordinary Danish peasants were drinking beer imported from Lübeck.[19] Though Wismar did establish an early foothold in the North other Hanse towns did not typically shift to the Scandinavian market until the fifteenth century when other export markets, such as ones in the Low Countries, tended to close to them. Denmark proved a difficult market to enter. King Eric V Glipping in 1283 issued a prohibition against the import of any German beer. The massive herring fishery along the shore near Falsterbo in the province of Scania was legally inside the kingdom of Denmark. The fishermen's camps there appear to have been only a very minor outlet for beer even though during the fishing season they were a market for a wide variety of trade goods sent from Lübeck.[20] The Hanse tried to pressure the Scandinavian kingdoms into trade concessions. The League prohibited the export of beer to Denmark in 1363, 1367, 1368, 1422, 1464, 1477 and 1490. In the fourteenth century the restrictions were combined with military action and led to success. In the fifteenth little came of the embargoes. By 1466 the Danish prohibition on imports had been changed

[18] Salzman 1964: 295.

[19] See Björn Poulsen's article above, p. 44.

[20] Weibull 1922: 26f, 51-80. See Björn Poulsen's article above, pp. 42-44, 47, 50.

to a heavy tax, 4 schillings per barrel or 22% of the selling price. At the same time the Danish king prohibited the import of German beer into certain towns. Later in 1489 Denmark prohibited the sale of foreign beer at the Malmö fall market, and in 1491 a new set of restrictions on imported beer followed.[21]

In Sweden in 1351 King Magnus VIII granted toll freedom for Wismar beer at Kalmar. The few townspeople in Scandinavian kingdoms, often immigrants from north German towns or descendants of immigrants, formed a market for the quality product. German shippers had much greater success in Norway, though. Bergen proved to be an important market for Wismar beer well before 1400. In 1284 German merchants put an embargo on export of grain, flour, and beer to Norway to force King Erik Magnusson into concessions. A famine the following year convinced the king and so those merchants came to control trade into the principal Norwegian port, Bergen.[22] The Hansards tried the strategy of an embargo repeatedly through the fourteenth century and were regularly successful. About 1400 Wismar exported some 10,000,000 litres of beer each year, much of it going to Norway. By the end of the fifteenth century, however, overseas sales had fallen to between 3,000,000 and 4,000,000 litres.[23] Drinkers in western Norway, especially around Bergen, still prefer beer with a relatively large quantity of hops. That taste probably is a result of German imports into Bergen which had to be heavily hopped to maintain quality during the sea voyage.[24]

Methods of shipping beer were relatively straightforward. Brewers packaged the beer in barrels, known since the sixth century and probably earlier. It was the only efficient choice for moving a liquid. Using barrels created problems of having to produce the casks, problems of loss if any staves were broken, problems of lost capacity since the barrels were round and the spaces they occupied were more or less square, and problems of standardisation of barrels. For brewers, shippers and governments to know the quantities involved in production and trade they needed a common measure of volume. In 1375 Lübeck, Wismar and other towns in the area agreed to use the Rostock barrel as the standard measure for beer. Though they might all be the same size, the barrels from each town carried dis-

[21] Techen 1915: 324-327, and Techen 1916: 182-183.

[22] Gelsinger 1981: 183, and Techen 1916: 176f, 182, 188f.

[23] Huntemann 1971: 13-19.

[24] Nordlund 1969: 225f.

tinctive brands or marks. It was not until 1480 that Hamburg gave up its own barrel size and joined in using the common measure. Units of measure were invariably a topic of government regulation.

Producing towns worried about maintaining markets and so worried about maintaining the quality of their product. To prevent damage to the good name of their beer, towns set up inspection systems for exports on departure. At Hamburg, for example, tasters would make sure the beer was acceptable before it could leave port. Towns also set limitations on who could produce for export. In some cases districts were specified exclusively for exporters. In some the time of the year for exports was set. In some there were limitations on how much of what kinds of grains brewers could use in making their beer. Typically regulations fiercely restricted imports of beer, as at Wismar from 1356, so that there was no threat to producers in the town from outside. Hamburg export brewers were not allowed to sell their product in the home market, so natives could not buy the best beer brewed in the town.[25] Those brewers could not make export beer before Saint Peter's Day, that is 22 February, at least from 1358 and probably earlier. In 1372 the town dropped the requirement. From 1381 no one could start up a brewery for export without permission of the town council. In 1411, Hamburg expanded restrictions on exporters, in essence introducing a licensing system, and set punishments for brewers who tried to export bad beer. In the same year the town also set a minimum time between brews. The brewing towns controlled prices, setting maximum prices, but often they were more interested in keeping the minimum at a certain level. Hamburg used what legislative powers it had to keep prices from falling in the Netherlands. There was no effort, apparently, to control the total volume of output for export brewers, only the quality.[26] At Wismar as early as 1322 the town set the wages of brewery workers, and from around 1420 the wages of the supervisors of those workers. All the varied restrictions in their many different forms may also have been part of an effort to prevent overproduction and so limit the wide swings in output typical of export industries in the Middle Ages.[27]

In general, towns regulated the trade in brewers' raw materials. Hamburg, for example, insisted that hops be sold only on a market controlled by town officials with no more hops sold than were needed for the making

[25] Bing 1909: 239f, and Techen 1916: 163, 205.

[26] Bing 1909: 253-255, 262, 271f, and Stefke 1979: 27-35, 50, 67f.

[27] Bing 1909: 244-247, and Stefke 1979: 46-49, 51-53, 129-131.

of beer. The purpose was to give all brewers equal access to raw materials and to prevent speculation in what could be a critical commodity. The fifteenth century saw much more extensive regulation than earlier years but the whole process of surveillance began when towns found they had a lucrative export good. The potential for trade meant a potential for prosperity and a potential for enhanced tax income. It is difficult to say whether town councils were more concerned with keeping up the quality of beer or keeping up the level of tax income. Fortunately for them often the two goals dictated the same policy.

Hopped beer had agents for its sale overseas, specialist merchants who concentrated their efforts on acting as middlemen between specific brewers in exporting towns and wholesalers and retailers in importing towns. They had a quasi-official and quasi-legal status. Overseas Hamburgers had factories or organizations of their beer merchants at Stavoren, dating from 1358, at Bruges and at Amsterdam. The group in Amsterdam formed their own *hanze* even before 1358. The group maintained a chapel in the Oude Kerk in the centre of the town.[28] The groups of factors even had their own regulations and statutes granted by Hamburg. The number of agents overseas fell over time as specialist beer importers tended to take over the trade. In 1365, 72 of Amsterdam's 78 beer importers came from Hamburg.[29] At Bruges, Hamburg traders concentrated so much on the beer trade that they even remained aloof from the organisation of merchants from towns of the Hanseatic League, maintaining a separate and much smaller organisation. In 1418 that League made clear that no goods could be sent to non-Hansards in Flanders and included beer in the list of goods. Such rules were strengthened throughout the fifteenth century,[30] but they had their origins in earlier arrangements like those ties of Hamburg brewers with their agents or *liggers* in Amsterdam. Those men were typically relatives of the brewers and principally and in some cases exclusively dealt with the sale of beer. There was cooperation among them, in one case an agent looking after the estate of another, all done with permission of the city government of Amsterdam which was granted at the request of Hamburg.[31] Though

[28] Daenell 1905, vol. 1: 267; Ebbing 1994: 44; Ketner 1946: 5, and Ter Gouw 1879, vol. 2: 309, vol. 5: 140.

[29] Daenell 1903: 10f; Daenell 1905, vol. 1: 266f, and Stefke 1979: 84-87.

[30] Bing 1909: 222f; Daenell 1903: 10f; Daenell 1905, vol. 1: 266f, vol. 2: 408-411; Smit 1917: 6f, and Stefke 1979: 84-87.

[31] *Oorkondenboek van Amsterdam tot 1400,* 1975: no. 522; Smit 1914: 45; Smit 1917: 6f, and Stefke 1983: 20f, 23-25.

such groups of agents and the associated regulations tend to turn up later—that is, they appear officially typically in the years after 1350 as the beer trade became more regularised and settled—still there is every indication that beer merchants and exclusive contracts with suppliers go back to the early days of the international exchange in beer.

Beer merchants used the common ships of the day. A bulk good sent out of German ports, beer was ideal for shipment in cogs. Undoubtedly beer did travel in cogs of many sizes. However, much of the trade in beer was coastal and even intracoastal. To get to Bruges from Hamburg the beer could go in large ships over the open sea or, more likely, in coastal traders to the Zuider Zee and then, after transshipment, in inland vessels along the rivers and lakes of the Low Countries to the final destination. Going to the east from Rostock or Wismar the beer would have travelled along the coast, along the south shore of the Baltic. Cogs probably dominated the Bergen trade and the direct trade to Bruges. Otherwise shippers could have sent beer out in small cogs or other types of sailing vessels, smaller boats of low tonnage and small crews.

It seems likely that in the closing years of the fourteenth century Hamburgers increasingly moved beer all the way to Sluis, the port of Bruges, without intermediate stops. Such a trend would explain the establishment of that organisation of agents at Bruges, like the one at Amsterdam, late in the century. Improvements in the quality of ships may have made sailing directly easier and safer. One English observer of the early fifteenth century said beer went straight to Flanders but he was talking about beer from Prussia, brought along with bacon, another foodstuff which was also very popular with Flemings. The Gdansk beer was probably heavier and stronger than competitors though not expensive.[32]

It is difficult to estimate the volume of trade in beer in the thirteenth and fourteenth centuries. The statistical evidence is sparse and rarely deals directly with shipment of beer. A 1376 survey, lost in a fire in 1842, had 1,075 Hamburgers stating their trades and of those 457 or almost 43% said they were beer brewers. Of the 457 brewers, 126 reported that they supplied the Amsterdam market while 55 reported they worked especially to supply Stavoren in Friesland. Almost 40% then concentrated their efforts on shipping beer to two ports in the northern Netherlands. Even those impressive figures understate the importance of beer production to Hamburg

[32] Bing 1909: 219, 227f; Stefke 1979: 123, 127f, 131; *De Tol van Iesekeroord* 1939: 10f, 14, and Warner 1921: 15f.

since by no means were all of the brewers identified in the survey. In that same year of 1376 Hamburg had no less than 104 master coopers. Many of those men produced barrels for the brewing industry.[33] The total output of fourteenth-century Hamburg brewers was about 24,000,000 litres per year. Export brewers appear to have even produced to order for Low Countries markets, making up an entire brew which then was loaded on board a ship and sent directly to Amsterdam. Some skippers and ships specialised in the coastal trade to Amsterdam. The 54 skippers who commanded 107 ships in 1352-1354 made an average of slightly over two trips each. Of those 54 skippers, 30 were from the Netherlands. In the second half of 1364, for the 98 ships which brought beer to Amsterdam, there were 63 skippers who made an average of about 1.5 trips each. In 1365 there were only 92 skippers who commanded 202 ships with an average of about 2.25 trips each. Shippers spread their cargoes across a number of vessels to decrease risk so the number of shippers varied from five to 20 per ship.[34]

Amsterdam was the chief port of entry for Hamburg beer exports. Indeed after 1323 the count of Holland, William III, required that imports come only through the ports of Amsterdam and Medemblik. It was an effort to direct the beer trade which presumably was growing and threatening the tax income he received from levies on domestically produced beer. In 1321 he had prohibited the import of Hamburg and eastern beer into three districts in the county, but two years later he rescinded the blanket prohibition and replaced it with a tax on imports. When Count William V renewed the toll in 1351 he mentioned only Amsterdam as a port of entry.[35] Hanse merchants paid a very light tax on beer imports but the volume of the trade presumably was enough to make the tax lucrative for the counts.

The result of the comital legislation, among other things, was to generate records of the import volume of beer going into the Low Countries. It is one of the rare cases where it is possible to know the volume of beer traded in the late Middle Ages. The beer toll records are among the surviving registers of the *Rentmeester van Amstel- en Waterland* for 1343 to 1370, with figures for the toll existing for only short periods during those 27 years. The name and often the residence of the skipper of each vessel

[33] Bing 1909: 243f; Smit 1914: 100; Stefke 1979: 119-122, and Stieda 1895: 30.

[34] Bing 1909: 250-252, and Smit 1914: 39-44, 47, 90f, 103, 107.

[35] Gemeente Archief Gouda, 37: 32; Doorman 1955: 18; Ebbing 1994: 44f; *Oorkondenboek van Amsterdam tot 1400,* 1975: no. 16, 602, 618; Smit 1914: 31, and Ter Gouw 1879, vol. 1: 356.

are listed as well as the shippers who were responsible for paying the toll and the number of barrels of beer in each ship. The vessels were of about 40 to 50 tons, that is in the middle range of ocean going ships of the day. The largest ships from the Hanse ports would have gone directly to Flanders.[36] The export of Hamburg beer to Holland, which was well underway by the 1320s, saw significant growth from 1343. There was a sharp setback in 1347. The general disruption of the European economy during the Black Death and a piratical war between Holland and Friesland combined to generate a disaster for beer shipments out of Hamburg. In 1351 exports returned to their former absolute level and continued at that level until the mid 1360s when they rose again and stabilised at a new plateau. It is that new higher level that is reflected in the Amsterdam records. Imports of beer to Amsterdam fell in the 1370s but rose again in the 1390s.[37] Imports in 1352-1354 were 31,319 tuns in 105 ships, a tun being about 150 litres. The seemingly large number of vessels can be explained only by their bringing more than just beer. In 1364 the figure was 17,514 tuns, that in 98 ships. For 1365-1366 it was 39,316 tuns. A quantity of beer avoided the toll collector but the exact quantity unaccounted for is not known. It would seem that by the 1360s, then, the average annual shipment from Hamburg to Amsterdam was almost 32,000 barrels or at least 5,600,000 litres, that is more than 20% of total Hamburg output in 1375 and probably more than half of all Hamburg exports.[38] Monthly shipments clearing customs at Amsterdam varied on average from 270,000 to 636,000 litres in the various tax periods for which data survive between 1358 and 1370. At a per capita consumption level of 300 litres per year, which is a reasonable if slightly generous estimate, those imports could have supplied a population of from 10,800 in a low average month to 25,500 people in a high one. The latter was enough beer to supply all the needs for a sizeable city. High quality imports sold to a minority so German hopped beer must have appeared on tables in many towns in the Low Countries.

Little of the beer presumably stayed in Amsterdam. Much of it went on further south and especially to Brabant and Flanders. Shippers had to move about 5,600 tonnes along the North Sea coast to Amsterdam on average each year. Given the size of vessels used in the trade, even with multiple voyages more than 20 ships would have been fully employed to move the

[36] Smit 1914: 48, and Smit 1917: 3-7.

[37] Bracker 1994: 28; Smit 1914: 89, and Stefke 1979: 63-83, 129-131, xlvi-liv.

[38] Bracker 1994: 29; Huntemann 1971: 14f, and Smit 1914: 37-39, 89.

beer alone. The ships travelled in convoy, varying in number from 25 to 3 in the 1350s. They did not sail in the winter and the shipping season was short, some 6 months in 1352-1353, in part because at that time Hamburg prohibited export before 22 February. The tax data do tend to underestimate the importance to commercial relations of the bulk trade in beer since the ships going between Hamburg and Amsterdam carried more than just the single cargo of beer.

Data on exports from Hamburg appear in the Hamburg *Pfundzollbuch* for February, 1369, to February, 1370. That source shows that beer made up a full one-third of all Hamburg exports by value. There are problems with the Hamburg records since the size of the barrel, the *fud*, which was the unit of tax is not certain. The records do show exports of 9,144.5 *fuder* of beer of which 4,262 or 46.6% went to Amsterdam. The destination of the other 53.4% of Hamburg exports is not obvious but a significant share must have found its way to the Low Countries either through Stavoren or Bruges. Hamburg tolls of 1399/1400 and 1417/18 show that the principal export commodity of Hamburg remained beer. It still went to the traditional markets of Holland and Friesland. Hamburg beer turns up in 1418 in toll records from the lower Scheldt.[39] In 1417 Hamburg exported 18,250,000 litres of beer. The figure for 1369 had been 13,260,000 litres so it is not possible to say that beer exports declined, even compared to the 1360s. As late as 1417 and even well beyond that date Hamburg brewing was still prosperous.[40] By around 1410 total production had risen to 30,000,000 litres and reached about 37,500,000 litres by about 1480. The 457 professional brewers of 1357 increased to some 520 in the fifteenth century. Though that figure was high, other north German towns had a large number of men who made a substantial proportion of their income from producing beer. At Bremen there were 300 brewers in the early fifteenth century, at Wismar some 200, and Lübeck 180.[41]

At the end of the fourteenth century and through the fifteenth the international trade in beer went through a transformation. The process was a slow one, already under way in the 1320s and not completed even at the end of the Middle Ages. The trade established by Bremen and Hamburg

[39] Dollinger 1964: 275; Stefke 1979: 88-90, 95, 117f; Stefke 1983: 23, and *De Tol van Iesekeroord* 1939: 165, 179.

[40] Huntemann 1971: 46; *Das Hamburger Pfundzollbuch von 1418,* 1972: 57f, and Stefke 1983: 23, 28-33.

[41] Abel 1981: 21, and Huntemann 1971: 11f, 14f, 18, 38f.

manufacturers and traders in the course of the thirteenth century was altered beyond recognition. The change came because of the rise of hopped beer brewing in other parts of Europe and, in the first instance, in Holland. Count William III in 1321 allowed the production of hopped beer in Holland, something illegal before that date. Brewers in various Dutch towns quickly tried their hands at producing the different type of beer. In the course of the fourteenth century Dutch brewers learned how to make hopped beer and by 1400 to make it as well as brewers in Bremen and Hamburg. The process was a slow one since local producers were not able to replace imports immediately. The chemistry of hops is such that the wrong quantities added at the wrong time can yield a beer of poor taste and without getting the desired antiseptic effect from the essential oils which preserves beer. It was possible to boil away the valuable chemicals if brewing went on too long. It was possible to be left with a bitter taste if boiling did not go on long enough.[42] As Dutch producers developed the ability to make hopped beer of high quality they began to export some of it to the Flemish market. Simply, over time beer from Holland supplanted beer from north Germany. The Dutch product was cheaper if for no other reason that it travelled over a much shorter distance to reach urban markets in those provinces just to the south. Complaints from German merchants in Bruges in the late fourteenth and fifteenth centuries about regulations, violations of rules and poor treatment suggest that German importers and imports were under pressure from Dutch competition. The threat from Dutch beer and Dutch shippers drove German traders to be more conscious of their privileges. In negotiations between the Hanseatic League and the Low Countries the duties on foreign beers turned up repeatedly as a bone of contention in the fourteenth and the fifteenth centuries. The Counts of Flanders did not always deal favourably with German beer. One of them even issued a prohibition of imports in 1370, though he had to rescind it soon thereafter, probably because the alternate suppliers in Flanders and Holland at that early date could not meet the demand for beer. Taxes levied on imports, like those beginning in 1379, proved a constant burden to merchants dealing in German beer. There was a long history of efforts by the Hanseatic League to get import duties on beer reduced. At Sluis in 1387, for example, the fee was about 50% of the value of beer. Hanse imports into Flanders were increasingly burdened through the first half of the fifteenth century with ever higher duties. The reasons for levying

42 De Clerck 1957: 60, 302-304.

them were financial but the results made what was high-priced beer prohibitively expensive for many and made even wine a reasonable alternative. In the 1450s the Hanse was able to get some relief but it proved to be temporary. Taxes on imports rose again in the last third of the century to even greater heights.[43]

In England resistance to hopped beer had been long established and whatever potential there was for a market was reduced as, first, Dutch producers began to ship beer to south-eastern England across the North Sea and as, second, Low Countries immigrants and their indigenous imitators began to produce hopped beer themselves. There are many signs of a rise in hopped beer output in the fifteenth century and a more rapid rise as the century went on. In Scandinavia, though markets for German hopped beer remained more resilient than in western Europe, still there was some replacement of imports by local production. While trade in beer northward might shrink there was probably some relative growth in beer shipments to the East, that is to the eastern Baltic.

The beer trade did not end in the fifteenth century. Rather there was a shift in the centres of production which in turn meant a shift in the routes followed by the trade. Distances became shorter and routes for German exporters were relatively more toward the north and east than to the west and south-west. There was also a shift in the types of beer traded. Since hopped beer of good quality could be produced in so many different places it made no sense to send that product over long distances. Shippers turned to more expensive, distinctive beers of the highest quality which would have had small but profitable sales in distant markets since they were better able to sustain the transport costs as part of the sale price. *Joopen* beer from Gdansk, a dark, thick, almost syrupy, heavy, strong beer sold in small quantities but found a place as much for medicinal as for nutritional purposes in Low Countries markets. It was a standard commodity for German and even Dutch merchants by the end of the fifteenth century. Gdansk *joopen* beer was the best example both of a shift in production, that is a technical response to the new market conditions, and a shift in type, that is moving to a higher priced commodity, and a shift in location, that is the development of a new route for the beer trade, from the eastern Baltic to western Europe. Beer did not stop being a commodity of large scale or long distance trade, but the trade of 1500 was very different from that of 1300.

It was technical change in the production of beer which created the

[43] Bing 1909: 232f, 237f, and Gemeente Archief Gouda, 37: 34f.

novel trade in that bulk good. Beer was a foodstuff that was hard to pack and difficult to handle. It did not travel well. The product of the technical change, hopped beer, was a drink for the well-to-do and for skilled labourers. At least it was a commodity with a broad geographic potential with possible consumers throughout northern Europe from the Loire to the Dwina and even beyond and virtually everywhere in between. The presence of that tradeable commodity undoubtedly was a critical element in the construction of a shipping and commercial network that spread out from the ports of Bremen, Hamburg, Rostock and Wismar.

Just as technical change had marked the start of the trade, the diffusion of that same technology led to the decline of the trade or, more precisely, the transformation of the trade. As producers elsewhere learned to make hopped beer and to make it as well as brewers in north German towns there was no need to trade it. That would apply first in Holland but slowly came to apply throughout northern Europe. Grain, or rather grains of various types, was the principal raw material for making beer. Grain was also a bulk good so there was always the question of whether or not it was better to ship the grain or the beer. Moving beer by land in the late Middle Ages added from 25% to 70% to the price for each 100 kilometres travelled. Since beer was more than 95% water, shipping the major ingredient by land or sea instead of all the water had to mean a sharp decrease in transport costs and so in the delivered price to the consumer. The barrier to shipping the raw material seems to have been, again, the technology of brewing. So long as brewers in the Hanse towns were the only ones who had mastered making beer with hops the beer had to be shipped. Acclimatization of the new technique to local conditions and of local producers and consumers to the methods and product was not immediate. The process took some time. What little data that does exist suggests that full mastery of the new technology occurred from about 1250 in north Germany, about 1390 in Holland, about 1450 in the southern Netherlands, and about 1520 in England. It was a matter of changing skills and tastes, of adjustment to the new product. First, consumers had to be convinced that the trade commodity was something to drink. Second, consumers had to be convinced that local imitations of the commodity were as good as the import. Once those two steps had been accomplished it was no longer necessary to trade beer over long distance. In the fifteenth century the trade in one bulky good—beer—was replaced by the trade in another bulky good —grain.[44]

[44] On the growth of the grain trade already in the fourteenth century, see Nils Hybel's article below, pp. 240f.

The Use of Pottery to Chart Trade Routes in the North Sea and Baltic Sea Areas

Alan G. Vince

This article will examine the interpretation of pottery distributions as they have been applied to the study of trade and contact between Scandinavia and the Baltic and the countries bordering the North Sea. Although it includes a short preamble on the theory and practice of using ceramic evidence, since this is an area of study of which documentary historians ought to be aware, in the main we will try to concentrate on the results of ceramic analysis, rather than on a critique of its methods.

Pottery is found in some quantities in excavations on medieval settlement sites around the North Sea and the Baltic, and its scientific study and publication has a history going back to the 1930s. However, until scientific analyses of the clays from which these pots were made became possible, the study of trade, as evidenced by pottery fragments, could not be taken very far, since it was not possible—except in the case of exotica such as the Alkaline Glazed ware from Lund[1]—to say for certain whether or not vessels were made locally copying foreign models, or were actual imports. Even once it became possible to reliably identify imported sherds (and there is still much work to be done here), it was still difficult to interpret a distribution map on which a dot might represent at one site a single sherd found in a collection of several thousand sherds whilst on another site it might represent the majority of the pottery found. Clearly, a means of quantifying

I would like to thank Per Kristian Madsen for his constant help and encouragement during my research. In addition, I would like to thank my many colleagues whose work on the pottery of north-west Europe and Scandinavia I have used here and elsewhere. In particular I am grateful to have been able to study pottery from sites such as Uppsala and Sigtuna in advance of their publication by Magnus Elfwendahl and Mats Roslund respectively. Finally, I would like to thank the British Academy and the Society of Antiquaries of London for supporting my fieldwork through research awards.

[1] Hurst 1968.

the frequency of pottery types in a collection is needed. Finally, even once these hurdles have been jumped, there remains the almost unknowable social context in which the pottery existed. Pottery was not a basic commodity such as grain or wood. It could be used for utilitarian functions: cooking, storage, fetching and carrying water, but it could also be used as a medium for display. Its function in society changed chronologically over the twelfth to fourteenth centuries and may well have differed geographically, for example between Uppsala, in central Sweden, and London, in the south-east of England.

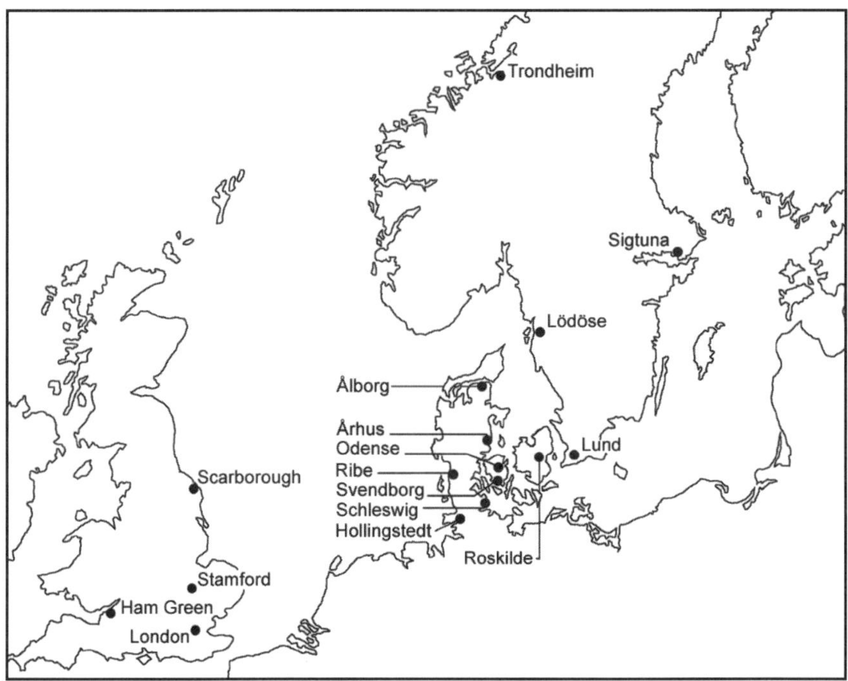

Figure 16. North-Western Europe and Scandinavia: Places involved in the pottery trade from the twelfth to the fourteenth centuries. Map: Lars Berggren.

Interpreting Pottery Distributions

Characterisation

Despite my comments on the use of visual appearance to identify the source of medieval pottery, this is in fact the first stage in any study. Siegburg stoneware, made in the Rhineland from the end of the thirteenth century onwards, has a distinctive appearance, and where a stoneware vessel is found with such an inclusionless white-firing clay body, together with a form or decoration paralleled in the publications of the vast waster heaps of Siegburg, then a Rhenish source can probably be assumed. In recent years though, it has become evident that stoneware was also made at sites in the north European plain, the production presumably diffusing from the Rhineland to serve the Hanseatic towns.[2]

The next stage in any study is the use of ceramic petrology. Medieval pottery vessels were not made solely of clay minerals but contain other rocks and minerals, some of which may be characteristic of particular areas. Finnish pottery may contain gabbro or diorite for example, and that from Sweden and Denmark can contain fragments of biotite granite. These rock fragments can often be seen by eye and reliably identified using a binocular microscope. Further detail can be obtained by using a thin-section of the pot, which can also be used to identify rocks and minerals too small or undiagnostic to identify in the hand.

Unfortunately, the main sources of pottery imported into Scandinavia and the Baltic Sea in the medieval period were located in areas with similar geological histories: tertiary or quaternary strata, in which flint, chalk, quartz and mica are predominant rocks and minerals. Furthermore, there are extensive areas of glacially-derived sand and gravel in Denmark, north Germany and the Low Countries. The odd fragment of granite, or sheaf of biotite, could be a glacial erratic, and is not in itself evidence for a Scandinavian or Baltic source for the vessel containing it.

Finally, samples of the pot can be crushed to a powder, and analysed using a technique that determines the chemical composition of the sample in terms of the basic elements present. Two such techniques are: neutron activation analysis (NAA) in which the samples are irradiated and the resulting radioactive decay detected and measured; and inductively coupled plasma spectroscopy (ICPS), in which a small quantity of the sample is vaporised and its composition measured by studying the emitted light spectrum.

2 Lindahl 1986; Gaimster 1997.

Despite the pioneering work of Anders Lindahl, at the University of Lund, there is still very little scientific analysis of the medieval pottery found in Scandinavia and the Baltic, but enough has been done to demonstrate the power of the techniques.[3]

Quantification

At Lincoln, London, and some other United Kingdom towns where permanent archaeological units exist, huge databases have been built up that contain information about the pottery finds.[4] Because every method of quantification devised to date has been shown to be flawed for some purposes, but suitable for others, it is normal for two or three complementary methods to be used.[5] A basic record can be simply to count sherds. If several sherds come from the same vessel, then this method can produce heavily skewed results, but if instead we record "sherd families" (that is, find and group together all the sherds from one pot buried on a site) it is very labour intensive, especially if the sherds were dispersed across the site. Using pottery weight instead of a sherd count can be more useful and in some cases quicker. Given estimates for the average weight of a vessel of a particular type, such data can be transformed, to give an indication of the relative quantity of pottery of different types present. The third method commonly used in the United Kingdom is the estimated vessel equivalent, or EVE. This method works on the assumption that a vessel would have only one rim and one base, and that if one measures the percentage of rim or base present in a sherd then this can be used to calculate the relative proportion of pottery types in a collection. In Scandinavia and the Baltic, such methods are (to the best of my knowledge) never used, and to produce comparative figures, even for the major collections: Schleswig, Lund, Århus, Ribe and the like, would take many person-months of work. Nevertheless, this is probably essential if the study of medieval pottery trade in the Baltic is to progress.

[3] Lindahl 1986.

[4] These databases are held at present by the organisations which created them: Lincoln—City of Lincoln Archaeology Unit; London—Museum of London Archaeological Service; York—York Archaeological Trust. Ultimately, they will probably be deposited with the local museum and perhaps available online.

[5] An introduction to these techniques and the theory behind them will be found in Orton, Tyers & Vince 1993.

Social context of pottery use

Even when such data is available, as one day undoubtedly they will be, there will remain the difficult problem of how much pottery was used in settlements in the medieval period. At Bergen and Trondheim, for example, it is likely that all of the medieval pottery found in the settlement was imported. Why this should have been so is an interesting point and certainly not simply a case of there being no clays suitable for potting available. At present, I want to point out the practical difficulties that this introduces for anyone studying pottery trade. At Bergen, for example, we might find that pottery from the Rhineland formed over half of all the pottery used in the fourteenth century, whereas, further south, at Lund or Malmö for instance, it might form as little as a quarter of the pottery used. (Both figures are made up, but the point is real enough.) In this example was there ever "more" Rhenish pottery in Bergen than Malmö? I suppose it all depends on what we mean by "more". A fishing village on the Öresund, for example, might also produce an assemblage in which 25% of the pottery found was Rhenish but in terms of trade it is clearly Malmö that would be the more important market. So, in addition to the relative proportion of pottery found (flawed as this might be as a measure), we also need to take into account the size of population of the settlement in the medieval period.

THE STATUS OF POTTERY AND POTTERY-PRODUCTION IN MEDIEVAL NORTH-WEST EUROPE

Given these difficulties in interpreting pottery data, a brief sketch of the status of pottery and its makers in north-west Europe will help us to better understand the mechanisms involved in its distribution.

From what we can infer from studies of twelfth- to fourteenth-century pottery assemblages, it seems that pottery making was never a domestic skill required of every family or settlement. Instead, there were a few centres specialising in pottery production. Some were rural, in which case the potters combined their craft with agriculture or woodland industry. Others were urban. There is no evidence from the British Isles that potters ever formed a guild or took apprentices, though it is likely that urban pottery production was organised in a similar manner to other industries. If so, then it is simply the low status of potters within the urban hierarchy which has led to the lack of surviving documentation.

Pottery itself is rarely mentioned in British medieval documentary sources, and was ignored by those making wills or probate inventories even well into the post-medieval period. Even in total, therefore, the value of pottery within a household was negligible in comparison with that of textiles or metal goods, which were often listed in some detail. Only when we look at Spanish pottery imported to England in the early fourteenth century is there a hint that pottery itself might have a value in its own right, as opposed to being a container for another product.[6] These pots, however, were in the main lustrewares from Malaga and of high technical quality in comparison to those made in north-west Europe.[7]

Despite the general impression, probably justified, that pottery was a low-value, low-status, commodity in the twelfth to fourteenth centuries, as it was in the centuries beforehand, and would remain until the advent of ceramics as an artistic medium in fifteenth-century Italy, there is abundant evidence that pottery was regularly traded over distances of 30-40 miles overland in England and over much longer distances around the coast.[8] Isolated vessels were carried over much longer distances. At the beginning of our period, for example, Stamford ware was occasionally to be found at sites in the Welsh borderland and Severn Valley, sites to which it must have been carried overland.[9]

TRADE IN POTTERY IN THE NORTH SEA/BALTIC AREAS BEFORE THE MID TWELFTH CENTURY

Although pottery was on occasion transported overland before the mid twelfth century, the norm in the British isles was for it to be obtained from sources within a radius of 10-20 miles from the settlement. Even at London, already beginning to be marked out from other British towns by its size and international contacts, the overwhelming majority of the pottery used in the town came from one or other of a series of rural centres which ringed the city.[10] The remainder was imported, mainly from the Meuse valley and the Rhineland.[11] This imported pottery was of a finer quality than the local wares, most of which were handmade vessels used for cooking. Away from

[6] Gerrard, Gutierrez & Vince 1995.

[7] Childs 1995.

[8] Vince 1983.

[9] E.g., Hen Domen castle, Montgomery (Barker 1982) and Hereford (Vince 1985a).

[10] Vince & Jenner 1991; Vince 1985b.

[11] Andenne-type ware, see Vince & Jenner 1991: 104-106. Paffrath ware, also known as Blue-grey or Blaugrau ware, see Vince & Jenner 1991: 103f.

the east coast, in the Severn valley, pottery production and distribution in the late eleventh and early twelfth centuries was also mainly very localised, except that sites in Wales and the Welsh border (such as Chepstow and Hereford), had no access to local pottery industries and were therefore supplied by centres further east.[12] Here too the majority of the pottery was handmade unglazed cooking ware, although, as on the east coast, the use of glaze was known, but not common. Pottery from production sites in Bristol and Gloucester has been found in later eleventh and twelfth-century contexts in Dublin, one of the few instances known of long-distance pottery trade at this time in western Britain.[13]

In the Scandinavian and Baltic world, there is a similar pattern. Pottery, by and large, was locally made (although the precise details of the sort of distances over which it was carried, and the distribution of production centres, is still being studied). Imports to the region consist of the occasional vessel from the Rhineland,[14] or amphora from the Black Sea coast (being studied by Mats Roslund, University of Lund).[15]

To summarise, therefore, in the century following the Norman conquest of England the majority of pottery was made and used locally (that is, within 10-20 miles of the site where it was used), except for rare overland trade (as with Stamford ware), and long-distance trade to ports such as London and Dublin. This appears to have been true also in Scandinavia. In both regions, whenever long-long-distance trade in pottery can be established, it is found at ports and major urban centres (such as Lund and Sigtuna), rather than in their rural hinterlands.

TRADE IN POTTERY IN THE NORTH SEA/BALTIC AREAS IN THE LATE TWELFTH AND THIRTEENTH CENTURIES

Some time towards the middle of the twelfth century, this pattern changed, quite rapidly. At London, where large datable assemblages of pottery span the twelfth century, this change can be seen clearly.[16] The overall propor-

[12] Vince 1991; Vince 1985a: 81f.

[13] Vince 1988.

[14] Mostly Paffrath ware vessels with some Blau-grau ware, see Lüdtke 1985 and Lüdtke 1989b.

[15] Recognised to date at Sigtuna, Lund and at Haithabu.

[16] Vince 1985b: 43f.

tion of glazed ware in use rose suddenly, and there was a widening of the range of shapes and decorations employed. In England, later twelfth-century glazed ware industries are known in the London area, Castle Hedingham in Essex, and Stamford.[17] For a generation or two, these industries were unusual, and this probably explains why their products are found in small numbers over wide areas of the country. The products of the Stamford industry, white-wares with bright green glazes, are distinctive, and their distribution is well known. The extent of the London industry was less clear until the 1980s, when it was recognised that a high proportion of the glazed wares found on Scottish port sites such as Aberdeen and Perth, were of London origin. More recently still, London wares have been identified at Waterford, on the southern Irish coast.[18]

This explosion of production and trade was not limited to eastern England. In the Rhineland, the later twelfth century saw the production of vessels ancestral to the thirteenth- and fourteenth-century stoneware jugs, and these were certainly traded as far as Amsterdam, whilst a number of production centres in Northern France, Belgium and the Netherlands began production on a large scale. In fact, the realisation that this production started in the later twelfth century was not made, or at least, not universally accepted, until the discovery of sherds of northern French Rouen ware were found in deposits dated by dendrochronology at Ribe.[19]

The early thirteenth century saw the consolidation and extension of the pattern established in the preceding fifty years. In western Britain, for example, the Ham Green kilns, situated at the mouth of the Bristol Avon, were certainly in operation from ca. 1200,[20] and recent dendrochronological work in Bristol would suggest that the industry extended much further back into the twelfth century.[21] Ham Green ware was traded widely by sea, as far as Dublin[22] (and sometimes even further; there is at least one sherd at Lund

[17] London-type ware and Coarse London-type ware, see Pearce, Vince & Jenner 1985. Hedingham ware is at present poorly documented, although a major, dated series from Colchester, Essex, is being prepared for publication by John Cotter. For Developed Stamford ware, see Simpson 1982.

[18] Vince 1994.

[19] Gaimster 1997.

[20] Barton 1963.

[21] Ponsford 1991.

[22] Barton 1988.

and another at the Bryggen in Bergen).[23] In the London industry there was a major stylistic change in the early thirteenth century, at which point highly-decorated vessels copying northern French wares became the norm.[24] All over lowland Britain, these fineware glazed pottery industries proliferated, and this whole process can be seen on a wider scale to have been happening simultaneously on both sides of the North Sea and English Channel.

It is during the later twelfth and early thirteenth centuries that imports into Scandinavia and the Baltic began in earnest. Although precise figures are not available, it seems that Rhenish and western European wares might have been present in similar quantities. There are differences between the range of imports found at different centres, and only three sites that I have personal knowledge of produced imports of this period in large quantities: Bergen,[25] Trondheim[26] and Ribe.[27] To these, we should probably be able to add Oslo and Lödöse, to judge from published sources.[28] There are hints that similar patterns might be found at Visby[29] and Sigtuna,[30] whilst Uppsala—founded in the later twelfth century—seems to have been first extensively occupied around the middle of this period, ca.1200. Alongside this evidence for large-scale regular trade in pottery (presumably as a sideline to other, more lucrative, trade) must be placed the evidence from other ports, such as Århus, Svendborg and Roskilde, which do not seem to have taken much part in this.[31]

[23] Unpublished, noted by the author whilst working on London area imports in 1986. There is a similarly far-flung vessel from Lund which must also have been exported via Bristol. Cf. Vince 1995b.

[24] Pearce, Vince & Jenner 1985: 131-134.

[25] Lüdtke 1989a.

[26] Reed 1990.

[27] Madsen 1991.

[28] Carlsson 1982. Photography and verbal description are not always sufficient to identify medieval pottery types, partly because there was a common pool of styles and forms.

[29] Personal communication by D. Gaimster.

[30] Sigtuna imports are being studied by Mats Roslund, University of Lund.

[31] A survey of published and unpublished material from Århus, Svendborg and Roskilde in 1994 revealed very few imports of late twelfth/early thirteenth-century date. There were none at all at either Århus or Svendborg and a handful at Roskilde, including developed Stamford ware.

TRADE IN POTTERY IN THE NORTH SEA/BALTIC AREAS IN THE LATE THIRTEENTH AND FOURTEENTH CENTURIES

In the second half of the thirteenth century there was another shift in ceramic production. Highly decorated glazed wares from then on became the norm over large areas of England, and even the cooking vessels could be glazed, and were normally thrown on a wheel. Similar changes took place in Northern France, Belgium, and the Netherlands, whilst in the Rhineland true stoneware production began and was accompanied by an increase in the scale of the pottery industry.

In England, pottery manufacture continued in the London area but production for export was probably concentrated in the hinterlands of the ports of Scarborough, Hull, Boston and King's Lynn. Unfortunately, a lot of this material looks very similar, and I have merely classified it as "English". In the archaeological literature it tends to be classified as "Scarborough ware", "York ware(s)", "Grimston ware" and the like.

The Low Countries

At this time, pottery from Flanders, and possibly sources further north, in Holland or Frisia, was exported in large quantities to Scandinavia and the Baltic. Reported finds from England are not numerous, and are mostly from east coast ports.[32] An indication of the scale and extent of this trade is given by the finds from Uppsala, where Prof. Frans Verhaeghe has recently identified the majority of the glazed red earthenwares found in medieval excavations in the town as Bruges products. The precise scale of this industry is not clear however, since much of the later medieval pottery of southern Scandinavia has a similar appearance, making use of shared manufacturing techniques and methods of decoration. Production waste from Bruges shows that the potters there fired their vessels twice, once as a biscuit firing, after slip and decoration had been added, and again after the vessels were glazed. This gave rise to a consistent red body, not matched for quality in most other western European red earthenware industries of the time. Bruges potters also had a distinctive way of applying

[32] Flemish redwares are remarkably scarce in eastern England, especially considering the documented contacts between Flanders and England at this time. This may partly be due to the fact that their similarity to English redwares means that vessels are not being recognised, and partly to the fact that there was little demand for decorated red earthenwares in a country that was itself exporting them. In either case the contrast with Jutland and the Baltic is remarkable.

white slip to their vessels, in which the slip was applied whilst the pot was still being thrown on the wheel. This gave rise to vessels where white slip can form a thick layer on the outside of the vessel, especially around the rim, whereas other parts of the pot have a very thin slip coating, through which can often be seen the red colour of the body. Such features are found on Scandinavian redwares as well as on the pots of the Bruges area, and are more likely to have been passed on from potter to potter through apprenticeship than by copying the products of a rival industry. It is likely, therefore, that the potters of Bruges had a strong influence on the development of the local pottery industries of Scandinavia and the Baltic. The exact nature of this influence is worthy of further study, and it may well be that it will be possible to chart the introduction of the glazed redware industry, initially by Flemish potters and its later adoption and development locally. However, it is clear that such is the similarity of local and imported glazed red earthenwares, that it will be some time before we can evaluate the contribution of trade rather than cultural diffusion in the relationships between the Baltic lands and Flanders.

Northern France

Pottery from a source in the Seine valley, possibly Rouen, is a distinctive import around the North Sea and into the Baltic in the later thirteenth and fourteenth centuries.[33] Sherds of this Late Rouen-type ware have been recorded at the ports and major towns of Bergen, Ribe, Ålborg, Århus, Svendborg, Roskilde, Lund and Visby as well as at rural sites, such as Løgumkloster in southern Jutland. At most of these places, these sherds are likely to have been the second most common western European import after Flemish wares, although at Bergen they were less common than English wares.[34]

---

[33] Lüdtke 1989b: 225 and fig. 4. The division into early and late wares can be clearly seen in Kenneth Barton's publication of material from Rouen museum. The later vessels are usually smaller, thinner-walled and with less elaborate designs, relying often on the overall application of a thin brown slip and irregularly-placed stamped pads of clay. Cf. Barton 1966, figs. 2-4, no 6 to 24.

[34] Deroeux, Dufournier & Herteig 1994: 163-208. Deroeux and Dufournier have demonstrated through chemical analysis that pottery of "Rouen type" falls into two distinct groups, one of which they identify as Rouen ware and the other they assign less precisely to the Seine valley. There is clearly much work to be done to clarify the classification of Seine valley products, although all were probably exported

Eastern England

In the early thirteenth century the Stamford kilns ceased production, and the main source of glazed pottery in Stamford itself became the Lyveden/Stanion industry, situated in the rural hinterland of Stamford.[35] In contrast to the earlier wares the products of these new industries were poorly made, using hand-forming techniques rather than the potter's wheel. Nevertheless, a few sherds of Lyveden/Stanion ware have been found in Scandinavia: at Bergen and at Ribe, for example.[36] At Bergen these vessels even included handmade cooking pots as well as the slip-decorated jugs for which the industry is generally known. Despite these finds, the middle of the thirteenth century seems to have marked the end of the Stamford area as a centre for the production of pottery for long-distance trade. It is likely that amongst the reasons for this change is the cessation of direct contact between the river port of Stamford and the North Sea, and the parallel rise in importance of the coastal ports of Boston and King's Lynn. Pottery continued to be made in the area, at Bourne, for example, into the post-medieval period, and a study of its distribution on archaeological sites shows this industry to have had a large inland market.[37]

---

through the port of Rouen.

[35] The Lyveden/Stanion pottery industry is known mainly through Geoffrey Bryant's and John Steane's excavations at the deserted medieval village of Lyveden, Northamptonshire. Subsequently, it has been recognised that almost identical vessels were produced in the neighbouring village of Stanion. Furthermore, very similar fabrics were produced at Bourne, in south Lincolnshire (Bourne A, B and C wares). In all cases, these rural industries probably supplied pottery for export through fenland ports such as Stamford and in Stamford itself the local pottery industry seems to have died out in the early/mid thirteenth century and these limestone-tempered wares were used in its place.

[36] Lyveden/Stanion ware has been found in Trondheim (see Reed 1990), at the Bryggen, Bergen (identified by the author in 1986—unpublished) and at Ribe. In both cases the ware forms a minute fraction of the pottery assemblage (a single sherd in the case of Ribe, see Vince 1995a). A number of sherds illustrated in Carlsson 1982 (fig.49) are also most likely to be Lyveden/Stanion ware, although their identity should be confirmed and their frequency established.

[37] The Bourne pottery industry started off in the late twelfth or early thirteenth century producing Bourne wares A to C, similar to those from Lyveden and Stanion, although without the applied clay and stamped decoration of the latter. The later ware, Bourne D, had a wider distribution, being common in both Lincoln and Boston, for example in the early post-medieval period.

Similarly, the later thirteenth- and fourteenth-century potteries supplying London seem only rarely to have supplied the export market. London-type ware products of the mid- to late-thirteenth century were found at the Bryggen in Bergen, but must have formed a much smaller proportion of the contemporary assemblages than London-area products had in the later twelfth and early thirteenth centuries.[38] A few sherds of Mill Green ware were found at the Bryggen, but apparently nowhere else in Scandinavia. Similarly, a few sherds of Kingston-type ware, a Surrey whiteware, were found at Bergen but have not yet been reliably identified elsewhere.[39] Clearly, the London area too ceased to be a pottery export centre on any scale during the second half of the thirteenth century. However, in contrast with Stamford, there is no suggestion that the port of London itself was any less active in this period, although a case could be made for it being outstripped by that of Bruges.

In their place, we find sherds of Scarborough ware, "Grimston-type" ware and other eastern and north-eastern English wares. Finds of Scarborough ware are common on coastal sites from south-eastern England right the way up along the east coast from London in the south to Caithness in the north and thence on to Norway.[40] They were probably carried along a

[38] Blackmore & Vince 1994.

[39] Kingston-type ware is a whiteware, however, and sand-tempered glazed wares with a white or off-white body are notoriously difficult to characterise.

[40] The classification of Scarborough ware is a complex problem. Excavations in the port of Scarborough itself have demonstrated that potting was a long-lived industry, starting in the twelfth century and continuing throughout the thirteenth century, at which point the industry died. However, "Scarborough Ware" is found at numerous east coast ports, as well as further inland, and is usually found in late thirteenth/early fourteenth-century assemblages. Either (a) the industry existed for ca. 100 years supplying local needs and then developed into an exporting industry at the end of the thirteenth century or (b) there is a discrepancy in the dating, either at Scarborough or at the consumer sites or (c) vessels identified as "Scarborough ware" include examples from other, later industries. A symposium on the problems of dating and characterisation of Scarborough ware was published in *Medieval Ceramics* 6, 1982: P. G. Farmer and N. C. Farmer, "The Dating of the Scarborough Ware Pottery Industry", pp. 66-87; Trevor Pearson, "The Dating of Scarborough Ware", pp. 88-93; Gareth Watkins, Charles Murray and Asbjørn Herteig, "Scarborough Ware from Hull, Aberdeen and Bergen: some Brief Comments on the Farmers' Chronology", pp. 94-99; P. G. Farmer and N. C. Farmer, "Summary and Conclusions", pp. 100-110; D. F. Williams and R. Tomber, "Ap-

linear trade route, in which manufactured goods and cereals were travelling northwards in return for dried fish and timber. There are very few examples indeed of these thirteenth/fourteenth-century English wares on sites which would have been supplied via the Öresund, although they do occur at both Ribe and Lödöse,[41] demonstrating that this trade route was not totally limited to western Norway.

The Rhineland

It is not possible to discuss late thirteenth- and fourteenth-century pottery trade into Scandinavia or the Baltic without mentioning Rhenish wares. Large quantities of Siegburg stonewares are found on all Scandinavian and Baltic sites of this period together with red-slipped stonewares which might be either from Langewehe, in the Meuse valley, or northwestern German sources. Few reliable reports of their frequency at these sites exist though, nor of how that frequency changed through time.[42]

Conclusions

Before the middle of the twelfth century there is little archaeological evidence for trade around the North Sea and between the North Sea littoral and the Baltic, and none at all for the movement of pottery. This trade seems to have fluctuated in direction and intensity and in the period immediately before ca. 1150 there is very little evidence at all. Whether this should be interpreted as an absence of contact or not remains an open question.

From the second half of the twelfth century onwards we see evidence for the importation to the Baltic and Scandinavia of pottery from a number of sources: Low Countries; Northern French; Eastern English and Rhenish. Of these, the strongest is undoubtedly the Low Countries, although work is still required to establish how much of this material came from Bruges

---

pendix 1: Petrological Examination of Scarborough Ware and other Medieval Pottery", pp. 111-119.

41 Carlsson 1982. The illustrated sherds of "Grimston/Scarborough type" ware from Lödöse include at least one likely Scarborough ware rim (fig 49, top right).

42 A major survey of the stonewares, and other later medieval ceramic imports in countries bordering the Baltic Sea has recently been completed by David Gaimster, Dept. of Medieval and Later Antiquities, British Museum.

and how much from other centres, in present-day Netherlands or even Scandinavia itself. Low Countries ceramics were also the probable inspiration for local pottery production in southern Scandinavia although here too much of the detail remains to be established. For example, can we demonstrate whether these new industries were formed by Danish or Swedish potters adopting forms and techniques by examining Flemish imports or whether the first glazed ware potters were actually immigrant artisans?

Rhenish pottery was next in importance. It had formed a sizeable proportion of non-local pottery at Hedeby in the eleventh century and in the early levels at Schleswig in the later eleventh or early twelfth century and grew in importance from there. Deposits dating to the fourteenth and fifteenth centuries in Ribe, Lund and Bergen, for example, were all dominated by Rhenish stonewares. One would imagine that the source of this stoneware within the Hanseatic world would be Lübeck, with the pottery coming overland from Hannover. Given the scale of production at Siegburg and in the countryside surrounding Cologne, it is likely that here we are looking at an organised export trade, one that had its origins back in the late eighth century with Badorf ware and continued without a break into the eighteenth century with Westerwald stoneware.

The wares which I have been tracking through Scandinavia, mainly from England and France, were very rarely found in anything like the quantities of either the Low Countries or Rhenish wares. It is probable that many in the Baltic were incidental imports, perhaps entering the Öresund as part of the personal belongings of crew or passengers. At Bergen, however, it is difficult to believe that there was not a trade in English pottery. Nevertheless, I doubt whether there was ever a cargo composed solely, or even mainly, of pottery vessels. These pots, I imagine, were slipped into mixed cargoes to make sure that a ship did not sail to the Baltic or the western Scandinavian coasts with empty space in its hold. If this was the case, then, it seems strange that we should find a distinct shift in the sources of pottery. Firstly, there is less pottery exported from river ports such as Stamford or London, and in their place are pottery vessels exported from coastal ports, such as King's Lynn, Hull and Scarborough. Secondly, there is a northwards shift in the location of the exporting ports. These patterns probably indicate a real difference in the organisation of trade between England, Scandinavia and the Baltic in the mid-thirteenth century to account for this change.

The Export of Limestone and Limestone Fonts from Gotland during the Thirteenth and Fourteenth Centuries[1]

Lars Berggren

It has long been known that stone products were exported from Gotland in the Middle Ages, primarily to the countries round the Baltic Sea. However, the scope of this activity and its economic significance have been seriously underestimated. The exports appear to have started on a very small scale in the second half of the twelfth century, consisting initially of a few special articles, chiefly baptismal fonts, which were probably carved according to precise instructions from individual customers. In the first half of the thirteenth century there was a striking rise in volume and a diversification of the product range; to meet the demands of a growing and increasingly anonymous market, the forms were simultaneously simplified and manufacture was standardised. Production appears to have reached its highest level in the period ca. 1250–1350, after which volumes declined and the product range was narrowed.

Anyone who regularly reads literature such as exhibition catalogues, church inventories, or similar works with a large proportion of medieval items will have been struck by the high frequency of mentions of objects of Gotlandic stone—and hence been able to draw the conclusion that the total volume of the export must have been very large. Yet no one hitherto has studied the medieval Gotlandic stone industry from this point of view.[2] The only category of Gotlandic export product that has attracted the attention of scholars to any extent is the baptismal fonts, the most distinctive article of the medieval stone industry. Although these fonts accounted for only a part of the range, however, they were exported to mainly the same desti-

[1] All the photographs and maps in this article are by the author. A preliminary typescript version of this paper has been available to Scandinavian colleagues since 1997.

[2] In three newspaper articles, however, William Anderson (1934) recognised the wide range of Gotlandic limestone exports.

nations and categories of purchaser as other articles, which means that the problems and questions that apply to the fonts are also relevant to the entire export sector of the stone industry. This study will therefore start with a few notes on the medieval stone industry in general, followed by a brief account of the history and results of earlier font research, with special emphasis on the parts that are relevant for Gotlandic stone exports and the design of the research project of which this article is one result. After this comes a presentation of the different types of fonts and a discussion of some of the problems associated with their dating. The rest of the article is then devoted to various aspects of the Gotlandic stone exports: their scope and volume, the organisation of manufacture, trade, and transports.

THE MEDIEVAL STONE INDUSTRY

Regular long- and medium-distance trade in large quantities of stone appears to have started in a number of different places in Europe in the twelfth and thirteenth centuries.[3] Some of this was good building stone, which satisfied the static requirements of the increasingly large and technically advanced building projects of the times, while some was homogeneous and easily shaped stone, which could be worked into the complex architectural and sculptural forms required by the new stylistic ideal; finally, other types of stone were in demand for their aesthetic properties, their colour and structure.

An early example of large-scale export of building stone is tufa from Andernach which, at least from the end of the twelfth century and into the second half of the thirteenth century, was transported down the Rhine to Deventer and Utrecht. There it was sold on and then used, among other purposes, to build hundreds of parish churches in the coastal region between the estuary of the Schelde in Flanders and Esbjerg on the west coast of Jutland. No less than 55 Danish churches were built wholly or partly of tufa from Andernach in the period ca. 1175–1250. The advantages of this stone were that it was easy to quarry, that it could be shaped by simple tools, and that because of its location by the Rhine and its low specific

[3] Soapstone from Norway and/or south-west Sweden, shaped in a wide variety of forms—vessels, ovens, baptismal fonts, etc.—was exported to Denmark and the southern part of the Baltic from the ninth century on (Skjølsvold 1961; Resi 1979); the same goes for millstones from Hyllestad (Carelli & Kresten 1997).

weight it was relatively easy to transport. It was a cheap but crude material, which was primarily imported to areas with little or no usable stone of their own; it was not suitable for elaborate architectural forms or sculptures.[4]

In contrast, the fine-grained limestones from the quarries in Caen, in north-western France, were admirably suited for precisely these purposes, and providing raw material for the most advanced buildings and the most refined sculptures of the time. Most of it, of course, stayed in France, but exports across the Channel to England probably reached considerable volumes not long after 1066 and then continued throughout the period.[5] The dense black-blue limestone from Namur was used locally for a whole range of purposes but, primarily in the form of a few specialised products, it was also traded over long distances. In the twelfth and thirteenth centuries, baptismal fonts were exported to France, England and the North Sea area; and during the following centuries finely worked slabs—with or without monumental brasses mounted on them—became the major article. These slabs, obviously produced in very large numbers, found their way as far as to Scotland and Scandiavia and far into the Baltic area.[6] The hard limestones from Purbeck in England and Buda/Esztergom in Hungary were in demand chiefly for their aesthetic qualities; the former could be polished and serve as a surrogate for the multicoloured marbles of the Mediterranean, while the latter, because of its deep red colour, was a cheap substitute for the symbolically charged but difficult-to-work porphyry.[7]

[4] On tufa from Andernach, see Haiduck 1992: 31ff. and Feveile 1996: 31–51.

[5] On Caen limestone, see Musset 1985: 219–235.

[6] On limestone from Namur/Tournai, see for instance Dunning 1944, Courtoy 1946, Tollenaere 1957, and Drake 1993; on the Flemish monumental brasses in the Baltic area, see Krüger 1992. Although the influences from the architecture and sculpture of Westphalia were felt all over the Baltic area very early, the Baumberg sandstone itself was exported in considerable quantities only towards the end of the fourteenth century, and then almost exclusively in the form of finished sculpture (Karrenbrock 1989: 497–505).

[7] Red Hungarian limestone was first quarried at the end of the twelfth century and was frequently used until the 1270s, when the deposits were exhausted. New deposits were quarried in the mid fourteenth century and the stone products—mostly grave slabs and architectural sculpture—were spread over a wider area; besides present-day Hungary and Austria they are found in Slovakia, Poland, Romania, Croatia, and Bosnia (Lövei 1992: 3–28). On the well-known limestone from Purbeck, also known as Purbeck marble, see Dru Drury 1948: 74–98, Leach 1978, and Blair 1991: 41–56.

In the Baltic region, Gotland was unrivalled as a centre of the stone industry; the island's total production probably also exceeded that of its contemporary Central and Western European counterparts. The rich supply of Silurian sandstones and limestones, suitable for a multitude of different sculptural and architectural purposes, together with the position as one of the most important junctions in Baltic trade, made Gotland into an easily accessible and relatively cheap supplier of stone to all the countries round the Baltic Sea.

Among the first stone products that left Gotland were a number of Romanesque fonts, dated to the second half of the twelfth century, and mostly sculpted in the soft, fine-grained sandstone from Burgsvik in the south of the island (Plate 7, Figure 17). During the same period, the limestone blocks that are used in a number of church doorways in southern Scania (Skåne) must also have left the island—although it is uncertain in what

Plate 3. Hedeskoga, Scania, Sweden: south portal, partly executed in limestone from Gotland.

Plate 4. Lerdal, Norway: grave-slab, now conserved in the Historical Museum, Bergen.

Plate 5. Grönbaek, Zealand, Denmark: altar slab and colonnettes of Gotlandic limestone.

form, worked or unworked (Plate 3).[8] The start of the next century saw sandstone being abandoned for the harder limestone, while simultaneously the forms of the products were simplified, the product range was widened, and workshop work was standardised. Most of the export goods were either finished or half-finished, for example, fonts, slabs for graves and altars, and various architectural elements such as plinths, quoins, mullions, columns, capitals, flagstones and floor tiles (Plates 4, 5). From the start of the thirteenth century until at least the end of the fourteenth century, that is, for two hundred years, the Gotlandic stone industry dominated this market throughout the Baltic region; subsequently the volumes appear to have fallen drastically, and at the same time the production of the more advanced products ceased almost completely.[9]

[8] The portals in Sjörup, Västra Nöbbelöv, and Hedeskoga; cf. Sundnér 1995: 241ff.
[9] From the fifteenth to the eighteenth century, the export of worked limestone from Gotland seems to have consisted mainly of grave slabs and flagstones, not to mention burnt and unburnt limestone for the production of mortar, which was exported in considerable quantities at least from the thirteenth century onwards (cf. notes 31, 43, 50 below).

RESEARCH INTO FONTS

There are several reasons why baptismal fonts have been studied so intensively. Some scholars have probably been fascinated by the fact that so little is known about this large and in many ways interesting category of objects: not a single known font can be dated with certainty on the basis of an inscription or unambiguous indications, and the written sources tell us virtually nothing about their manufacture, acquisition, and installation. The fact that great toil was often expended on their design and decoration—in keeping with the central position of the font in medieval Christian symbolism and liturgy—also made them ideal objects on which modern-day art historians could exercise their skills in stylistic and iconographic analysis. In addition, the great age of the fonts, in combination with their extremely high degree of preservation,[10] made them a category of object that in the Darwinist spirit of the times could be systematised, categorised, and classified into neat evolutionary series which in turn could serve—it was hoped—as instruments for dating other objects, such as the church buildings themselves. For more than a hundred years, then, Scandinavian and German scholars, mostly art historians, have studied the Gotlandic fonts, mainly with a view to finding missing links, adjusting chronologies, and attributing individual fonts to masters, workshops, and schools.

It was in Germany that the first questions were formulated about the origin and place of manufacture of the Gotlandic fonts. In 1854 Friedrich Lisch had realised that the limestone fonts in Mecklenburg could not be made from indigenous stone, since there were no "Kalksteinblöcke von so grossem kubischen Inhalte". He also doubted that there could have been local artists "welche so schöne Werke ausführen konnten, zu denen nicht allein Steinmetzfertigkeit, sondern auch grosse Kunstbildung gehörte", and thus reached the conclusion either that the stone could have been imported in blocks and then been worked into fonts, or that finished fonts were imported. It was then natural to assume, he thought, that they came from Scandinavia, possibly Norway, which at that time was often considered a suitable *Urheim* for all Germanic culture.[11] In the 1880s, both Theodor

[10] Hallbäck 1978 reckons that about three-quarters of the original West Swedish, that is, primarily Romanesque, fonts are preserved. The figure should really be even higher for the Gothic fonts, since in many cases they replaced Romanesque ones. Cf. also Svanberg 1995: 122ff.

[11] Lisch 1854: 407.

Hach and Richard Haupt were fully aware that it was Gotlandic stone, but at least the former thought it likely that the actual carving had been done in the Lübeck region.[12] The first time the Gotlandic limestone fonts were seen as a separate group was in Ernst Sauermann's dissertation *Die mittelalterlichen Taufsteine der Provinz Schleswig-Holstein*, published in Flensburg in 1904, where the author argues that the fonts were carved in Gotland and exported as finished products to Schleswig-Holstein.[13]

All these scholars called for a total inventory of the fonts in question. This task was undertaken at the start of the twentieth century by the Swedish art historian Johnny Roosval. Some of his findings were presented in 1918 in his classic opus *Die Steinmeister Gottlands: Eine Geschichte der führenden Taufsteinwerkstätte des schwedischen Mittelalters, ihrer Voraussetzungen und Begleit-Erscheinungen*, although here the emphasis is almost entirely on the Romanesque sandstone fonts.[14] Roosval continued this work in the 1920s and 1930s but never achieved an assembled survey of all the fonts including the Gothic limestone ones. In the 1940s the task was taken over by his pupil and co-worker Oscar Reutersvärd, who for several decades collected and published more material. In the study *The Fountain of Paradise and the "Paradise Fonts" of Gotland* (1967) and a number of smaller articles he dealt with specific problems connected with various types of fonts and the interpretation of individual iconographic elements.[15]

In actual fact, traditional research, working primarily with stylistic and iconographic comparisons, focusing on the construction of evolutionary chains of development, may be said to have reached the end of the road

12 Hach 1882a: 432–434, Hach 1882b: 445-446, and Haupt 1888: 196.

13 Sauerman 1904: 15ff.

14 Roosval's *Die Steinmeister* is still the most comprehensive survey of medieval Gotlandic stone sculpture in general, and of the Romanesque baptismal fonts in particular; the Gothic limestone fonts, however, receive very limited attention. Influenced by Roosval's work, Richard Haupt then presented the Gotlandic limestone fonts as a special group in the later volumes of his inventory *Die Bau- und Kunstdenkmäler der Provinz Schleswig-Holstein* (vol. 5, 1924: 29ff., 597ff., and vol. 6, 1925: 21ff., 526ff.). Gotlandic fonts in Germany were also dealt with by Annemarie Mehnert in her dissertation *Mittelalterliche Taufsteine in Vorpommern* (1934); those in Denmark were listed by Mackeprang 1941 (although his identifications of the stone are not always correct). Pudelko 1932 treated Gotlandic fonts in a separate chapter, but had nothing to say about the material.

15 See Reutersvärd 1967, 1969, and 1975.

with a couple of dissertations from the mid 1970s.[16] Some of the reasons for this became clear when Annette Landen at the start of the 1980s surveyed all that had so far been written about the Gotlandic limestone fonts —including archival material from different countries, institutions, and individuals, as well as Oscar Reutersvärd's unpublished manuscripts and annotations. It turned out that, of the roughly 800 fonts stated in various places to be of Gotlandic limestone, little more than fifty had been presented with information on dimensions, iconography, type of stone, and location. For the vast majority there were only isolated data, and checks showed that these were often highly unreliable, sometimes downright wrong. In many cases, different writers provided contradictory information about the stone and the original or current location; often it was not even possible to identify the fonts they described or to confirm their existence. In other words, the whole discussion of the typology and relative chronology of the fonts had been conducted on the basis of limited and unreliable information.

It was also clear from the inventory what difficulties had been involved, and to some extent still are, in the study of export fonts. Their large number and wide geographical spread made it impossible in practice for a single scholar to acquire first-hand knowledge of more than a limited part of the stock, and at the same time the amount of available secondary information was minimal and the quality of what did exist was often dubious. In particular, there is always uncertainty about the grounds on which a certain font is classified in the literature as "Gotlandic". It may mean that it is ascribed to a Gotlandic stonemaster, that it is generally speaking of "Gotlandic type", or that the stone itself has been identified as Gotlandic. It is very unusual, however, for the classification to be based primarily on the stone; on the contrary, it can be observed that the lack of geological knowledge on the part of the scholars has mostly led to fonts of "typically Gotlandic" form being described as Gotlandic regardless of the actual provenance of the stone, while atypical examples of blatantly obvious Gotlandic stone are rarely attributed to the same category.[17] This methodological confusion did not just fundamentally distort the picture of Gotlandic font

[16] Fåhreus 1974 and Stenström 1975 both focus on specifically Gotlandic conditions and problems, considering the problem of exports only to a limited extent.

[17] It is common that both grey and red Gotlandic limestones are mistaken for granite. Examples are the fonts in Satrup (Schleswig-Holstein), Bad Doberan, Eickelberg, Gnoien, Gross Brütz (Mecklenburg).

production as a whole, but also made it impossible to compile a reliable inventory of fonts.[18]

Having studied this maze of mutually contradictory theories, terminologies, and classifications accumulated over the years, Annette Landen and I decided to try to tackle the font problem from a partly new angle. The project we started in 1993 had the aim of documenting all medieval fonts of *Gotlandic limestone*, whatever their type, style, or other more or less subjective criteria. In practice, this meant that virtually every single font of allegedly Gotlandic type or extraction had to be examined *in situ* to determine the provenance of the stone, but in methodological terms it was nevertheless a gain, since the right of each individual font to be included in the group could be objectively established. The basic condition, however, was that the Gotlandic limestone could be identified as such using relatively simple and cheap methods.

The bedrock of Gotland consists almost entirely of marine sediments deposited during the Silurian period (435–395 million years before the present) to give a total thickness of about 600 metres. At that time, the sea-bottom that would later be Gotland lay close to the equator and the sediment was built up in shallow, warm marine environments similar to what is found today around the coast of Australia.[19] Layer sequences from the same period are preserved at a number of places on earth, but in Europe they are virtually restricted to Gotland.[20] Among geologists the island is rightly famous for its incredible wealth of well-preserved fossils, especially crinoids, stromatoporids, bryozoans, and different variants of early tabulate and rugose corals (Plate 6). Since most of these fossils are comparatively easy to identify, they are also of crucial significance for the implementation of the font project: with their help even a trained amateur can decide with

[18] The inability to distinguish between the provenance of the stone and that of the stonemaster has led to a number of curious consequences. In his study of the so-called "paradise fonts", for example, Oscar Reutersvärd lets the font in Strängnäs Cathedral give its name to a special group of fonts as being "most representative" of its category (Reutersvärd 1967: 73 and 82f.). The problem is that this particular font is *not* made of Gotlandic stone.

[19] On the Gotlandic bedrock, see for instance Hede 1960: 44–89, and Laufeld 1974a.

[20] There is also a part of the same stratigraphic sequence in Estonia, more precisely on the island of Saaremaa/Ösel, but for the present purposes it can probably be ignored.

Plate 6. Grönbaek, Zealand, Denmark: macrophoto of the font showing the limestone with parts of crinoids and stromatoporids.

reasonable certainty—often with the naked eye, or at least with a simple hand microscope—whether a given stone comes from Gotland or not.[21]

The flora and fauna of the sea bed changed gradually in the course of the millions of years during which the sediments were deposited, which means that each individual layer in the sequence has its own set and composition of typical inhabitants. Moreover, since the whole bedrock is gently tilted so that the oldest layers are exposed on the north-west coast and the youngest ones in the south (Figure 17), it is normally possible to determine at least in which of the main zones a block was quarried. In many cases the precision may be much greater: some kinds of stone that were popular for fonts occur in only one or two very narrow belts running across the island.

Armed with this knowledge, we have now worked our way through over two-thirds of the fonts. A consequence of applying the stone criterion is that more than 100 fonts previously classified as Gotlandic have been eliminated, but since just as many Gotlandic fonts have been identified as such for the first time, the total number of registered fonts today remains largely unchanged.

[21] Occasionally, we have to deal with blocks containing no identifiable fossils at all, but then there is the further possibility of having them examined by an expert in micro-fossil analysis. This method is described in Laufeld 1974b: 4ff.

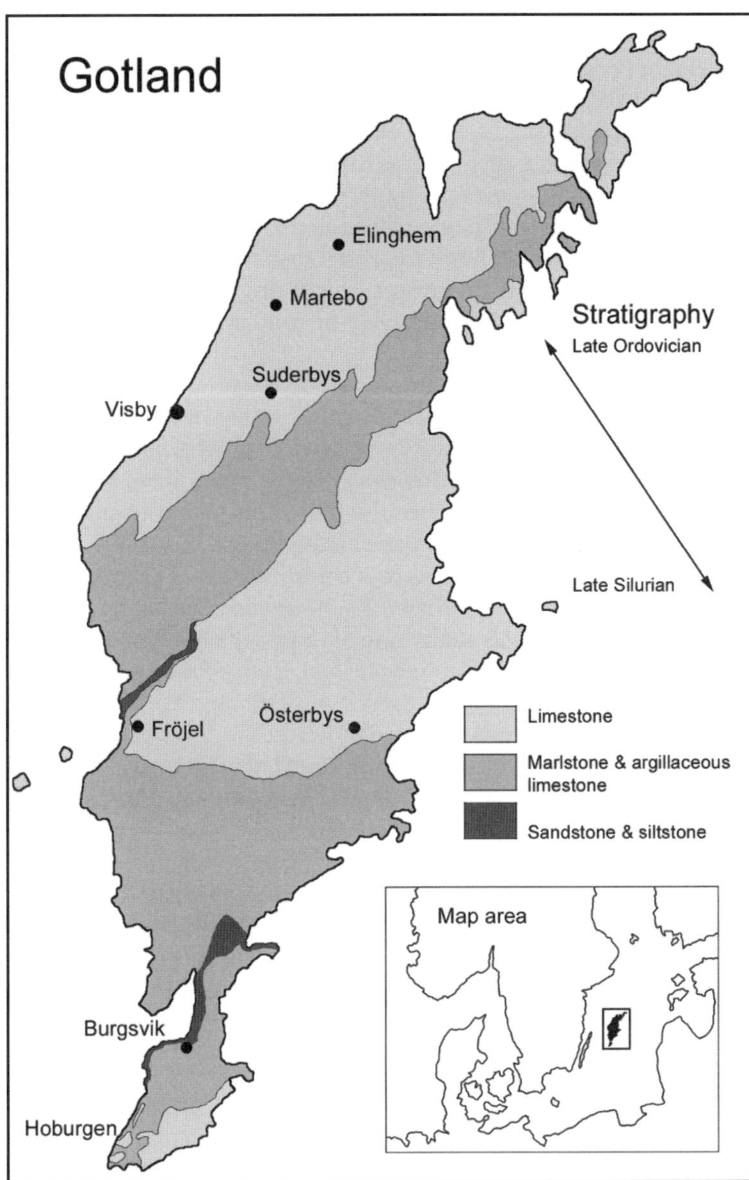

Figure 17. Map of Gotland showing main rock areas and places mentioned in the text.

Font Types and Their Dating

There is no doubt broad agreement that fonts were exported from Gotland during most of the Middle Ages, from around the middle of the twelfth century and probably into the fifteenth century. However, their chronology and division into types are disputed, although few would question the rough classification into Romanesque fonts, mostly cut from sandstone, and Gothic fonts, almost exclusively made of limestone. In the following presentation, the typological division has been simplified so that the roughly 800 fonts are divided into eight main groups, the dating and relative chronology of which can be regarded as relatively uncontroversial.

1. The first group consists of the Romanesque fonts, about which more has probably been written than about any other group of fonts. There are many descriptions, attributions to different masters or workshops, theories of their origin and dating and position in variously constructed series, but here we have found it sufficient to ascribe the whole group to the period ca. 1150–1210. The fonts in question are mostly found in local Gotlandic contexts, but they were also exported to a certain extent. There are about 50 such fonts altogether in Gotland and 25–30 outside the island. Most of them are made of relatively soft sandstone of Burgsvik type, but not all—as earlier scholars automatically assumed. In fact, many Romanesque fonts which are said in the literature to be carved in sandstone are really wholly or partly made of fine-grained, much harder, limestone.[22] An example is the famous font by master Sigraf in Åkirkeby on Bornholm (Plate 7): the bowl, decorated with flat reliefs, is carved of limestone, while the material of the three-dimensionally sculptured base is sandstone.

2. The second main group consists of the late Romanesque fonts, dated between ca. 1200 and 1250, which in turn comprise three sub-groups: fonts with figural scenes (28), fonts with convex fields twisted round the bowl (6), and fonts with arcade bows on the sides of the bowl (16). The figural fonts are still conceived and carved in a decidedly Romanesque way, but

[22] Differences in workability have been overemphasised. Romanesque sculptors often used fine-grained limestones, similar in structure to sandstone, or they chose calcareous sandstones. Unfortunately, the presumed differences in workability have often been allowed to play a large role in the dating discussion in which it has been supposed that the use of sandstone always indicates a more primitive stage representing low tool development.

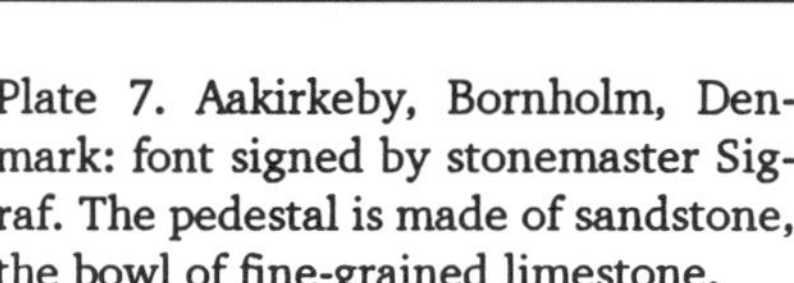

Plate 7. Aakirkeby, Bornholm, Denmark: font signed by stonemaster Sigraf. The pedestal is made of sandstone, the bowl of fine-grained limestone.

Plate 8. Borrby, Scania, Sweden: late Romanesque font, ascribed to "Calcarius Secundus".

they differ from their predecessors in their more restrained and surface-bound idiom, and because they are made of limestone (Plate 8). The "spiral frieze fonts" (*virvelfrisfuntar*) are viewed by several scholars as precursors of the later so popular "paradise fonts" (see below), since a couple of the gadrooned bowls are placed on pedestals of Romanesque type. The characteristic feature of "arcade fonts" is a simple, flat Romanesque arcade running round the side of the bowl; the relative lack of further decoration, together with the usually clearly Gothic profile of their pedestals, determine their place in the chronology as predecessors of the next main group.

3. In the third main group containing two different types of chalice-shaped fonts dated ca. 1200– 1275, the tendency to flatness was carried to its extreme. Stripped of all plastic surface decoration, their simple hemispherical or biconical bowls (41 and 113 respectively) and slender, elegantly swung pedestals have smooth, sometimes even polished, surfaces

Plate 9. Elinghem, Gotland, Sweden: font on its original podium in the deserted church.

(Plate 9). The whole group is fairly homogeneous, and the individual fonts stray but little from the master design(s). Although their size may vary considerably, not so the proportions. Here it should also be noted that with the chalice fonts, the design of the pedestals was set for all the subsequent font types; it was to remain almost unaltered throughout the period while the form of the bowls changed.

4-6. Some time around the middle of the thirteenth century, the production of the plain bowls seems to have ceased, and a new form—also borrowed from chalices—was introduced. Their most characteristic features—the convex fields separated by ribs on the side of the bowl, and the scotia just below the rim—clearly belong in the domain of sumptuous metalwork. A number of different denominations are used for these fonts: in Sweden they are usually called *paradisfuntar* (paradise fonts), in Germany the bowls are referred to as *Muschelcuppen*, and other names are used in other countries.[23] Totalling 289 more or less completely preserved specimens, they supposedly dominated the production for the rest of the thirteenth and probably also the first half of the fourteenth century. Because of the length of their period in

[23] The designation "paradise font" (*paradisfunt*) was introduced by Oscar Reutersvärd in the first study of these fonts (1967). One of Reutersvärd's arguments for this designation refers to the prime characteristic of these fonts, the border of convex fields, which he claims is a motif found on classical paradise vases and incorporated in early Christian iconography—often together with the tree of life, the cross, and so on—as a symbol of eternal life. The Danish archaeologist Mackeprang (1941) used the term "sepal fonts" (*Bægerbladsfonte*), while the oldest designation, "mussel cups" (*Muschelcuppen* in German, *musselcuppor* in Swedish), was introduced by Roosval in 1918. See also Landen 1993.

Plate 10. Emmelsbüll, Schleswig-Holstein, Germany: four-lobed Paradise font.

Plate 11. Nordborg, Als, Jutland, Denmark: detail of the Paradise font.

production and the comparatively large size of the category, these fronts have been subdivided into three separate groups.

In the beginning the bowls were normally rather high, often somewhat more than hemispherical, but later they became increasingly lower and wider. At the same time, the shape of the upper end of the convex fields went through a development parallel to that in architecture: the rounded arches (group 4: Plates 10, 11) first changed into pointed (group 5: Plate 12), then trefoil arches (group 6: Plates 13, 14). Discs, roses, and other forms were introduced as a kind of capital at the spot where the ribs widened into spandrels, and the spandrels themselves were filled with a variety of ornaments, mainly geometrical—trefoils and quatrefoils—but also simple leaves and the like; occasionally one may find small, rather crudely executed animals and human heads. Group 4 is constituted by the 152 fonts with rounded, group 5 by the 45 with pointed, and group 6 by the 92 with trefoil (or more elaborated) arches.

Plate 12. Asnaes, Zealand, Denmark: Paradise font.

Plate 13. Koszalin, Poland: Paradise font. Cfr. Plate 14.

Plate 14. St. Giles, Bruges, Belgium: bowl of a Paradise font. Cfr. Plate 13.

Plate 15. Lubiana, Poland: the bowl of a Fröjel font (now in the National Museum, Szczecin).

7. After the middle of the fourteenth century the dominance of the paradise fonts was broken by the introduction of a number of new types, here classed together as main group seven. Most of them were relatively wide and shallow, some of them round or polygonal, without any kind of ornament, but the majority are polygonal and figured in flat relief. These late fonts may be divided into five sub-groups, the first of which is made up of 12 uncommonly wide and shallow bowls; the second contains 24 non-figurative, polygonal ones; the third is constituted by 5 rather thick, sturdy bowls, decorated with a mixture of stars, wheel-crosses, lions, and lilies—some of which are demonstrably made with the same template; in the fourth, the 5 bowls are encircled by rows of apostles, standing frontally, divided by columns. In the fifth sub-group, counting 32 items, we find the enigmatic fonts of the Fröjel type, named after the famous font in a small village church in southern Gotland.

If the customary dating of this last group, to ca. 1400, is correct at all, their decoration must be interpreted as a deliberate revival of the Romanesque idiom.[24] Processions of strange creatures march round the bowls:

[24] According to Roosval (1928: 53ff.) these fonts show a certain change of style in Gotlandic sculpture, which he calls "contra-Gothic" and dates to the period 1335-

Plate 16. Wilamòw, Poland: polygonal font of the Fröjel type. Cfr. Plate 15.

quadrupeds with hooves or paws, with or without horns, often with segmented bodies, and with tongues and tails ending in luxuriant palmettes; there are fantastic birds with huge beaks and claws, and sometimes ludicrous grinning faces—half human, half animal. They are mostly placed in fields bordered by ribs and arches decorated with bands of pellets or nailheads (Plates 15, 16).

8. Last, but unfortunately not least, we have a group of fonts and parts of fonts which, although they are all made of Gotlandic limestone and obviously belong to the period 1250–1400, cannot be assigned with any certainty to any of the above groups. These objects can be subdivided into the following categories: (a) occasional bowls (whole or fragmentary, in some cases with their pedestal) with a form and decoration differing from the types described above (27 items), and (b) only pedestals or parts of pedestals (139).

As has already been pointed out, the dating of the font types is uncertain, for several reasons. Since there are virtually no written sources available, scholars have tried to anchor the relative chronology, arrived at by means of stylistic analyses, in real time by grasping at a few highly questionable historical straws. One such has been the occurrence of discharge holes. On the basis of a couple of dates for the dedication of churches in Gotland, and proceeding from the hypothesis that fonts were acquired in connection with the building (or rebuilding) of these churches, it has been thought possible to establish that fonts made before ca. 1250 had holes to

---

1370. Oscar Reutersvärd speaks of a "Romanesque Renaissance", also anti-Gothic in character, and would date the group as late as around 1425-30 (Reutersvärd 1969: 107–114, and Reutersvärd 1975: 37–40).

allow christening water to be drained, while fonts made after that time were not provided with this facility.[25] Although the initial dating is dubious, and although there is no evidence whatever that any such change occurred anywhere but in Gotland, fonts—to say nothing about churches—all over Scandinavia have been dated according to this criterion. The fact is, however, that the presence or absence of discharge holes does not follow the typology of the fonts, whether in Gotland or elsewhere, and the problem that arises then is that either the dating of the font types is incorrect or else the question of discharge holes is irrelevant.[26]

Another straw to which scholars have clung, one that concerns the relative as well as the absolute chronology, is the idea that font bowls some time after the mid thirteenth century started to become increasingly wide and shallow, and that the relation between the width and depth of the bowl can give a rather precise indication of the age of the font. Behind this reasoning there is once again a loosely based assumption, namely, that there was a general switch at this time from baptism by total immersion (*immersio*) to merely pouring water over the head (*affusio*), and that the bowls consequently did not need to be made so deep. The reasoning is problematic, not just because there are numerous shallow Romanesque

[25] Fonts are normally thought of as having been acquired in connection with the building or rebuilding of a stone church. This may be the case but it is far from certain. Many such churches at this time had already had a predecessor built of timber, for which the font may very well have been procured. It also happens not infrequently that a church takes over an older font from another church, for example, if the latter has acquired a new font or if parishes have been amalgamated.

[26] Apart from our own observations during the inventory work, it may be mentioned that the numerous Romanesque granite fonts in Denmark usually lack a discharge hole; the same applies to the large group of Jutlandic fonts, dated to the twelfth century, with bowls resembling those of the Gotlandic paradise fonts. In Norway there is moreover a group of five hourglass-shaped fonts of wood, dated by C14 to 1150–1350, all of which have discharge holes; a sixth wooden font, with no discharge hole, was made after the Reformation. This piece of information has kindly been communicated by Mona Bramer Solhaug (February 1998), who carried out the analysis in connection with research for her dissertation on medieval baptismal fonts in Norway (*Middelalderens døpefonter i Norge*). In her studies she has also found that a large proportion—surprisingly large in view of the significance attached to the phenomenon—of the Romanesque fonts lack a discharge hole; at the same time, many of the Gothic ones have such a hole (her studied group includes about 200 stone fonts).

bowls and just as many deep Gothic ones, but also because the basic assumption cannot be proved. The sources adduced by the proponents of the thesis are mostly post-Reformation, whereas contemporary sources provide evidence for both forms of baptism.[27] In fact, it seems that both variants —and also several intermediate forms—were practised at the same time in different places; and we know nothing about the practice in Gotland. The whole question is further complicated if we adopt the generally held view that the basic form of the Gothic fonts was modelled on the communion chalice. In the first half of the thirteenth century chalices were wide and shallow, but in the second half of that century they were made almost hemispherical, and then in the fourteenth century they became higher and deeper,[28] thus describing a course of development diametrically opposed to that presumed for the fonts.

From this it need not be concluded that the entire established chronology must be rejected. It is probably correct in broad outline, although some of the grounds for it may be highly questionable. What must be emphasised instead is that, even if we should succeed in exactly dating individual fonts, we must stick to the broad lines when it comes to dating the types. Research into fonts and other stone products has mostly proceeded from the notion of small, exclusive production taking place in a few workshops where changes in fashion had a great impact, if not quickly then at least contemporaneously, so that the different types succeeded one another in good evolutionary order. Until a decade or two into the thirteenth century there may be some foundation in reality for this picture, but for the

[27] The evidence for immersion baptism, taken in the strict and total sense of the term, dwindles on examination to the fact that several generations of scholars have repeated the story. Johnny Roosval, for example, an authority for generations of font scholars in several countries, was not the first person whose description of baptism relied on Olaus Petri's *Svensk döpelse* from 1529 (Roosval 1918: 6). This is not the place, however, for a detailed investigation of medieval practice and terminology; this will be found in the forthcoming project publication. It should nevertheless be pointed out (a) that the term *immersio* in the Middle Ages was scarcely interpreted as necessarily meaning *total* immersion, (b) that virtually all contemporary depictions of baptism show sprinkling and not immersion—which previous observers have explained away with reference to the difficulty of rendering immersion in pictures—and (c) that a large number of both Romanesque and Gothic fonts are far too small for total immersion (the inner diameter of the bowl is often less than 50 cm).

[28] Andersson 1963: 168ff.

time thereafter it is highly improbable. The reasons for this will be dealt with in the following pages.

DISTRIBUTION AND VOLUMES

Each dot on the map (Figure 18) represents a font of Gotlandic limestone. They are seen to be spread all round the Baltic and the North Sea, with the greatest concentrations in the Mälaren valley, medieval Denmark and the German Baltic coast; the geographical extremes are in Bergen, Tartu, Umeå, Wilamów and Bruges. The interesting thing here, however, is that the map shows more than the distribution of fonts. For each dot may also be said to

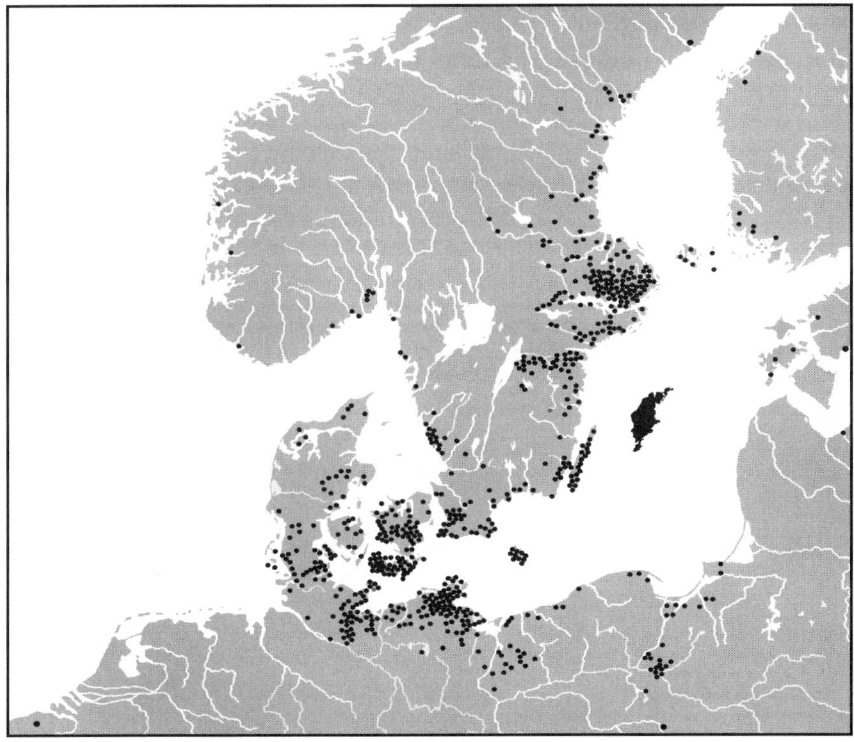

Figure 18. Distribution of Gotlandic limestone fonts. Each dot represents a whole or partially preserved font. Map: Lars Berggren and Annette Landen.

represent between one and twenty-five sizeable slabs of Gotlandic stone (Plate 4), and usually an occasional other object of the same material—perhaps just a piscina or a couple of colonnettes, but sometimes an entire socle or a whole floor.

This statement is founded on information collected in the course of our field studies of Gotlandic fonts, when we also register all objects of Gotlandic stone found in their vicinity. The reason for that is of course that the font and the other objects may have been part of the same order, perhaps the same delivery, and that, for example, a dated gravestone could help to give us a closer date for the font. As regards dating, this has not yet yielded results worth mentioning here, but a large quantity of data has been accumulated which says something about the scale and spread of Gotlandic stone exports as a whole.

In reality, neither the quantity nor the variety of products should surprise us. The structure and quality of Gotlandic limestone varies greatly, which means that one can find stone to suit the most diverse purposes. There are fine-grained, homogeneous kinds which, like the stone from Caen, are suitable for sculptures with fine details (Plates 11, 17). There are softer, more coarse-grained kinds that are excellent for ashlar, column drums, and architectural profiles. There are hard kinds in beds of precisely the right thickness for floor tiles, grave slabs, inscription tablets, altarpieces, and the like. More or less monochrome variants are found, from

Plate 17. Martebo, Gotland, Sweden: scene on the south doorway–the Harrowing of Hell.

Plate 18. Österbys, Gotland, Sweden: limestone quarry with beds of varying thickness.

white, via grey, greenish, yellowish, or bluish, to a deep red (which was used for high status purposes and probably, like the Hungarian stone mentioned at the beginning, probably served as a substitute for porphyry), but normally the stone is polychrome, with groundmass (*matrix*) and larger fossil parts in various colours.

The only thing that limits the usefulness of Gotlandic stone in certain contexts is that the beds are generally rather thin: a thickness of 50 cm is very uncommon, and 60 cm is rare indeed (Plates 18, 19).[29] This is incidentally the explanation why fonts are almost always made of three separate parts: the bowl is of course made in one part, while the pedestal is made of two (shaft and base). If the stone was not intended to take much structural pressure but had a mainly decorative function, as in the case of mullions and portal colonnettes, one could also use pieces of stone cut parallel to the sedimentation horizon.

[29] Limestone deposits are divided more or less horizontally into layers, generally known as beds, of different character which have been formed under varying conditions; the beds may vary considerably in form, colour and quality within the same quarry. The term "bed", or "quarry-bedded", is also used to denote the horizontal plane on which it should normally be used in building. Rockwell 1993: 150.

Plate 19. Suderbys, Gotland, Sweden: medieval limestone quarry–surface bed with wedge-holes and grooves for splitting blocks. The size of the blocks indicates that they were intended for column-drums.

As regards volumes in general, we may illustrate this with a few simple arithmetical examples. If we cautiously assume that the registered fonts—excluding the podium slabs that were not infrequently part of the ensemble (as shown in Plate 9)—originally weighed an average 0.7 tonnes, their total weight was roughly 500 tonnes.[30] The figure may not sound impressive, but if we reckon, equally cautiously, that for every exported font there were about five grave slabs, and that these weigh on average 4 tonnes (they normally lie between 1.5 and 15 tonnes), the result is of the order of 15,000 tonnes—and then we have only counted the slabs found in and around churches where there is a surviving Gotlandic font, that is, probably a relatively small part of the total. If one then begins to calculate other categories of artefact, one soon realises that the total amount of stone products that left Gotland during the period is a matter of not tens of

[30] This is calculated on the basis that one cubic metre of normal limestone equals three tonnes. The podium, normally consisting of two, sometimes three, circular slabs, weigh much more than the baptismal font itself. In Elinghem (Plate 9), for example, the two slabs weigh approximately 2.4 tonnes, or about four times as much as the font.

thousands but hundreds of thousands of tonnes.[31]

This leads to interesting consequences in at least two different areas. First: since fonts were just one product among many in a large-scale stone industry mainly geared to export, the view prevailing among art historians in particular—that font manufacture was an exclusive and small-scale pursuit—is untenable. Second: since the scope of the stone industry and the spread of its products were on a scale far exceeding what historians have hitherto reckoned with—a small number of artistic luxury products of very limited commercial interest—its economic significance in the framework of Baltic trade especially has to be radically revised.

The Transition Phase

If the customary datings of the different font types are combined with their geographical distribution, we arrive at some interesting, albeit scarcely surprising, results (Table 5). It may be observed that the relatively few Romanesque export fonts (group 1) almost only occur in eastern Sweden and Denmark, while a large number of the late Romaneque and early Gothic types (groups 2–3) are found in western Sweden, Denmark, the western part of the southern Baltic coast, and Norway; later groups (4–7) dominate in Germany and especially in today's Poland. Another thing that is immediately noticeable is the concentration in areas lacking their own usable stone (and hence a stone-working tradition), and how the market is successively expanded in a way that seems to follow the periods of Christianisation and church building in the different areas.

Of the Romanesque fonts, only 34 per cent were exported, while the figure for all the later groups is between 89 and 100 per cent. Also worth noting here is that just one stonemaster, working around 1200, accounts for the vast majority of exported Romanesque fonts.[32] It thus appears as if production, at least until a decade or so into the thirteenth century, was mainly geared to the domestic market in Gotland, but that there subsequently was a change to manufacture for export. This was due to several

[31] The calculation should also take into account the fact that a considerable part of the exported stone consisted of stone intended for burning to make mortar, or ready-burnt lime. All the sources cited below in note 43 also mention the import of *cymentum* and *lapis* or *lapides*.

[32] Of the 26 exported Romanesque fonts, no less than 18 (i.e., 70 per cent) could be attributed to the same stonemaster: Sigraf. Cf. Svanberg 1995: 205ff.

TABLE 5. FONTS OF GOTLANDIC STONE: GROUPS, NUMBERS, DISTRIBUTION

Groups	Total	Exported	Percent Exported
1: Romanesque fonts, mainly in sandstone, 1150-1210	76	26	34
2: Late Romanesque limestone fonts (3 sub-groups), 1200-1250	50	45	90
3: Chalice fonts (types 1-2), 1225-1275	154	137	89
4: Paradise fonts (types 1-2), 1250-1300	152	141	93
5: Paradise fonts (types 3-4), 1275-1325	45	45	100
6: Paradise fonts (types 5-6), 1300-1350	92	85	92
7: Late Gothic fonts (5 sub-groups), 1300-1400	78	74	95
8: Limestone fonts, or parts of such, not ascribable to any of the above groups, 1250-1400	166	158	95

Note that the time intervals for the different groups differ in size and that they overlap in time to varying extents. The table and the charts thus do not clearly show the changes in volume through time.

factors. One was probably that the first wave of church building in Gotland at the end of the twelfth century was ebbing out, which created employment problems for specialist stone craftsmen. However, the fact that trade in the same period was developing rapidly meant that transport became easier and cheaper and that the circle of potential customers was widened. The better economic conditions in combination with the simplified communication between commissioner and producer, meant that, for at least a small number of skilled stonemasters and their workshops, opportunities opened for export to new overseas markets.

During this phase it was still a matter of a relatively small number of objects, primarily fonts, manufactured to the wishes of demanding and well-off customers. The Romanesque fonts, with their fantastic world of distorted monsters and biblical scenes, must have commanded extremely high prices and appear to have been destined for churches with very high status, often associated with royal power or the upper spheres of the ecclesiastical hierarchy.[33] Since the early Gothic font types are largely found in the same areas as the Romanesque ones, it is conceivable that also in this phase there was more or less direct contact between the commissioner and the producer, but that this gradually changed to production for an anonymous market. To meet the increasing demand, the number of types was reduced, the design was simplified, and the production process was standardised; producing items at the special request of an individual commissioner became the exception rather than the rule.

In the first half of the thirteenth century we can observe how the Romanesque forms, although surviving, were successively simplified (group 2). This process has been described, above all by art historians, as being primarily the result of changes in the spiritual climate and the aesthetic ideals, from the uninhibited Romanesque to the ascetic Gothic (group 3). Yet it is probable that economic factors were at least as weighty; production at competitive prices for an anonymous market required simplification and rationalisation for greater efficiency, which led to the development of a small number of standard types. The producers arrived at these types, not so much by designing completely new forms as by gradually eliminating labour-intensive and expensive elements such as figural motifs and complex ornament. What remained was a number of already established basic forms: the gently rounded, smooth pedestal, the also smooth biconical or hemispherical bowls, with or without gadrooning—all easy to make for stoneworkers with a normal basic workshop training, and all viable on the market because of their familiar symbolic form, that of the chalice, and at a competitive price.[34] This development probably took place over a rela-

[33] For instance, Åkirkeby (Bornholm), Borby and Sörup (Schleswig-Holstein), Skelby (Falster).

[34] The change from the wealth of sculpted figures and ornament of the Romanesque to the completely smooth types in group 3 does not appear so abrupt if we remember that the latter were probably always painted (see also note 40 below), perhaps in a way that carried on the earlier tradition. It may also be noted that metal-imitating forms were in fashion; during the thirteenth century there is a proliferation all over Britain of imitation in pots of metal ewers: church cruets, lobed cups, acquamaniles, cooking pots with sharp everted rims, and so forth. Le Patourel (1979: 176) associates this with higher standards of living and consequent ambitions for status.

tively long period, during which the new standard types coexisted with increasingly simplified versions of the Romanesque idiom, and when manufacturer–customer relations were weakened and the required standards of sculptural skill were gradually lowered, although to differing extents in different workshops.

It is certainly no chance that the transition from sandstone to limestone took place at the start of this phase. The latter was easy to work into the simpler forms coming into fashion, its superior strength and resistance to weathering were of great importance for the huge quantity of architectural products, and, in addition, it was much better able than sandstone to withstand the strain that long transports inevitably involved. Nor is it likely due to chance that signatures disappear completely from fonts at this time. While it is true that the Romanesque stonemasters did not regularly sign their products, we have almost 800 limestone fonts and not one is signed.

MANUFACTURE

Despite the absence of written evidence, certain conclusions can nevertheless be drawn about the organisation of font manufacture. There can hardly have been centralised serial production in one or two places in Gotland, as some scholars seem to suppose, since the variations in fossil content clearly indicate that the stone of the fonts was quarried in a large number of different places. The island is in fact full of medieval quarries where stone for fonts may have been taken out; more than 500 have been registered to date, and since the stonemasons of the period normally used only stone from the topmost beds, there are probably many still to be discovered (Plate 19).[35] In addition, there are also large variations in the execution of

[35] In most cases, the quarriers simply cleared the surface from soil and unusable stone and took out whatever blocks they needed from the topmost bed. The aspect of such a quarry today is often no more than a slight depression in the ground the true nature of which is very easily overlooked. This notwithstanding more than 540 quarries are indicated on the geological maps published by *Sveriges Geologiska Undersökningar*, The Geological Survey of Sweden (for instance SGU Ser Aa 152, 1922; Aa 156, 1925; Aa 160 and 164, 1927; Aa 169, 1928; Aa 170, 1929; Aa 171, 1933; Aa 180, 1936, by H. Munthe et al.). Of these probably 34 quarries were of great importance for building stones of different types; see the survey of medieval quarries in Gotland made on behalf of *Riksantikvarieämbetet* (National Heritage Board), Stockholm: Falk 1989; Falk et al. 1989; Falk et al. 1990. Cf. also Shaikh et

the fonts: their proportions, decoration, and cutting differ much more than has previously been believed. There are in fact no two fonts with exactly the same dimensions, but one can notice a tendency for them to fall into small sub-groups of two, three, or up to a maximum of ten individuals. Within these small groups the fonts are almost identical in appearance, with just minor differences in proportions, profiles, and working, and the constituent stone is almost always so similar in structure and fossil content that it presumably not only comes from the same quarry but also from the same bed. A good example of such a group, although with an unusually wide geographical spread, is the one consisting of the four paradise fonts now in Bruges in Belgium, Koszalin in Poland, Pöide in Estonia, and Dagsberg in Östergötland, Sweden (Plates 13, 14).[36]

Yet not even where the similarities are greatest, and where one can actually presume that the same hand held the chisel, can we talk of serial production in the sense of exact reproduction as regards dimensions, proportions, and profiles. It is instead a matter of what almost any trained stoneworker could achieve more or less freehand, using what happened to be available in the quarry. This is suggested by the absence of exactly repeated forms, just as the high frequency of irregularities and makeshift solutions cannot be explained by irregularities or damage in the actual stone.[37] A standard type was followed, but not a precise model copied in slavish detail; only for a few fonts is there unambiguous evidence of the use of templates, and then only for figural scenes.[38] If manufacture was mainly the work of non-specialists relying on workshop knowledge and tradition, it could explain why several of the font types remained in production so long: each workshop stuck to its own standard model which was only slow-

al. 1990, 175–291; Löfvendahl 1995, 17–25.

36 Cf. Landen 1997: 91. Given that the font in Bruges appears as a solitaire on the distribution map, it is perhaps best to point out that objects of Gotlandic stone are by no means rare in that town.

37 An argument for freehand manufacture is that the bowls are often noticeably askew, that the fields can vary greatly in width, and that the dividing ribs are often not plumb. It was very common to make even complicated standard works without templates, both in classical times and in the Middle Ages (Rockwell 1993: 133ff.).

38 The trees and heraldic lions that occur on the so-called lily-tree fonts (which form part of group 7) are made using one and the same template (fonts in Roholte and Valløby in Zealand, Denmark, and in St Nicholas' Church in Stralsund, Vorpommern). Judging from traces on a substantial number of fonts, the stonecarvers much preferred the compasses as guiding instrument.

Plate 20. Suderbys, Gotland, Sweden: nearly finished holy water or font bowl abandoned in the quarry.

ly modified through time. In the design both of the basic model and of the individual fonts, of course, different workshops may have been inspired by different sources and different commissioners' wishes.

All the available evidence seems to suggest that the fonts were manufactured in small workshops which worked for a limited time at a particular quarry making fonts as well as other products. Judging by the finds in the quarries of several different products in varying degrees of working, it was normal that most of the work was carried out in or very close to the quarry. At several places one can find objects like the bowl in the quarry in Suderbys, a few kilometres from Visby (Plates 19, 20); for some reason it was abandoned at an advanced stage and left lying just a few metres from the place where the block had been quarried. Also at the same place are a number of column bases in varying degrees of finishing.

This does not mean, however, that all the products left the quarries, or even Gotland, in a finished state. As regards the fonts, Swedish art historians have generally preferred to assume that they all left the island in a fully finished state;[39] an assumption that seems quite natural once one has

[39] This view is held by both Roosval 1918 and Reutersvärd 1967. The former described the paradise fonts as a commodity which spread like "oil on the waterroads" (Roosval 1918: 202).

classified the fonts as exclusive *objets d'art*—which of course could not be thought of as having left the sculptor's studio unless fully completed! This line of reasoning was further strengthened by the (national romantic) belief that it was the aesthetic quality of the stone material itself that lay behind the international popularity of the fonts; since the intrinsic beauty of the stone only revealed itself after careful polishing, and the polishing process, besides requiring considerable professional skill, clearly counted among the ultimate artistic touches to the work. Consequently, painting was always seen as the dastardly work of later periods, and any defects in the stone-working were a result of secondary cutting.

It is scarcely possible to maintain this picture if we see the fonts as only one of many products of a large export industry, many of which for obvious reasons could not be completely finished until they were installed in their final location. While it is certainly true that *some* of the fonts were polished in a way that suggests a desire to emphasise the natural colour and structure of the stone, this applies above all to the rather few examples made of the relatively rare, intensely red stone that could aspire to imitate porphyry. The vast majority of the fonts are carved from much less interesting kinds of stone and were at most smoothed off with rough abrasives like sandstone. A too glossy surface was in fact seldom desirable, since most of the fonts were intended to be painted, and this finishing treatment was unlikely to have been done before the font had reached its final destination.[40] Moreover, quite a few fonts were probably delivered in a state that can only be described as semi-worked. An example is the font from Sæbø in Norway, where the heads and the torus of the shaft were never finished—probably because it cracked in transport (Plate 21). Another is found at Langå in Jutland; here the work was broken off after the stoneworker had incised the outline of a typical paradise frieze into the surface of the smooth, round bowl and had just carved out the first convex field. Finally, some fonts are so badly worked that they can hardly have been exported as such; the only reasonable explanation is that local inexperienced hands have tried their ability on semi-worked or rough-hewn blocks.[41]

[40] A very large proportion of the investigated fonts have remains of both priming and painting. Although it has not been possible to establish when the painting was done, there is a great deal to suggest that the frequently occurring red paint is original, or at least medieval. Haastrup 1995 gives an account of the scope of painted Romanesque fonts in Denmark. Cf. also Kryger 1977.

[41] The problems of determining where a specific font (in Neuburg, Mecklenburg)

Plate 21. Saebö, Norway: unfinished pedestal with cracks in the upper part (now in the Bergen Historical Museum).

The fact that the different parts of fonts often fit badly together, and that the fossil content of the different components can vary greatly, may indicate that they were not always manufactured and sold as whole units; the different elements may have been produced separately and only brought together when they were to be shipped or set up in a church. The large number of Gotlandic bowls, shafts, and bases, which obviously served as "spare parts" for fonts made of other material, usually local sandstone or granite, can also be seen as evidence for fairly large-scale manufacture of separate components, although of course it may to some extent be a matter of reusing rejected pieces. It cannot be ruled out, then, that what is today a complete Gotlandic font was bought in stages, so that, for example, an existing Romanesque pedestal was first furnished with a Gothic bowl and that on a later occasion it was supplemented with a pedestal in matching style. It also appears that churches sometimes "updated" their font, by replacing an older Gotlandic bowl with one of a more modern design.[42]

---

has been carved are exemplified in Landen 1999.

[42] Remains of two or more Gotlandic fonts occur, for example, in Rerik (Mecklenburg), Chelmno (Poland), Roslagsbro (Uppland), Skanör and Falsterbo (Scania).

Trade and Transport

It could be concluded from the above that the sale of Gotlandic stone products was carried on roughly like modern mail order, and to the extent that the comparison is relevant for Hanseatic trade as a whole, it is probably also relevant for trade in stone. Yet in this area too, the written sources tell us practically nothing; not a single font is mentioned in customs rolls or other contemporary records, and Gotlandic stone in general is mentioned only a few times, and then in such a way and in such contexts that very little information useful for our purposes can be extracted.[43] The only thing that can be established with great precision is where the stone came from and where it ended up; as for what happened in between, we can only gain an idea by studying other sources. However, the long period we are talking about here, roughly 250 years during which both the organisation and the physical conditions of trade and transport underwent major changes, in combination with the absence of fixed datings, means that our conclusions must be of a very general and preliminary nature.

The fact that stone is so rarely mentioned in the customs records is interesting in itself, although of course we must remember that few sources at all survive in the areas where the imported stone is most frequent. A parallel case is timber: although we know that large volumes were imported to Lübeck, timber is very seldom mentioned in the local customs records of Hanseatic cargoes, and it has therefore been concluded that the trade in the Baltic region was mainly in the hands of local merchant-farmers or other free agents. If the trade in stone and stone products was conducted in a similar way it could explain at least in part why stone is also so rarely mentioned in official documents, and moreover it seems reasonable in view of what has already been said about the organisation of the stone industry in Gotland. It may be objected that there are other categories of objects which escaped registration without the involvement of peasant-merchants or other local agents. One example, comparable at least with the more lavish fonts, is the Flemish monumental brasses, which have left no

[43] Several payments for Gotlandic stones are registered in a list of goods bought in Rostock in 1283 (Kämmerei-Rechnung, see *Mecklenburgisches Urkundenbuch 1281–1296,* 1865: 108, no. 1705). In the year 1368 a number of stones were transported by four different shippers from Gotland to Lübeck (*Die hansischen Pfundzollisten des Jahres 1368,* 1935, no. 93, 394, 680, 681); at the castle of the Teutonic Knights in Marienburg payment for four "Gotlandic stones" is registered in 1409 (*Das Marienburger Tresslerbuch der Jahre 1399–1409,* 1896: 542).

traces at all in customs lists and poundage books—despite being numerous and costly items with a wide geographical spread.[44]

Yet there are other possibilities. One is that only commercial goods were subject to tariffs and private objects—among which fonts and gravestones may be included—therefore slipped through without dues or registration. Another is that stone for large building projects often did not need customs clearance, for instance if the king himself was the commissioner, or if he (or his proxy) issued special privileges for the building in question, as not infrequently happened. In addition to this, imports by the bishops always took place under special privileges, and the ecclesiastical economy to a large extent constituted a separate economic system which left no traces in the secular records. Finally one may wonder to what extent stone was a normal component in the commercial flow of goods subject to customs duties. Surely it was mainly a case of deliveries direct from Gotland to a particular destination or commissioner; there may have been several middlemen, but it is hard to conceive that there was any large retail trade in such heavy goods, for the sheer practical difficulty of handling them.[45]

Evidence in favour of the stone products having spread via the Hansa comes from the fact that the pattern of distribution of at least the limestone fonts (groups 2–8), as regards both geography and chronology, agrees very well with the general pattern of Hanseatic trade. It is also clear that places connected by commercial and/or family ties to Gotlandic merchants engaged in Hanseatic activities, to a very high extent are also provided with fonts or other objects of Gotlandic stone. This is of course not surprising: the contacts needed to acquire the desired products were already established, which greatly facilitated ordering, payment, and delivery. There may, perhaps, also have existed a positive interest on the part of the merchants in supplying products of Gotland, either at favourable prices or even as donations, to places with which they had ties of kinship. Finally, it has been noted that the German-speaking merchants of Visby often had family connections with the rural population of Gotland, which means that at least some of them probably were in a position to control the whole business process from quarry to customer.[46]

44 For Flemish monumental brasses in the Baltic area, see Krüger 1992: 195.

45 It is also possible that stones often escaped custom duties for other reasons, for instance by being classified as ballast; see also below, p. 183. Cf. Buckland & Sadler 1990: 114–125.

46 Cf. Wase 1997.

Because of the lack of source material, the commercial value of the stone products cannot be determined, but one thing is certain: they were expensive. In a letter dated 13 September some year between 1315 and 1326, the Gotlandic burgher Gerhard Swede complains bitterly of the loss of his "best stones" by shipwreck, probably on the way to Königsberg.[47] We shall never find out what type of stones they were, or what profit Swede lost in the sea, but it is clear that he regarded the loss as a heavy one. The notes in the Lübeck poundage book from 1368 may give some indication of the price level. We find here cargoes containing stone from Gotland noted on four occasions, two of which concern *lapides* in indefinite plural form, not saying very much about the relation between weight and price, while the other two cases seem to be about single stones (*lapis*). One of the latter is valued at 30 Lübeck *mark*, the other at no less than 102, which corresponds roughly to the value of 8 and 25 *tunnae butiri* (butter) respectively, or 32 and 106 *tunnae carnis* (meat) respectively. We do not know how big or how worked these stones were (or whether the degree of working affected the valuation), but they can hardly have been small objects. From what we have observed while compiling our inventory, we can guess that the record refers to a couple of all the gravestones with a weight of between two and twenty tonnes which occur frequently in Lübeck and the surrounding district.[48]

The freight was probably the greatest cost, although it was scarcely as complicated and expensive as previous scholars have assumed—in fact, exaggerated notions about the difficulty and cost of transport have contributed to the picture of Gotlandic stone exports as a small and exclusive trade. In contrast to what has hitherto been presumed, weight was no intrinsic problem, at least not as regards sea transport. Not even in the case of very heavy objects were there any serious obstacles, which is shown—if nothing else—by the fact that grave slabs with a weight between fifteen and twenty tonnes were shipped from Gotland to places like Lübeck and Bergen in the thirteenth and fourteenth centuries. Merchant ships of normal size in those days could take at least fifty tonnes, and we need not assume any special difficulty in stowing the cargo, since special frameworks were normally built for each load.[49] Even much smaller vessels could trans-

[47] *Preussisches Urkundenbuch 1309–1335*, 1939: 379, no. 566.

[48] *Die hansischen Pfundzollisten des Jahres 1368*, 1935: nos. 93, 394, 680, 681.

[49] Cf. Jan Bill's article in this volume, especially p. 94ff. Among the few marine archaeological remains we may mention a ship of cog type, loaded with floor tiles

port normal-sized gravestones and fonts. That something was technically feasible does not mean, however, that it was economically profitable. What we are talking about is not isolated exclusive items but the large and continuous production and export of a long series of different products, most of which cannot be described as outright luxury goods, and which therefore could hardly have sustained very high transport costs.

An explanation that is not infrequently suggested for this economic anomaly is that the stone could have been used as ballast. The problem with this is that ballast is by definition without economic interest; it is taken in when need arises and thrown out when no longer necessary. But since the stone and the stone products evidently had a commercial value, and no doubt in most cases were intended for specific destinations, they cannot have been used as ballast in the strict sense of the word. All the types of ship that were common during the period were capable of sailing virtually without ballast if carefully stowed, but it became necessary to lower the centre of gravity as soon as large quantities of bulky but light goods (such as stockfish or furs) were loaded; even with large cargoes of heavier goods (such as tar, timber, or perhaps grain), it could be necessary to stabilise the ship with a smaller quantity of even heavier material, such as stone.[50] Thus a relatively light and profitable commodity could not fill a ship on its own, but had to be supplemented with a heavier and perhaps less profitable commodity, or pure ballast, and vice versa. Pottery, for example, was a light but not very profitable item, but it could still yield an

---

and grave slabs of Estonian limestone (probably from the quarry in Lasnamagi, near Tallinn/Reval), which was wrecked in the mid fifteenth century at Ny-Hellesund in southern Norway. On the basis of what is stated in the preliminary reports from the investigation (*Norsk Sjøfartsmuseums årbok* 1986: 11–12), it can be calculated that the cargo weighed at least 48 tonnes. Another stone-carrying ship, dated dendrochronologically to 1328, was found in 1996 at Hiddensee near Rügen. Although the greater part of the stone cargo was probably salvaged soon after the shipwreck, at least ten tonnes of the stone remained at the time of the excavation (personal communication from Friedrich Lüdtz, Archeologisches Landesmuseum, Schwerin). For medieval techniques for transporting and loading stone blocks, see Rockwell 1993: 166ff.

50 The cargo that included the stone block for 30 *mark* also contained *cymentum* (lime) to a value of 4 *mark*, 15 *tunnae teres* (tar) worth 9 *mark*, 43 *mark's* worth of *butirum* (butter), almost 70 *mark's* worth of *pisces* (fish: herring or stockfish) and two *tunnae cum opere* (probably greywork) worth no less than 450 *mark*—in total 606 *mark* (*Die hansischen Pfundzollisten des Jahres 1368*, 1935: no. 394).

economic surplus if it was allowed to fill the remaining space when stone, beer, or other heavy goods made up the main cargo. Since single commodity cargoes were probably quite rare,[51] and given the large number of ships carrying such mixed cargoes that annually called on Gotland for trade and transshipment, there was surely often both the need and the opportunity to arrange transport of stone products at relatively low prices—primarily as ordered goods, but perhaps also out of pure speculation.

In other words, all the other commercial activity was a precondition for the stone exports, and it is thus no chance that Gotlandic stone exports appear to decline at least as drastically as transit trade in the second half of the fourteenth century. In this the Black Death no doubt played a less crucial role than changes in the technical, economic, and political spheres, since the volumes of goods on alternative routes grew considerably during the same period.[52] Another relevant factor is that competition in the simple stonecutting sector probably increased towards the end of the fourteenth century, when grave slabs and floor tiles in particular were exported in larger quantities from both Öland and Estonia.[53]

Conclusion

It is not possible at present to make even a rough estimate of the total volume of exports during the period, but as regards worked stone products alone—such as fonts, gravestones, and various types of architectural items —it must have been of the order of hundreds of thousands of tonnes. In addition, there were probably as large amounts of burnt or unburnt limestone for mortar manufacture. The relative ease with which Gotlandic stone can be identified, however, suggests that there may be good opportunities in the future to obtain a good picture of both the distribution and the total

[51] Hutchinson 1994: 96.

[52] Cf., for example, Wendy Childs' and Nils Hybel's articles in this volume.

[53] The Öland stone industry also seems to have started producing for export in the thirteenth century, but, due to the thin bedding of the local stone, almost exclusively concentrated on flagstones, steps, gravestones and the like (see Wilson 1983, p. 102). In the seventeenth and eighteenth centuries, sandstone from Gotland once again came into great demand—now for use in buildings, portals, and sculptures—especially on the Swedish mainland, but also in the southern parts of the Baltic Sea area (see Cedergren 1991). During the same period the export of worked limestone articles also increased, as did the quantities of burnt lime.

volumes. Because of the almost total absence of written sources, nothing can be said with certainty about how production, sales, or transports were organised, but we may well hope that increased awareness of the scale and significance of the stone trade will ultimately result in a better picture of these aspects as well. For unlike the most of the commodities traded, the stone objects are still there to be studied with the different methods that scholars from the interested disciplines choose to adopt. In this paper, a combination of geological, historical and art historical analyses has helped us to reach at least two important conclusions: firstly, that the scope and economic significance of the trade in stone and stone products have been seriously underestimated; and, secondly, that as far as worked stone products are concerned, a change from small-scale high-value goods to bulk trade seems to have occurred around the middle of the thirteenth century.

Timber for Cloth: Changing Commodities in Anglo-Baltic Trade in the Fourteenth Century

Wendy R. Childs

Introduction

Many new markets and new commodities appeared in long-distance trade during the period of economic expansion which touched all western Europe during the twelfth and thirteenth centuries. The period also laid foundations for the sophisticated organisation of international commerce and transport.[1] These offered continued opportunities even in the less expansionary times of the mid to late fourteenth century, and allowed further specialisations and new markets to develop.[2]

Two commodities which saw changes in their trade patterns during the fourteenth century sufficient to be called "new" were Baltic timber and English cloth. Both commodities were on the international market before 1300, but both flourished and reached wider markets in the fourteenth century. Both were fairly cheap and benefited from the more stable markets and cheaper sea transport which was available. By the end of the fourteenth century they had become complementary goods for exchange in the eastern Baltic trade. This paper concentrates particularly on England's timber trade because, unlike the cloth trade, it has not yet received in England the study

[1] Crucial to the development of markets in bulky products was the development of long-distance sea routes, and especially regular sailings in and out of the Baltic and the Mediterranean. The passage round Jutland was already used by the mid-thirteenth century by Frisian ships and was increasingly used from the 1260s; the regular passage through the Straits of Gibraltar to Flanders began in the 1270s.

[2] Much specialisation was due to local natural resources, but the economic expansion also allowed men to choose whether to specialise in agriculture and industry. Two good examples are the viticulture of Gascony and the cloth industry of the Flemish towns.

it deserves.[3] The pattern of the trade is not unexpected and reflects the pattern in other countries round the North Sea, but a separate study is worthwhile since it can draw on the evidence of the English customs accounts, which allow more precise quantitative and comparative analyses. Like most medieval records the use of customs accounts presents difficulties of under-recording and of terminology and definition. Timber, for instance, is specified by measure and by value, but the size of the measure may vary, and the value may be aggregated in that for the whole cargo. Nonetheless the accounts provide regular information for two periods, 1303-1330 and 1377-1402, which allows the scale of trade and the periods of change to be established more closely, and thus provides a basis of comparison for other studies.[4]

THE PATTERN OF ENGLAND'S TIMBER TRADE

The main receiving ports for timber on a large scale were on the east coast of England. England imported some timber and forest by-products from Spain, Gascony, and Ireland, but its big timber suppliers were in Scandinavia and the Baltic. It is not surprising that among the ports Hull and Lynn were the main importers. Both were naturally good distribution points with high local demand, being exceptionally well-situated on river systems which stretched into relatively unwooded hinterlands. Table 6 shows the relationships of the ports to each other. In 1303-1330 Lynn was the most important with imports often over £500 a year, followed by Hull with imports regularly over £300 and once nearly £600; despite close links with Scandinavia and the Hansards, Boston's imports were rarely worth more than £100 a year; Great Yarmouth's were similar; and London's were also low. In the late fourteenth century, imports at Hull and Lynn remained

[3] Studies are available for other areas, and some use information from English sources; see Bugge 1925. I am grateful to Bjørn Poulsen for this reference, but unfortunately I have been unable to make as much use of it as I would have wished because of language difficulties.

[4] English national customs accounts survive from 1275 but cover general goods (including timber) only from 1303, and then only for alien merchants. The general goods of English merchants were taxed at first temporarily then permanently in the later fourteenth century under the poundage duties. The most useful accounts for the timber trade are the original returns from the individual ports (Public Record Office, London, King's Remembrancer's Customs Accounts, E122). These provide details of shipping, commodities and merchants.

TABLE 6: THE SCALE OF IMPORTS OF TIMBER AND FOREST BY-PRODUCTS (PITCH, TAR, ASHES)

Insufficient accounts survive to provide full statistical data. Examples are provided to illustrate the scale of the trade in the various ports, and to indicate the probable overall import level. The numbers of pieces include all timber irrespective of size. Timber was measured by the long hundred of 120 pieces and this is used in all the following tables; for actual pieces the number given should be increased by 20%. Where timber appears in the cargoes but the amount is not specified, this is indicated by a plus sign (+). Values are given to the nearest £ sterling. Where timber values have not been specified but values have been included in the aggregated value of a cargo, the minimum and possible maximum valuations have been given (for example £7–£200). In most cases the actual value is clearly much less than the possible maximum. Accounts covering less than 12 months are marked with an asterisk (*). All accounts are in the Public Record Office, London (PRO).

TABLE 6A. 1303-1330: PETTY CUSTOM ACCOUNTS (ALIEN TRADE ONLY)

Date	Port–major	Timber and Bowstaves			By-Products (by value) (£)	Total Value (£)
		timber (pieces)	bow-staves	value (£)		
1303-04*	Hull	37,000	11,900	137	92	229
1304-05	Hull	90,500	14,050	239	333	572
1305-06	Hull	84,400	21,200	175	190	365
1306-07	Hull	55,500	8,000	135	253	368
1307-08	Hull	86,500	2,200	203	102	305
1308-09	Hull	14,800	10,600	48	68	116
1309-10*	Hull	21,300	–	63	4	67
1310-11	Hull	62,600	3,800	145	139	284
1322-23	Hull	5,900	–	32	1	33
1324-25	Hull	+	–	6–83	1–151	42–183
1303*	Lynn	+	–	447–868	86	502–924
1303-04	Lynn	+	+	119–388	5–113	124–501
1304-05	Lynn	+	–	60–485	(with timber)	60–485
1305-06	Lynn	31,900	–	79	9	88
1306-07	Lynn	+	–	233	24	257
1308-09	Lynn	+	+	20–37	1–160	21–97
1322-23	Lynn	⟩ 23,000	–	340–482	97–239	579–601
1323-24	Lynn	44,000	–	240	126	355
1324-25	Lynn	62,000	–	402	129	531

Date	Port–minor	Timber and Bowstaves			By-Products (by value) (£)	Total Value (£)
		timber (pieces)	bow-staves	value (£)		
1303*	Bost	+	+	75–127	1–176	76–303
1303-04*	Lndn	–	–	–	–	–
1306-07*	Lndn	500	–	4	3–23	7–27
1308-09*	Lndn	+	–	1–28	1–46	1–73
1308-09	Ipsw	+	–	1–41	–	1–41
	Bost	+		12–80	4–38	16–118
1309-10*	Bost	+	+	26–154	(⟨78)	26–154
1310-11	Gt Y	+	+	119–426	13–69	132–504
1324-25*	Gt Y	+	–	36–103	58–77	105–170
1324-25	Ipsw	oars in mixed cargo	–	1–30	1041	2–71
1325-26*	Gt Y	+	–	45–59	37–44	82–103
1326-27	Ipsw	+	–	5–25	1–25	6–50
1326-27	Ipsw	+	–	5–25	1–30	6–55

TABLE 6B. 1380-1402: PETTY CUSTOM AND POUNDAGE ACCOUNTS

Date	Port–major	Timber and Bowstaves			By-Products (by value) (£)	Total Value (£)
		timber (pieces)	bow-staves	value (£)		
1383-84*	Hull	109,500	15,900	364	208	572
1391-92	Hull	34,000	–	98	76	174
1398-99	Hull	22,000	2,500	60+	60+	120–160
1401*	Hull	17,800	7,600			
1390-91	Lynn	157,500	3,900	451	114	565
1396-7**	Lynn	19,300	–	57	26	83
1383-84*	Lndn	36,300+	600	140+	100+	240+
1389	Lndn	44,000	+	353	134	487

Date	Port–minor	Timber and Bowstaves			By-Products (by value) (£)	Total Value (£)
		timber (pieces)	bow-staves	value (£)		
1389-90	N'c	9,000+	–	63+	37+	100–209
1401-02*	N'c	4,900	300	40	13	53
1383-84"	Bost	+	–	4–1030	26–1030	30–1030
1390-1**	Bost	1,014	–	3	1–8	4–11
1392-93	Bost	–	–	–	–	–
1392-93	Gt Y	29,500	–	141	38	179
1387-88	Ipsw	200	–	3	16	19

The details are as follows.:

Boston: 5/9 (1303, 6 months only), 6/3 (1308-9, 10 months only), 6/5 (1309-10, 2 months only), 7/17 (1383-4, 10 months only), 7/23 (1390-1), 7/30a (6 months only). In this period custom accounts which cover alien trade only are marked **.

Great Yarmouth: E122/148/15 (1310-11, 13 months; bowstaves worth £54 came from Gascony), 148/27 (1324-5, 9 months only), 148/30 and 149/9 (1325-6, 10 months only), E122/149/27 (1392-3)

Hull: E122/55/16 (1303-4; full amounts given for 3 months only, but timber was also included in cargoes valued at £668 in the first 9 months of the account), 55/17 (1304-5), 55/19 (1305-6), 55/23 and 56/3 (1306-7), 134/1 (1309-10; 2 months only), 56/10 (1310-11), 57/10 (1322-3), 56/26 (1324-5), E122/59/8 (1383-4), 59/24 (1391-2), 159/11(1398-9), 60/2 (1401, 3 months only)

Ipswich: E122/50/8 (1308-9), 50/12 (1324-5), 50/13 (1325-6), 50/17 (1326-7), E122/50/33 (1387-8)

London: E122/68/11 (1304, 6 months only), 68/21 and 69/1 (1306-7, 10 months only), 69/3 (6 months only), E122/71/8 (1384, 3 months only), 71/13 (1389, 9 months only)

Lynn: E122/93/3 (1303-7), 93/4 (1308-9, 11 months only), 93/17 (1322-3), 93/19 (1323-4), 93/22 (1324-5), E122/94/12 (1390-1), 94/16 (1396-7)

Newcastle: E122/106/16 and 17 (1389-90), 106/3 and 134/7 (1401-2)

high, London's became significant, but the others remained minor ports, although import values rose a little.[5]

The value of timber imports was modest compared with many other goods, but was nonetheless significant in several of the ports. At Newcastle in the late fourteenth century a relatively small amount made up 8 per cent of total import values, while in London at that period timber imports worth four times as much as Newcastle's were unimportant at a fraction of 1 per cent. At Hull and Lynn timber was always significant. In the early period in each port it amounted to some 10 per cent of import values. In the later period at Hull the increased value had decreased in importance to about 6 to 8 per cent of import values, but at Lynn relatively stable import values increased in importance to reach 15 to 16 per cent.[6] Hull and Lynn remained the most active provincial ports in the timber trade, and it is not surprising to find that their merchants became the most aggressive English traders in the eastern Baltic.[7]

Assessing the scale of commodities by volume is always difficult because of the variability of weights and measures, and timber is no exception. Then as now the term "board" could designate any length of sawn timber, and simple numbers of pieces can conceal important differences and shifts from larger to smaller timber or vice versa. Nonetheless they provide some idea of scale and are provided in Table 6. Imported timbers ran into many thousands of pieces a year.[8] In the early period Hull and Lynn each at times imported 44,000, 55,000, or 72,000 pieces. Altogether imports at all the English ports together must reach 100,000 pieces or more a year. In the 1380s and early 1390s imports at Hull or Lynn alone could reach over 100,000 pieces and in some years total imports at all ports must

[5] The values quoted here are of timber and forest by-products combined.

[6] The customs accounts (Public Record Office, London) for 1303-1330 and 1377-1402 on which this paper is based are as follows: Newcastle: E122/106/16,17, 18, 23, 24, 134/7; Hull: E122/55/16,17,19, 23, 56/3, 7, 10, 26, 57/1, 10, 59/1, 8, 24, 25, 60/2, 159/11; Boston: E122/5/9, 6/3, 5, 20, 7/17, 23, 30; Lynn: E122/93/3, 4, 7, 17, 19, 22, 94/9, 12, 16, 95/12; Great Yarmouth: E122/148/15, 27, 30, 149/9, 22, 27; Ipswich: E122/52/38, 50/8, 12, 17, 19, 29, 33; London: E122/68/21, 69/1, 3, 15, 71/8, 13, 16.

[7] Their importance in Prussia in 1385 is shown when 84% of the English goods arrested there belonged to merchants operating through these two ports.

[8] Numbers throughout this paper are given in the long hundred of 120 pieces (and thus long thousand of 1,200 pieces) in which timber was measured. For the actual number of pieces therefore all given numbers should be increased by 20%.

have reached well over 200,000 pieces. By the mid-fifteenth century the peak of imports was past, and this fits with the known decrease in exports from Danzig.[9] Forest by-products, pitch, tar and ashes, were normally imported by the barrel, which varied in size but not as widely as the size of a piece of hewn or sawn timber. Pitch and tar imports (Table 7) reached several thousand barrels a year and could surpass timber in value. In 1306-1307 over 3000 barrels were unloaded in Hull alone, and in the 1380s England's total imports probably still reached more than 3000 barrels a year, since over 1000 barrels a year regularly reached each port of Hull, Lynn, and London.

There can be little doubt that there was a rise in both timber and by-product imports over the century, despite the drop in population. It is reflected in both the values and the pieces imported. The precise scale is unclear, since the possibilities of changing valuations and of shifts in the size of timber complicate the picture, and the true scale of increase was almost certainly lower than the apparent rise from perhaps 100,000 to 200,000 or 250,000 pieces a year. This is because the imports in the earlier period were by alien merchants only, but the imports in the later period included those of English merchants, who then handled about two thirds of the imports.[10] In the earlier period English merchants certainly traded abroad, indeed had traded with Norway from the early thirteenth century, but the scale of their untaxed and unrecorded trade is unknown. However, evidence from a range of sources suggests that it was relatively low until the 1320s, and it is highly unlikely that English merchants in the early period were carrying anything like two-thirds of England's imports. Possible changes in the valuations and size of timber also pose a problem for com-

[9] At Hull imports rarely reached 12,000 pieces a year after 1450; Lynn's were higher and in 1464-65 possibly 49,000 pieces of wainscot and clapholt were imported; at Newcastle imports sometimes nearly reached 20,000 pieces, and at London in 1480-81 alien imports alone reached 5,500 pieces (Childs 1986: passim; Owen 1984: no.410; Wade 1995: passim; Cobb 1990: passim). For Danzig see Dollinger 1970: 232.

[10] English activity varied in different ports. For instance in 1390-91 at Lynn 87% of timber merchants were English; in 1383-84 at Hull at least 76%; in 1383-84 at Boston the majority were clearly English; in 1392-93 at Yarmouth at least 47%, and possibly 65%, were English; only in Newcastle and London were fewer than 50% English: in 1389-90 at London only 25% and at Newcastle only 20%. In London most timber merchants were Hansards, but in Newcastle most were from the Low Countries.

TABLE 7: PITCH AND TAR IMPORTS (BY THE BARREL)[11]

Early fourteenth century:

	1305-06	1306-07	1307-08	1308-09	1310-11	1323-24	1324-25
Hull	738	3112	823	161	741		
Lynn	21	369				385	167+
Lndn		27		51			+
Gt Y					6+		
Ipsw							
Boston							
Total	759	3508	823	212	747+	385	167+

Later fourteenth century:

	1383-84	1388	1389	1390-91	1392-93	1396-97	1398-99
Hull	1320						450
Lynn				1134		852+	
Lndn			1075				
Gt Y		195			328		
Ipsw		10					
Boston	+			+			
Total	1320	205	1075	1134	328	852	450

parisons over the century, but there is no indication that the problem is great enough to invalidate the visible rising trend. To assume a real rise in timber imports is probably safe, even if the rise is not massive and cannot be precisely quantified.

The customs accounts offer excellent information on the varieties of hewn, sawn and manufactured timber goods which England received. Table 8 shows the range and indicates change over time. Timber came from both Norway and the Baltic but over the century there was a decisive shift towards Baltic timber. In 1303-1330 most timber from both areas was recorded as boards. Then as now, boards could vary greatly in size, but building accounts most frequently mention purchases of lengths of about 8 to 10 feet (2.5 to 3 m). These would be reasonably straightforward to handle,

[11] Sources are as for Table 6.

TABLE 8. TIMBER TYPES AS RECORDED IN ENGLISH CUSTOMS ACCOUNTS[12]

1303-1330	1380-1399
	Timber in bulk
—	*meremium* / timber
borde / boards	*borde, bordes*
borde abietes / boards of fir	—
borde ad cistas / coffer boards [see *chistholt*]	—
borde ad mensas, de mensul', ad mensul' / table boards	—
borde de lim' / boards of lime	*lyndbordes*
borde de sappo/sape / boards of fir	*borde de fer*
borde estrenses / estrich boards [from Estland, possibly Estonia]	*borde estrense*
borde fracte / broken boards	—
borde longe / long boards	—
borde parve / small boards	—
borde quercine / oak boards	*borde quercine*
barelbord'; borde ad barill'/ad barillos faciendum / barrel boards [see *tunnestaves; tunholt*]	*barelbordes*
bulkebord' / balk-boards	—
fow bordes (sic) / ?	—
hekebord' / hatchboards	—
lattebord' / lathe-boards	—
merk' bordes	—
—	*bechenbordes*
—	*cogbordes*
—	*flatbordes*
—	*penybordes*
—	*tenfoteborde*
cheverons, cheveruns, cheverouns de sape / rafters [of fir]	*raftes / raughtres* / rafters
planc' / planks (large boards)	*plankys*
—	*deles, delys* / deals; large boards
spire, spires, sperres / spars	*sparres, sperres, sparrez de firre*
spira parva / small spars	—
—	*sperres quercin'* / oak spars
stawes / staves	—

[12] Sources are as for Table 6.

tignum / tyngnum de sappo / sape / beams [of fir]	—
tunnestaves [see *barelbord'*, *tunholt*]	—
bodikholt (sic; *recte bowholt'* ?) / wood for bows	—
boghholt', *boweholt'* / wood for bows	—
chistholt', *kystholt'* [see *bord' ad cistas*]	—
litholt', *lutholt'* / wood for barrel-ends?	*lidholt*
melvyngholt', *melvyng bord'* boards from Elbing	—
remeholt' / wood for oars and possibly for rudders	*remeholt*
righolt' / rails, spars [*rigald*; from *regelholt*, or possibly Riga]	*righolt*
stapeholt	*stepeholt*
tunholt, *tunneholt'* [see *barelbord'*, *tunholt*]	*tunneholt'*
waynescot / wainscot, oak boards for waggons	*waynescot*
—	*botumholt* / large timber for ships' hulls?
—	*cambholt* / wood for making wool combs?
—	*clapholt* / small oak boards
—	*clipclapp*
—	*knarrholt*

Naval and military timber

ores / remes / virones / oars [see *remeholt*]	*ores / remes*
mastes / masts	*mastes*
—	*spretes* / sprits or poles
boustaves / bow-staves [see *bowholt*]	*bowstaves*

Other manufactured goods

algea, gates, trowes / troughs	*trowes*
scopes / scoops	*scopys*
cista / chests, coffers	*cista*
moldes / moulds	*moldys*
mensa / tables	*tabula parva* small tables (or small boards)

possibly in bundles of about 8 or 10 x 2 x 2 feet (2.5 or 3 x 0.6 x 0.6 m) weighing about one third of a ton. This could be handled by about eight men.[13] The Norwegian balk boards (*bulkbords*) were most probably larger roughly squared beams, and from Norway also came small boards, lathe boards (*lattbords*), and boards for tables. Some Norwegian boards were possibly of oak, but others were specified as of fir (*bord' de sappo*). From the Baltic came *borde estrenses* (in English *estrich* boards, a word which is known to include wainscot and righolt).[14] Also from the Baltic came hatch boards (*hekebords*), oak and lime boards. Boards for making barrels and chests unloaded from ships of Harderwijk, Deventer and Zutphen, were probably also of Baltic origin. As well as the large balk boards Norway sent other large pieces, spars, beams (*tignum*), and rafters (*chevrons*), all at various times specified as of fir (*de sappo*). Planks (normally of oak) came not by the long hundred, but in small numbers of six, eight, or perhaps a dozen, and were clearly of substantial size.[15] These were generally imported from the Baltic.

The growing influence of Baltic timber is already apparent in the occasional use of German words for timber which were normally recorded in an English form: barrel-boards and tun-staves were also recorded as *tunholt*, and boards for chests as *chistholt*,[16] but in the early fourteenth century Baltic terminology was far from dominant. By the 1380s and 1390s considerable changes had taken place and the language used for timber in England (as in Scandinavia and the Low Countries) was now heavily dependent on German words. The word "board" rarely appeared now, except for occasional non-standard timber which was still described in the vernacular English, notably *ten-fot-bords* and *cogbords* (probably for ship-building).[17] Norwegian timber was still imported as spars, planks, masts, and rafters (the former *chevrons*), but *deles* now appeared frequently instead of

13 Tipping 1994: 4.

14 Salzman 1967: 246.

15 English building accounts show that planks were normally of oak and about 10 feet (3 m) long by 18 inches (45 cm) wide and perhaps 1.5 inches (4 cm) thick; but some reached greater sizes of 12 to 13 feet (3.5 to 4 m) long by 3 feet (90 cm) wide and up to 6 inches (15 cm) thick (Salzman 1967: 242).

16 Salzman 1967: 258f.

17 The older English names such as *estrich bords* continued to be used inland by carpenters in the building trade (Salzman 1967: 257).

"planks",[18] and tunholt, wainscot, and righolt made up the vast majority of bulk imports. To these and the earlier words such as *melvyngholt*, *remeholt*, and *clapholt* were added *knarrholt*,[19] *bothumholt*,[20] *stepeholt*,[21] *cambholt*,[22] and *clippclapp*.[23]

Apart from bulk timber a number of manufactured goods arrived, some of naval and military significance. Masts came mostly from Norway, occasionally through the Low Countries, and almost never from the Baltic. They were usually imported in small numbers of up to three or four dozens, but "small masts" were sometimes sent by the hundred (it is unlikely that these were timbers large enough for main masts). Oars on the other hand rarely came from Norway, but often came through the Low Countries in the early period, and later directly from the Baltic. They were imported in larger numbers than masts, by the hundred and half hundred, although total imports rarely reached more than one or two hundred a year. Bowstaves were even more important. They were very regular shipments from the Baltic, which could draw on Carpathian yew. Imports ran into thousands each

[18] Like planks these were large pieces handled in small numbers. Almost certainly most were of fir, since the word in modern English has come to mean fir or pine wood.

[19] *Knarrholt* has been defined as narrow oak boards (Nirrnheim 1910: xlv). It has also been suggested that it was knotty wood, but examples of its use in English building accounts for doors and shutters suggest that its quality was good (Salzman 1967: 247).

[20] This is clearly large timber and may be for ship-building.

[21] Unidentified.

[22] This was imported by John Cambmaker, and was probably for making wool-combs.

[23] Unidentified. The name suggests a similarity with clapholt, but clapholt was valued, like tunholt, at only 10d the hundred, while the high price of *clippclapp*, often 30s to 33s 4d the hundred suggests more than mere barrel-staves. The problem of terminology worsens in the fifteenth century. At London it becomes cheap: in 1420-21 *clippclapp* was valued as cheaply like barrel-staves or tunholt, and clapholt was recorded by the last valued at 20s. If clapholt runs at 3000 to the last as in the "Noumbre of Weyghtes", this is also cheap at about 8d the hundred (Gras 1918: 467, 481, 486, 498, 501; The Noumbre of Weyghtes. British Library, Cotton Ms. Vespasian E.ix, fol. 99v, now published by Jenks 1992b: 307). At Lynn, however, clapholt was still recorded and valued at 20s and 26s 8d the hundred, which makes it similar to wainscot and fits with the use of clapholt as good-quality panelling wood in the fifteenth and sixteenth centuries (Owen 1984: no.410; Gras 1918: 617, 676-679).

year. At Hull over 21,000 were imported in 1305-06 and nearly 16,000 in 1384. These were clearly significant military supplies for England's wars with Scotland and France.

Most small manufactured goods were described by various words such as *trowe*, *gate*, *algea*, *molde*. It is not clear exactly what shape or size these "troughs" were. Useful wooden containers could range from small vessels no more than three or four inches (8 to 10 cm) across to substantial platters eighteen inches (45 cm) long or more. Scoops were also fairly frequent imports, and chests and tables appeared occasionally, forerunners of the large numbers of coffers, counting and playing tables, trenchers, cupboards, and musical instruments which came to provincial ports from the Baltic and the Low Countries in the fifteenth century.

Forest by-products were pitch and tar, essential for ship-building and for many other waterproofing jobs, and wood-ashes for fixing dyes in the cloth industry. These were shipped by the barrel and last (normally 12 or 13 barrels to the last). Tar (*bitumen*) had occasionally been a part of Norwegian cargoes, but most tar, pitch, and wood-ashes came from the Baltic. In recent times Prussian and especially Finnish tar have been reckoned the best quality,[24] and undoubtedly greater access to these better-quality Baltic supplies in the fourteenth century helped to destroy the small Norwegian trade.

The swing from Norwegian to Baltic supplies in the fourteenth century was almost complete. At the beginning of the fourteenth century both areas were very active suppliers, and to about 1311 the ratio of Norwegian to Baltic timber was about 3 : 2 at Hull and Lynn (and sometimes nearer 2:1 in Hull). By the 1320s the balance had probably already tipped into the Baltic's favour, and by the late fourteenth century it certainly had done so. Table 9 illustrates the dramatic swing. In Hull in 1310-1311 imports from Norway still reached over 42,000 pieces valued at over £72, while Baltic pieces were fewer than 24,000 although they also reached £70; by 1383-1384 Norwegian imports barely reached 1,300 pieces worth considerably less than £30, while Baltic imports reached 118,000 pieces (including bowstaves) valued at £378.[25] For the rest of the Middle Ages imports of Norwegian softwood were rare except for small amounts at Newcastle and Hull.

[24] Layton 1996: 87.

[25] The comparison by number of pieces is, of course, very imprecise because the size of timber varied greatly.

TABLE 9. TIMBER IMPORTS TO HULL, 1310-1311 AND 1383-1384

All numbers are given in the long hundred of 120; actual numbers are therefore 20% higher. "Under £30" and "inc(luded)" indicate that the values of timber imports are aggregated into general cargo values. Source: PRO E122/56/10, 59/8.

1310-1311	Number	Value: £ s d	1383-1384	Number	Value £ s d
From Norway (brought by Norwegian and Baltic ships):					
Boards	11, 850	21.17.8	Planks	200	
Chevrons	28,500	43.14.0	Lignum	60	
Spars	2,000	2.6.8	Spars	1,004	
Masts	100	4.16.0	Masts	16	
Total	42,450	72.14.4	Total	1,280	under £30
From the Baltic (brought by Baltic ships):					
Hatchboards	1,000	1.10.0	—		
Wainscot	4,720	11.16.0	Wainscot	71,460	215.13.2
Tunhold	8,500	10.5.0	Tunholt	21,400	10.8.4
Christholt	94	7.0	Righolt	8,640	65.17.0
Oars	200	1.8.0	Bothumholt	360	2.1.8
			Planks	16	1.5.1
			Lignum	12	inc.
			Deals	5	inc.
Total	14,514	25.6.0	Total	102,038	295.5.3
Probably from the Baltic (via the Low Countries):					
Boards	4,900	35.5.0	—		
Bowstaves	3,800	4.8.0	Bowstaves	15,900	82.11.8
Oars	196	2.19.0	—		
Total	8,896	42.12.0	Total	15,900	82.11.8
Origin unclear (via the Low Countries):					
Masts	45	4.0.0			
Grand Totals					
	66,405	144.12.4		119,218	407.16.11

TABLE 10. EXAMPLES OF THE ORIGINS OF SHIPS WHICH IMPORTED TIMBER TO ENGLAND[26]

Early fourteenth century:

	Norway	[Germany]	Hamburg	Lübeck	Wismar	Rostock	Stralsund	Greifswald	Gotland	Reval
Into Hull (including Ravenser and Scarborough)										
1305-06	7	4	1	2	—	—	3	—	—	—
1306-07	3	3	1	2	—	1	4	—	—	—
1307-08	8/12	3	3	1	1	—	1	—	—	—
1308-09	1	1	2	1	—	—	1	1	—	—
1310-11	5	2	1	1	—	2	1	—	1	—
Into Lynn										
1305-06	12	—	5	—	—	—	1	—	4	1
1306-07	5/7	2	3	—	—	—	3	—	1	—

Later fourteenth century:

	Norway	Bremen	Hamburg	Lübeck	Wismar	Stettin	Danzig	Elbing	Königsberg	England
Into Hull										
1383-84	2	—	5	—	—	—	6	1	2	3
1398-99	2	—	—	—	—	—	8	1		1
Into Lynn (2 also came from "the Sound")										
1390-91	—	1	2	1	3	1	12	1	—	7

The shift in the trade is clearly reflected in the shipping used, and this is illustrated in Table 10 with examples from Hull and Lynn. The shift had already begun in the thirteenth century, as more ships sailed around Jutland after the 1250s. Before then any references to timber cargoes mention

[26] Sources: PRO E122/55/19, 23, 57/1, 56/7, 0, 59/8, 159/11 (Hull); E122/93/3, 94/12 (Lynn).

only Norwegian involvement, like the ten Norwegian ships at Grimsby in 1230 with fir boards,[27] but by the end of the thirteenth century references to timber cargoes frequently mention Baltic ships. There were for instance over 96,000 boards on the fifty-five ships of Friesland and the Baltic bound for Flanders which were driven by storms to Newcastle, Scarborough, and Ravenser in 1294; only one of them seems clearly to be carrying a Norwegian cargo of fir rafters and whetstones.[28] In the fourteenth century vessels from four areas were involved in the timber trade: the Low Countries and Friesland, Norway, the Baltic ports, and England. Low Country and Friesland shipping, skippered by masters from Sluys to Stavoren, was a constant element throughout the century. Most vessels brought small amounts of timber in mixed cargoes from the Low Country ports, but a few, especially those of Harderwijk and Stavoren in the early fourteenth century and those of Veere later, brought larger cargoes and probably came directly from the Baltic. Norwegian shipping, however, declined and shifted in emphasis. At the beginning of the century a dozen or more ships from Stavanger, Bergen, and Trondheim on the west coast imported balk boards and chevrons by the thousands. At the end of the century only one or two ships a year from Tønsberg and Oslo are visible.[29] Baltic shipping also changed dramatically. Ships from western ports (Stralsund, Rostock, and Lübeck), some of which in the early period had imported Norwegian goods, gave way to those from eastern ports (Danzig, Elbing, and Königsberg). English ships had been active in Norwegian trade from the early thirteenth century,[30] but their entry into the Baltic trade is more difficult to trace. Evidence of their sailing into the Baltic is scarce before the 1350s, but is

[27] *Calendar of Close Rolls 1227-1231*, 1902: 367.

[28] Davies 1953: 185f.

[29] The ships brought small cargoes of the larger sorts of timber. At Hull in 1382-83 two Tønsberg ships brought 1000 spars, 4 masts, 12 small masts, 60 beams, and ca. 200 planks; in 1398-99 two Oslo ships brought spars, planks, and small masts worth under £7; in 1401 an Oslo ship brought spars and masts valued at £5 (Public Record Office E122/59/8, 159/11, 60/2). At Newcastle in 1402 an Oslo ship brought 26 dozen planks and 7 C 20 (i.e., 860) spars valued at ca. £6 (Public Record Office E122/134/7). Newcastle remained one of the few ports to receive Norwegian timber in the fifteenth century: in 1499-1500 two and possibly three Tønsberg ships brought spars, rafters, bumkins, bill-shafts and hazel rods valued at £12 (Wade 1995: 258, 278f).

[30] *Rotuli Litterarum Clausarum 1204-1224*, 1833: 464b, 607b; *Calendar of Patent Rolls 1232-1247*, 1906: 100; *Calendar of Close Rolls 1247-1251*, 1922: 424.

clear thereafter and by the end of the fourteenth century they were active in importing Baltic timber to Hull, Lynn, and London. At Boston and Yarmouth, where the timber trade was weaker and Hamburg and Lübeck links remained strong, they appeared more rarely with Baltic cargoes. This shift in English activity exactly mirrors the expanding exports from Danzig which were at their peak from the 1350s.[31]

Customs valuations (originally based on the merchants' declared purchase prices) repay examination, and samples are shown in Table 11. Variations in values were wide because they reflected differences of size, of quality of wood, or of finish, few of which we can now establish. Lengths and thicknesses of timber depended on the quality of the standing timber before it was cut, as well as on the felling and sawing practices of several different areas in Germany, Poland, and Livonia, but regular trade tends to encourage convergence of measures, and the valuations may help to indicate broad categories of imports, differing prices between different supply areas, and trends in prices in these areas.[32] In the early fourteenth century valuations ranged from 60s per hundred for the most expensive timber to 5d per hundred for the cheapest. What it is important to note is that although Norway was still supplying a large amount of timber, the Baltic forests were already supplying the widest range from the most expensive, of good size and quality for building and ship-building, to the cheapest, for making barrels. The most expensive timber of all at this period was a cargo of lime boards at 60s the hundred. Oak planks at the equivalent of 37s 6d the hundred and oak righolt at about 20s the hundred were also expensive. In the middle range came estrich boards. In the cheaper timber came wainscot, normally under 6s the hundred, Elbing boards, hatch boards, and right at the bottom tunholt at 5d to 1s 6d the hundred. Norwegian fir boards fell into two distinct categories probably based on size, the most expensive of which reached 20s the hundred. The cheaper spars similarly fell into two categories; Norwegian rafters at 2s 6d to 5s the hundred are among the cheaper woods; and surprisingly the balk boards, which by

31 Wazny 1992:331.

32 Timber was counted by the long hundred of 120 pieces. It should be noted that valuations at Lynn are generally higher than at Hull, and those at London higher still. All should be based on the merchants' declared purchase prices, so this may reflect different markets for different types of timber in these ports, but it might also suggest that at the end of the fourteenth century customs collectors were beginning to use conventional rates of valuations, a practice which became widespread in the fifteenth century.

TABLE 11. TIMBER VALUATIONS IN THE ENGLISH CUSTOMS ACCOUNTS

Valuations (given here in shillings and pence sterling) were based on the merchants' sworn declarations of purchase prices, and thus reflect purchase prices abroad (not English market prices). They had not yet become conventionalised, and certainly still relate to the market. Variations within a category were sometimes wide, the most expensive could be twice or even three times the value of the cheapest. These reflect variations of size, quality, or finish which we cannot now establish, but the valuations are still useful for broad comparative purposes. The table shows the most common valuations, all by the long C (120). Valuations at Lynn tend to be slightly higher than at Hull, and valuations at London often higher than at both. They all, however, show the same relative positions. Sources are as for Table 6.

All ports, 1303-1330 (timber in descending order of valuation)

lime boards	60s
planks	37s 6d (3d farthing each)
righolt	20s
boards (Norwegian)	3s to 6s and 16s to 20s
fir boards (Norwegian)	2s to 6s 8d and 16s to 20s
estrich boards	6s 8d through 10s and 12s to 17s 4d
chistholt	10s
spars [Norwegian]	5s and 12s
wainscot	4s 6d to 6s and 12s (occasionally)
Elbing (melvyng) boards	4s
hekebords	3s
chevrons (Norwegian)	2s 6d to 5s
balk-boards (Norwegian)	2s 6d
boweholt	2s or less
tunholt	5d to 1s 6d (once 3s)
oars	2d, 3d and 5d each (via the Low Countries)
bowstaves	2s to 3s the C (ca. halfpenny each; also sometimes 1s 6d or 4s)
masts	96s 4d for C (about 9d each if the C was 120
pitch and tar	1s 6d to 3s the barrel, and 15s to 40s the last

Hull and Lynn, 1380-1402 (timber in descending order of valuation)

cog-boards	120s (1s each)
oak boards	53s 4d
deals	40s (4d each; sometimes 3.5d and once 7d = 70s)
lime boards	40s (4d each)
planks	20s and 40s; once 50s (2d, 4d or 5d each)

bothumholt	26s 8d (Hull) to 30s (Lynn)
righolt	13s 4d to 16s 8d (once 11s 8d at Hull, 20s at Lynn)
ten-foot-boards	10s
wainscot	6s 8d (sometimes 4s 10d to 5s 5d (Hull) and 7s (Lynn)
spars	6s
tunholt	10d to 1s (sometimes 6d to 8d, once 1s 8d)
clapholt	10d (but also 5s)
oars	ca. 1d each (direct from the Baltic)
bowstaves	10s
masts	1s 9d each
pitch and tar	1s 8d the barrel, and 13s 4d or 16s 4d the last
wood ashes	26s 8d the last

London (timber in descending order of valuation)

deals	40s to 50s (4d, 5d each; also 6d, 7d more often than in Hull and Lynn)
lime boards	40s (4d each)
clipclapp	30s to 33s 4d
remeholt	33s 4d
knarrholt	28s 2d
righolt	19s 2d to 24s 2d
wainscot	11s 2d to 14s
spars	8s and 13s 4d
cambholt	6s 8d

definition seem to be larger beams, were very cheap at 2s 6d the hundred. The relative cheapness of Norwegian wood may reflect cheaper transport costs.

In the late fourteenth century valuations still varied widely, but there was more standardisation in the valuation of the commonest types of timber. This may have been promoted by regular trade or be due to conventional customs rates. Some timber was even more expensive. Fifteen *cogbords* (presumably major ship-building timbers) valued at 1s each were the equivalent of 120s the long hundred, twice as expensive as any other imports, and as expensive as small masts. Baltic lime boards, planks, and deals at 4d, 5d, and 6d each (the equivalent of 40s, 50s, 60s the hundred) were obviously highly valued, and some oak boards and *bothumholt* were also quite highly placed. Righolt had perhaps become a little cheaper, but wainscot had risen in value. Tunholt had also risen slightly in value, but remained the cheapest timber. Relative valuations of the commonest timber partly reflected their size, and this is confirmed by known timber measures. The last of timber was defined as 60 deals, or 100 righolts, or 200 wainscots, or 600 bowstaves, or 3000 clapholts.[33]

Most masts ranged from 1s or 2s each and are sometimes called "small masts". At this price some are only two or three times more expensive than the most expensive planks and boards, but some reached 4s each which suggests a greater size, although still far from the one great mast imported to London from the Low Countries and valued at 13s 4d. The decreasing valuation of oars are interesting because it suggests transport costs were important. In the early fourteenth century oars nearly always came through the Low Countries and were valued quite highly at 1d, 2d, 3d and even 5d each. Their high value was partly because the timber had to be of considerable length (18–24 feet/5.5–7.3 m) and included labour costs for shaping, but it was also partly because of transport costs. Oars came through the Low Countries and were either transported overland through Lübeck and Hamburg or transshipped at a Low Country port. They thus incurred considerable handling charges, but because good oars were in demand the high costs did not prohibit trade. Direct trade, however, was cheaper and at the end of the century when oars arrived at Hull from the Baltic on Danzig ships their valuation never rose above 1d each. Bowstaves, on the other hand, rose dramatically in valuation. In the early fourteenth century valuations might reach 4s the hundred, but were normally 2s to 3s (that is 4 or 5 bowstaves to 1d); at the end of the century they were normally valued at 6s 8d and even 10s the hundred (about 1d each). This undoubtedly reflected England's increasing demands during the Hundred Years War.

These then are the main patterns of the trade. Most timber imports went to Hull and Lynn, with London becoming active in the later fourteenth century. A very wide variety of hewn and sawn timber was imported with an equally wide range of valuations, although much was of relatively small size. There was a marked shift from Norwegian to Baltic supplies, which is visible in the timber imports themselves, the terminology used by the customs collectors in their records, and in the ships used to carry timber.

The information visible in documentary evidence can be effectively expanded by important recent developments in dendrochronology research.[34]

[33] Jenks 1992b: 307.

[34] I am extremely grateful to Cathy Groves of the Archaeological Science Research School, University of Sheffield, for introducing me to the current work by dendro-

Dendrochronology's essential role in dating timber is widely recognised but it also has other uses. One of these is provenancing timber. The possibility of this was established in the mid-1980s,[35] and since then research has been moving fast. The increasing number and sophistication of dendrochronology databases across northern Europe allow much more precise matching of timber and area, and show the complexity of multiple production and export areas in the Baltic.[36] A considerable number of the artifacts so far examined have been from the later fourteenth and fifteenth centuries when eastern Baltic, especially Polish, areas were dominant, but of even more interest are surviving examples of the earlier, less precisely known, western trade. Particularly exciting are the painted boards in the nave at Peterborough Cathedral. Eleven of these, felled and used after ca. 1230, are not of English origin. Not only are they the earliest recorded surviving imports, but they came from northern Germany or Denmark rather than from the eastern Baltic.[37] Their presence fits in the pattern of the thirteenth-century timber trade with its emphasis on western supplies. These boards were probably brought overland to Hamburg or the Low Country ports for onward transport to England, but within a generation similar boards could have become part of cargoes coming directly by sea from the western Baltic ports.

INFLUENCES ON THE ANGLO-BALTIC TIMBER TRADE

It is now time to raise some wider questions. How did the trade fit the wider trade patterns of England and of northern Europe? Why did the change occur? Why did England need to import timber? Why should there be an increase in the later fourteenth century? How important were the imports to England as a whole?

England was not isolated and took part in the general developments on Europe's commercial routes. It had an extremely long history of commercial contact with the rest of northern Europe, and in the thirteenth century the east coast ports enjoyed extensive trade with Norway, the Low Countries, north-eastern France, and Germany by way of the Rhine. England benefited

---

chronologists.

35 Baillie et al. 1985; Eckstein 1986; Fletcher 1986.

36 Hillam & Tyers 1995: 400f; Bonde et al. 1997: 203. Work on dating pine is also beginning (Groves 1997), which should also be of great interest to the medieval timber trade.

37 Groves 2000.

like many other areas from the expansion of trade and the opening of sea passages in the thirteenth century. The regular passage through the straits of Gibraltar after the 1270s resulted in even east coast ports being visited by Italian ships, but it was the passage round Jutland which effected them more closely. In this the English ports were simply experiencing changes similar to those in other ports around the North Sea. Bruges too now expected to receive Baltic cargoes of timber, furs, wax, and iron directly by sea, as on the fleet of fifty-five ships blown into Newcastle, Scarborough and Ravenser when bound for Flanders in 1294; and the well-known list of goods available there at about this time includes timber (*merriens*) from Norway and Germany.[38]

Access to the Baltic by sea was commonplace by the early fourteenth century, but access had been developed mainly for western Baltic trade and need not inevitably lead to increased trade in eastern Baltic timber. How far access was developed depended on many other factors. Resources, demands, costs, prices, and technology all play their part, and political pressures can also be a major influence.

Undoubtedly simple changes in transport costs with the regular use of the passage round Jutland were important for the spread of bulky Baltic timber into North Sea ports. The increasing reference to Baltic timber in the later thirteenth century fits well with the first sailings around Jutland by about 1250. Even so the new accessibility of Baltic timber through the use of sea transport does not make inevitable a shift to the almost exclusive use of eastern Baltic timber in England. The North German timber which had come through the Low Countries could now come by sea;[39] and Bergen and Trondheim were nearer to England in sailing distance than Danzig and Riga,[40] and transport from there should be comparable in cost. However, the technical developments in Hanseatic vessels which created some of the best bulk carriers in Europe tipped the balance. The main hull changes which produced these vessels had already taken place in the thirteenth century and cannot by themselves explain movements in the fourteenth century, but continued refinements and increasing size no doubt made

[38] Gilliodts van Severen 1904-1906, vol. 1: no.14.

[39] Salzman's earliest references to "estrich" boards in 1260 and to "Almain" timber in 1275 (Salzman 1967: 245, 247) can now be pushed back by over two decades in the light of Groves' work on Peterborough Cathedral (Groves 2000).

[40] Layton 1996: 72.

Baltic shipping cheaper than Norwegian.[41]

Hansard merchants reinforced this economic advantage by political dominance in Scandinavia, first in Denmark and then in Norway. The Norwegian timber trade had been combined with the west coast codfish and skin trades, and a typical Norwegian cargo was that brought by merchants of Bergen to Ravenser in 1306: 7,000 balk boards and nearly 18,000 fish. However, the Hansards who came to dominate Bergen were interested only in stockfish for German markets, and it is perhaps significant that when they also sent cargoes from Norway to England they similarly ignored timber: in 1307 three Baltic ships brought Norwegian stockfish to Ravenser, but not a single board.[42] If stockfish was creamed off by the Hansards, then the export of timber alone was less attractive, although a few Norwegians carried on a small trade into the fifteenth century.[43]

Transport costs and political influence were important, but even more so were the characteristics of Baltic resources. Baltic timber and forest by-products came in almost unlimited amounts, great variety, excellent quality, and at reasonable cost. The slow-growing oak in the eastern forests provided tall clean timber, which was also easier to work than the intensively grown timber in England and was probably cheaper at source.[44]

England was not particularly short of timber overall, but there were temporary, local, and specialised shortages which encouraged imports. The expansion of population in the thirteenth century certainly increased general demand for building and shipbuilding timber of all sorts. To satisfy these demands, timber might have to be carried considerable distances, but land transport was expensive for bulky goods. Thus, imports by sea could be as cheap as domestic timber if that had to be hauled any distance overland. It is undoubtedly significant that Hull and Lynn were the most important entry ports for timber. Both had largely unwooded hinterlands and excellent river networks for distribution by water transport. The steady growth of York in the fourteenth century encouraged imports through Hull, and the use of timber in East Anglian buildings identified by Oliver Rackham

[41] See Jan Bill's article above, pp. 101-105, 109-112. Hanseatic vessels were some of the most efficient in Europe. Some were crewed at the rate of 1 man per 10–12 tuns, compared with Spanish and English ships crewed at 1 man to 3–5 tuns, and Mediterranean galleys at 1 man to 1 tun.

[42] Public Record Office, London, E122/55/19, 56/3.

[43] See above note 29.

[44] I am indebted to Bruce Campbell for discussion on the matter of land values during the conference.

both stimulated and depended on cheap overseas supplies through Lynn.[45] General demand in England could be satisfied by the forests of north-east Europe, and so could the specialised demands for certain types of woods which were always scarce in England. Fir was not grown in England at all and softwoods were regularly imported, although as yet no Norwegian pine has been identified in medieval buildings despite the many fir rafters (*chevrons*) imported.[46] Outsize oak was also scarce. For most purposes this did not matter, since relatively young trees between 20 and 70 years of age could provide up to about 20 feet (6 m) of clean timber. This was adequate for most building needs, and this size was readily renewed in managed woodland. In much shorter supply were "outsize" oaks providing 30 to 50 feet (9 to 15 m) of usable timber, which was needed for great cathedral buildings and for the massive supports of post mills. Timber up to 35 feet (10.6 m) could be found in mature trees in England, but owners were often reluctant to fell them except for special purposes, so it was expensive. Baltic forests could easily supply slow growing, large, clean oak, and possibly some of the larger beams which were counted individually were of this large size, but it must be emphasised that most oak imports were in fact of relatively small timber. Sawn boards such as wainscots, righolt, and tunholt were the most usual cargoes and priced attractively enough for consumers with their own managed woodland, such as Norwich Cathedral Priory, to prefer to buy foreign wainscot and righolt.[47] Good yew for bowstaves was also scarce and eastern sources predominated, because the other major supplier, Spain, was frequently a French ally and could not therefore be relied on for military supplies.

At the end of the fourteenth century with declining population after the Black Death, a slackening in general demand might be expected, but English imports were not only sustained but increased. Why? Paradoxically, this may be partly due to the population decrease. It has long been argued

[45] Rackham emphasised the almost profligate use of timber in East Anglia, although it was one of the least well-wooded areas in England (Rackham 1980: 163 and note). This may be a sort of conspicuous consumption, but it may also indicate the ease with which the area could obtain foreign timber through King's Lynn.

[46] Rackham estimated that 97 percent of timber in surviving medieval buildings is oak, although some pine doors have survived (Rackham 1980: 145, 147, 151). Recently interest in dating and analysing pine has increased (Groves 1997), and the results will be of considerable interest to all working on the medieval timber trade.

[47] Rackham 1980: 159.

that declining population resulted in an increasing per capita income, which made possible a rising standard of living. A rising standard of living was likely to stimulate demand for better housing with better fittings—doors, shutters, screens and panelling—and thus a sustained demand for timber.

Further stimuli to import may have been comparative price and cost structures in England and the Baltic which maintained and even possibly increased the profitability of the trade. Accurate assessments of profitability demands long runs of detailed accounts for production, transport and handling costs, which are not easily available. Information can be patchy. For instance, there appears to be little evidence of fourteenth-century Baltic freight rates. Fifteenth-century rates indicate that transport costs raised the price of timber by 79 per cent, far more than for rye (68 per cent) or cloth (10 per cent),[48] which looks punitive, but obviously was no deterrent.[49]

Relevant and directly comparable price data are difficult to find. The valuations in the customs accounts look promising as they should reflect the merchants' buying price in the Baltic and are recorded in the pound sterling. In theory they could be used to compare directly with sterling selling prices in England, but in practice this cannot be done. Firstly, the size and quality of the timber were rarely specified, so we cannot securely compare like with like; secondly, there is some possibility that the valuations by the later fourteenth century are beginning to become conventional; and thirdly, most known English timber prices are retail prices to the end-user, which include further transport costs, middleman profits, and labour charges. Nonetheless, even if it proves impossible to quantify actual profits, it is possible to discuss the broad relationship of prices in the Baltic and in England.

Many prices in England rose after the Black Death. If these rose faster than prices abroad, this would offer timber merchants increasing profits, and stimulate trade. However, the rate of the price rise in timber has caused some difference of opinion: Salzman suggested that prices rose rapidly between 1338 and 1442 especially for large timber,[50] but detailed

[48] Dollinger 1970: 157f.

[49] Even if timber had originally ridden on the back of other goods (which is unproven), it soon became an integral part of Baltic cargoes—sought by the English as well as sent by the Germans. Complaints of half-empty ships all concerned ships returning to the east.

[50] Planks for groundsills 24 feet (7.3 m) long cost 1s 2d in 1338 and those of 30 feet (9.15 m) long cost 13s 4d in 1442 (a 12 fold rise); 12-foot (3.65 m) joists rose

information in his own work shows a relatively slow increase in the prices of wainscot and lesser timbers (which were the boards which were most often imported) and only from the mid-fifteenth century did timber prices began to rise fast.[51] Rackham's broader survey of building timber in England shows a rise in the 1340s to 1360s, but no further appreciable rise in the price of building oak until the sixteenth century;[52] and Ian Friel's examination of royal ship-building accounts shows similarly slack timber prices at least to the mid-fifteenth century.[53]

Despite the differences of opinion, it is clear that prices in England were not falling at the end of the fourteenth century, but at this period they were falling in some parts of the Baltic. General prices, including timber, fell sharply in Prussia through the 1390s and up to ca. 1405; after a rise from then until 1418, they again fell for much of the fifteenth century.[54] Such a fall would be to the advantage of the timber merchants. A further factor leading to market specialisation is often a longer-term structural difference in labour costs (a phenomenon well known today, when European clothing manufacturers seek cheap labour not only in other countries, but also on other continents). The labour input in the production of timber and its by-products was not negligible—felling, sawing and splitting timber, distilling resin for pitch and tar, and hauling the timber to the rivers. Labour costs are therefore a factor worth considering. Labour costs in transport were minimised by the use of excellent river access to production areas, notably in Poland where the Vistula made central Poland easily accessible from Danzig, and also in Riga which could reach well into the

---

from 2.5d to 12d each (a 6 fold rise); small lathes trebled in price, and wainscots (*estrich* boards) doubled (Salzman 1967: 206-208).

51 They were bought at Windsor in 1351 for 1.5d each and near London in 1366 for 3.5d each, but at Hull and Wallingford in 1360 and 1375 they were still ca. 2d and 2.5d each. This seems to indicate a steady mark-up of ca. 150% to 200% for retail prices over the customs valuations. By 1432 at Cambridge wainscots cost just over 5d each, and by 1533 they were 1s each in London (Salzman 1967: 245f).

52 Rackham 1980: 162-164, 171. He drew heavily but not exclusively on Cambridge and East Anglia (where ease of access to imports might have kept prices down), but there is no reason to doubt the broad trends.

53 Friel 1995: 65-67, and Table 4.

54 Dollinger 1970: 216f. Wainscots were valued at the customs ports at about a halfpenny each in the early century, and between a halfpenny and one penny each in the later fourteenth century. This seems to keep pace with English prices rather than Baltic ones.

Daugava basin.[55] It is also possible that generally labour costs in the late fourteenth century were lower in real terms in the east than in England, because land an food costs were cheaper in a more recently colonised area, and the population had not been damaged by the Black Death to the same degree as in western Europe. More comparative work on land values and labour costs is needed to verify this last point,[56] but it remains possible that a significant price-cost differential between the eastern Baltic and England was an added factor encouraging imports, especially of the less expensive, smaller timber.

Although the importance of timber imports in England's overseas trade is relatively straightforward to estimate (and is not high), their impact on the English economy as a whole is impossible to assess. Without English production figures, we have nothing to compare the imports with; but imports, even of 200,000–250,000 pieces, would not go far. However their use was clearly more significant than the scale of trade would suggest. Specialised products such as softwoods, bowstaff wood, pitch, tar, and ashes provided essential military, naval, and industrial supplies, and the use of foreign timber was also wide-spread enough for words such as "deal" and "wainscot" to become part of the English language. In the immediate hinterlands of Hull and Lynn imports had even greater significance. The use of timber for decoration as well as building in East Anglia, on which Rackham remarked, was undoubtedly the result of the area's easy access to Norwegian and Baltic timber through Lynn. Indeed, if timber prices generally remained low in East Anglia and in the ship-yards, as Rackham and Friel find, then imports may have contributed to this, although again we cannot quantify to what extent.[57]

Many questions remain, and there is room for further study of English demand patterns, of the relationship of English and Baltic prices, of comparative labour costs and land values, and of transport costs. But the gen-

55 Wazny 1992: 331; Zunde 1998: 71, 73.

56 I am indebted to a reader of my paper for pointing me towards Sarnowski 1993, but the Prussian and English material will still need considerable future work to find a common basis for comparison, which would allow firm conclusions about comparative labour costs to emerge.

57 Rackham used much data from East Anglia and especially from Cambridge in his study. His finding of low retail prices for oak is, perhaps, therefore not surprising, since imports contributed greatly to supplies in the immediate hinterlands of the ports. Whether imports were sufficient to keep down prices over the whole of England is more difficult to assess.

eral pattern of England's timber trade is reasonably clear from the evidence of the customs accounts, taken together with other documentary and archaeological evidence for building and shipbuilding.

ENGLISH CLOTH EXPORTS TO THE BALTIC

The rising imports of timber in the later fourteenth century were further stimulated by one other factor. Good return cargoes became available with the revival of the English cloth industry. Indeed, the timber trade may have been partly driven by the English search for markets for their rising cloth output and their need, in their turn, to find useful return goods.

In the early fourteenth century England had had little to send directly to the Baltic. Her cloth exports were small,[58] and her main export was wool, which went to the Flemish industrial cities rather than to the Baltic. In the late fourteenth century the situation was transformed with the development of the English cloth export industry. Annual exports rose fast from about 1,000 cloths in 1350 to nearer 40,000 in the 1390s.[59] Increased output meant that new markets were needed since Flemish cities would not buy competing English cloth. Finding new markets was not particularly difficult for the English. The small amount of English cloth exported between 1303 and 1330 had been handled by Spaniards, Italians, Gascons, Frenchmen, Norwegians, merchants from the Low Countries and from Germany (from Köln, Hamburg, Lübeck, Rostock, Greifswald, and Osnabrück). Through them it reached all Europe, and English merchants could therefore address known markets which stretched from the Mediterranean to the Baltic.[60] Iberia and the Mediterranean could be as easily exploited as the Baltic through cheap sea transport; but for the English east coast ports the

[58] Exports of standard cloths by aliens rarely reached 700 a year in the early fourteenth century. Together with non-standard cloths worth about £2,000 a year, and a small amount of exports by English merchants total exports might have reached 1,500 a year, but cloth exports were a drop in the ocean compared with the value and scale of the wool trade (Childs 1996).

[59] Carus-Wilson & Coleman 1963: 75-88, 138-155. The increase was encouraged by English kings' manipulation of trade for war finance (embargoes and increased wool-taxes); by internal troubles in Flanders (which damaged textile production); and by the attractive variety and cost of English output. See also Bridbury 1982: passim.

[60] Ordering was known in the fifteenth century and was undoubtedly frequent before then; see Wolff 1983; *Calendar of Close Rolls 1468-76*, 1953: no.709.

Baltic was geographically closer. Quite possibly 50 per cent of England's exports were finding their way into German markets at the end of the century, many of them through the Baltic ports.

English merchants handled 50 to 66 per cent of English cloth exports,[61] and actively marketed them abroad. Numbers of merchants and factors in Baltic ports could be substantial. When English goods were arrested in Prussia in 1385, 115 English merchants were affected, 85 per cent of whom were merchants who traded through Hull and Lynn.[62] The English merchants clearly preferred the eastern to the western Baltic markets, where they found the rivalry of Lübeck and Hamburg in Skåne (Scania) and Bergen irksome, and they particularly favoured Danzig.[63] From there return cargoes of wax, furs, and iron were all good possibilities, but so was timber and pitch, and at Hull and Lynn it was English merchants not Hansards who dominated the timber trade. When the English merchants demanded the right to trade in Reval, Pernau, and Livonia in 1388, which the Hansards complained was a new demand, they were no doubt looking as much for direct access to sources of timber and forest by-products (which bulked large in their home imports), as for furs (which did not).[64]

Cloth, like timber, was offered in good variety to consumers. In the late fourteenth century, the English merchants sold medium to good quality broadcloth and many cheaper sorts.[65] These included narrow cloths (the so-called "straits"), unfulled broadcloth, worsteds and says of various widths, russets, beaver cloth, damdukes, chalons, and kerseys. This range was simply a continuation from the early fourteenth century, when the smaller amount of exports similarly included the full range from top-quality scarlets on a par with Flemish cloths to cheaper worsteds, serges and says, blanket, frieze cloth, wadmal, kerseys, bluet, brunet, and russets, some of which

[61] Hansards were fairly slow to exploit the trade, but by the 1380s they exported between 15 % and 20 % of England's total cloth exports, and in the 1390s they sometimes took over 30% (Carus-Wilson & Coleman 1963: 75-88, 138-155).

[62] *Hanserecesse* 1875: 404. Forty-five were Yorkshire merchants trading through Hull, 34 traded through Lynn , and 36 came from the rest of England.

[63] The fortunes of the English in the Baltic have been recently re-examined by Jenks 1992a, and Lloyd 1991.

[64] Veale 1966: 69f; London took almost all Baltic furs and 90% were handled by Hansards.

[65] Changes in the tax system increasingly obscure the variety. Kerseys and "straits" were officially included in the cloth tax after 1390, although russets and some other narrow cloths continued to be valued for a while.

cost only a few pence a yard.[66] It is interesting that the customs valuations of English cloth in the later fourteenth century remained relatively low, despite the general rise in labour costs; indeed, valuations for some scarlets actually fell to 10s a yard, which suggests declining quality, or increasingly efficient production, or possibly both.[67] In the later fourteenth century there was still plenty of cloth at the cheap end. The increasingly popular kerseys were normally valued at 2.25 to 3.25d a yard, as cheap as anything in the early part of the century.

The cheaper cloths were frequently exported to the Baltic, and it was, of course, exactly these which benefited from the most efficient transport. Cloth is not always included among goods dependent on cheap transport, but it should be. Costs were crucial for less expensive cloths as medieval merchants clearly understood. One merchant who sent cloth from Flanders to Italy at the end of the fourteenth century wrote that "cloths of high value can bear the costs of transport by land, the others not", and another estimated that while land transport increased the price by 21.75 per cent, sea transport did so only by 15.2 per cent, and some merchants who sent cloth by land "have lost all the profit". Clearly four per cent made a great difference to profits.[68] This was no doubt the reason for the Hansards' objection to the change in English export duties in 1388-90.[69] On a batch of 24 kerseys worth about £8 the tax increased from 2s to 8s, an increase from 1.25 per cent to 5 per cent of the value—a difference of 3.75 per cent. This was not drastic, but it was close to the four per cent difference which the merchants dealing between Flanders and Italy had remarked on. The shift might have brought the cheaper cloths very near to a crucial threshold, but it was not enough to stop the trade. Cloth continued to be exchanged for timber.

[66] Worsteds cost 3.5d to 4.5d an ell; says were very cheap at 2.5d an ell. A yard was 36 inches (90 cm) long, and an ell was ca. 39 inches (1 m) long.

[67] The major changes in cloth types in the early fourteenth century are considered in Chorley 1987, and Munro 1991. Excavations in London have provided ample evidence of a move in the later fourteenth century to tabby weaves. These were cheaper to weave, but when fulled could make very desirable cloths. Crowfoot et al. 1992: 26-55.

[68] Fryde 1976: 348; reprinted in Fryde 1983.

[69] Instead of by value, the cloths were charged by the piece, at the rate of three kerseys or two narrow cloths to the standard cloth of assize. This meant that Hansards paid 1s for three kerseys instead of 3d for four kerseys normally valued together at about £1.

Conclusion

Several points can be made in conclusion. New commercial specialisation continued to emerge in the fourteenth century, promoted by particular combinations of natural resources, possibly cheaper production costs, greater skills, and more efficient transport services. The Baltic timber trade and the English cloth trade illustrate the "new markets" and "new commodities" of that century. Both commodities were available before 1300, but both came into their own in the later fourteenth century. Timber from the eastern Baltic overwhelmed the Norwegian trade in England, and English imports continued to rise at least until the 1390s. English cloth exports soared from 1,000 cloths a year in the first half of the century to 40,000 in the 1390s. The two commodities worked harmoniously together, and the expansion of English exports undoubtedly helped further to encourage the Anglo-Baltic timber trade by providing attractive return cargoes. The exact profitability of the trades would be difficult to quantify, but the increasing trade in both commodities suggest that profits were clear and worth having in both directions. Although profits on timber may have been quite small per piece, that did not matter if profits were regular and secure. Small regular profits were much appreciated by medieval business men. The advice offered in the English merchant manual known as the *Noumbre of Weyghtes* would apply to both these trades:

> Lyghte wynnynge make ane hevy pourse.
> Many smalle make a grete.[70]

[70] Noumbre of Weyghtes, fo.97v in Jenks 1992b: 306.

The Foreign Grain Trade in England 1250-1350

Nils Hybel

It is well known that the Baltic region supplied the urban centres in Western Europe with grain in the later middle ages, but it is an open question when this grain trade became a regular traffic. The history of the North European interregional grain market before ca. 1350 is obscure. The sources are very sparse and even though distinguished scholars drew attention to this field many years ago, there is still a lack of systematic research. This article attempts to throw new light on the topic. It presents an analysis of the English *new custom* preserved in the Public Record Office in London, a source that has never been studied for this purpose. I will concentrate on the grain trade between the Baltic region and England before 1350, but other aspects of the foreign grain trade in England will also be considered, for instance the connections with Norway, Flanders, France and Southern Europe.

CARTA MERCATORIA 1303

In 1303 King Edward I negotiated the *Carta Mercatoria* with representatives of the foreign merchants visiting England, who were granted more liberal conditions for their residence and trading. In return new duties were imposed upon them, among these a poundage on the import and export of general merchandise. The treaty gives the reasons for the poundage as follows: "And as some of the aforesaid merchants handle other wares, for instance avoirdupois and other fine goods, such as cloths of Tars', silk, cendals, hair and divers other wares and horses also and other animals, corn and other things and merchandise of many kinds which cannot easily be given a fixed custom, those merchants have agreed to give us and our heirs on each pound of silver of the valuation or worth of things and merchandise of this kind, by whatsoever name they are, 3d in the pound."[1]

[1] *English Historical Documents* 1975: 515.

The *Carta mercatoria* and subsequent customs accounts provide the first solid evidence of *ad valorem* custom duties in Northern Europe. Before 1303 duties were levied either per number or per quantity/lot. In England neither the fifteenth of King John nor the New Aid of 1266 can be proved conclusively to have been *ad valorem* duties. The *Carta Mercatoria* itself does not explain why *ad valorem* duties were being brought into use. It indicates a multiplicity of commodities and a profound monetary element in English foreign trade, but medieval tariff rates from other parts of Northern Europe enumerate similar numbers of various commodities without introducing *ad valorem* duties.[2]

Italian influence on the English customs system must be taken into consideration in order to understand this phenomenon. Italian merchants visited England at least from the beginning of the thirteenth century and they soon were involved in the collection of customs dues.[3] In the first years of the 1270s the New Aid of 1266 was farmed out to merchants from Florence and in the spring of 1275 the import duties were collected by Luke de Lucca.[4] After the introduction of the poundage Italian assignees, such as the Frescobaldi, received the incomes from customs dues as refund arrangements on loans given to the crown.[5] *Ad valorem* duties were known in antiquity and in the North Italian city-states poundage duties were used long before the English poundage was implemented.[6] Thus, it appears that the concept of poundage was imported by Italian merchants in the second half of the thirteenth century or perhaps even earlier. Hanseatic merchants probably transmitted the concept of poundage from England to Germany. Poundage was at least introduced in Lübeck and Hamburg in the late

[2] For instance the customs tariff rates given in 1252 by countess Margarethe of Flanders and Hennegau for Damme, Sluys and Bruges. See Gilliodts van Severen 1904-1906, vol. 1: no. 56, p. 41.

[3] In 1252 Pope Innocent IV asked the English king to protect two merchants from Sienna who wanted to set up in business in England, and in the following years the presence of more Italians is detectable in *Rymer's Fœdera* 1869.

[4] *Calendar of Patent Rolls 1266-72*, 1908-1913: 223, 442, 617; *Calendar of Fine Rolls 1272-1307*, 1911: 46f.

[5] *Calendar of Fine Rolls 1307-1319*, 1912: 44; Kaeuper 1973.

[6] In 1210 the consuls in Genoa for instance imposed a customs tax (*collecta*) of 2d. per 3 pound value sent by sea for six years to pay for the aid to Henry of Malta's attempt to recover Crete. "Colligere denarios duos per libram de mobilia que per mare portata vel missa fuerit semel in anno usque ad annos sex proximos venturos." *Annales Ianuenses* 1901: 114f.

1360s.[7] In Scandinavia *ad valorem* duties were brought into use much later. This system of taxation cannot be traced in Denmark before about 1500. A poundage proper was perhaps never enforced in Scandinavia in the Middle Ages.[8]

Customs rolls have survived for a great number of English ports from after Edward I issued the *Carta Mercatoria* in 1303 until the poundage was suspended, due to public criticism, from 20 August 1309 to 2 August 1310, and finally abandoned in 1311. There are even unbroken series of rolls from these early years of poundage, and from the 1320s after its reintroduction by Edward II in 1322. Apparently customs dues were collected very carefully and the accounts kept with much enthusiasm. The rolls are written in beautiful hands, carefully arranged and surprisingly detailed. Even in remote fishing hamlets, such as Whitby and Ravenser, determined customs collectors made entries relating to the landing of a few hundred herring, paying a duty of 3 d. The customs rolls are not merely sources for the study of trade but also of shipping and the medieval seasonal herring fishery. Not least important, they give us a glimpse of the administrative talents of the English Crown at the beginning of the fourteenth century.[9]

It is not easy to understand the background on which Eileen Power, Michael Postan and other earlier historians questioned the reliability of the early English customs rolls. They appear as reliable as any medieval record and give us at least an impression of the trends in foreign trade in England. Perhaps they even give a realistic image of the grain trade in England in the hands of the foreign merchants in the first decades of the fourteenth century. But let us first turn our attention to the second half of the thirteenth century, before the introduction of the poundage in 1303.

[7] *Die Hansischen Pfundzollisten des* Jahres *1368*, 1935; Nirrnheim 1910.

[8] Poundage was perhaps introduced by the Hanseatics after they, as part of the peace treaty of Stralsund 1369-1371, got two thirds of the incomes of the Scanian castles Helsingborg, Malmö, Skanör and Falsterbo for fifteen years. A custom roll from Malmö for 1375 is preserved. The structure of this roll suggests that it is a poundage roll, even though it does not include any valuations of merchandise trans ported, merely totals of the customs duties paid. See Jahnke 1997.

[9] Hybel 1996.

GRAIN TRADE BEFORE 1300

As we have just seen the *Carta Mercatoria* itself suggests that England was involved in the international grain trade at the time the treaty was signed. Grain itself was mentioned as one of the wares that occasioned the poundage because it could not "easily be given a fixed custom." In fact, the foreign grain trade in England seems to have been quite well established in the thirteenth century.

The first indication of imports of grain to England can be found in a royal order from 1257. In that year, Henry III authorised payment for oats bought for the royal household from Flemish and German merchants. Three years later firmer evidence of imports appears in a letter to the Dunwich bailiff in which the king orders the release of the German vessel *Salomon of Hamburg* loaded with grain and other merchandise bound for London.[10] The first document does not of course provide evidence of the actual import of oats. But it is very likely that oats were imported from Flanders for they played an important role from the twelfth century onward as a commercial crop in the reclaiming of the poor, light and sandy soils of central Flanders.[11] From the latter document it is reasonable to deduce that German grain was imported either from Western Germany or from the Baltic region and transshipped via Lübeck-Hamburg. Archaeological and documentary evidence suggests that in the thirteenth century Lübeck was an important grainport in the international trade between the Baltic region and Western Europe.[12]

The export of grain from Pomerania to England is indicated in a letter issued in 1278 by Wislaw II of Rügen and Stralsund.[13] Another document issued by Wislaw II in the same year, concerning various rules in the port of Stralsund, leaves the impression that the export of rye to Flanders and England was quite normal by this time and had been going on for some time.[14] In 1278 English grain prices were, according to David Farmer's re-

[10] *Hansisches Urkundenbuch* 1, 1876: no. 502, 554.

[11] Thoen 1997.

[12] See Rolf Hammel-Kiesow's article in this volume.

[13] In this letter it is ordained that freight and handling charges on rye and other merchandise are payable before departure in the port of Stralsund or at the arrival in Flanders or England. *Pommersches Urkundenbuch* 2, 1881: no. 1091, pp. 367-68.

[14] In the document among other things the handling charge of grain in Stralsund is stated together with an estimated sailing time of fourteen days to Flanders and England for a fast ship with good wind. *Hansisches Urkundenbuch* 1, 1876: no. 810.

construction, at an average level.[15] When they rose slightly in the early years of the 1280s, the mayor and citizens of London made an agreement (in 1282) with the German Hansa on various matters: the Germans were, for example, granted the liberty of importing and selling grain in the city.[16]

In the first half of the 1280s the grain yields on the estates of the bishops of Winchester were some 10 to 30% below average, and from Bohemia and Poland we have reports of famine lasting several years.[17] According to Farmer, the English grain prices in the years 1281-1284 were some 20-30% higher than average. When prices were at their highest in 1283-1284, Edward I granted protection and safe conduct for one year for Richard de Alemannia, the king's merchant and citizen in Lynn, to travel to Norway and "Estland" to buy grain and other merchandise for sale in England.[18] Richard hardly expected to buy grain grown in Norway since that country was supplied with grain from Northern Germany and presumably also England. The vigorous attempts made by the German emperor, German princes and Hanseatic towns to persuade Edward I to take part in the blockade of Norway from December 1284 to 1285 support the idea that English grain was exported to Norway in exchange for Norwegian fish and timber.[19] Richard de Alemannia's intention might have been to buy imported German grain in Norway but probably he was unable to do so because of the German blockade.

More likely it was his plan to purchase grain in "Estland". But what was meant by "Estland"? Hardly Estonia, which in Danish is called "Estland".

[15] Farmer 1988: 787-791 (Statistical Appendix, Table A.).

[16] "...et quod blada sua, que per eos adduci contigerint vendenda, in civita hosti tare possint et vendere in hospiciis et granariis suis per quadraginta dies a hospita cionis predicte, nisi per dominum regem vel majorem et cives propter caristiam bladi vel aliam causam necessariam hospitacio predicta inhibeatur expresse." *Hansisches Urkundenbuch* 1, 1876: no. 902.

[17] Titow 1960; Curschmann 1900; Alexandre 1987.

[18] Public Record Office, London (PRO): C. 66, 103.

[19] On 14 December 1284 Rostock asked Edward I to ban the export of grain and legumes to Norway. In a letter dated three days later Wismar put forward the same request. In two letters from 1285 the German Emperor Rudolf I and John, duke of Sachsen, asked the English king to prohibit exports from England to Norway and so did Lübeck and Henry, duke of Brandenburg, with a cry of help against the ravage of the Norwegians so that the German merchant could visit England as they had done before. *Hansisches Urkundenbuch* 1, 1876: no. 959, 961, 966, 967, 974, 975.

The "Estland" referred to presumably denoted the shores from Estonia to Prussia or probably the southern shores of the Baltic Sea from Prussia to Lübeck. Later, in a letter from ca. 1315 (concerning the capture by German merchants of a ship belonging to Ade le Clerk, citizen of King's Lynn) Stralsund, Lübeck and Greifswald are mentioned as towns in "Estland".[20] A document from 1321 shows that "Estland" was also used in the more general meaning of "the parts beyond the North Sea", including Denmark.[21] We will return to this document.

We have seen how only two of these four cases of the export of grain from the Baltic region to England in the second half of the thirteenth century coincide with poor harvests and famine in parts of Europe and a rather high English price level in the first half of the 1280s. This does not, of course, allow us to deduce that imports of grain from the Baltic region to England only took place when English prices were extraordinarily high. Years of crop failure, famine, war and high prices sometimes stimulated the grain trade, but a simple price/trade mechanism seems not to have been in operation. Thus, in the 1290s, when grain prices rose again after a drop of some 20% below the average level of the late 1280s, no evidence of imports from the Baltic can be found. Anyhow, grain was imported to England. From the last decade of the thirteenth century there are a few indications of imports from Ireland.[22] Grain seems to have been imported from Ireland to England and Wales from time to time in the preceding decades and a few documents prove that occasionally grain was also imported from France.[23]

In the thirteenth century England was not only *importing* grain; as we have seen it was also *exporting* grain. Long before the Hanseatic blockade

[20] *Rotuli Parliamentorum* 1832: 317,6.

[21] *Diplomatarium Danicum*, 2nd ser., vol. 8, no. 347.

[22] Two of them are related to the King's expedition into Wales in 1294. In the same year the Earl of Norfolk's clerk was granted safe conduct for buying victuals and other necessities in Ireland and bringing them to England. Two years before the Welsh campaign Henry le Mareschal and Robert de Wyleby, citizens and king's merchants of Dublin, were licensed to bring 200 crannocks of grain from Ireland to England and sell it. *Calendar of Close Rolls 1288-96*, 1900-08: 374; *Calendar of Patent Rolls 1281-1292*, 1893-95: 489; *1292-1301*, 1893-95: 216.

[23] Thus in 1271, 1276, 1277, 1278, 1280, 1283, 1284. *Calendar of Close Rolls 1272-79*, 1900-08: 272, 314; *Calendar of Close Rolls 1279-88*, 1900-08: 273; *Calendar of Patent Rolls 1266-1272*, 1908-13: 526; *Calendar of Patent Rolls 1272-1281*, 1901: 254, 403; *Calendar of Patent Rolls 1281-1292*, 1893-95: 116, 59.

of Norway, during the North European famine of 1224-1226,[24] Henry III gave permission for grain to be exported from Lynn to Norway, Denmark and Flanders.[25] Permission to export grain to Denmark was exceptional, as too was permission to export to Flanders. There are no further indications of grain exports to Denmark in any records from the thirteenth and the first decades of the fourteenth century. Neither are there any further signs of grain exported from England to Flanders before the French wars in the 1290s.[26] Likewise there are no records of exports of grain and other victuals from England to her continental possessions before the French seized Gascony in 1294. But during the following years of conflict, grain and other necessaries were frequently shipped from England, and sometimes from Ireland, to Gascony for the maintenance of the king's subjects.[27] We do not know how much grain was exported to Gascony and Flanders in this critical situation, but the mere fact that exports took place indicates that England, even in times of high prices, had a surplus of grain to sell abroad. The above mentioned attempts of the German king and princes and the Hanseatic league to drag England into the blockade of Norway in 1284-1285 support this assumption.

Besides these requests from the Germans, the fairly numerous records of Anglo-Norwegian trade relations in the late thirteenth century only include one document mentioning grain directly.[28] Nevertheless, it seems plausible to suggest that in the thirteenth century English grain supplemented the North German supply of grain to Norway, in return for Norwegian fish and timber. The same thing can hardly be said about supplies

[24] From the Netherlands, most of Germany, Eastern France, Denmark and England there are reports of storms, destruction of crops, murrain, hard winters and famine in the years 1224-1226.

[25] *Diplomatarium Danicum*, 1st ser., vol. 6, no 28.

[26] In February 1297 closed letters were sent to the sheriffs in Dorset, Northumberland, Cumberland, Lancaster, York, Lincoln, Norfolk, Suffolk, Essex, Kent, Sussex, Southampton, Somerset, Gloucester, Devon, Cornwall and Middlesex to announce that exports of corn, victuals and other goods was permitted from all ports and markets to Flanders. *Calendar of Close Rolls* 1296-1302, 1900-08: 15.

[27] Thus in 1296 and 1297. *Calendar of Patent Rolls 1292-1301*, 1893-95: 242, 244, 245, 292, 398.

[28] It is an order issued in February 1276 from Edward I to the sheriff in Norfolk to buy two hundred quarters of the best grain and hand it over to the king's servant Matheus de Columbariis to be taken to Norway. *Diplomatarium Norvegicum*, vol. 19, 1910: no. 290.

of foreign grain to Holland, Zeeland and Flanders. In the thirteenth century, the Netherlands were dependent on grain from the Baltic region, Germany and Northern France. Only in critical political situations was England now and again a source of supply. There is no evidence of regular English grain deliveries to the Netherlands. This impression seems confirmed by a list, dated to the last third of the thirteenth century, of the merchandise imported to Bruges and Flanders from various countries. Imports from England are described as wool, hides, lead, timber, coal and cheese; grain is not mentioned.[29]

By the end of the thirteenth century, Hanseatic merchants from the Baltic Sea region had visited England for many years. Merchants from Lübeck and other towns along the coasts of the Baltic Sea seem to have begun to visit the English North Sea ports and London from the beginning of the thirteenth century and this traffic became increasingly regular.[30] From 1281 the Hanseatic merchants of the Baltic Sea region amalgamated with the Westphalians in London and the Hanseatic *Kontor* was founded. Grain was one of the commodities they shipped to England, but they were hardly the only ones to do so.

In a royal Danish charter from the mid-thirteenth century the so-called *ummelandsfart* appears. The charter, mentioning those "gui umlandsfarœ dicuntur", was issued by King Abel on 24 September 1251. The original is kept in the town archive of Kampen and an undated confirmation of the document is in the town archive of Utrecht indicating that these *umlandsfarœ* were Dutchmen.[31] The charters reveal that the *ummelandsfahrere* were skippers from the Netherlands who quite simply could not use the Lübeck-Hamburg route. However, there were also English or perhaps even Hanseatic skippers avoiding the troublesome Lübeck-Hamburg transshipment by sailing through the Danish straits into the Kattegat and round the Skaw into the North Sea. This direct route from the Baltic to the North Sea must have been an advantageous alternative for German bulk carriers loaded with timber, corn, stone, etc. (cf. p. 57).

[29] *Hansisches Urkundenbuch* 3, 1882-86: 419, note 1.

[30] Thus, in 1248, Henry III was allowed to postpone the payment of his debt to merchants from "Estland" and Gotland. In 1252 he gave safe conduct and protection for traders from Hamburg and in 1265, 1269, 1275 and 1276 to Lübeck. *Calendar of Patent Rolls 1247-1258*, 1908: 7, 155; *1258-1266*, 1908-13: 565; *1266-1272*, 1908-13: 322; *1272-1281*, 1901: 83, 171.

[31] *Diplomatarium Danicum*, 2nd ser., vol. 1, no. 50.

Flemish and English merchants were probably doing business in the Baltic Sea region in the later part of the thirteenth century, but judging by a list of the duties on rye, wheat and barley exported from Greifswald, Hanseatic merchants dominated the grain market. This document from 1275 makes a distinction between German merchants and merchants from Norway and Balticum but it does not mention either English or Flemish traders. Two letters issued in 1294 by Zwolle and Kampen addressed to Lübeck perhaps illustrate the situation in the decades before 1300. The two Dutch towns are thanking Lübeck for enforcing the old tradition that the Frisians and Flemish should not sail the waters of the Baltic Sea, and they request Lübeck to try to keep the English out of the *Mare Orientale* too.[32] But all in vain; the English could not be kept out of the Baltic Sea. A few years later, in 1304, the Danish King Erik Menved agreed to compensate Johannes of Great Yarmouth for the loss he had suffered through a shipwreck in Danish waters.[33] As will be seen below there is still more evidence of Englishmen in the Baltic region in the first decades of the fourteenth century.

While it seems quite obvious that foreign merchants handled the major part of the English foreign grain trade, in particular imports from the Baltic Sea, it is impossible to determine the balance of trade with grain in the thirteenth century. It was probably positive, as it was in the first decade of the fourteenth century, as far as the balance can be reconstructed from the poundage accounts.

Quantifying the Grain Trade 1304-1347

The port covered by the best series of accounts is Kingston-upon-Hull which covers imports to Hull from July to September 1304 and imports and exports from October 1304 to the suspension of the poundage in September 1309. Hereafter imports and exports are covered from October 1310 to the abolishment of the poundage in September 1311. After the reintroduction of the poundage in 1322, there are rolls covering the years October 1322 to September 1323, and October 1324 to September 1325. The latter is a combined export and import account. In the roll for the year 1322-1323 there are only import entries. Finally there is a register of the outgoing vessels from Hull and their cargo in the period November 1346 to August

[32] *Hansisches Urkundenbuch* 1, 1876: no. 1154, 1155, 1275.

[33] *Diplomatarium Danicum*, 2nd ser., vol. 5, no. 347.

1347. On the basis of this excellent series, the balance of the grain trade at Kingston-upon-Hull can be shown (Table 12).

TABLE 12. HULL: EXPORTS/IMPORTS OF GRAIN, 1304-1347[34]

	Exports in quarters	Imports in quarters
1304-05	7,719	0
1305-06	424	4,582
1306-07	5,218	0
1307-08	3,165	256
1308-09	268	1,746
1310-11	3	85
1322-23	0	2,693
1324-25	0	10,751
1346-47	4,416	0
Total	21,213	20,113

During the years 1304 to 1311 there was a marked decrease in the export of the grain from Hull. They fell from 7,719 quarters in 1304-05 to 268 quarters in 1308-09 and to 3 quarters in 1310-11. Imports also fell from 4,582 quarters in 1305-06 to a mere 85 quarters in 1310-11. The total balance of the grain trade for Kingston-upon-Hull in the years 1304-1311 is exports of 16,797 quarters and imports of 6,669 quarters; the average per year for exports is 2,799.5 quarters, and for imports 1,111.5 quarters.

Chart 1, based on Table 12, shows that the grain trade at Kingston-

[34] In 1310-11 there are entries of 14 trayas exported and 24 imported; these are converted to quarters—1 traya = 1/5 quarter. In 1308-09 39 *Last* (*laest*) siligio and in 1322-23 24.5 *Last* siligio are entered; these are also converted to quarters—1 *Last* = 42 quarters. There is no information on the quantity of grain imported in 1324-25, only the dutiable value. This is converted to quarters on the basis of the relationship between quantity and dutiable value for oats (2.03s per quarter) and rye (2.4s per quarter) in the year 1322-23, and the corresponding relationship for wheat (6.3 pr quarter) in the year 1308-09. According to Farmer the average price level was 130 in 1308-09, 156 in 1322-23 and 146 in 1324-25 (Farmer 1988, pp. 790f.) Frumentum, siligio, ordei and a bit of seminis are the crops found in the rolls: PRO E.122, 55/16; 55/17; 55/19; 55/20; 55/23; 56/2; 56/3; 56/7; 56/10; 56/14; 56/26; 57/1; 57/2; 57/10; 6/1; 193/14.

upon-Hull almost died out in the years up to and including 1310-11. It also shows a remarkable swing in the balance of trade after 1308-09 and in particular after the reintroduction of the poundage in 1322. In the two years 1322-23 and 1324-25 13,444 quarters of grain were imported while exports had come to a complete standstill. Unfortunately there are no customs rolls from the following period. But judging from the list of ships leaving the port in 1346-47, grain was apparently being exported again at the same level as in the first years of poundage.

These trends seems to have been more or less the same in most of the other North Sea and Channel ports such as King's Lynn, Boston, Ipswich and Sandwich. Contrary to Hull only more patchy series of accounts have survived from these ports. Lynn seems, in contrast to its reputation in his-

CHART 1. HULL: EXPORTS/IMPORTS OF GRAIN 1304-1347

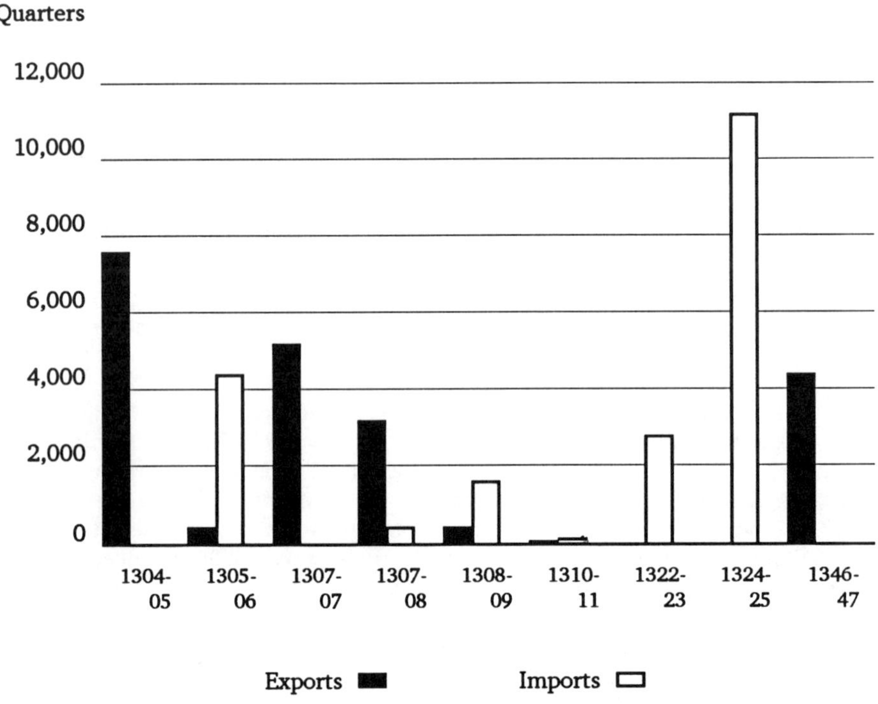

torical literature, merely to have been, next to Hull, the second most important grain port for the foreign merchants. From Lynn and the associated East Anglian ports there are accounts of the customs on general merchandise covering the first two successive phases of poundage for the years 1303 to 1309 and 1322 to 1326. Of the eleven relevant rolls examined, five relate to Lynn and all the ports to Yarmouth while six refer to Lynn only.

The first roll begins in February 1303. It is a combined export and import account. All the entries for grain seem to concern exports (*exendo*) even though nine out of the fifty-one grain entries do not state if they concern import or export dues. Another problem is that in twelve cases it is not possible to separate grain from other merchandise, as everything is entered and evaluated as one item. In the next very long roll covering the period from July 1304 to September 1307, we are confronted with the same problem in the part up to October 1306. Furthermore the roll is damaged and very difficult to read from July to October 1304. Thus, no statistical calculations of the grain trade can be based on the accounts from these East Anglian ports before October 1306. One of the subsequent rolls also presents problems. In the account for the year 1308-09 there is no information on quantities; we only have evaluations. Therefore Table 13 shows the balance of the grain trade in the East Anglian port in pounds sterling.

TABLE 13. LYNN AND ASSOCIATED PORTS: EXPORTS/IMPORTS OF GRAIN, 1306-1326[35]

	Value of Exports	Value of Imports
1306-07	£ 456	£ 9
1308-09	235	156
1322-23	0	118
1323-24	0	150
1324-25	0	1,057
1325-26	40	70

Table 13 indicates that the export of grain from this port also declined in the first phase of the poundage before 1311, and that here too exports also seem virtually to have died out in the 1320s. Imports are detectable before the poundage was suspended and, like at Hull, they peaked in 1324-

[35] PRO: E. 122, 93/3; 93/4; 93/17; 93/19; 93/22; 93/25; 93/28.

25. Only 5,280 quarters were imported at Lynn in that year, i.e., merely half the quantity imported at Hull in the same year. Exports from Lynn were at their highest in 1306-07 when about 2,700 quarters of grain were shipped from the port. For the same year more than 5,200 quarters were exported from Hull.

Judging from the more scanty series of poundage rolls from Ipswich, the grain trade at this port was less important than at Lynn. Still, the same trend is detectable as at Hull and Lynn. Only two rolls have survived from the first phase of the poundage, for the years 1304-05 and 1308-09. The account from 1308-1309 consists of two fragments, but a large part of them is illegible. Neither exports nor imports of grain is accounted for in the legible parts of these documents. The beginning of the roll covering the year from October 1304 to September 1305 is damaged and illegible, but from the middle of December to the beginning of July, when the grain trade ends, it is possible to calculate the total value of grain exports to be well over £300, while only one import entry of £4 appears.[36]

The first account after 1322 leaves the impression that the foreign merchants' activities in the port of Ipswich were in decline. In the year 1324-25 only three outgoing and forty-two incoming vessels were cleared; only four of the latter were loaded with grain. More or less the same situation appears from the account for the following year; very few export entries and no exports of grain at all, and thirty-six incoming vessels of which only three carried grain. Also from Ipswich the export of grain by foreigners stopped in the 1320s. There are no signs of grain exports in the last two accounts from 1326-27 and 1331-32. Imports of grain were very modest in the first year, with a value of £16, but in 1331-32 it increased to £150.[37]

The pattern at Boston differs from that at the other North Sea ports—Hull, Lynn and Ipswich. In contrast to these ports, there are no imports of grain detectable in the Boston accounts during the years following the reintroduction of poundage in 1322, and it can hardly be explained by a lack of or insufficient source material, even though some of the rolls are mere fragments. For imports we have a fragment of an account covering the period from 20 October to 13 November 1326 followed by a roll running from 24 October to 25 April 1327. The last import account covers January to the end of June 1334.[38]

[36] PRO: 122, 50/8; 52/38.

[37] PRO: 122, 50/12; 50/13; 50/17; 50/19.

[38] PRO: 122, 6/2; 6/21; 7/5.

Also contrasting with the other North Sea ports, the export of grain from Boston continued during some of the 1320s and 1330s. There is one export account from 1324-25, two from 1326-27 and one from 1333-34, although only two of the rolls show any exports of grain.[39] In the one running from May to August 1327 there are entries of grain exported with a total value of about £50. In the account for 1333-34 grain exports occur in March, April and May, with a total value of about £180.

Neither does there seem to have been any imports of grain to Boston in the first phase of the poundage like in the other North Sea ports. In the three import accounts from this period—1303, 1308-1309 and August to September 1309—not a single grain entry can be found.[40] But not surprisingly grain was shipped out of Boston. It is actually more surprising to discover that grain occurs only in the first two of the four surviving export accounts from 1303, 1303-1304, 1308-1309 and August to September 1309.[41] As at Hull and Lynn, grain exports seem to have died out at the end of the decade. From the beginning of March to the end of September 1303, wheat worth well over £200 was exported from Boston, and from the beginning of October of the same year to the end of June 1304 only less than half that amount was exported. From this point until May 1328 there is no trace of grain exported from Boston.

Moving down to the Channel ports, the Public Record Office in London possesses thirty-one customs rolls from Sandwich and the ports to Winchelsea from the years 1303–1348. Only nine of them include the poundage and in six of these there is evidence of grain trade in the years 1302-1303, 1304-1305, 1307-1308, 1324-1325 and 1327-1329. For the first year there is one account, covering the period February to May 1303, which contains no entries for grain at all, and two fragmented rolls, one of which is imperfectly preserved and very hard to read. The fragments are probably two parts of an integral account covering May to September 1303, showing no grain exports but four small entries for oats which must be interpreted as import entries, although it is not stated explicitly whether they are imports or exports.[42]

Two accounts cover the following year, 1304-1305. One is an account of anchoring, sales and passage dues at Sandwich from September to De-

39 PRO: 122, 6/19; 6/22; 7/1; 7/5.

40 PRO: 122, 5/9; 6/3; 6/5.

41 PRO: 122, 5/7; 5/10; 6/2; 6/8.

42 PRO: 122, 124/8; 124/10; 124/11.

cember 1304, mentioning no more than three cases of grain, but it is not possible to determine whether they were imports or exports.[43] The other account is now missing from the Public Record Office, but fortunately it was published by N. S. B. Gras in 1918.[44] It begins with the export of wool and the importing of cloth and wax, followed by an account of the poundage where a few import entries can be found. The export of general merchandise is extensive, but unfortunately in numerous cases it is impossible to distinguish grain from other merchandise. Thus no calculations can be made of the total value of the export of grain; but grain was important since it is mentioned in most of the two hundred-odd entries.

The account for 1307-08 is much more adequate. It is divided into an import and an export account. There are no grain imports traceable at any of the ports, but not surprisingly there are notable exports from Sandwich from the beginning of April to August 1308. These exports were much less than in 1304-05, when there were about two hundred entries of grain. In 1307-08 there were only seventeen entries of grain and in five of these grain and other merchandise are combined making a total dutiable value of about £100.[45] Thus, like in Hull and Lynn, grain exports from Sandwich and the associated Channel ports seem to have been in decline in the first decade of the fourteenth century, even though exports were at a much lower level than in the North Sea ports. In 1307-08 the value of the grain exports from Hull was about £720.

After the reintroduction of the poundage in 1322, the Channel ports show a pattern similar to that of the North Sea ports. In 1324-25 the dutiable value of grain imports was £378 65 s.[46] This was the year when imports peaked at Hull with the importation of 10,751 quarters fixed at £1,488 dutiable value, and in Lynn where the value of the imports was fixed at £1,061. The grain imported through the Channel ports in the 1320s was at a much lower level than that imported to the North Sea ports. After 1325, like at Lynn, imports of grain seem to have faded out. There are a few entries in the spring and early summer of 1327 but none in the account running from October 1328 to January 1328.[47]

[43] PRO: 122, 124/14.

[44] Gras 1918: 302-346.

[45] PRO: 122, 124/18.

[46] PRO: 122, 124/29.

[47] PRO: London: 122, 124/30.

THE SWING FROM EXPORTS TO IMPORTS

In the first years of the poundage the balance of the English foreign grain trade was positive, but the poundage rolls from the North Sea and Channel ports suggest that the balance turned from exports to imports in the last years of the first decade of the century. At all the ports examined, exports of grain either faded or died out from the year 1308-09 and at the most important grain ports—Hull and Lynn—imports increased from that year on. On 5 January 1307 a ban on the export of grain, animals and other victuals, horses, arms, silver and gold was sent to Great Yarmouth and several other ports. But this royal order hardly explains the fall of the English grain exports. Either the ban was ignored or the king granted a lot of exemptions. In any case it did not appear to have great immediate influence on the export of grain from the ports examined here. In Hull and Lynn exports continued uninterrupted in the months after the ban was imposed; as well in the following year there is a rather notable amount of grain exports from both ports. The swing in the English overseas trade did not set in until 1308-09.

This turning-point corresponded with rising grain prices. Reconstructions of English prices show that from 1309-10 to 1310-11 they were about 40 to 60% above the average level of the period from 1330-31 to 1346-47[48] and complaints of high prices were frequently heard in the years before the poundage was abolished in 1311. In the New Ordinance lifting the customs on foreigners in 1311, it is said that because of the new customs "merchants come more rarely and bring less goods into the land and foreign merchants stay for a longer time than they use to, by which staying things are made that much dearer than they used to be, to the detriment of the king and his people."[49] As we have seen the poundage did not prevent imports of grain from increasing, and as far as the rise of prices is concerned, foreign merchants seem to have been made scapegoats in times of dearth. The high prices were in all probability caused by poor weather and crop failures rather than the presence of foreigners. Calculations of grain yields on the estates of Winchester Cathedral indicate that the yields in 1310 were 16% below average and the bailiff's report states that the weather was dry in 1309 and very dry in 1310.[50]

48 Farmer 1988: 787-791 (Table A).

49 *Statutes of the Realm* 1810: Les noveles Ordenances, 1311.

50 Titow 1960.

The poundage hardly had a negative effect on the volume of the grain trade although the total volume decreased temporarily at the end of the first decade of the fourteenth century. In the long run the grain trade increased greatly because of the increase in imports after the reintroduction of the poundage in the 1320s. At Hull the volume in 1304-05 was 7,719 quarters (see Table 12). In 1308-09 it had fallen to 2,014 quarters and in 1324-25 it had peaked at 10,751. The fluctuations at Lynn were similar. In 1306-07 the dutiable value of the grain imported and exported by foreign merchants was £465, in 1308-1309 £391 and it peaked, like at Hull, in 1324-25 at £1,061 (Table13). The reason why the trade dwindled at the end of the first decade of the fourteenth century was probably the same as the cause of the high prices—poor weather and crop failure. Moreover not only England was affected; the climate was unfavourable to crops all over Northern Europe in the years around 1310.

Danish annals give information of drought and failure of crops in 1311.[51] From Flanders there are reports of a very hard winter and high prices of grain and wine in 1309, and Hessen in Germany was ravaged by famine that year.[52] The Lübeck chronicler Detmar informs us of high prices in England and Flanders in 1310, and fears that a time of dearth will be transmitted to the German towns along the southern shores of the Baltic Sea. Thus, he confirms the swing of English prices, and perhaps also the turning-point of the foreign grain trade in the English North Sea and Channel ports. Detmar also tells us of many merchants coming to Venden to buy grain and that the export of grain was forbidden from Wismar, Rostock, Stralsund and Greifswald to prevent rising prices.[53] General climatic difficulties in Northern Europe blocked the overseas grain trade.

The impact of the troubles with the Scots and the great European famine in the years from 1315 to 1317 on the English grain-market is illuminated by innumerable letters. A ban on the export of grain, fish and other victuals was issued in 1317 and repeated in 1318 and 1319. In 1319 the ban was caused by an allegation that foreigners had exported English grain to the Scots, more than any scarcity of it in England. Thus, the bailiffs of the Tolbooth of Lynn were instructed that foreign merchants could only ex-

51 Hybel 1997.

52 Curschmann 1900.

53 *Chronik des Franciscaner Lesemeisters Detmar* 1829.

port grain if they pledged that they would not supply the Scots.[54] During these critical years the king tried to attract foreign merchants to the country by issuing an increasing number of letters of protection and safe conduct to individual merchants and by giving residence permits to all foreign merchants (except subjects of his enemies) coming into the realm with corn and other merchandise.[55] Attempts were also made to supplement the English grain market with supplies from France, Spain, Portugal and even Italy and Sicily. As mentioned earlier Italian merchants had been in the country for many years and so had Spanish and Portuguese.[56] Merchants from southern Europe relieved the situation during the famine from 1315 to 1317. They supplied England with thousands of quarters of wheat from southern Europe, which did not suffer from heavy rainfalls from 1314 to 1316.[57]

But these were years of exceptional circumstances. The more regular English grain imports hardly came from Italy, Spain and Portugal. A closer study of the information given by the customs rolls provides strong arguments that the majority of the regular imports through the North Sea ports came from the Baltic region which, as in the extraordinary years around

[54] PRO: C. 54, 134; *Calendar of Close Rolls 1313-1318*, 1892-1898: 588; *1318-1323*, 1892-1898: 132, 134, 136.

[55] PRO: C. 66, 144.

[56] In 1248 Henry III, for instance, was granted a respite for the refund of his debt to Spanish merchants; and two letters of protection and safe conduct for Portuguese merchants were issued in 1258. *Calendar of Patent Rolls 1247-1258*, 1908-1913: 613; *1258-1266*, 1908-1913: 258.

[57] In a 1316 document about the capture by French pirates of a vessel from Genoa carrying wheat, oil and honey, it is mentioned that because of the recent scarcity of corn and other victuals in his realm the king has given special privileges to Sicily, Spain and Genoa and other merchants from the east and the west in order that they might bring such victuals into his kingdom. A writ of Peter Bard, bailiff of Sandwich, and Nicholas, clerk of Antony Passaigne of Genoa, states that this Genoese merchant had called at the port of Sandwich with about 2,500 quarters of wheat and other merchandise in 1316. The wheat probably came from Italy and/or Spain. In the following year Edward II addressed the rulers of Spain with a request that the same Anthony Passaigne of Genoa could buy 1,000 bushels of wheat in Spain and ship it to England. In the same year the rulers of Genoa were requested by the English king that another member of the Passaigne family, Leonard, should be allowed to fit out five galleys with armed men, arms and victuals to be used in the Scotch wars. PRO: C. 54, 134; C. 66, 145; 146; *Calendar of Close Rolls 1313-1318*, 1892-1898: 452.

1310 and also during and after the 1315-1317 famine, seems to have stopped exporting grain to England, to judge by the remarkable absence of documents concerning the Baltic grain trade in these years.

The Origins of the Imports

From Table 14 it can be calculated that during the entire period of 1304-1309, about 94% of the exports from Hull consisted of wheat (*frumentum*), although two years differ from this general pattern. In 1305-06 wheat made up only 69% while the export of rye rose to 28%. In 1308-09 the proportion of wheat exported fell to about 66% of the total while rye made up 12% and barley 22% of the grain exports from Hull. In both these years imports far exceeded exports—92 and 89% respectively of the total amount of grain passing through the port. A share of the relatively small exports in these years therefore probably consists of the re-export of rye and barley imported to Hull—at least rye, since much rye was imported in both years, while barley was only imported in 1305-06 and not in 1308-09, and because rye was the most important crop imported.

TABLE 14. EXPORTS OF GRAIN FROM HULL, 1304-1347
DISTRIBUTION OF CEREALS IN QUARTERS

	Frumentum Wheat	Ordei Barley	Avene Oats	Siligio Rye	Brasei Malt
1304-05	7630	9	0	80	0
1305-06	294	0	0	119	0
1306-07	5218	0	0	0	0
1307-08	2040	0	0	9	1117
1308-09	177	58	0	33	0
1310-10	0	0	0	3	0
1346-47	3082	0	0	0	0
Total	18441	67	0	244	1117

Wheat was also the dominant commercial crop in the exports from the other North Sea ports. In 1306-07 only wheat was exported from Lynn, and wheat made up nearly 90% of the total export of grain in 1308-1309. In 1325-26 about 90% of the grain exported from Lynn was wheat. Also in the best preserved of the two existing Ipswich accounts from before 1311, that from 1304-05, wheat made up nearly all the grain exported. As far as it is possible to distinguish between the crops in the accounts from Boston, wheat was also the main crop to be exported from this port. Wheat was no doubt the most important crop to be exported from all the North Sea ports.

As for imports, we find a completely different cereal distribution. Table 15 shows that from 1305 to 1325 rye and oats were the main cereal imported via Hull. Rye made up 68% and oats 24% of total imports, whereas wheat made up merely 6%. The most important crops imported at Hull were definitely rye and oats. More or less the same thing can be said about Lynn and Ipswich but, as we have seen, there were no grain imports at Boston at all.

TABLE 15. IMPORTS OF GRAIN INTO HULL, 1304-1325
DISTRIBUTION OF CEREALS IN QUARTERS

	Frumentum Wheat	Ordei Barley	Avene Oats	Siligio Rye
1305-06	640	104	2,736	1,102
1307-08	0	0	76	0
1308-09	100	0	510	1,110
1310-11	80	110	185	0
1322-23	0	282	1,362	1,050
1324-25	644	0	522	9,585
Total	1,464	496	5,391	12,847

When imports peaked at Lynn in 1324-25 the distribution of grain was rye 75%, barley 5%, oats 14%, wheat 5% and mixed grain less than 1%. When imports rose before the suspension of the poundage in 1308-1309 the distribution was rye 32%, barley 1%, oats 37%, wheat 21% and mixed grain 9%. At Ipswich it is only possible to reconstruct the distribution of grain from the 1324-25 account: imports of rye and oats were 53% and of barley 47%.

The distribution of cereals found in the customs accounts from the North Sea ports suggests certain areas of origin for the grain imported to England. We found evidence of imports of oats from the Netherlands to England in 1257 and pointed out that this crop was suitable for growning on the reclaimed salt land of the Low Countries, whereas rye was the major crop in continental Northern Germany. Rye in particular was the most important crop in the region colonised in the twelfth and thirteenth centuries north-east of the Elbe and in arable south-eastern Scandinavia—the Danish islands and Scania. As we also saw earlier, rye is frequently mentioned in documents providing information on imports of grain from these parts beyond the North Sea. The customs rolls give further, similar indications of the origins of the rye imported to England.

In 1305-06, the first year imports exceeded exports at Hull, Hamburg is the home port most frequently mentioned for skippers and merchants importing rye and oats at Hull. This grain could, of course, have come from a variety places, but perhaps the emphasis on Hamburg indicates trans-shipments from the Baltic Sea via the normal Hanseatic Lübeck-Hamburg axis. Some of the entries seem to support this assumption: "navis Boyd de Estland" arrived at Hull on 20 April carrying rye and oats of his own and also of Johannis de Hamburg, who arrived the same day as the master of another ship loaded with rye and oats. Apparently they tried to cope with the dangers at sea by sailing in convoy and spreading the risk by sharing out the cargo.

In 1308-09, the next year showing extensive imports at Hull, there are striking indications of grain imported from Pomerania. On 13 June "navis Walter de Strallesond" (Stralsund) arrived with 240 quarters of rye. On 22 June "navis Engelbrecht de Grippeswald" (Greifswald) arrived with 28 *Last* rye—part of the cargo belonging to the merchant Henry from the same town. Two days later "navis Jacobi de Scaner" (perhaps Skanör in southern Scania) arrived with 18 *Last* rye belonging to the merchant Helerimus de Grippeswald and 10 *Last* rye belonging to the merchant Henry de Wymar (Wismar). Many other examples from the customs rolls could be mentioned indicating that skippers and merchants from home ports stretching from Lübeck in the West to Wismar, Stralsund and Greifswald, and Thorn (Torun) in Prussia in the East were delivering grain to the English market in the first three decades of the fourteenth century.

Therefore, the contents of Edward II's order from 1323 to the merchant Nikolaus Pape of Hamburg comes as no surprise. With reference to the Scottish Wars, Nikolaus is instructed to buy grain and victuals on his journey to "Estland" and Prussia. In the same year King Edward also gave a letter of protection and safe conduct to the Esterling Godekin von Reval.[58] At this time the town seems to have been exporting grain for years. As early

[58] *Hansisches Urkundenbuch* 2, 1879: no. 399.

as in 1297 the Danish King Erik VI Menved ordered that restrictions on exports of grain from Reval could only be imposed in exceptional cases.[59]

Not surprisingly the grain imported to the Channel ports—from Sandwich to Winchelsea—came from other parts of the world. It is unfortunately not possible to examine the distribution of the cereals imported to these ports. In most cases entries only record grain (*bladis*) and when there is more specific information only wheat and oats are named. In the accounts from Sandwich and the ports to Winchelsea, there is not a single entry concerning rye or barley. Taken together with the fact that there are no North-east German or Baltic but only French and Flemish names in these rolls, it is reasonable to conclude that the grain imported to the Channel ports consisted primarily of wheat (and secondarily of oats) from Northern France and Flanders.

THE REGULARITY OF THE GRAIN TRADE

The English overseas grain trade was indeed not restricted to years of poor crops, war and high grain prices. Such climatic and political disturbances influenced trade, of course, but they did not automatically stimulate it. In the 1290s war seems to have dampened the interregional grain trade. No simple price-trade mechanism was in operation. We saw that there was no unequivocal correlation between amount of trade in grain and the rise of prices in the thirteenth century, and nor was there any in the fourteenth century. English exports from Hull dwindled from the late 1290s to 1308 in a period of stable prices. Likewise it is perhaps surprising that in the first year showing extensive imports at Hull (1305-06) the English price level was normal. The high prices connected with the North European drought around 1310 and the wet seasons in Northern Europe (1314 to 1316) blocked the Anglo-Baltic grain trade but, on the other hand, the latter catastrophe paved the way for the introduction of South European wheat to the English grain market.

Political intervention played its part, but export regulations did not necessarily have much influence on the grain trade and price formation. As mentioned earlier, on 5 January 1307 the king issued a letter to Yarmouth and many other ports stating that grain and other victuals, animals, horses, arms, gold and silver were only to be exported with the king's permission,

59 *Diplomatarium Danicum*, 2nd ser., vol. 4, no. 260.

except to Gascony.[60] Nevertheless the export of grain from the North Sea ports continued on quite an extensive scale. Caution must be used in determining the effect of the royal bans on exports. Thus, the political factor hardly explains the total standstill of grain exports in the 1320s from the ports examined. In 1322 a general ban on the export of grain was issued by the king "as corn is now dear in the realm, and it is feared that it will be dearer in future if it be permitted to be taken out of the realm" and in view of the approaching summer campaign in Scotland. Sometime in 1325 or in the immediately preceding years, merchants from Flanders, Brabant, Spain and Germany were forbidden to export victuals from England.[61]

In the following two years grain prices fell to quite a low level. If this drop was due to export restrictions, or was a consequence of grain deliveries from abroad, or other factors is hard to decide. But the grain deliveries from overseas no doubt had an impact on the English grain market even though, considering the gross national production, the volume of imports was not overwhelming. When imports to Hull peaked at nearly 11,000 quarters in 1324-25 it matched perhaps the production of 10 to 15 manors like Elton Manor under the Ramsey Abbey. On the other hand the 11,000 quarters could feed about 1,500 people and in a medieval urban perspective that is a lot. Furthermore it must be kept in mind that we only have information on imports of grain by foreigners in the customs rolls.

In the wool trade the last third of the thirteenth and the first third of the fourteenth century seem to have witnessed a significant evolution of denizen advance.[62] The growth of the English merchants' share in the country's overseas grain trade was perhaps not that considerable. But, as we have seen earlier, documents at least provide evidence that English skippers and merchants were engaged in shipping in the Baltic sea from the last quarter of the thirteenth century, and they definitely participated in the grain trade with places beyond the North Sea in the critical years around 1310.[63] English involvement in the overseas grain trade is further proved

[60] *Calendar of Close Rolls 1302-1307*, 1900-1908: 527.

[61] *Calendar of Close Rolls 1318-1323*, 1892-1898: 691; *1323-1327*, 1892-1898: 224-225.

[62] Miller & Hatcher 1995: 233.

[63] A closed letter from 1310 informs us about the wreck on the Norwegian coast of a ship from Grimsby on its journey back to England from "Estland" loaded with grain and victuals. Two years later we hear of the confiscation of an English merchant's merchandise in Stralsund. *Calendar of Close Rolls 1307-1313*, 1892-1898: 325; *Hansisches Urkundenbuch* 2, 1879: no. 206.

by a case of piracy from 1321.[64] A dispute about freight rates from 1327 indicates English involvement in shipping of grain from Thorn in Prussia to England, but perhaps even more important it is proof of regular navigation between Prussia and Norway, Scotland, Flanders and England.[65] There is in fact plenty of evidence that from about 1310 English merchants increasingly took part in the grain trade with the Baltic region.[66]

Even if Englishmen imported grain on a scale comparable with that of imports by foreigners, the total amount imported to England must have been very modest. Nevertheless it might very well have influenced the English prices. The mere knowledge that imported grain was available at a low cost might have had some effect. Edward II at least seems to have been influenced by such intelligence when on 20 April 1325, before he came to

64 The document states that the merchant Petri de Wellewyk from Ravenser was on his way back to England with grain and other merchandise loaded "in Estland apud Aldeburg in Denemarch"—maybe Ålborg in Northern Jutland. *Calendar of Close Rolls 1318-1323*, 1892-1898: 309.

65 Hinricus Blake, presumably an Englishman, had booked thirty-nine *Last* and three barrels of rye on Herbordus Hamer's and Hinricus de Brema's ships for Bergen but when they came to the port of Skagen, Blake decided to sail for England instead. Blake was perhaps informed by sailors or merchants calling at Skagen on their way to the Baltic that the prices were favourable in England. If so, the journey probably took place in 1324 or before the 1325 harvest when the English price level was some fifty per cent above average. After arrival in England they could not agree on the rate of freight, and Harbordus and Henricus collected information about the rates from Thorn to England from other skippers. Eventually the case was brought before the bailiff in Falsterbo; perhaps it was a proviso in the charter party to bring possible conflicts before this court. During the trial two German skippers, Ricquardus Schonenberch and Nicolaus Detmars, stepped forward and testified about the freight rates from Thorn to Scotland and Flanders. *Diplomatarium Danicum*, 2nd ser., vol. 9, no. 447.

66 In 1329 we hear of the good ship *La Godeyere* of Newcastle being arrested in Copenhagen on her journey back to England from Stralsund. A similar case is reported in 1339 when *La Cuthbert* of Hartlepool on her way to "Estland" was captured on the Danish coast. Two years before, Edward III had sent a letter to the lady of Wolgast, Greifswald and Stralsund about seizure of the merchandise of an English merchant in these towns. Three years later another English merchant was molested in Königsberg in Prussia. There are several indications that English merchants visited the German towns in 1342. See note 70. *Calendar of Close Rolls 1327-1330*, 1896-1913: 537; *1337-1339*, 1896-1913: 130; *1339-1341*, 1896-1913: 345; *Diplomatarium Danicum*, 2nd ser., vol. 10, no. 109, 110, 111; vol. 12, no. 149.

London, he instructed the mayor and aldermen that grain prices in the city should be adjusted to the prices of grain purchased from grain merchants "as the king understood that grain of divers sorts had been brought to the city from Flanders in great quantity."[67] It is hardly a coincidence that the king gave such an order in this particular year. As we have seen, imports of grain via the North Sea and Channel ports was at its highest in 1324-25; and it was a year of high grain prices—some fifty percent above average. At that time the English grain prices turned.

After a temporary rise from about 1330 to 1332, grain prices fell and remained at a constant low level up to the Black Death. Seen in a longer perspective the prices in the period 1325 to 1350 were some 10 to 30 percent below the level of prices in the first quarter of the fourteenth century. Comparing prices of wheat, rye, barley, oats and peas in the years 1300-01 to 1324-25 with the period 1325-26 to 1349-50 the price level decreased by about thirty percent. If the extremely high prices in the years 1315-16, 1316-17 and 1321-22 are dropped from the calculations the price levels in the second quarter were about ten percent below those of the first quarter of the fourteenth century.[68]

One precondition for this reduction in prices must have been a continuation of the regular Baltic-North Sea grain route established during the last quarter of the thirteenth and the first quarter of the fourteenth century, and of the importing of grain from Western continental Europe. England was at war during most of this period of moderate grain prices after 1325-26; so even though we do not have much evidence of grain imports after the disappearance of the customs rolls, it seems plausible to suggest that imports continued after the outbreak of the Hundred Years War. Only a few poundage rolls from the late 1320s are preserved and practically none from the 1330s and 1340s. Therefore, grain imports can in principle be illustrated only using piracy cases, just as before the poundage and when it was suspended in the second decade of the fourteenth century. A number of documents from the 1320s and 1330s concerning attacks on ships carrying grain from the continental dominions of England and Portugal show that imports did not stop after the disappearance of the poundage rolls.[69] Continuity in imports from the Baltic region is indicated by letters from the councils in

67 *Calendar of Close Rolls 1323-1327*, 1892-1898: 286.

68 Hybel 1994.

69 *Calendar of Close Rolls 1323-1327*, 1892-1898: 616; *1327-1330*, 1896-1913: 409; *1330-1333*, 1896-1913: 158; *1333-1337*, 1896-1913: 644; *Calendar of Patent Rolls 1330-1334*, 1893-1905: 169.

Stralsund, Greifswald, Lübeck and Wismar to Edward III, and by royal orders to the bailiffs of Boston from the 1340s.[70]

The 1330s and 1340s were marked by export bans. It can be argued that such political action helped to keep the English grain prices down. On the other hand we have seen above that export restrictions were not always observed; sometimes bans were violated daily, as shown below, but the bans certainly produced adequate historical source material for the study of the export trade. Thus, various permissions to export grain to Ireland, Scotland, Bordeaux, Norway and places beyond the sea indicate that sometime in the years 1330-32, when grain prices rose temporarily, a ban on exporting grain from England was issued by the king.[71] In 1333 all sheriffs in England were instructed that grain exports were prohibited, except by royal grant of exemption.[72] In the following years up to the beginning of the Hundred Years War, a large number of such dispensations were granted for exports to Norway, Gascony, Spain, Ireland, Aquitaine, Bayonne, Scotland, Flanders, Zeeland, Brabant, Hainault and Friesland.[73]

On the outbreak of the Hundred Years War a ban was introduced on exports of grain to the king's enemies as a usual measure in times of war. It seems to have been proclaimed in October 1336 since a merchant from Hainault on the 25th of that month was permitted to remove two hundred quarters of wheat from England because they had been loaded on his ship

[70] These documents relate to a ban on the export of grain and victuals from the German Baltic ports due to the war in 1342 between the Hanseatic towns, on the one hand, and the Swedish-Norwegian king on the other. The councils in the German towns complained that William de Lethenay Ravenser had violated the ban by loading grain, timber, wax, copper and other merchandise in Stralsund on a ship, owned by Jacok Davidsson from Sluys, with the intention of shipping this merchandise to England. Apparently William got away but was later captured. In a 1344 letter to the bailiffs in Boston the king claimed that William had been attacked near the coast of Ravenser by a body of Hanseatic ships from Lübeck, Wismar, Stralsund, Greifswald, Rostock, Hamburg, Kampen, Königsberg and Danzig. The ship was taken to "the parts beyond, to Strallesund", and William was put into prison. *Calendar of Close Rolls 1343-1346*, 1896-1913: 296, 408, 414, 415; *1346-1349*, 1896-1913: 519, 520, 521. *Diplomatarium Danicum*, 3rd ser., vol. 1, no. 341.

[71] *Calendar of Close Rolls 1330-1333*, 1896-1913: 205, 275, 309; *Calendar of Patent Rolls 1330-1334*, 1893-1905: 302, 372, 414.

[72] *Calendar of Close Rolls 1333-1337*, 1896-1913: 83.

[73] *Calendar of Patent Rolls 1330-1334*, 1893-1905: 415, 419, 420, 421, 423-425, 425, 428, 429,431, 487, 542, 544; *1334-1338*, 1893-1905: 57, 80, 171.

before the proclamation was published.[74] Later references to the ban issued in 1343 and 1345 maintain that neither native nor foreign merchants were allowed to export grain and that the ban was daily disregarded. They also mention that Gascony, Ireland, Flanders, Brittany, Brabant, Spain, Holland, Zeeland and Germany were excepted.[75]

These proclamations, together with the list of outgoing vessels from Hull in 1347, illustrated by Chart 1, and numerous export licences from the period 1337 to 1350, prove that the export of grain from England did not come to an end in the 1320s. The decline of exports around 1310 and the total standstill in the 1320s, as shown by the customs accounts, were intervals in the history of the overseas English grain trade. As we have already seen, exports to Norway, the continental English dependencies, the Netherlands, and even Spain, were taken up again in the late 1320s and in the first half of the 1330s. Judging from the increasing number of export licences issued, and the alleged violations of the export ban issued at the beginning of the Hundred Years War, exports seem to have grown in the years immediately after 1336. In the Calendar of Patent Rolls 1334-1338 eighteen such licenses can be found, while in the Calendar covering the years 1338-1340 only four were given to export grain to Norway, Germany, the Netherlands, Spain and the English dependencies on the continent.[76]

In 1338 a trade agreement between England and Flanders was renegotiated, and in the following decade many export licences and letters of protection and safe conduct relating to the export of grain to Flanders and Zeeland were issued.[77] However, the majority of these licences and letters from the 1340s concerned the supply of the King's men on his continental dependencies, particularly after 1345.[78] Only a few are granted to German

[74] *Calendar of Patent Rolls 1334-1338*, 1893-1905: 333.

[75] *Calendar of Patent Rolls 1343-1345*, 1893-1905: 186; *1345-1348*, 1893-1905: 30.

[76] *Calendar of Patent Rolls 1334-1338*, 1893-1905: 333, 337, 339, 340, 351, 414, 536-539, 542, 543, 546, 553, 571, 572; *1338-1340*, 1893-1905: 20, 46, 51, 53.

[77] *Calendar of Close Rolls 1337-1339*, 1896-1913: 515, 590; *1339-1341*, 1896-1913: 349, 503, 504; *1341-1343*, 1896-1913: 627, 628, 694, 695; *1343-1346*, 1896-1913: 81, 315, 316, 334, 384, 390, 478, 479, 482; *1349-1354*, 1896-1913: 15, 184; *Calendar of Patent Rolls 1340-1343*, 1893-1905: 579; *1348-1350*, 1893-1905: 501, 502, 510, 550.

[78] *Calendar of Patent Rolls 1340-1343*, 1893-1905: 28, 579; pp. 131, 220; *1345-1348*, 1893-1905: 198, 206, 207, 209, 210, 212, 213, 216, 225, 246, 251, 280, 28, 282, 283, 287, 291, 403; *1348-1350*, 1893-1905: 20, 34, 147, 469, 485, 555, 556,

merchants.[79] Some exports of grain to Norway continued despite its prohibition in the already-mentioned ban imposed at the beginning of the Hundred Years War. [80] There exist two export licences for grain from London and Boston to Spain from 1346. Also in the 1340s various measures were taken to prevent the illegal export of grain from England. Commissioners were, for example, appointed to arrest ships loaded with corn and bound for Normandy or other hostile parts beyond the sea, or in other respects violating the king's restrictions on grain exports.[81]

According to Table 12 and Chart 1, exports from Hull in 1347 reached the level they had in the first decade of the century. If illegal exports were a reality, and we also take into account the deliveries to the king's men at war on the continent as well as the export licenses issued, it can be concluded that exports of grain from England on the eve of the Black Death were of some importance. In this light it is interesting to read the statement of reasons for the general ban on the export of grain and animals issued in 1350 after the plague had struck England. The ban was not motivated by disturbances caused by the heavy death tolls, but "the frequent exportation of corn and animals" that had led to "a great scarcity of those things."[82]

In contrast to the thirteenth and the first decade of the fourteenth century, the Netherlands—Flanders, Zeeland, Holland and Brabant—seem to

---

570.

[79] One of them, from 1340, allowed German and Flemish merchants to export wheat and other cereals up to an amount of five hundred quarters to Germany and Flanders. Another tells of German merchants loading 40 quarters of grain in Newcastle for export to Geldern in 1343. *Calendar of Close Rolls 1339-1341*, 1896-1913: 349; *Hansisches Urkundenbuch* 2, 1879: 343, appendix no. 77.

[80] In 1341 two persons apparently of German origin, Thomas and William Melckebourn, were appointed "to arrest and forfeit any ships or boats laden with corn, victuals and armour intended to be taken to the king's enemies in Scotland, Norway or elsewhere, found in the ports in the counties of Lincoln, Norfolk and Suffolk, where as is said some merchants at present daily ship such thing contrary to the king's proclamation." In 1344 a closed letter instructs the mayor and bailiffs of Lynn that the burgesses of the town were permitted "to take to Norway as much as they wish of certain kinds of corn." In 1348 an English merchant is licensed to export one thousand quarters of grain to Norway. *Calendar of Close Rolls 1343-1346*, 1896-1913: 274; *Calendar of Patent Rolls 1340-1343*, 1893-1905: 212; *1348-1350*, 1893-1905: 287.

[81] *Calendar of Patent Rolls 1343-1345*, 1893-1905: 279, 286, 294: *1345-1348*, 1893-1905: 30, 97,98, 373, 390; *1348-1350*, 1893-1905: 67, 68, 311, 518.

[82] *Calendar of Close Rolls 1349-1354*, 1896-1913: 199, 233.

have been among the chief recipients during the revival of English grain exports after about 1330. The original main importing country—Norway—was subject to English export restrictions from the mid 1330s, but it seems to have been such a good export market that restrictions could not prevent English grain continually being imported to the country illegally, or by special royal grant. The Hundred Years War and the provisioning of the king's men on the continent also played an important role in English exports of grain in particular, in the late 1340s.

In light of the many export licences and violations of the export bans in the second quarter of the fourteenth century, it can hardly be concluded that warfare and political intervention in the overseas grain market were the sole commercial factors keeping English grain prices at a moderate level in the decades prior to the Black Death. The political restrictions on the export of grain cannot have been the most important factor in this respect. The constant importing of grain and in particular the established Baltic-North Sea route must also be taken into account.

Conclusion

The Baltic-North Sea grain route was in full operation by the beginning of the fourteenth century at the latest. Grain grown in the more or less newly colonised hinterlands of the Hanseatic towns on the south-eastern shores of the Baltic Sea was shipped to the North Sea region either directly through the Danish sounds and *ummeland* the Skaw, or was transshipped via the traditional Lübeck-Hamburg link between north-eastern and north-western Europe. Rye began to flow from these new parts of Europe some time in the thirteenth century and at the turn of the century they supplied even grain-growing eastern England.

From the end of the thirteenth century the overseas grain trade through the English North Sea ports was dominated by the export of wheat to Norway. In the first decade of the fourteenth century exports declined. But the decline of exports detectable around 1310 and the complete standstill in the 1320s were intervals in a continuous exporting of grain from England. On the eve of the Black Death the level of exports probably matched that at the beginning of the century. In contrast to the thirteenth and the first decades of the fourteenth century, the Netherlands seem to have been chief recipient of English wheat from about 1330.

During the first decade of the fourteenth century imports of rye and oats to the English North Sea ports became increasingly important. In the following troubled decade these imports were supplemented by the importing of wheat from France, Spain, Portugal and Italy. Imports of rye at the North Sea ports and wheat at the Channel ports reached a maximum level at the same time as wheat exports from England hit bottom in the middle of the 1320s. After the disappearance of the poundage rolls, England continually imported grain from her continental dependencies and Portugal; continuity in imports from the Baltic region can also be proved. During the whole period the grain supplies to the North Sea ports came from Germany and the Baltic region while the Channel ports were supplied from France, Spain, Portugal and Italy.

Unfavourable climate, war and high prices affected the overseas grain trade but the interregional exchange of grain was not restricted to abnormal years. Climatic or political disturbances did not automatically stimulate the grain trade; on the contrary they sometimes retarded it. The English foreign grain trade fluctuated but it continued year after year. Imported grain was available under fluctuating economic circumstances, and it can be argued that the imports had an effect on local prices and on the level of prices on a more general scale. One possible reason for the rather moderate level of grain prices in the decades before the Black Death was the increasing imports of grain in the first quarter and the continuation of such imports in the second quarter of the fourteenth century. However, the price-building effect of the grain imported to England should not be exaggerated. The quantities imported were very modest and the major part consisted of rye and oats, while the crop generally exported from England was wheat.

On the face of it, it seems unreasonable that grain was imported to the grain-growing eastern districts of England. Further research will hopefully uncover the conditions under which it was possible and profitable to ship it the long way from "Estland".

Bibliography

UNPUBLISHED SOURCES

Copenhagen, Rigsarkivet: Reg. 108 A. Nr. 25. 1518-22. Toldregnskaber fra Aalborg og Rødby.

Gouda, Gemeente Archief Gouda: 37, A. Van Der Poest Clement, *De Bierbrouwerijen van Gouda in middeleeuwn en 16e eeuw*, incomplete and unpublished doctoral dissertation, 1959.

Hoorn, Gemeente Archief Hoorn: 481 [287-9].

London, British Library: Add. MS 15524.

London, Public Record Office: C 54

——: C 66

——: E 122 (King's Remembrancer's Customs Accounts)

——: E159/68

——: E364/92 A, M and N.

Lübeck, Altes Senatsarchiv: Lastadie 4/1.

Lübeck, Archiv der Hansestadt Lübeck: Hansestadt Lübeck, Schonenfahrer. Befrachtungsbuch der Aalborgfahrer 1576-1604.

Oxford, Bodleian Library: MS Bodley 401, f. 55v.

Roskilde, Institute for Maritime Archaeology, National Museum of Denmark: File no. MAJ 98.

PUBLISHED SOURCES AND SECONDARY LITERATURE

Abel, Wilhelm. (1978a) *Agrarkrise und Agrarkonjunktur*. Hamburg, 1978.

____. (1978b) *Geschichte der deutschen Landwirtschaft vom frühen Mittelalter bis zum 19. Jahrhundert*. Stuttgart, 1978.

____. *Stufen der Ernährung. Eine historische Skizze*. Göttingen, 1981.

Acta Processus Litium inter Regem Danorum et Archiepiscopum Lundensem, edited by Alfred Krarup and William Norvin. Copenhagen, 1922.

Adey-Davies, Simon. "The Invisible Ship. Distinguishing Ship Building Traditions within the Archaeological and Historical Records." MA thesis, University of Southampton, 1997.

Agats, Arthur. *Der hansische Baienhandel*. Heidelberg, 1904.

Alexandre, Pierre. *Le Climate en Europe au Moyen Âge*. Paris, 1987.

Andersen, Per Kohrtz. *Kollerupkoggen*. Thisted, 1983.

Anderson, William. "Den gotländska kalkstenens utbredningsområde." *Gotlands-Posten*, 16, 18, and 19 May 1934. Also published separately: Visby, 1934.

Andersson, Aron. "Kalk och paten." *Kulturhistoriskt lexikon för nordisk medeltid.* Malmö, 1963.

Andrén, Anders. *Den urbana scenen: Städer och samhälle i det medeltida Danmark.* Malmö, 1985.

——. "State and Towns in the Middle Ages: The Scandinavian Experience." In *Cities & the Rise of States in Europe A.D. 1000 to 1800*, edited by Charles Tilly and Wim P. Blockmans, 128-149. San Francisco & Oxford, 1994.

Annales Ianuenses. Edited by Luigi T. Belgrano and Cesare Imperiale di Sant'Angelo. Vol. 2. Genoa, 1901.

Arup, Erik. *Danmarks Historie*. Vol. 1. Copenhagen, 1925.

Ashurst, P. R. "Hops and their Use in Brewing." In *Modern Brewing Technology*, edited by W. P. K. Findlay, 31-59. London, 1971.

Atkin, M. A. "Land Use and Management in the Upland Demesne of the De Lacy Estate of Blackburnshire, c.1300." *Agricultural History Review* 42 (1994): 1-19.

Atlas over Fyns kyst i jernalder, vikingetid og middelalder, edited by Ole Crumlin-Pedersen, Erland Porsmose, and Henrik Thrane. Odense, 1996.

Bailey, Mark. "Sand into Gold: The Evolution of the Foldcourse System in West Suffolk, 1200-1600." *Agricultural History Review* 38 (1990): 40-57.

Baillie, M. G. L., J. Hillam, K. R. Briffa, and D. M. Brown. "Redating the English art-historical tree-ring chronologies." *Nature* 315 (1985):1-3.

Barfod, Jørgen H. *Flådens fødsel* (Marinehistorisk Selskabs skriftrække, vol. 22). Copenhagen, 1990.

Barker, Philip. *Hen Domen, Montgomery: a Timber Castle on the Welsh Border*. London, 1982.

Bartholin, Thomas S. "Viking Ships from Norway." *Maritime Archaeology Newsletter from Roskilde, Denmark* 10 (1998): 36-37.

——. *Dendrokronologisk undersøgelse af The Big Ship og The Second Big Ship fra Bryggen i Bergen* (Nationalmuseets Naturvidenskabelige Undersøgelser, rapport, vol. 16). Copenhagen, 1999.

Bartley, K., and B. M. S. Campbell. "*Inquisitiones Post Mortem*, G.I.S., and the Creation of a Land-use Map of Pre Black Death England." *Transactions in G.I.S.* 2 (1997).

Barton, Kenneth J. "A Medieval Pottery Kiln at Ham Green, Bristol." *Trans Bristol Gloucestershire Archaeological Society* 82 (1963): 95-126.

——. "Medieval Pottery at Rouen." *Archaeological Journal* 123 (1966): 73-85.

——. "The Medieval Pottery of Dublin." In *Keimelia: Studies in Medieval Archaeology and History in Memory of Tom Delaney*, edited by Gearoid Mac Niocall and Patrick F. Wallace, 271-324. Galway, 1988.

Behrmann, Thomas. " 'Hansekaufmann', 'Hansestadt', 'Deutsche Hanse'? Über hansische Terminologie und hansisches Selbstverständnis im späten Mittelalter." In *Bene vivere in communitate. Beiträge zum italienischen und deutschen Mittel-*

alter. Hagen Keller zum 60. Geburtstag überreicht von seinen Schülerinnen und Schüler, edited by Thomas Scharff and Thomas Behrmann, 155-176. Münster, New York, München & Berlin, 1997.

Bender Jørgensen, L.: see Jørgensen, Lise Bender.

Bendixen, E.B. *Tyskernes handel paa Norge og det hanseatiske Kontor i Bergen*. Vol. 1. Bergen, 1915.

Benecke, Norbert. "Zur frühmittelalterlichen Heringsfischerei im südlichen Ostseeraum—ein archäologischer Beitrag." *Zeitschrift für Archäologie* 16 (1982): 283-290.

Beresford, Maurice. *New Towns of the Middle Ages: Town Plantation in England, Wales and Gascony*. Gloucester, 1988.

Berkenvelder, F. C. "Frieslands Handel in de late Middeleeuwen." *Economisch-Historisch Jaarboek* 29 (1963): 136-187.

Bill, Jan. (1991a) "Gedesbyskibet. Middelalderlig skude- og færgefart fra Falster." *Nationalmuseets Arbejdsmark* (1991): 188-198.

____. (1991b) "Vikingeskibe som experimentelt arbejdsområde." In *Kontaktstencil XXXIII. Experimentell Arkeologi. Rapport från Kontaktseminariet i Hällnäs, Västerbotten, 8-14 oktober 1989*, 33-48. Umeå, 1991.

____. "Getting into Business—Reflections of a Market Economy in Medieval Scandinavian Shipbuilding." In *Shipshape. Essays for Ole Crumlin-Pedersen. On the Occasion of his 60th Anniversary February 24th 1995*, edited by O. Olsen, J. Skamby Madsen and F. Rieck, 195-202. Roskilde, 1995.

____. (1997a) "Ships and Seamanship." In *Oxford Illustrated History of the Vikings*, edited by Peter Sawyer, 182-201. Oxford. 1997.

____. (1997b) "Small Scale Seafaring in Danish Waters AD 1000-1600." Ph.D. diss., Institute of Archaeology and Ethnology, University of Copenhagen, 1997.

Bill, Jan, Bjørn Poulsen, Flemming Rieck, and Ole Ventegodt. *Dansk søfarts historie. Vol 1. Indtil 1588. Fra stammebåd til skib*. Copenhagen, 1997.

Bill, Jan, Morten Gøthche, and Hanne Marie Myrhøj. "Nordeuropas største skibsfund." *Nationalmuseets Arbejdsmark* (1998): 136-158.

Birkedahl Christensen, P.: see Christensen, P. Birkedahl

Bing, Wolf. *Hamburgs Bierbrauerei vom 14. bis zum 18. Jahrhundert*. Hamburg, 1909.

Bitsch, Birka Ringbøl. *Malmgryder i Danmark*. Højbjerg, 1997.

Blackmore, Lyn, and Alan G. Vince. "Medieval Pottery from South East England Found in the Bryggen Excavations 1955-68." In *The Bryggen Papers Supplementary Series 5*, edited by Asbjørn Herteig, 9-160. Bergen, 1994.

Blair, John. "Purbeck Marble." In *English Medieval Industries: Craftsmen, Techniques, Products*, edited by John Blair and Nigel Ramsay, 41-56. London, 1991.

Blake, J. B. "The Medieval Coal Trade of North East England: Some Fourteenth-Century Evidence." *Northern History* 2 (1967): 1-26.

Blanchard, Ian S. W. "Economic Change in Derbyshire in the Late Middle Ages, 1272-1540." Ph.D. diss., University of London, 1967.

———. "The Continental European Cattle Trades: 1400-1600." *Economic History Review* 39 (1986): 427-460.

Bødker Enghoff, I.: see Enghoff, Inge Bødker.

Bonde, Niels. *Præliminær dendrokronologisk undersøgelse af seks skibsvrag fra Roskildes gamle havneområde* (Nationalmuseets Naturvidenskabelige Undersøgelser, rapport, vol. 15). Copenhagen, 1997.

Bonde, Niels, Ian Tyers, and Tomasz Wazny. "Where Does the Timber Come From? Dendrochronological Evidence of the Timber Trade in Northern Europe." In *Archaeological Sciences* 1995 (Proceedings of a Conference on the Application of Scientific Techniques to the Study of Archaeology, Liverpool July 1995; Oxbow Monograph 64), edited by Anthony Sinclair, Elizabeth Slater, and John Gowlett, 201-204. Oxford, 1997.

Bracker, Jörgen. "Hopbier uit Hamburg Het verhaal van een middeleeuwse succesformule." In *Bier! Geschiedenis van een volksdrank*, edited by R. E. Kistemaker and V. T. Van Vilsteren, 28-33. Amsterdam, 1994.

Bridbury, A. R. *Medieval English Clothmaking. An Economic Survey*. London, 1982.

———. *The English Economy from Bede to the Reformation*. Woodbridge, 1992.

Britnell, Richard H. "Commercialisation and Economic Development in England, 1000-1300." In *A Commercialising Economy: England 1086 to c.1300*, edited by Richard H. Britnell and Bruce M. S. Campbell, 7-26. Manchester, 1995.

Bronnen tot de Geschiedenis van den Oostzeehandel (1122-1499). Edited by H. A. Poelman. Vol. 1-2 (Rijks Geschiedkundige Publikatiën 36). 'S-Gravenhage, 1917.

Buchwald, Vagn Fabricius. "Jernfremstilling i Danmark i middelalderen – lidt om bondeovne og kloder." *Aarbøger for Nordisk Oldkyndighed og Historie* (1992): 265-286.

———. "Om proveniensbestemmelse, med særlig henblik på hallandske kloder." In *Medeltida danskt järn. Framställning av och handel med järn i Skåneland och Småland under medeltiden*, edited by Sven-Olof Olsson, 108-126. Halmstad, 1995.

Buckland, P.C., and Jon Sadler. "Ballast and Building Stone: A Discussion." In *Stone: Quarrying and Building in England AD 43–1525*, edited by David Parsons, 114-125. Chichester, 1990.

Buell, Reinhard. *Das große Buch vom Wachs*. München, 1977.

Bugge, Alexander. "Gotlændingernes handel med England og Norge omkring 1300." *Historisk tidskrift* (Oslo) 5 (1899): 145-180.

———. "Die nordeuropäischen Verkehrswege im frühen Mittelalter und die Bedeutung der Wikinger für die Entwicklung des europäischen Handels und der europäischen Schiffahrt." *Vierteljahrschrift für Sozial- und Wirtschaftsgeschichte* 4 (1906): 227-277.

———. "Skibsfarten fra de ældste tider til omkring aar 1800." In *Den norske sjøfarts historie fra ældste tider til vore dage*. Vol. 1. Oslo, 1923.

———. *Den norske Trælasthandels Historie*. Vols. 1-2. Skien, 1925.

Calendar of Close Rolls preserved in the Public Record Office. London, 1892-1953.

Calendar of Fine Rolls preserved in the Public Record Office (1272-1307 and 1307-1319). London, 1911-12.

Calendar of Liberate Rolls preserved in the Public Record Office (1226-1260). Vols. 1-4. London, 1916-1959.

Calendar of Memoranda Rolls preserved in the Public Record Office (1326-1327). London, 1968.

Calendar of Patent Rolls preserved in the Public Record Office. London, 1893-1913.

Campbell, Bruce M. S. "Agricultural Progress in Medieval England: Some Evidence from Eastern Norfolk." *Economic History Review*, 2nd series, 36 (1983): 26-46.

——. (1995a) "Ecology Versus Economics in Late Thirteenth- and Early Fourteenth-Century English Agriculture." In *Agriculture in the Middle Ages: Technology, Practice, and Representation*, edited by Del Sweeney, 76-108. Philadelphia, 1995.

——. (1995b) "Measuring the Commercialisation of Seigneurial Agriculture *circa* 1300." In *A Commercialising Economy: England 1086-1300*, edited by R. H. Britnell and Bruce M. S. Campbell, 132-193. Manchester, 1995.

——. "Economic Rent and the Intensification of English Agriculture 1086-1350." In *Medieval Farming and Technology: The Impact of Agricultural Change in Northwest Europe*, edited by Grenville Astill and John Langdon, 225-250. Leiden, 1997.

——. "Constraint or Constrained? Changing Perspectives on Medieval English Agriculture." *Neha-Jaarboek voor economische, bedrijfs- en techniekgeschiedenis* (1998): 15-35.

——. (2000a) "Britain 1300." *History Today* 50, nr 6 (2000): 10-17.

——. (2000b) *English Seigniorial Agriculture 1250-1450.* Cambridge, 2000.

——, ed. *Before the Black Death: Studies in the 'Crisis' of the Early Fourteenth Century.* Manchester, 1991.

Campbell, Bruce M. S., and John P. Power. "Mapping the Agricultural Geography of Medieval England." *Journal of Historical Geography* 15 (1989): 24-39.

Campbell, Bruce M. S., James A. Galloway, Derek Keene, and Margaret Murphy. *A Medieval Capital and its Grain Supply: Agrarian Production and its Distribution in the London Region c.1300*, Historical Geography Research Series, no. 30. 1993.

Carelli, Peter, and P. Kresten. "Give Us This Day Our Daily Bread. A Study of Late Viking Age and Medieval Quernstones in South Scandinavia." *Acta Archaeologica* 68 (1997): 109-137.

Carlsson, Kristina. *Importkeramik i Gamla Lödöse. Lödöse – västsvensk medeltidsstad 3:2.* Stockholm, 1982.

Carus-Wilson, Eleanor M. "The Medieval Trade of the Ports of the Wash." *Medieval Archaeology* 6-7 (1962-63): 182-201.

——. "Die Hanse und England." In *Hanse in Europa. Brücke zwischen den Märkten. 12.-17. Jahrhundert* (Kölnisches Stadtmuseum, exhibition-catalogue), 85-106. Köln, 1973.

———. "The German Hanse in the Economy of the Medieval England." In *Aspekte der deutsch-britischen Beziehungen im Laufe der Jahrhunderte* (Veröffentlichungen des Deutschen Historischen Instituts in London, vol. 4), edited by P. Alter and P. Kluke, 14-23. Stuttgart, 1978.

Carus-Wilson, Eleanor M., and Olive Coleman. *England's Export Trade 1275-1547.* Oxford, 1963.

Cedergren, Allan. *Gotländsk sandsten i tid och rum.* Visby, 1991.

Childs, Wendy R. "Documentary Evidence for the Import of Spanish Pottery to England in the Later Middle Ages: Twelfth to Sixteenth Centuries." In *Spanish Medieval Ceramics in Spain and the British Isles,* edited by Chris Gerrard, Alejandra Gutierrez and Alan G. Vince, 25-32. Oxford, 1995.

———. "The English Export Trade in Cloth in the Fourteenth Century." In *Progress and Problems in Medieval England: Essays in Honour of Edward Miller,* edited by Richard Britnell and John Hatcher, 121-147. Cambridge, 1996.

———, ed. *The Customs Accounts of Hull, 1453-1490.* Yorkshire Archaeological Record Series, 144. 1986.

Chorley, P. "The Cloth Exports of Flanders and Northern France during the Thirteenth Century: a Luxury Trade?" *Economic History Review* 40 (1987): 349-379.

Christensen, Aksel E. "Danmark." In *Det nordiske syn på forbindelsen mellem Hansestæderne og Norden,* 55-96. Århus, 1957.

———. "Das Artlenburg-Privileg und der Ostseefernhandel Gotlands und Lübecks im 12. und 13. Jahrhundert." *Nerthus* 2 (1969): 219-237.

Christensen, Arne Emil. "Boat Finds from Bryggen." In *The Bryggen Papers. Main series,* vol. 1 (The archaeological excavations at Bryggen, "The German Wharf" in Bergen 1955-68), edited by Asbjørn Herteig, 47-278. Bergen, 1985.

———. "Hanseatic and Nordic Ships in Medieval Trade. Were the Cogs Better Vessels?" In *Medieval Ships and the Birth of Technological Societies.* Vol. 1: *Northern Europe,* edited by Christiane Villain-Gandossi, 17-23. Malta, 1989.

Christensen, Margrit. *Kleinbürgerlicher Wohnungsbau in Lübeck. Grundstücksentwicklung, Baustruktur und Sozialtopographie im 16. und 17. Jahrhundert* (Häuser und Höfe in Lübeck). Neumünster (forthcoming).

Christensen, P. Birkedahl and E. Johansen. "En handelsplads fra yngre jernalder og vikingetid fra Sebbersund." *Aarbøger for Nordisk Oldkyndighed og Historie* (1991): 199-229.

Chronik des Franciscaner Lesemeisters Detmar. Edited by F. H. Grautoft. Hamburg, 1829.

Clarke, Helen. "English and Baltic Trade in the Middle Ages. An Evaluation of the Evidence." In *Society and Trade in the Baltic during the Viking Ages* (Acta Visbyensia VII), edited by Sven-Olof Lindquist, 113-118. Visby, 1985.

Cobb, H., ed. *The Overseas Trade of London. Exchequer Customs Accounts 1480-1.* London Record Society, 27. 1990.

Cordes, Albrecht. *Hansischer Gesellschaftshandel.* Köln, Wien & Weimar, 1998.

Courtoy, F. "Le travail et le commerce de la pierre à Namur avant 1500." *Namurcum* (Chronique de la Société archéologique de Namur) 21 (1946): 17-29.

Crowfoot, E., F. Pritchard, and K. Staniland, eds. *Textiles and Clothing c.1150-c.1450*. Vol. 4 of *Medieval Finds from Excavations in London*. London, 1992.

Crumlin-Pedersen, Ole. "Some Principles for the Recording and Presentation of Ancient Boat Structures." In *Sources and Techniques in Boat Archaeology* (British Archaeological Reports, Suppl. Series, vol. 29), 163-178. Greenwich, 1977.

——. (1979a) "Danish Cog-finds." In *The Archaeology of Medieval Ships and Harbours in Northern Europe* (British Archaeological Reports, International Series, vol. 66), 17-34. Oxford, 1979.

——. (1979b) "Lynæsskibet og Roskilde søvej." In *13 bidrag til Roskilde by og omegns historie*, edited by Frank A. Birkebæk, 65-77. Roskilde, 1979.

——. "Cargo Ships of Northern Europe AD 800-1300." In *Conference on Waterfront Archaeology in North European Towns* (Bergen 1983), edited by Asbjørn E. Herteig, 83-93. Bergen, 1985.

——. *Schiffstypen aus der frühgeschichtlichen Seeschiffahrt in den nordeuropäischen Gewässern* (Untersuchungen zu Handel und Verkehr der vor- und frühgeschichtlichen Zeit in Mittel- und Nordeuropa. Teil V. Der Verkehr. Verkehrswege, Verkehrsmittel, Organisation. Abhandlungen der Akademie der Wissenschaften in Göttingen. Philologisch-Historische Klasse, Dritte Folge, vol. 180). Göttingen, 1989.

——. *Viking-Age Ships and Shipbuilding in Hedeby/Haithabu and Schleswig*. Vol. 2 of *Ships and Boats of the North*. Schleswig & Roskilde, 1997.

——. "Ships as Indicators of Trade in Northern Europe 600-1200." In *Maritime Topography and the Medieval Town*. 5th International Conference on Waterfront Archaeology, Copenhagen 1998 (Publications from the National Museum, Studies in Archaeology & History, vol. 4), edited by Jan Bill and Birthe L. Clausen, 11-20. Copenhagen, 1999.

Curshmann, Fritz. *Hungernöte im Mittelalter*. Leipzig, 1900.

Czaja, Roman. "Udzial wielkich miast pruskich w handlu hanzeatyckim do polowy XIV wieku." *Zapiski Historyczne* 60 (1995): 21-38, 43-55.

Daenell, Ernst. "Der Ostseeverkehr und die Hansestädte von der Mitte des 14. bis zur Mitte des 15. Jahrhunderts." *Hansische Geschichtsblätter* 30 (1902): 1-47.

——. "Holland und die Hanse im 15. Jahrhundert." *Hansische Geschichtsblätter* 31 (1903): 3-41.

——. *Die Blütezeit der deutschen Hanse*. Vols. 1-2. Berlin, 1905.

Daly, Aoife. *Dendrokronologisk undersøgelse af skibsvrag fra Lynæs, Frederiksborg Amt* (Nationalmuseets Naturvidenskabelige Undersøgelser, rapport, vol. 39). Copenhagen, 1998.

——. *Dendrokronologisk undersøgelse af skibsvrag fra Lynæs A, Frederiksborg Amt* (Nationalmuseets Naturvidenskabelige Undersøgelser, rapport, vol. 12). Copenhagen, 1999.

———. *Dendrokronologisk undersøgelse af skibsvrag ,Kollerup kogge', Nordjyllands Amt.* (Nationalmuseets Naturvidenskabelige Undersøgelser, rapport nr 2, 2000). Copenhagen, 2000.

Danmarks Gamle Landskabslove med Kirkelovene, edited by Johannes Brøndum-Nielsen and Poul Johannes Jørgensen. Vols. 1-8. Copenhagen, 1933-61.

Danmarks Gamle Købstadslovgivning, edited by E. Kroman and P. Jørgensen. Vols. 1-5. Copenhagen, 1951-61.

Danmarks Gilde- og Lavsskråer fra Middelalderen, edited by C. Nyrop. Vol. 1. Copenhagen, 1899-1900.

Danske Helgeners Levned, edited by Hans Olrik. Copenhagen, 1893-94.

Davies, J. Conway. "Shipping and Trade in Newcastle upon Tyne, 1294-1296." *Archaeologia Aeliana* 4th series 31 (1953): 175-204.

Davis, R.H. *The Medieval Warhorse: Origin, Development and Redevelopment.* London, 1989.

De Clerck, Jan. *A Textbook of Brewing.* Transl. by K. Barton-Wright. Vols. 1-2. London, 1957-1958.

Deane, Phyllis, and W. A. Cole. *British Economic Growth 1699-1959.* Cambridge, 2nd ed., 1969.

Deroeux, Didier, Daniel Dufournier, and Asbjørn E. Herteig. "French Medieval Ceramics from the Bryggen Excavations in Bergen, Norway." In *The Bryggen Papers Supplementary Series 5,* edited by Asbjørn Herteig, 161-208. Bergen, 1994.

Diplomatarium Danicum. 1st-4th series. Copenhagen, 1938- .

Diplomatarium Norvegicum. Edited by C. C. A. Lange et al. Vols. 1-21. Christiania, 1849-Oslo, 1976.

Dollinger, Philippe. *Die Hanse.* Transl., 4th ed. Stuttgart, 1989.

———. *La Hanse.* Paris, 1964.

———. *The German Hansa.* Transl. London, 1970.

Donkin, Robin A. "Changes in the Early Middle Ages." In *A New Historical Geography of England,* edited by H. C. Darby, 75-135. Cambridge, 1973.

———. *The Cistercians: Studies in the Geography of Medieval England and Wales.* Toronto, 1978.

Doorman, G. *De Middeleeuwse Brouwerij en de gruit.* The Hague, 1955.

Drake, Colin Stuart. "The Distribution of Tournai Fonts." *The Antiquaries Journal* 73 (1993): 11-26.

Drescher, Hans. "Grapen des 12.-13. Jahrhunderts aus Lübeck. Arbeiten Lübecker Giesser?" In *Lübeck 1226: Reichsfreiheit und frühe Stadt,* edited by O. Ahlers, A. Graßmann, W. Neugebauer and W. Schadendorf, 307-320. Lübeck, 1976.

Dru Drury, G. "The Use of Purbeck Marble in Medieval Times." In *Proc. Dorset Nat. Hist. and Arch. Soc.* 70 (1948): 74-98.

Dunning, G. C. "The Distribution of Black Tournai Fonts." *The Antiquaries Journal* 24 (1944): 66-68.

Ebbing, H. "Bier op transport De binnenvaart door Holland en de ontwikkeling van de Hollandse brouwnijverheid tot 1500." In *Bier! Geschiedenis van een volksdrank*, edited by R. E. Kistemaker and V. T. Van Vilsteren, 39-50. Amsterdam, 1994.

Eckstein, D., T. Wazny, J. Bauch, and P. Klein. "New evidence for the dendrochronological dating of Netherlandish paintings." *Nature* 320 (1986): 465f.

Ehbrecht, Wilfried. "Universitas Civium. Ländliche und Städtische Genossenschaftsformen im mittelalterlichen Nordseeküstenraum." In *Civitatum Communitatis. Studien zum europäischen Städtewesen: Festschrift Heinz Stoob zum 65. Geburtstag*, vol. 1, 115-145. Köln & Wien, 1984.

Ellmers, Detlev. *Frühmittelalterliche Handelsschiffahrt in Mittel- und Nordeuropa* (Offa-Bücher, vol. 28.). Neumünster, 1972.

——. "The Cog of Bremen and Related Boats." In *The Archaeology of Medieval Ships and Harbours in Northern Europe* (British Archaeological Reports, International Series, vol. 66), 1-16. Oxford, 1979.

——. "Die Entstehung der Hanse." *Hansische Geschichtsblätter* 103 (1985): 3-40.

——. "Die Bedeutung der Friesen für die Handelsverbindungen des Ostseeraums bis zur Wikingerzeit." *Emder Jahrbuch* 66 (1986): 5-64.

Enemark, Poul. (1981a) "Hestehandel." In *Kulturhistorisk Leksikon for Nordisk Middelalder*, 524-532. Vol. 6. Copenhagen, 1981.

——. (1981b) "Kramhandel." In *Kulturhistorisk Leksikon for Nordisk Middelalder*, 240-244. Vol. 9. Copenhagen, 1981.

——. (1982a) "Salthandel, Danmark." In *Kulturhistorisk Leksikon for Nordisk Middelalder*, 704-710. Vol. 14. Copenhagen, 1982.

——. (1982b) "Ölhandel, Danmark." In *Kulturhistorisk Leksikon for Nordisk Middelalder*, 703-710. Vol. 20. Copenhagen, 1982.

——. *Sortbroget kvæg – baggrund og udvikling*. Viby, 1983.

——. "Lybæk og Europa: Skæbnemodstandere eller handelspartnere?" In *Kongemagt og samfund i middelalderen. Festskrift til Erik Ulsig*, edited by Poul Enemark, Per Ingesman and Jens Villiam Jensen, 161-189. Aarhus, 1988.

——. "Vesteuropa, Lübeck og dansk handel i senmiddelalderen." *Historisk Tidsskrift*, pp. 361-401. Copenhagen, 1992.

Engberg, Niels, and Vagn F. Buchwald. "Værktøjskisten fra Veksø." *Nationalmuseets Arbejdsmark* (1995): 62-75.

Enghoff, Inge Bødker. "Denmark's First Herring Industry?" *Maritime Archaeology Newsletter from Roskilde, Denmark* 6 (May 1996): 2-4.

Englert, Anton. *The Dating and Origin of the "Big Ship" from Bergen*. (The Bryggen Papers, Supplementary series.) Forthcoming.

English Historical Documents. Edited by Harry Rothwell. Vol. 3. London, 1975.

Ersgård, Lars. *"Vår marknad i Skåne": Bebyggelse, handel och urbanisering i Skanör och Falsterbo under medeltiden*. Lund, 1988.

Erslev, Kristian, ed. *Testamenter fra Danmarks Middelalder indtil 1450*. Copenhagen, 1901.

Falk, Lennart. *Byggnadsstenbrott på Gotland.* Report, Riksantikvarieämbetet (Central Board of National Antiquities). Stockholm, 1989.

Falk, Lennart, and Mats Arup. *Medeltida byggnadssten på Gotland.* Part 2. Report, Riksantikvarieämbetet (National Heritage Board) 1990:35, Stockholm, 1990.

Falk, Lennart, Fredrik Jerre, and Mats Arup. *Medeltida byggnadssten på Gotland.* Part 1. Report, Riksantikvarieämbetet (National Heritage Board). Stockholm, 1989.

Farmer, David L. "Prices and Wages." In *The Agrarian History of England and Wales.* Vol. 2. *1042-1350,* edited by H. E. Hallam, 716-817. Cambridge, 1988.

____. "Marketing the Produce of the Countryside, 1200-1500." In *The Agrarian History of England and Wales.* Vol. 3. *1348-1500,* edited by Edward Miller, 324-430. Cambridge, 1991.

Feveile, Claus. "Tufstenskirkerne i Sydvestjylland—set i arkæologisk, handelshistorisk belysning." In *By, marsk og geest* 8. Årsberetning 1995. Den antikvariske Samling i Ribe 1996, 31-51. Ribe, 1996.

Fischer, David Hackett. *The Great Wave: Price Revolutions and the Rhythm of History.* Oxford, 1996.

Fletcher, J. "Dating of art-historical artifacts." *Nature* 320 (1986):466.

Friel, Ian. *The Good Ship. Ships, Shipbuilding and Technology in England 1200-1520.* London, 1995.

Fritze, Konrad. *Die Hansestadt Stralsund. Die beiden ersten Jahrhunderte ihrer Geschichte* (Veröffentlichungen des Stadtarchivs Stralsund 4). Schwerin, 1961.

____. "Entstehung, Aufstieg und Blüte der Hansestadt Stralsund." In *Geschichte der Stadt Stralsund,* edited by Herbert Ewe, 9-102. Weimar, 1984.

Fritze, Konrad, Johannes Schildhauer, and Walter Stark. *Die Hanse.* Berlin, 1974.

Fryde, E. B. "The English Cloth Industry and the Trade with the Mediterranean c. 1370-c.1480." In *Produzione, Commercio e Consumo dei Panni di Lana,* 343-367. Florence, 1976. Reprinted in E. B. Fryde, *Studies in Medieval Trade and Finance.* London, 1983.

Fryde, Natalie. "Deutsche Englandkaufleute in frühhansischer Zeit." *Hansische Geschichtsblätter* 97 (1979): 1-14.

____. "Arnold fitz Thedmar und die Entstehung der großen deutschen Hanse." *Hansische Geschichtsblätter* 107 (1989): 27-42.

Fåhreus, Fredrik. *Dopfuntarna, deras tillbehör och placering på Gotland under medeltiden: En inventering.* Stockholm, 1974.

Gaimster, David. *German Stoneware 1200-1900.* London, 1997.

Galloway, James A., Derek Keene, and Margaret Murphy. "Fuelling the City: Production and Distribution of Firewood and Fuel in London's Region, 1290-1400." *Economic History Review,* 2nd series, 49 (1996): 447-472.

Gardiner, Mark. "The Geography and Peasant Rural Economy of the Eastern Sussex High Weald, 1300-1420." *Sussex Archaeological Collections* 134 (1996): 125-139.

Gelsinger, Bruce E. *Icelandic Enterprise: Commerce and Economy in the Middle Ages*. Columbia, South Carolina, 1981.

Gerrard, Chris, Alejandra Gutierrez, and Alan G. Vince, eds. *Spanish Medieval Ceramics in Spain and the British Isles*. Oxford, 1995.

Gilliodts van Severen, L. *Cartulaire de l'ancienne Estaple de Bruges. Recueil de documents concernant le commerce intérieur et maritime, les relations internationales et l'histoire économique de cette ville*. Vols. 1-4. Bruges, 1904-1906.

Gladitz, Charles. *Medieval Stud Management: Studies in Horse Breeding, East and West*. Dublin, 1997.

Grantham, George. "Time's Arrow and Time's Cycle in the Medieval Economy: The Significance of Recent Developments in Economic Theory for the History of Medieval Economic Growth." Paper presented at the Fifth Anglo-American Seminar on the Medieval Economy and Society. Cardiff, 1995.

———. "*Contra* Ricardo: The Macroeconomics of Pre-Industrial Agrarian Economies." *European Review of Economic History* 3 (1999): 199-233.

Gras, Norman Scott Brien. *The Early English Customs System. A Documentary Study of the Institutional and Economic History of the Customs from the Thirteenth to the Sixteenth Century*. Cambridge, Mass. 1918.

———. *The Evolution of the English Corn Market from the Twelfth to the Eighteenth Century*. Cambridge, Mass., 1926.

Greigh, James. "Plant Foods in the Past. A Review of the Evidence from Northern Europe." *Journal of Plant Foods* 5 (1983): 179-214.

Groves, Cathy. "The Dating and Provenancing of Imported Conifer Timbers in England: the Initiation of a Research Project." In *Archaeological Sciences* 1995 (Proceedings of a Conference on the Application of Scientific Techniques to the Study of Archaeology, Liverpool July 1995; Oxbow Monograph 64), edited by Anthony Sinclair, Elizabeth Slater, and John Gowlett, 205-211. Oxford, 1997.

Groves, Cathy. *Tree-ring Analysis of Timbers from Peterborough Cathedral, Peterborough, Cambridgeshire: Boards from the Painted Nave Ceing—Phase 2*. Ancient Monuments Laboratory Report 37. London, 2000.

Haastrup, Ulla. "Bemalede romanske døbefonte i det middelalderlige Danmark." (Kirkearkæologi i Norden 5, Viborg, Danmark 1993) *hikuin* 22 (1995): 7-26.

Hach, Theodor. (1882a) "Aus dem Kulturhistorischen Museum. I. Ein alter Taufstein." *Lübeckische Blätter* 24, no. 77 (1882): 432-434.

———. (1882b) "Die Taufsteine zu Schlutup und Hamberge." *Lübeckische Blätter* 24, no. 79 (1882): 445-446.

Hallbäck, Sven Axel. *Medeltida dopfuntar i västra Sverige*. Systematisk del. Skara, 1978.

Das Hamburger Pfundzollbuch von 1418. Edited by Rolf Sprandel. Köln, 1972.

Hamburgisches Urkundenbuch. Edited by Johann Martin Lappenberg. Vol. 1. Hamburg, 1907.

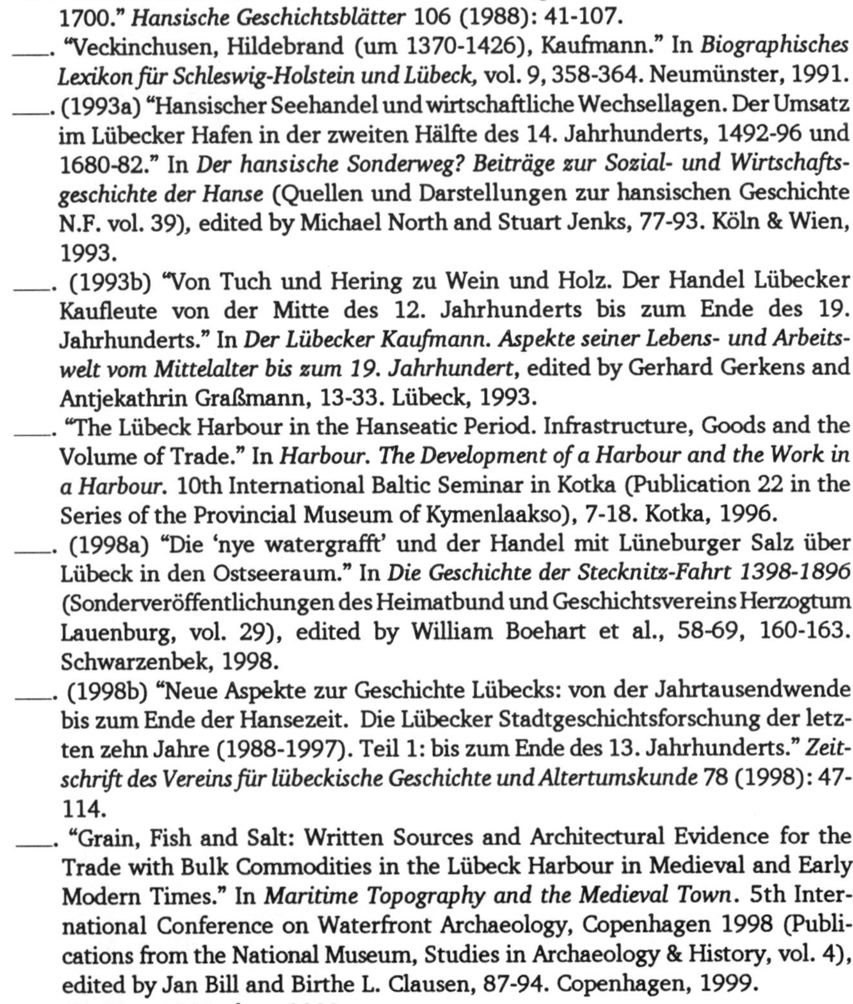

Hammel-Kiesow, Rolf. "Wittenborg, Johann (1320/25-1363), Kaufmann, Bürgermeister." In *Biographisches Lexikon für Schleswig-Holstein und Lübeck,* vol. 6, 303-305. Neumünster, 1982.

____. "Häusermarkt und wirtschaftliche Wechsellagen in Lübeck von 1284 bis 1700." *Hansische Geschichtsblätter* 106 (1988): 41-107.

____. "Veckinchusen, Hildebrand (um 1370-1426), Kaufmann." In *Biographisches Lexikon für Schleswig-Holstein und Lübeck,* vol. 9, 358-364. Neumünster, 1991.

____. (1993a) "Hansischer Seehandel und wirtschaftliche Wechsellagen. Der Umsatz im Lübecker Hafen in der zweiten Hälfte des 14. Jahrhunderts, 1492-96 und 1680-82." In *Der hansische Sonderweg? Beiträge zur Sozial- und Wirtschaftsgeschichte der Hanse* (Quellen und Darstellungen zur hansischen Geschichte N.F. vol. 39), edited by Michael North and Stuart Jenks, 77-93. Köln & Wien, 1993.

____. (1993b) "Von Tuch und Hering zu Wein und Holz. Der Handel Lübecker Kaufleute von der Mitte des 12. Jahrhunderts bis zum Ende des 19. Jahrhunderts." In *Der Lübecker Kaufmann. Aspekte seiner Lebens- und Arbeitswelt vom Mittelalter bis zum 19. Jahrhundert,* edited by Gerhard Gerkens and Antjekathrin Graßmann, 13-33. Lübeck, 1993.

____. "The Lübeck Harbour in the Hanseatic Period. Infrastructure, Goods and the Volume of Trade." In *Harbour. The Development of a Harbour and the Work in a Harbour.* 10th International Baltic Seminar in Kotka (Publication 22 in the Series of the Provincial Museum of Kymenlaakso), 7-18. Kotka, 1996.

____. (1998a) "Die 'nye watergrafft' und der Handel mit Lüneburger Salz über Lübeck in den Ostseeraum." In *Die Geschichte der Stecknitz-Fahrt 1398-1896* (Sonderveröffentlichungen des Heimatbund und Geschichtsvereins Herzogtum Lauenburg, vol. 29), edited by William Boehart et al., 58-69, 160-163. Schwarzenbek, 1998.

____. (1998b) "Neue Aspekte zur Geschichte Lübecks: von der Jahrtausendwende bis zum Ende der Hansezeit. Die Lübecker Stadtgeschichtsforschung der letzten zehn Jahre (1988-1997). Teil 1: bis zum Ende des 13. Jahrhunderts." *Zeitschrift des Vereins für lübeckische Geschichte und Altertumskunde* 78 (1998): 47-114.

____. "Grain, Fish and Salt: Written Sources and Architectural Evidence for the Trade with Bulk Commodities in the Lübeck Harbour in Medieval and Early Modern Times." In *Maritime Topography and the Medieval Town.* 5th International Conference on Waterfront Archaeology, Copenhagen 1998 (Publications from the National Museum, Studies in Archaeology & History, vol. 4), edited by Jan Bill and Birthe L. Clausen, 87-94. Copenhagen, 1999.

____. *Die Hanse.* München, 2000.

Das Handlungsbuch von Hermann und Johann Wittenborg. Edited by Carl Mollwo. Leipzig, 1901.

Hanserecesse: Die Recesse und andere Akten der Hansetage, series 1, 1256-1430. Edited by K. Koppmann. Vols. 1-8. Leipzig, 1870-97.

Die hansischen Pfundzollisten des Jahres 1368. Part 1: *Das lübische Pfundzollbuch von 1368*. Edited by Georg Lechner. Vol. 10 of *Quellen und Darstellungen zur hansischen Geschichte*. Neue Folge. Lübeck, 1935.

Hansisches Urkundenbuch. Edited by K. Höhlbaum et. al. Vols. 1-11. Halle, Leipzig & München 1876-1916.

Hårdh, Birgitta. *Wikingerzeitliche Depotfunde aus Südschweden. Probleme und Analysen*. (Acta Archaeologica Lundensia, Series tertia in 8° minore, no. 6). Bonn & Lund, 1976.

Häpke, Rudolf. "Friesen und Sachsen im Ostseeverkehr des 13. Jahrhunderts." *Hansische Geschichtsblätter* vol. 19 (1913): 163-192.

Hasse, Max."Neues Hausgerät, neue Häuser, neue Kleider—eine Betrachtung der städtischen Kultur im 13. und 14. Jahrhundert sowie ein Katalog der metallenen Hausgeräte." *Zeitschrift für Archäologie des Mittelalters* 7 (1979): 7-83.

van Haster, Henk. "Umwelt und Nahrungswirtschaft in der Hansestadt Lübeck vom 12. Jahrhundert bis in die Neuzeit. Ein Überblick über bisherige paläoethnobotanische Untersuchungen." *Lübecker Schriften zur Archäologie und Kulturgeschichte* 21 (1991): 203-223.

Hatcher, John. *The History of the British Coal Industry. Vol. 1. Before 1700: Towards the Age of Coal*. Oxford, 1993.

Hatting, Tove. "Animal Bones from Svendborg." *Journal of Danish Archaeology* 6 (1987): 213-217.

Haupt, Richard. *Die Bau- und Kunstdenkmäler der Provinz Schleswig-Holstein*. Vols. 1-2. Kiel, 1887-1888.

——. *Geschichte und Art der Baukunst im Herzogtum Schleswig*. Vol. 5 of *Die Bau- und Kunstdenkmäler der Provinz Schleswig-Holstein*. Heide in Holstein, 1924.

——. *Geschichte und Art der Baukunst in den Herzogtümern Holstein und Lauenburg sowie den Fürstentümern Lübeck und Ratzeburg*. Vol. 6 of *Die Bau- und Kunstdenkmäler der Provinz Schleswig-Holstein*. Heide in Holstein, 1925.

Haverkamp, Alfred et al., ed. *England and Germany in the High Middle Ages. Challenge and Change* (Greece and Rome Studies, 3). Oxford. 1996.

Hede, J. Ernhold. "The Silurian of Gotland." In *The Lower Palaeozoic of Scania. The Silurian of Gotland*, by G. Regnéll and J. E. Hede, 44-89. International Geological Congress, 21st Session. Stockholm, 1960.

Heinsius, Paul. *Das Schiff der hansischen Frühzeit* (Quellen und Darstellungen zur hansischen Geschichte, Neue Folge, vol. 12). Weimar, 1956.

Helle, Knut. "Trade and Shipping between Norway and England in the Reign of Håkon Håkonsson (1217-1273)." *Sjöfartshistorisk årbok* (1967): 1-34.

——. "Neueste norwegische Forschungen über deutsche Kaufleute in Norwegen und ihre Rolle im norwegischen Außenhandel vom 12. bis 14. Jahrhundert." *Hansische Geschichtsblätter* 98 (1980): 23-38.

Hellerup Madsen, E.: see Madsen, Erik Hellerup.

Henn, Volker "Entfaltung im Westen: 'Hansen' auf den niederländischen Märkten." In *Die Hanse. Lebenswirklichkeit und Mythos* (Exhibition-catalogue, vols. 1-2), edited by Jörgen Bracker. Vol. 1: 42-45. Hamburg 1989.

Hennings, Hans Harald. "Die Lübecker Kornhäuser zu Beginn des 14. Jahrhunderts." In *Städtewesen und Bürgertum als geschichtliche Kräfte. Gedächtnisschrift für Fritz Rörig*, edited by Ahasver von Brandt, 311-339. Lübeck, 1956.

Hillam, J., and I. Tyers. "Reliability and repeatability in dendrochronological analysis: tests using the Fletcher archive of panel-painting data." *Archaeometry* 37, 2 (1995): 395-405.

Hocker, Frederick Martin. "Technical and Organizational Development in European Shipyards 1400-1600." In *Maritime Topography and the Medieval Town*. 5th International Conference on Waterfront Archaeology, Copenhagen 1998 (Publications from the National Museum, Studies in Archaeology & History, vol. 4), edited by Jan Bill and Birthe L. Clausen, 21-32. Copenhagen, 1999.

Hogan, M. Patricia. "Clays, *Culturae* and the Cultivator's Wisdom: Management Efficiency at Fourteenth-Century Wistow." *Agricultural History Review* 36 (1988): 117-131.

Hoheisel, Wolf-Dieter, and Uwe Baykowski. "A Full-Scale Replica of the Hanse Cog of 1380." In *Crossroads in Ancient Shipbuilding*. Proceedings of the Sixth International Symposium on Boat and Ship Archaeology in Roskilde 1991, edited by Christer Westerdahl, 257-264. Oxford, 1994.

Holm, Poul. "Catches and Manpower in the Danish Fisheries c. 1200-1995." In *The North Atlantic Fisheries 1100-1976. National Perspectives on a Common Resource*, edited by Poul Holm, David J. Starkey, and Jón Th. Thor, 177-206. Esbjerg, 1996.

Holst, Jens-Christian. "Beobachtungen zu Handelsnutzung und Geschoßbildung an Lübecker Steinhäusern des Mittelalters." *Jahrbuch für Hausforschung* 35 (1986): 93-144.

Hørby, Kai. *Status Regni Dacie: Studier i Christofferlinjens ægteskabs- og alliancepolitik 1252-1319*. Copenhagen, 1977.

Hough, J. S. *The Biotechnology of Malting and Brewing*. Cambridge, 1985.

Huntemann, Hans. *Das deutsche Braugewerbe vom Ausgang des Mittelalters bis zum Beginn der Industrialisierung. Biererzeugung—Bierhandel—Bierverbrauch*. Nürnberg, 1971.

Hurst, John G. "Near Eastern and Mediterranean Medieval Pottery found in North West Europe." In *Archaeologica Lundensia* 3 (1968): 195-204.

Hutchinson, Gillian. *Medieval Ships and Shipping*. London, 1994.

Hybel, Nils. "Godssystemerne i England, Danmark og på kontinentet ca. 1200-1350." *Historie* 1 (1994): pp. 40-60.

———. "Sildehandel og sildefiskeri i den nordvestlige Nordsø i begyndelsen af det 14. århundrede." *Søfart, Politik og Identitet* (Festskrift til Ole Feldbæk), edited by Hans Jeppesen et al. 27-42. Copenhagen, 1996.

———. "Klima, misvækst og hungersnød i Danmark 1311-1319." *Historisk Tidskrift* (Copenhagen) 97:1 (1997): 29-40.

Hyland, Ann. *The Medieval Warhorse. From the Crusades to the End of the Middle-Ages*. Herndon, Virginia, 1997.

Irsigler, Franz. "ind machdem alle lant beirsvoll": Zur Diffusion des Hopfenbiers im westlichen Hanseraum." In *Nahrung und Tischkultur im Hanseraum*, edited by Günter Wiegelmann, and Ruth-E. Mohrmann, 377-397. Münster & New York, 1996.

Jacobsen, N. H. *Skibsfarten i det danske Vadehav. En erhvervsgeografisk Studie.* Copenhagen, 1937.

Jahnke, Carsten. "Die hamburg-lübeckischen Pfundgeldlisten von 1458/59 und 1480-1487." *Zeitschrift des Vereins für Lübeckische Geschichte und Altertumskunde* 76 (1996): 27-53.

———. "Pfundzollrechnungen im Ostseeraum. Bestand und Fragen der Auswertung." In *Die preußischen Hansestädte und ihre Stellung im Nord- und Ostseeraum des Mittelalters*, edited by Hubert Nowak and Janusz Tandecki, 153-170. Torun, 1998.

———. "Heringsfang und -handel im Ostseeraum des Mittelalters." Ph.D. diss., University of Kiel, 1997 (also published as *Das Silber des Meeres..., Köln,* 2000; see below).

———. *Das Silber des Meeres. Fang und Vertrieb von Ostseehering zwischen Norwegen und Italien vom 12. bis zum 16. Jahrhundert* (Quellen und Darstellungen zur hansischen Geschichte, Neue Folge 49). Köln, 2000.

———, ed. "Die Malmöer Schonenzolliste des Jahres 1375." *Hansische Geschichtsblätter* 115 (1997): 1-107.

Jenks, Stuart. "The English Grain Trade, 1377-1461." In *Les techniques de conservation des grains à long terme*, 501-526. Paris, 1985.

———. (1992a) *England, die Hanse und Preussen*. Vols. 1-3. (Quellen und Darstellungen zur Hansischen Geschichte.) Köln, 1992.

———. (1992b) "Werkzeug des spätmittelalterlichen Kaufmanns: Hansen und Engländer im Wandel von *memoria* zur Akte (mit einer Edition von *The Noumbre of Weyghtys*)." *Jahrbuch für fränkische Landesforschung*, 52 (1992): 283-319.

———. "Die Welfen, Lübeck und die werdende Hanse." In *Die Welfen und ihr Braunschweiger Hof im hohen Mittelalter*, edited by Bernd Schneidmüller, 483-522. Wiesbaden, 1995.

———. "Der hansische Salzhandel im 15. Jahrhundert im Spiegel des Danziger Pfundzollbuchs von 1409." In *"Vom rechten Maß der Dinge." Beiträge zur Wirtschafts- und Sozialgeschichte. Festschrift für Harald Witthöft zum 55. Geburtstag* (Sachüberlieferung und Geschichte vol.17), edited by Rainer S. Elkar et al., 257-284. St. Katharinen, 1996.

Jensen, Jørgen Steen. "Udmøntningens størrelse." In *Danmarks middelalderlige skattefund c. 1050-c.1550*, edited by Jørgen Steen Jensen et al., 104-107. Copenhagen, 1992.

Jensen, Stig. "Handel med dagligvarer i vikingetiden." (Handel og udveksling i Danmarks oldtid) *hikuin* 16 (1990): 119-138.

Jessen, Julius. "Das älteste Schleswiger Stadtrecht." *Beiträge zur Schleswiger Stadtgeschichte* 41 (1996): 7-22.

Jöns, Hauke. "Zur Eisenverhüttung in Schleswig-Holstein in vor- und frühgeschichtlicher Zeit." *Offa: Berichte und Mitteilungen zur Urgeschichte, Frühgeschichte und Mittelalterarchäologie* 49/50 (1992/1993): 41-55.

Jørgensen, Lise Bender. *North European Textiles until AD 1000*. Århus, 1992.

Kalkar, Otto. *Ordbog til det ældre danske Sprog (1300-1700)*. Vol. 1. Copenhagen, 1881.

Kancelliets brevbøger 1551-55. Rigsarkivet. Copenhagen, 1885-86.

Kancelliets brevbøger 1566-70. Rigsarkivet. Edited by L. Laursen. Copenhagen, 1893-95.

Karrenbrock, Richard. "Baumberger Sandstein: Ausstrahlung westfälischer Kunstschaffens in den Ostseeraum." In *Die Hanse. Lebenswirklichkeit und Mythos* (Exhibition-catalogue, vols. 1-2), edited by Jörgen Bracker. Vol. 1: 497-505. Hamburg, 1989.

Kattinger, Detlef. "Tyska och Gotländska köpmäns handel på Novgorod och i England under 1100-och 1200-talet." *Gotländskt Arkiv* 64 (1992): 131-142.

___. "Deutsche Kaufmannshansen im Nord- und Ostseeraum und die Entstehung der hansischen Kontore im 12. und 13. Jahrhundert." *Zeitschrift für Geschichtswissenschaft* 42, n. 10 (1994): 883-898.

___. "Selef Susse—gotländsk handelsman under hansan." *Gotländskt Arkiv* 69 (1997): 163-172. (With an English summary.)

___. *Die Gotländische Genossenschaft. Der frühhansisch-gotländische Handel in Nord- und Westeuropa* (Quellen und Darstellungen zur hansischen Geschichte N. F. vol. 47). Köln, Weimar & Wien, 1999.

Keene, Derek. (1989a) "Haus in London: Von der Guildhall zum Stalhof." In *Die Hanse. Lebenswirklichkeit und Mythos* (Exhibition-catalogue, vols. 1-2), edited by Jörgen Bracker. Vol. 1: 47f. Hamburg, 1989.

___. (1989b) "Medieval London and its Region." *London Journal* 14 (1989): 99-111.

___. (1989c) "New Discoveries at the Hanseatic Steelyard in London." *Hansische Geschichtsblätter* 107 (1989): 15-26.

Kerling, N. J. M. *Commercial Relations of Holland and Zeeland with England from the Late 13th Century to the Close of the Middle Ages*. Leiden, 1954.

Ketner, F. *Handel en Scheepvaart van Amsterdam in de Vijftiende Eeuw*. Leiden, 1946.

Kiesselbach, Th. "Grundlagen und Bestandteile des ältesten Hamburger Schiffsrechts. *Hansische Geschichtsblätter* 28 (1900): 49-96.

Kjersgaard, Erik. *Mad og øl i Danmarks Middelalder*. Copenhagen, 1978.

Kohrtz Andersen, P.: see Andersen, Per Kohrtz.

Kong Valdemars Jordebog. Edited by Svend Aakjær. Vols. 1-3. Copenhagen, 1926-1945.

Krieger, Karl Friedrich. "Der Rechtsschutz der deutschen Hansekaufleute in England unter König Eduard I. (1272-1307)." In *Stadt und Land in der Geschichte des Ostseeraums. Wilhelm Koppe zum 65. Geburtstag überreicht von Freunden und Schülern,* edited by Klaus Friedland, 33-50. Lübeck, 1973.

——. "Die Anfänge des Seerechts im Nord- und Ostseeraum." In *Der Handel der Karolinger- und Wikingerzeit.* Part 4 of *Untersuchungen zu Handel und Verkehr der vor- und frühgeschichtlichen Zeit in Mittel- und Nordeuropa* (Abhandlungen der Akademie der Wissenschaften in Göttingen, phil.-hist. Klasse, 3. Folge, Nr. 156), edited by D. Düwel et al., 246-265. Göttingen, 1987.

Krøniker fra Valdemarstiden. Edited by Jørgen Olrik. Copenhagen, 1900-01.

Krüger, Klaus. "Flämische Grabplatten im Ostseeraum: Kunstdenkmäler als historische Quelle." In *Die Niederlande und der europäische Nordosten: Ein Jahrtausend weiträumiger Beziehungen (700–1700),* edited by Hubertus Menke, 167-208. Neumünster, 1992.

Kryger, Karin. "Middelalderens bemalede stenskulptur i Danmark." *hikuin* 3 (1977): 183-194.

Kumlien, Kjell."Bergsbruk." In *Kulturhistorisk Leksikon for Nordisk Middelalder,* 482-490. Vol. 1. Copenhagen, 1980.

Kunze, Karl. "Das erste Jahrhundert der deutschen Hanse in England." *Hansische Geschichtsblätter* 18 (1889): 129-152.

——, ed. *Hanseakten aus England. 1275-1412* (Hansische Geschichtsquellen, vol. 6). Halle/Saale, 1891.

Lahn, Werner. *Die Kogge von Bremen.* Vol. 1. *Bauteile und Bauablauf* (Schriften des Deutschen Schiffahrtsmuseums, vol. 30). Hamburg, 1992.

Landen, Annette. "Dopfuntar så in i Norden." *Kulturmiljövård* 5 (1993): 40-45.

——. "Gotländsk stenexport." In *Medeltid,* edited by Erik Osvalds, 81-93. Lund, 1997. (2nd ed., 1999.)

——. "Die mittelalterliche Taufe der Dorfkirche in Neuburg bei Wismar." *Mecklenburgische Jahrbücher* 114 (1999): 5-15.

Langdon, John L. *Horses, Oxen and Technological Innovation: The Use of Draught Animals in English Farming from 1066-1500.* Cambridge, 1986.

——. "Inland Water Transport in Medieval England." *Journal of Historical Geography* 19 (1993): 1-11.

Laufeld, Sven. (1974a) *Reference Localities for Paleontology and Geology in the Silurian of Gotland.* Sveriges Geologiska Undersökningar (The Geological Survey of Sweden), series C, no. 705. 1974.

——. (1974b) *Silurian Chitinozoa from Gotland.* Ph.D. diss., University of Lund 1974. In *Fossils and Strata,* no. 5. Oslo, 1974.

Layton, I. G. "The Origins of Britain's Tar and Pitch Imports, 1700-1920. The Role of Maritime Freights in Patterns of Trade and Production." *Northern Seas Yearbook 1996* (Fiskeri- og Søfartsmuseets studieserie nr 8), edited by P. Holm, O. Janzen, J. Thór, 72-104. Esbjerg, 1996.

Le Patourel, Jean H. E. "Pottery as Evidence for Social and Economic Change." In *Medieval Settlement: Continuity and Change,* edited by P. H. Sawyer, 169-179. London, 1976.

Leach, R. *An Investigation into the Use of Purbeck Marble in Medieval England.* 2nd edition, privately printed. Crediton, 1978.

Leciejewicz, Lech. "Z denara otrzymasz wóz świeżych śledzi." In *Nummus et historia. Pieniadz Europy średniowiecznej,* edited by Stefan K. Kuczyński et al., 103-109. Warsaw, 1985. (For the version in German, see Leciejewicz 1991.)

Leciejewicz, Lech. "Zum frühmittelalterlichen Heringshandel im südlichen Ostseegebiet." *Zeitschrift für Archäologie* 25 (1991): 209-214.

Lesnikov, M. P. "Beiträge zur baltisch-niederländischen Handelsgeschichte am Ausgang des 14. und zu Beginn des 15. Jahrhunderts." *Wissenschaftliche Zeitschrift der Karl-Marx-Universität Leipzig* 7 (1957/58): 613f.

Liber Albus: The White Book of the City of London, 1419. Edited by H. Riley. Compiled by J. Carpenter and R. Whittington. London, 1861.

Liebgott, Niels-Knud. "Telt, hytte, bod. Eksempler på primitive bebyggelsesformer i vikingetid og middelalder." In *Strejflys over Danmarks Bygningskultur. Festskrift til Harald Langberg,* 9-22. Copenhagen, 1979.

———. *Dansk Middelalderarkæologi.* Copenhagen, 1989.

Lindahl, Anders. *Information Through Sherds: a Case Study of the Early Glazed Earthenware from Dalby, Scania.* Lund, 1986.

Lindström, Gustav. *Anteckningar om Gotlands medeltid.* Vol. 2. Stockholm, 1895.

Liv-, Est- und Churländisches Urkundenbuch. Edited by Friedrich Georg von Bunge. Vol. 1 (part I). Reval, 1853.

Liv-, Est- und Curländische Urkunden-Regesten bis zum Jahre 1300. Edited by Friedrich Georg von Bunge. Leipzig, 1881.

Lloyd, Terence H. *The English Wool Trade in the Middle Ages.* Cambridge, 1977.

———. *Alien Merchants in England in the High Middle Ages.* Brighton, 1982.

———. *England and the German Hanse. 1157-1611. A Study of their Trade and Commercial Diplomacy.* Cambridge, 1991.

Löfvendahl, Runo. "Gotländsk byggnadssten." In *Gotlands Län: Natursten i byggnader.* Riksantikvarieämbetet (National Heritage Board), Statens historiska museer, 17-25. Stockholm, 1995.

Lopez, Robert S. *The Commercial Revolution of the Middle Ages, 950-1350.* Englewood Cliffs, 1971.

Lövei, Pál. "A tömött vörös mészkö—'vörös márvány'—a középkori Magyarországi müvészetben" (Summary: Der dichte rote Kalkstein—'der rote Marmor'—in der Kunst des mittelalterlichen Ungarn). *Ars Hungarica* 2 (1992): 3-28.

Lüdtke, Hartwig. *Die mittelalterliche Keramik von Schleswig. Ausgrabung Schild 1971-1975.* Schleswig, 1985.

———. (1989a) *The Bryggen Pottery I: Introduction and Pingsdorf Ware.* (The Bryggen Papers, Supplementary Series 4.) Bergen, 1989.

———. (1989b) "Fünf Karten Verbreitung mittelalterlicher Keramik in Skandinavien." *Hammaburg* n.s. 9 (1989): 215-226.

Mackeprang, Mouritz. *Danmarks middelalderlige Døbefonte.* Copenhagen, 1941.

Maddicott, J. R. *The English Peasantry and the Demands of the Crown, 1294-1341*, Past and Present Supplement, I (1975). Reprinted in *Landlords, Peasants and Politics in Medieval England*, edited by T. H. Aston, 285-359. Cambridge, 1987.

Madsen, Erik Hellerup. "Salt og salthandel i østersøområdet i tidlig middelalder." *hikuin* 3 (1977): 269-294.

Madsen, Hans Jørgen. "Møllesten til Norden." *Skalk* 6 (1967): 9-11.

———. "The Earliest dated Finds of Glazed Pottery in Ribe." *Medieval Ceramics* 9 (1985): 57-64.

———. "Handelskeramik fra middelalderens Grønnegade." *By, Marsk og Geest* 2 (1991): 3-33.

Das Marienburger Tresslerbuch der Jahre 1399–1409. Königsberg, 1896.

Marsden, Peter. *Ships of the Port of London, Twelfth to Seventeenth Centuries AD* (English Heritage Archaeological Report, vol. 6). London, 1996.

Mate, Mavis. "Profit and Productivity on the Estates of Isabella de Forz (1260-92)." *Economic History Review*, 2nd series, 33 (1980): 326-334.

Mayhew, N. J. "Modelling Medieval Monetisation." In *A Commercialising Economy: England 1086-1300*, edited by R. H. Britnell and B. M. S. Campbell, 55-77. Manchester, 1995.

McGrail, Sean. (1993a) "The Future of the Designated Wreck Site in the R. Hamble." *International Journal of Nautical Archaeology* 22 (1993): 45-51.

———. (1993b) *Medieval Boat and Ship Timbers from Dublin* (Medieval Dublin Excavations 1962-81. Ser. B, vol. 3). Dublin, 1993.

McNamee, Colm. *The Wars of the Bruces: Scotland, England and Ireland 1306-1328*. East Linton, 1997.

Mecklenburgisches Urkundenbuch (-1400). Vols. 1-25. Schwerin, 1863-1977.

Mehnert, Annemarie. *Mittelalterliche Taufsteine in Vorpommern*. Greifswald, 1934.

Miller, Edward. "Farming in Northern England." *Northern History* 11 (1975): 1-16.

Miller, Edward, and John Hatcher. *Medieval England: Towns, Commerce and Crafts 1086-1348*. London, 1995.

Mortensøn, Ole. *Renæssancens fartøjer – sejlads og søfart i Danmark 1550-1650* (Meddelelser fra Langelands Museum). Rudkøbing, 1995.

Moulin, Léo. "Bière, houblon et cervoise." *Bulletin de l'Académie Royale de Langue et de Littérature Françaises* 59 (1981): 111-148.

Munro, John H. "Wool-Price Schedules and the Qualities of English Wools in the Later Middle Ages, c.1270-1499." *Textile History* 9 (1978): 118-169.

———. "Industrial Transformations in the North-West European Textile Trades, c. 1290-c. 1340: Economic Progress or Economic Crisis?" In *Before the Black Death: Studies in the 'Crisis' of the Early Fourteenth Century*, edited by Bruce M. S. Campbell, 110-148. Manchester, 1991.

———. *Textiles, Towns and Trade. Essays in the Economic History of Late Medieval England and the Low Countries*. Aldershot/Hampshire, 1994.

Munthe, H. et al. *Sveriges Geologiska Undersökningar*. Series Aa 152, 1922; Aa 156, 1925; Aa 160 and 164, 1927; Aa 169, 1928; Aa 170, 1929; Aa 171, 1933; Aa 180, 1936.

Musset, L. "La pierre de Caen: extration et commerce, XIe-XVe siècles.' In *Pierre et métal dans le bâtiment au Moyen Age*, edited by O. Chapelot and P. Benoit, 219-235. Paris, 1985.

Müller-Boysen, Carsten. *Kaufmannsschutz und Handelsrecht im frühmittelalterlichen Nordeuropa.* Neumünster, 1980.

Nedkvitne, Arnved. (1976a) "Handelssjøfarten mellom Norge og England i høymiddelalderen." *Sjøfartshistorisk Årbok. Norwegian Yearbook of Maritime History* (1976): 7-252.

___. (1976b) "Utenrikshandelen fra det vestafjelske Norge." Ph.D. diss., University of Bergen, 1976.

___. (1983a) "Der Strukturwandel im nordeuropäischen Seehandel vom 12.-14. Jahrhundert; seine Bedeutung für die norwegischen Seehandelsstädte." In *Seehandelszentren im nördlichen Europa* (Lübecker Schriften zur Archäologie und Kulturgeschichte, vol. 7), 261-269. Bonn, 1983.

___. (1983b) "Utenrikshandelen fra det vestafjelske Norge 1100-1600." Bergen, 1983. Typescript.

Nielsen, Herluf. "Luksusforordning." In *Kulturhistorisk Leksikon for Nordisk Middelalder*, 2-5. Vol. 11. Copenhagen, 1981.

Nightingale, Pamela. "The Growth of London in the Medieval English Economy." In *Progress and Problems in Medieval England: Essays in Honour of Edward Miller*, edited by Richard Britnell and John Hatcher, 89-106. Cambridge, 1996.

Nihlén, John. *Studier rörande äldre svensk järnhantering med särskild hänsyn till Småland.* Stockholm, 1932.

Nilsson, T. "Stentinget. En indlandsbebyggelse med handel og håndværk fra yngre jernalder og vikingetid." *Kuml* (1990): 119-132.

Nirrnheim, H. *Das Hamburgische Pfundzoll Buch von 1369.* Hamburg, 1910.

Nordlund, Odd. *Brewing and Beer Traditions in Norway. The Social Anthropological Background of the Brewing Industry.* Oslo, 1969.

North, Michael. *Das Geld und seine Geschichte. Vom Mittelalter bis zur Gegenwart.* München, 1994.

Olrik, Jørgen. "Øm Klosters Krønike. Exordium Caræ Insulæ." *Aarhus Stifts Aarbøger* (1932): 1-99.

Olsen, Olaf, and Crumlin-Pedersen, Ole. "The Skuldelev Ships. A Report of the Final Underwater Excavation in 1959 and the Salvaging Operation in 1962." *Acta Archaeologica* 38 (1968): 73-174.

Olsson, Sven-Olof, ed. *Medeltida danskt järn. Framställning av och handel med järn i Skåneland och Småland under medeltiden.* Varberg, 1995.

Oorkondenboek van Amsterdam tot 1400. Edited by P. H. J. Van Der Laan. Amsterdam, 1975.

Oosting, Rob. "De opgraving van het vlak van een kogge bij Rutten." In *Raakvlakken tussen scheepsarcheologie, maritieme geschiedenis en scheepsbouwkunde* (Flevobericht, vol. 280), edited by Reinder Reinders, 57-63. Lelystad, 1987.

Orduna, Jette. *Middelalderlige klædeplomber*. Højbjerg, 1995.

Ormrod, W. M. "The Crown and the English Economy, 1290-1348." In *Before the Black Death: Studies in the 'Crisis' of the Early Fourteenth Century*, edited by Bruce M. S. Campbell, 149-183. Manchester, 1991.

Orton, Clive, Paul Tyers, and Alan G. Vince. *Pottery in Archaeology*. Cambridge, 1993.

Owen, D., ed. *The Making of King's Lynn*. London, 1984.

Overton, Mark. *Agricultural Revolution in England: The Transformation of the Agrarian Economy 1500-1850*. Cambridge, 1996.

Overton, Mark, and Bruce M. S. Campbell. "Productivity Change in European Agricultural Development." In *Land, Labour and Livestock: Historical Studies in European Agricultural Productivity*, edited by Bruce M. S. Campbell and Mark Overton, 1-50. Manchester, 1991.

——."Norfolk Livestock Farming 1250-1740: A Comparative Study of Manorial Accounts and Probate Inventories." *Journal of Historical Geography*, 18 (1992): 377-396.

——. "Production et productivité dans l'agriculture anglais, 1086-1871." *Histoire et Mesure* 11, no. 3/4 (1996): 255-297.

Parker, Vanessa. *The Making of King's Lynn: Secular Buildings from the 11th to the 17th Century*. King's Lynn Archaeological Survey, 1. London and Chichester, 1971.

Pasteur, Louis. *Studies on Fermentation. The Diseases of Beer, Their Causes, and the Means of Preventing Them. A Translation ... of "Etudes Sur La Biere," with Notes, Index and Original Illustrations by Frank Faulkner, author of "The Art of Brewing", etc. and D. Constable Robb*. London, 1879.

Pearce, Jacqui E., Alan G. Vince, and M. Anne Jenner. *A Dated Type-series of London Medieval Pottery: Part 2, London-type Ware*. London, 1985.

Pelham, R. A. "Timber Exports from the Weald during the Fourteenth Century." *Sussex Archaeological Collections* 69 (1928): 170-182.

——. "The Foreign Trade of Sussex, 1300-1350." *Sussex Archaeological Collections* 70 (1929): 93-118.

——. (1936a) "Medieval Foreign Trade: Eastern Ports." In *An Historical Geography of England before A.D. 1800*, edited by H. C. Darby, 298-329. Cambridge, 1936.

——. (1936b) "Fourteenth-Century England." In *An Historical Geography of England before A.D. 1800*, edited by H. C. Darby, 230-265. Cambridge, 1936.

Persson, Karl Gunnar. *Pre-Industrial Economic Growth: Social Organization and Technological Progress in Europe*. Oxford, 1988.

Pinkse, V. C. C. J. "Het Goudse Kuitbier, Gouda's Welvaren in de Late Middeleeuwen 1400-1568." In *Gouda Zeven Eeuwen Stad*, 91-128. Gouda, 1972.

The Pipe Roll of the Bishopric of Winchester 1301-02. Edited by Mark Page. (Hampshire Record Series, 14.) Winchester, 1996.

Pitz, Ernst. "Einstimmigkeit oder Mehrheitsbeschluß? Ein heimlicher Verfassungsstreit um die Vollmachten der Ratssendeboten auf den Hansetagen." In *Verwal-*

tung und Politik in den Städten Mitteleuropas. Beiträge zu Verfassungsnorm und Verfassungswirklichkeit in altständischer Zeit (Städteforschung A/34), edited by Wilfried Ehbrecht, 115-146. Köln, Weimar & Wien, 1994.

Platt, Colin. *Medieval Southampton: The Port and Trading Community, A.D. 1000-1600.* London, 1973.

Pommersches Urkundenbuch. Edited by Rodgero Prümers. Vol. 2. Stettin, 1881.

Ponsford, Michael. "Dendrochronological dates from Dundas Wharf, Bristol and the dating of Ham Green and other medieval pottery." In *Custom and Ceramics: Essays presented to Kenneth Barton*, edited by E. Lewis, 81-103. Wickham, 1991.

Postan, Michael M. "Village Livestock in the Thirteenth Century." *Economic History Review*, 2nd series, 15 (1962): 219-249. Reprinted as pp. 214-248 in M. M. Postan, *Essays on Medieval Agriculture and General Problems of the Medieval Economy.* Cambridge, 1973.

——. "Economic Relations between Eastern and Western Europe." In M. M. Postan, *Medieval Trade and Finance*, 305-341. Cambridge, 1973.

——. "The Trade of Medieval Europe: The North." In *Trade and Industry in the Middle Ages.* Vol. 2 of *The Cambridge Economic History of Europe*, edited by M. M. Postan and Edward Miller, 168-305. 2nd ed. Cambridge, 1987.

Poulsen, Bjørn. "Møntbrug i Danmark 1100-1300." *Fortid og Nutid* 28 (1979): 281-285.

——. "Wirtschaftliche und rechtliche Aspekte des nordfriesischen Salzes im Spätmittelalter und in der frühen Neuzeit." In *Das Salz in der Rechts- und Handelsgeschichte*, edited by Jean-Claude Hoquet and Rudolf Palme, 279-292. Schwaz, 1991.

——. (1996a) "Fra middelalder til renæssance: Vækst og strukturændringer i søfarten på Aalborg 1518-1583." In *Søfart, politik, identitet. Festskrift til Ole Feldbæk*, 43-64. Copenhagen, 1996.

——. (1996b) "Skibet og ploven. Ribe og Vestslesvig i senmiddelalderen." *Byarkæologi* (Ribe) 3 (1996): 14.

——. "Agricultural Technology in Medieval Denmark." In *Agrarian Technology in the Middle Ages: North-West Europe*, edited by Grenville Astill and John Langdon, 115-145. Leiden, 1997.

——. "The Herring Fisheries off Heligoland, c.1330-1550." *North Atlantic Fisheries. Markets and Modernisation, Studia Atlantica* 2 (1998): 7-37.

Power, Eileen. *The Wool Trade in English Medieval History.* Oxford, 1941.

Power, John P., and Bruce M. S. Campbell. "Cluster Analysis and the Classification of Medieval Demesne-Farming Systems." *Transactions of the Institute of British Geographers*, New Series, 17 (1992): 227-245.

Prestwich, Michael. *War, Politics and Finance under Edward I.* London, 1972.

Preussisches Urkundenbuch, 1309–1335. Vol. 2. Königsberg, 1939.

Probst, Niels. "Hovedskibet Maria 1514-25, et rekonstruktionsforsøg." *Marinehistorisk Tidskrift* 2 (1990): 3-32.

___. "The Introduction of Flushed-planked Skin in Northern Europe – and the Elsinore Wreck." In *Crossroads in Ancient Shipbuilding.* Proceedings of the Sixth International Symposium on Boat and Ship Archaeology, Roskilde 1991, edited by Christer Westerdahl, 143-152. Oxford, 1994.

Pudelko, Georg. *Romanische Taufsteine.* Berlin, 1932.

Rackham, O. *Ancient Woodland.* London, 1980.

Rahlf, Thomas. *Getreide in der Sozial- und Wirtschaftsgeschichte vom 16. bis 18. Jahrhundert. Das Beispiel Köln im regionalen Vergleich* (Kleine Schriften zur Geschichte und Landeskunde, vol. 3). Trier, 1996.

Rasmussen, Poul. *Mål og vægt.* Copenhagen, 1967.

Raven van Barnekows räkenskaper för Nyköpings fögderi 1365-1367, edited by Birgitta Fritz and Eva Odelman. Stockholm, 1994.

Ravensdale, Jack R. *Liable to Floods: Village Landscape on the Edge of the Fens, 450-1850.* Cambridge, 1974.

Reed, Ian W. *1000 Years of Pottery: An Analysis of Pottery Trade and Use.* Meddelelser 25 (Riksantikvaren, Utgravingskontoret for Trondheim). Trondheim, 1990.

"Regnskabet for Ribebispens gård Brink 1388-89", edited by Bjørn Poulsen and Fritz S. Pedersen. *Danske Magazin* 6:3 (1993): 316-336.

Reincke, Heinrich. "Die Deutschlandfahrt der Flandrer während der hansischen Frühzeit." *Hansische Geschichtsblätter* 67/68 (1942/1943): 51-164.

Reinders, H. Reinder, and Rob Oosting. "Mittelalterliche Schiffsfunde in den Ijsselmeerpoldern." In *Ländliche und städtische Küstensiedlungen im 1. und 2. Jahrtausend.* Wilhelmshavener Tage, nr 2, Dokumentation des Vortragszyklus 23.-25. Oktober 1987, 106-122. Wilhelmshaven, 1989.

Resi, Heid Gjöstein. *Die Specksteinfunde aus Haithabu.* (Berichte über die Ausgrabungen in Haithabu 14.) Neumünster, 1979.

Reutersvärd, Oscar. *Paradisets källa och de gotländska "paradisfuntarna": Ett bidrag till studiet av vattensymboliken på de medeltida dopfuntarna.* (With an English translation: *The Fountain of Paradise and the "Paradise Font" of Gotland: A Contribution to the Study of Water Symbolism on Medieval Fonts.*) Lund, 1967.

___. "Fröjel-Falsterbofunten i Hälsingborg." In *Kring Kärnan* X. Hälsingborgs museums publikation 1969, 107-114. Hälsingborg, 1969.

___. "Fyra Olavsframställningar på de så kallade Fröjel-Falsterbofuntarna från 1400-talets början." In *Fra Sankt Olav til Martin Luther.* Foredrag fremlagt ved det tredje nordiske symposion for ikonografiske studier, Bårdshaug den 21-24 augusti 1972, edited by Martin Blindheim, 37-40. Oslo, 1975.

Ringbøl Bitsch, B.: see Bitsch, B. Ringbøl.

Rockwell, Peter. *The Art of Stoneworking: A Reference Guide.* Cambridge, 1993.

Rönnby, Johan, and Jonathan R. Adams. *Östersjöns sjunkna skepp. En marinarkeologisk tidsresa.* Stockholm, 1994.

Roosval, Johnny. *Die Steinmeister Gottlands: Eine Geschichte der führenden Taufsteinwerkstätte des schwedischen Mittelalters, ihrer Voraussetzungen und Begleit-

Erscheinungen. Kungliga Vitterhets, Historie och Antikvitetsakademien, Monografiserien 11. Stockholm, 1918.

___. *Medeltida skulptur i Gotlands Fornsal*. Stockholm, 1928.

Roover, R. de. "The Organization of Trade." In *Economic Organzisation and Policies in the Middle Ages*. Vol. 3 of *The Cambridge Economic History of Europe*, edited by Michael M. Postan et al., 42-118. Cambridge, 1979.

Rörig, Fritz. "Die Hanse und die nordischen Länder." In *Hansische Beiträge zur deutschen Wirtschaftsgeschichte* (Veröffentlichungen der Schleswig-Holsteinischen Universitätsgesellschaft Nr. 12), 157- 173. Breslau, 1928.

___. *Vom Werden und Wesen der Hanse*. Leipzig, 1940.

___. (1958a) "Das älteste erhaltene deutsche Kaufmannsbüchlein." In Fritz Rörig, *Wirtschaftskräfte im Mittelalter*, edited by Paul Kaegbein, 167-215. Weimar, 1958.

___. (1958b) "Die Entstehung der Hanse und der Ostseeraum." In Fritz Rörig, *Wirtschaftskräfte im Mittelalter*, edited by Paul Kaegbein, 542-603. Weimar, 1958.

___. (1958c) "Großhandel und Großhändler im Lübeck des 14. Jahrhunderts." In Fritz Rörig, *Wirtschaftskräfte im Mittelalter*, edited by Paul Kaegbein, 216-246. Weimar, 1958.

___. (1958d) "Reichssymbolik auf Gotland. Heinrich der Löwe, Kaufleute des Römischen Reiches, Lübeck, Riga und Gotland." In Fritz Rörig, *Wirtschaftskräfte im Mittelalter*, edited by Paul Kaegbein, 490-541. Weimar, 1958.

___. *Wirtschaftskräfte im Mittelalter*, edited by Paul Kaegbein. Weimar, 1958. Reprint Wien, Köln & Graz, 1971.

Roskildebispens Jordebøger og Regnskaber. Edited by C. A. Christensen. Danske middelalderlige regnskaber. 3d ser., vol. 1. Copenhagen, 1956.

Rotuli Litterarum Clausarum 1204-1224. Edited by T. Hardy. Record Commission. London, 1833.

Rotuli Parliamentorum. Vol. 2. London, 1832.

Russell, Josiah Cox. *Medieval Regions and their Cities*. Newton Abbot, 1972.

Ryder, M. L. "Medieval Sheep and Wool Types." *Agricultural History Review* 32 (1984): 14-28.

Rymer's Fœdera. Edited by T. D. Hardy. Vol. 1. London, 1869.

Salzman, L. F. *English Industries of the Middle Ages*. (1st ed. 1915.) New edition, enlarged and illustrated. London, 1964.

Sarnowski, Jürgen. *Die Wirtschaftsführung des Deutschen Ordens in Preussen (1382-1454)*. Köln, Weimar & Wien, 1993.

Sartorius Freiherr v. Waltershausen, Georg. *Urkundliche Geschichte des Ursprungs der deutschen Hanse*, edited by Johann Martin Lappenberg. Vols. 1-2. Hamburg, 1830.

Sauermann, Ernst. *Die mittelalterlichen Taufsteine der Provinz Schleswig-Holstein*. Flensburg, 1904.

Saul, Anthony. "Great Yarmouth in the Fourteenth Century: A Study in Trade, Politics, and Society." Ph.D. diss., University of Oxford, 1975.

——. "English Towns in the Late Middle Ages: The Case of Great Yarmouth." *Journal of Medieval History*, 8 (1982): 75-88.

——. "The Herring Industry at Gt. Yarmouth, c.1280-c.1400." *Norfolk Archaeology*, 38 (1983): 33-42.

Saxo Grammaticus. *Danmarks Krønike*, edited by Fr. Winkel Horn. Copenhagen, 1913.

Scheftel, Michael. "Skizzen zu einer Geschichte des privaten Profanbaus in Lübeck." In *Lübeckische Geschichte*, edited by Antjekathrin Graßmann, 757-762. Lübeck, 1997.

Schich, Winfried. "Der Ostseeraum aus der Sicht der mittelalterlichen Siedlungsgeschichte—mit besonderer Berücksichtigung der 'Seestädte' an der südwestlichen Ostseeküste." *Siedlungsforschung* 15 (1997): 53-79.

Schildhauer, Johannes. "Zur Verlagerung des See- und Handelsverkehrs im nordeuropäischen Raum während des 15. und 16. Jahrhunderts. Eine Untersuchung auf der Grundlage der Danziger Pfahlkammerbücher." *Jahrbuch für Wirtschaftsgeschichte* 4 (1968): 187-211.

Schlosser, Hans. *Braurechte, Brauer und Braustätten in München. Zur Rechts- und Sozialgeschichte des spätmittelalterlichen Brauwesens*. Elsbach am Main, 1981.

Schulz, Friedrich. *Die Hanse und England von Eduards III. bis auf Heinrichs VIII. Zeit*. (Abhandlungen zur Verkehrs- und Seegeschichte, vol. 5). Berlin, 1911. Reprinted (Scientia Verlag) Aalen, 1978.

Schäfer, Dietrich. *Die Hansestädte und König Waldemar von Dänemark. Hansische Geschichte bis 1370*. Jena, 1879.

——. *Die deutsche Hanse*. Leipzig & Bielefeld, 1903.

Scriptores Minores Historiae Danicae Medii Ævi. Edited by M. CL. Gertz. Vols. 1-2. Copenhagen, 1917-22.

Seifert, Dieter. *Kompagnons und Konkurrenten. Holland und die Hanse im späten Mittelalter*. Köln, Weimar & Wien. 1997.

Shaikh, Naz Ahmed, Åke Brun, Lars Karis, Göran Kjellström, Ulf Sivhed, Arne Sundberg, and Nils-Gunnar Wik. *Kalksten och dolomit i Sverige*. Del 3. *Södra Sverige*. Sveriges Geologiska Undersökning (The Geological Survey of Sweden). Rapporter och meddelanden 56. Uppsala, 1990.

Shaw, R. Cunliffe. *The Royal Forest of Lancaster*. Preston, 1956.

Simpson, Gavin. "Two Medieval Pottery Kilns." In *Excavations in Stamford Lincolnshire 1963-1969* (Society for Medieval Archaeology Monograph Series 9), edited by Chris Mahany, Alan Burchard and Gavin Simpson, 145-172. London, 1982.

Skjølsvold, A. *Kleberstensindustrien i vikingetiden*. Oslo 1961.

Skyum-Nielsen, Niels. *Fruer og Vildmœnd*. Vol. 1 of *Dansk Middelalderhistorie 1250-1340*. Copenhagen, 1994.

Smit, H. J. *De Opkomst van den Handel van Amsterdam, Onderzoekingen naar de economische ontwikkeling der stad tot 1441*. Amsterdam, 1914.

———. "De Registers van den Biertol te Amsterdam." *Historisch Genootschap te Utrecht. Bijdragen en Mededelingen* 38 (1917): 1-97.

Snooks, Graeme D. "The Dynamic Role of the Market in the Anglo-Norman Economy and Beyond, 1086-1300." In *A Commercialising Economy: England 1086-1300*, edited by R. H. Britnell and Bruce M. S. Campbell, 27-54. Manchester, 1995.

Søgaard, Helge. "Nogle bidrag til øllets ældre kulturhistorie." *Brygmesteren* 10 (1953): 261-284.

Spufford, Peter. "The Scale of Commercial Activity"; paper given at the Lübeck conference "Stand und Aufgaben der hansischen Geschichtsforschung" in 1993.

———. "Trade in Fourteenth-Century Europe." In *The New Cambridge Medieval History*, vol. 6, *c.1300-c.1415*, edited by Michael Jones, 155-208. Cambridge, 2000.

Statutes of the Realm. Vol. 1. London, 1810.

Steen Jensen, J.: see Jensen, Jørgen Steen.

Steensberg, Axel. *Bondehuse og vandmøller i Danmark gennem 2000 år*. Copenhagen, 1952.

Steenstrup, Johannes. *Studier i Kong Valdemars Jordebog*. Vols. 1-2. Copenhagen, 1873-74.

Stefke, Gerald. *Ein städtisches Exportgewerbe des Spätmittelalters in seiner Entfaltung und ersten Blüte. Untersuchungen zur Geschichte der Hamburger Seebrauerei des 14. Jahrhunderts*. Hamburg, 1979.

———. "Die Hamburger Zollbücher von 1399/1400 und '1418'. Der Werkzoll im 14. und Frühen 15. Jahrhundert und die Ausfuhr von Hamburger Bier über See im Jahre 1417." *Zeitschrift des Vereins für Hamburgische Geschichte* 69 (1983): 1-33.

———. "Der Bierexport auf mittlere und größere Distanz vom 14. bis zum frühen 16. Jahrhundert." In *Die Hanse. Lebenswirklichkeit und Mythos* (Exhibition-catalogue, vols. 1-2), edited by Jörgen Bracker. Vol. 1: 468-72. Hamburg, 1989.

Stenholm, Leifh. *Ränderna går aldrig ur: en bebyggelsehistorisk studie av Blekinges dansktid*. Lund, 1986.

Stenström, Tore. *Problem rörande Gotlands medeltida dopfuntar*. Umeå, 1975.

Stieda, W. "Das Böttcherei-Gewerbe in Alt-Rostock." *Beiträge zur Geschichte der Stadt Rostock* 1-2 (1895): 29-52.

Stoob, Heinz. *Die Hanse*. Graz, Wien & Köln 1995.

Sundnér, Barbro. "Byggnadssten i Skåne." (Kirkearkæologi i Norden 5, Viborg, Danmark 1993) *hikuin* 22 (1995): 231-248.

Sutton, Anne F. "The Early Linen and Worsted Industry of Norfolk and the Evolution of the London Mercers' Company." *Norfolk Archaeology* 40 (1989): 201-225.

Svanberg, Jan. "Stenskulpturen." In *Den romanska konsten* (Signums svenska konsthistoria), 117-227. Lund, 1995.

Svenwall, Nils. *Ett 1500-talsfartyg med arbetsnamnet Ringaren*. Stockholm, 1994.

Techen, Friedrich. "Das Brauwerk in Wismar." *Hansische Geschichtsblätter* 21 (1915): 263-352.

___. "Das Brauwerk in Wismar." *Hansische Geschichtsblätter* 22 (1916): 145-224.

Ter Gouw, J. *Geschiedenis van Amsterdam*. Vol. 1-5. Amsterdam, 1879.

Thoen, Erik. "The Birth of 'The Flemish Husbandry': Agricultural Farming in Medieval Flanders." In *Medieval Farming and Technology. The Impact of Agricultural Change in Northwest Europe*, edited by Grenville Astil and John Langdon, 69-88. Leiden, 1997.

Thunæus, Harald. *Ölets historia i Sverige*. Vols. 1-2. Stockholm, 1968-70.

Tipping, C. "Cargo handling and the medieval cog." *Mariner's Mirror* 80 (1994): 3-15.

Titow, J. "Evidence of Weather in the Account Rolls of the Bishopric of Winchester 1209-1350." *The Economic History Review*, 2nd ser., 12 (1960): 360-407.

De Tol van Iersekeroord. Documenten en Rekeningen 1321-1572, edited by W. S. Unger. The Hague, 1939.

Tollenaere, Lisbeth. *La sculpture sur pierre de l'ancien diocèse de Liège a l'époque romane*. Université de Louvain, Recueil de travaux d'histoire et de philologie, ser. 4, fasc. 11. Louvain, 1957.

Trow-Smith, R. *A History of British Livestock Husbandry to 1700*. London, 1957.

Ulriksen, Jens. "Teorier og virkelighed i forbindelse med lokalisering af anløbspladser fra germanertid og vikingetid i Danmark." *Aarbøger for Nordisk Oldkyndighed og Historie* (1990): 69-101.

Unger, Richard W. *The Ship in the Medieval Economy 600-1600*. London & Montreal, 1980.

___. "Technical Change in the Brewing Industry in Germany, the Low Countries and England in the Late Middle Ages." *The Journal of European Economic History* 21 (1992): 281-313.

Urkundenbuch der Stadt Lübeck (-1470). Vols. 1-11. Lübeck, 1843-1905. (Vols. 1-2 reprinted in 1976.)

van Uytven, Raymond. "Politiek en economie: de crisis der late Xve eeuw in de Nederlanden." *Belgisch Tijdschrift voor Filologie en Geschiedenis* 53 (1975): 1097-1149.

Varenius, Björn. *Det nordiska skeppet. Teknologi och samhällsstrategi i vikingatid och medeltid* (Stockholm Studies in Archaeology, vol. 10). Stockholm, 1992.

Veale, E. M. *The English Fur Trade in the Late Middle Ages*. Oxford, 1966.

Vellev, Jens. *Saltproduktion på Læsø, i Danmark og i Europa*. Viborg, 1993.

Venge, Mikael. *Fra åretold til toldetat. Middelalderen indtil 1660*. Vol. 1 of *Dansk Toldhistorie*. Copenhagen, 1987.

Ventegodt, Ole. "Skånemarkedets sild." *Maritim Kontakt* 14 (1990): 3-19.

Viborgbispen Gunners Levned. Transl. by Hans Olrik. Copenhagen, 1892.

van Vilsteren, V. T. "De oorsprong en techniek van het brouwen tot de 14de eeuw." In *Bier! Geschiedenis van een volksdrank*, edited by R. E. Kistemaker and V. T. van Vilsteren, 7-19. Amsterdam, 1994.

Vince, Alan G. *The Medieval Ceramic Industry of the Severn Valley*. Southampton, 1983.

___. (1985a) *The Ceramic Finds. Part 2*. In vol. 3 of *Hereford City Excavations: The Finds. Council for British Archaeology Research Report 56*, edited by R. Shoesmith, 34-82. London, 1985.

___. (1985b) "The Saxon and Medieval Pottery of London: A Review." *Medieval Archaeology* 29 (1985): 25-93.

___. "English Medieval Pottery in Viking Dublin." In *Keimelia: Studies in Medieval Archaeology and History in Memory of Tom Delaney*, edited by Gearoid Mac Niocall and Patrick F. Wallace, 254-270. Galway, 1988.

___. "The medieval pottery." In *Excavations at Chepstow 1973-1974*, edited by R. Shoesmith, 93-139. Cardiff, 1991.

___. *The Petrology of some Medieval Pottery from Waterford*. CLAU Archaeological Report, no 188. Lincoln, 1994.

___. (1995a) "English Pottery Imports in Medieval Denmark." *By, Marsk og Geest* 8 (1995): 23-29.

___. (1995b) "The Study of Imported Medieval Pottery in Southern Scandinavia." *META* 1 (1995): 660-4.

Vince, Alan G., and Anne Jenner. "The Saxon and Early Medieval Pottery of London." In *Aspects of Saxo-Norman London. 2: Finds and Environmental Evidence* (London & Middlesex Archaeological Society Special Paper 12), edited by Alan G. Vince, 19-119. London, 1991.

Vlek, Robert. *The Mediaeval Utrecht Boat. The history and evaluation of one of the first nautical archaeological excavations and reconstructions in The Low Countries* (British Archaeological Reports, International Series, vol. 382). Oxford, 1987.

Vlierman, Karel. *'...Van Zintelen, van Zintelroeden ende Mossen ...' Een breeuwmethode als hulpmiddel bij het dateren van scheepswrakken uit de Hanzetidj. Scheepsarcheologie I.* (Flevobericht 386, Nederlands Instituut voor Scheeps- en onderwater Archeologie, Rijksdienst voor het Oudheidkundig Bodemonderzoek). [Lelystad], 1996.

Vogel, Walter. (1915a) *Die Geschichte der deutschen Seeschiffahrt*. Vol. 1: *Von der Urzeit bis zum Ende des 15. Jahrhunderts*. Berlin, 1915.

___. (1915b) *Kurze Geschichte der deutschen Hanse* (Hansische Pfingstblätter, 11). München & Leipzig, 1915.

Vogel, Volker. "Die Anfänge des Schleswiger Hafens." *Beiträge zur Schleswiger Stadtgeschichte* 22 (1977): 21-28.

___. *Schleswig im Mittelalter: Archäologie einer Stadt*. Neumünster, 1989.

Vogtherr, Hans-Jürgen. "Hamburger Faktoren von Lübecker Kaufleuten des 15. und 16. Jahrhunderts." *Zeitschrift des Vereins für Lübeckische Geschichte und Altertumskunde* 73 (1993): 39-138.

Von Thünen's Isolated State, an English edition of *Der isolierte Staat* by Johann Heinrich von Thünen, translated by Carla M. Wartenberg, edited by Peter Hall. Oxford, 1966.

Wade, J., ed. *The Customs Accounts of Newcastle-upon-Tyne*. Surtees Society, 202. 1995.

Waites, Bryan. "The Medieval Ports and Trade of North-East Yorkshire." *Mariners Mirror* (1977): 137-152.

Walendowski, Henryk. "Posadzki szwedzkie w budownictwie Poznana (xvi-xviii w.)" (Swedish Floors from the 16th to the 18th Centuries in Poznan). *Przegląd Geologiczny* 7 (1996): 671-674.

Warner, George, ed. *The Libelle of Englyshe Polycye. A Poem on the Use of Sea-Power, 1436*. Oxford, 1921.

Wase, Dick. "Det medeltida gutniska borgerskapet." In *Gotlandia Irredenta. Festschrift für Gunnar Svahnström zu seinem 75. Geburtstag*, edited by Robert Bohn, 289-301. Sigmaringen, 1990.

———. "Gotländska hanseaters förbindelser till 1350: En studie över den tyska släkten Cosvelt och dess krets." *Gotländskt Arkiv* 69 (1997): 143-162.

———. *Farmän, bönder och gotländskt borgerskap. En studie i interna gotländska förhållanden under medeltiden*. Stockholm, 1998.

Waugh, Scott L. *England in the Reign of Edward III*. Cambridge, 1991.

Wazny, T. "Historical Timber Trade and its Implications on Dendrochronological Dating." In *Tree Rings and Environment*. Proceedings of the International Dendrochronological Symposium, Ystad 3-9 September 1990 (LUNDQUA Report 34, Lund University, Department of Quaternary Geology), edited by Thomas Bartolin, Björn Berglund, Dieter Eckstein, and Fritz Schweingruber, 331-333. Lund, 1992.

Weczerka, Hugo. "Verkehrsnetz und Handelsgüter der Hanse." In *Hanse in Europa. Brücke zwischen den Märkten 12. bis 17. Jahrhundert* (Kölnisches Stadtmuseum, exhibition-catalogue), 41-56. Köln, 1973.

Weibull, Carl. "Lübecks Schiffahrt und Handel nach den nordischen Reichen 1368 und 1398-1400." *Zeitschrift des Vereins für Lübeckische Geschichte und Altertumskunde* 47 (1967): 5-98.

Weibull, Curt. *Lübeck och Skånemarknaden. Studier i Lübecks Pundtullsböcker och Pundtullskvitton 1368-1369 och 1398-1400*. Lund, 1922.

Wernicke, Horst. "Kaufmannshanse und Stadtentstehung im Ostseeraum während des 12./13. Jahrhunderts." In *Frühgeschichte der europäischen Stadt* (Schriften zur Ur- und Frühgeschichte, vol. 44), edited by Heinrich Brachmann and Joachim Herrmann, 309-313. Berlin, 1991.

van Werveke, Hans. "Die Beziehungen Flanderns zu Osteuropa in der Hansezeit." In *Die Deutsche Hanse als Mittler zwischen Ost und West*, by Ahasver von Brandt, Paul Johansen, Hans van Werveke, Kjell Kumlien and Hermann Kellenbenz (Wissenschaftliche Abhandlungen der Arbeitsgemeinschaft für Forschung des Landes Nordrhein-Westfalen, vol. 27), 59-77. Köln & Opladen 1963.

van der Wijk, P. H. "Beschouwingen over het Utrechtse schip." *Jaarboek Oud Utrecht* 1933: 28-47.

Wilson, Eva. "Swedish limestone paving in 17th and 18th century English buildings." *Post-Medieval Archaeology* 17 (1983): 95-109.

Witney, K. P. "The Woodland Economy of Kent, 1066-1348." *Agricultural History Review* 38 (1990): 20-39.

Witthöft, Harald. "Wägen und Messen." In *Die Hanse. Lebenswirklichkeit und Mythos* (Exhibition-catalogue, vols. 1-2), edited by Jörgen Bracker. Vol. 1: 549-553. Hamburg, 1989.

Wolff, P. "Three samples of English Fifteenth-Century Cloth." In *Cloth and Clothing in Medieval Europe. Essays in Memory of Professor E. M. Carus-Wilson*, edited by N. B. Harte and K. G. Ponting, 120-125. London, 1983.

Yrwing, Hugo. *Gotland under äldre medeltid. Studier i hanseatisk-baltisk historia.* Lund, 1940.

——. (1954a) *Kungamordet i Finderup: Nordiska förvecklingar under senare delen av Erik Klippings regering*. Lund, 1954.

——. (1954b) "Till frågan om tyskarna på Gotland under 1100-talet." *Historisk tidskrift* (Stockholm) 74 (1954): 411-421.

——. "Salt och saltförsörjning i det medeltida Sverige." *Scandia* 34 (1968): 219-242.

——. *Gotlands medeltid.* Visby, 1978.

——. *Visby. Hansestad på Gotland.* Visby, 1986.

Zunde, Maris. "Wood Export from Medieval Riga and Possibilities for Dendrochronological Dating." In *Proceedings of the International Conference, Dendrochronology and Environmental Trends*, edited by Vida Stravinskiene and Romualdas Juknys, 67-74. Kaunus, 1998.

The Contributors

LARS BERGGREN, senior researcher in the Department of Art History and Musicology at the Lund University, Sweden. One of his main research interests is medieval sculpture and stone industry.

JAN BILL, senior researcher in the Centre for Maritime Archaeology at the Danish National Museum in Roskilde, Denmark. He has specialised on Viking Age and medieval seafaring.

BRUCE CAMPBELL, chair of Medieval Economic History in the Department of Economic and Social History, The Queen's University of Belfast, UK. His field of research is medieval English agrarian history.

WENDY R. CHILDS, reader in Medieval History, School of History, University of Leeds, Leeds, UK. Her main research interest is in England's overseas trade in the Middle Ages.

ROLF HAMMEL-KIESOW , director of the Forschungsstelle für die Geschichte der Hanse und des Ostseeraums, Archiv der Hansestadt Lübeck, Germany. His field of research is urban history in medieval and early modern times.

NILS HYBEL, professor in the Department of History at the University of Copenhagen, Denmark. He has specialised in historiography and medieval social and economic history.

ANNETTE LANDEN, researcher in the Department of Art History and Musicology at the Lund University, Sweden. She is engaged in research on medieval baptismal fonts from Gotland.

BJÖRN POULSEN, professor in the Department of History, University of Aarhus, Denmark. He is engaged in research on social and economic history of medieval and early modern Denmark, and the Duchy of Schleswig.

RICHARD UNGER, professor in the Department History, University of British Columbia in Vancouver, Canada. He works principally in economic history and the history of technology.

ALAN VINCE, Managing Editor of Internet Archaeology, University of York, UK. He has specialised in the study of pottery from archaeological excavations and the publication of archaeological fieldwork.

Index of Persons and Places

Subject Index